Confluence of Literature India-Vietnam

CONFLUENCE OF LITERATURE
India-Vietnam

Editor
Geetesh Sharma

Sub-Editors
Prem Kapoor
Kusum Jain
Dr. Pravamayee Samantaray

RAJKAMAL PRAKASHAN

ISBN : 978-93-93768-26-1

Price : ₹1495

First Edition : 2022

Published by

Rajkamal Prakashan Pvt. Ltd.

1-B, Netaji Subhash Marg, Darya Ganj

New Delhi-110 002

Branches : Ashok Rajpath, Opp. Science College, Patna-800 006
1st Floor, Darbari Building, M.G. Marg, Prayagraj-211 001

website : www.rajkamalprakashan.com
e-mail : info@rajkamalprakashan.com

Printed by

B.K. Offset
Navin Shahdara, Delhi-110 032

Cover Design : Ashok Verma

CONFLUENCE OF LITERATURE : INDIA-VIETNAM
Edited by Geetesh Sharma

Geetesh Sharma

(6th August, 1932 - 2nd May, 2021)

This anthology is dedicated to
The 50th Year of Diplomatic Relations
between India and Vietnam
and to our mentor and guide Late. Geetesh Sharma,
who dedicated the major part of his life towards promotion of
goodwill and mutual relations between India and Vietnam.

CONTENTS

Editor's Note

Indian culture had its great influence over certain parts of central and south Vietnam till fifteenth century. So, when we go through its folk stories and poetry, we find a unique similarity in Indian and Vietnamese literature. However, there had been a basic difference too. Although Vietnam is known as a Buddhist country, its culture has always been a secular one. 'TET' is the biggest festival of Vietnam, but it also has no relation with religion. So far as I know, Vietnam is a unique country of its kind in the world.

When liberation war against the French colonialists started in Vietnam, it had its strong impact over its literature and culture. Writings, thought process and behaviour in Vietnam underwent a basic change and it all started with propaganda literature. Ho Chi Minh used to proudly admit that yes, it was a propaganda literature but it was deeply attached with the literate, illiterate and common people. Such language was used in the literature, which even an illiterate could easily comprehend.

As mentioned earlier it was Ho Chi Minh, who had inspired people's literature. He himself was also a poet, writer, dramatist, composer, who directed a symphony besides being a war strategist. He not only participated in the war but led it from the front and at the same time penned down poems and fictions. A great poet of VietnamHuu Thinh, whom I regard as my own brother, had once told me that he had participated in the liberation war of Vietnam with pen in one hand and gun in another. He had shot down many American bomber planes with his gun. During nights he used to write poems.

During the liberation war from 1945 to 1975 whatever popular literature was written, did not have the description of war alone, poems and novels relatable to human compassion and concern were also written.

After the unification of Vietnam, its literature underwent another change, that was for peace, friendship and development. It brought about prosperity to the people. When people had a taste of freedom and prosperty they wrote poetry and fiction relatable to love and sex.

In this collection there are 16 Vietnamese poems and eight stories selected by the great poet of Vietnam, Huu Thinh, who also happens to be the President of Vietnam Writer's Union. So far as I understand he has completely desisted to include Vietnamese literature related to free love and sex. He might have thought that it would provide a wrong message. However, the collection of writings that he has selected for this number are penned by eminent literators belonging to senior as well as new generations.

This is the first opportunity that the Indian readers are getting to acquaint themselves with the Vietnamese literature, as no such endeavour was undertaken before on government or non-government level. Naturally, the credit for this number goes to Vietnam Writer's Union and Indo-Vietnam Solidarity Committee.

'People to people diplomacy' is a much talked about term, but despite most cordial and close relations no enveavour was ever made to acquaint the people of both the nations with each other's literature.

It goes beyond mention that the already deep cordial bilateral relations between India and Vietnam need to be further strengthened as such relations not only unite the hearts of the people but leave an everlasting impact too.

By going through the Vietnamese writings, l am sure, the Indian readers would not only be acquainted with the Vietnamese literature but with Vietnamese society as well.

So far as, the Calcutta and its suburbs based literature of Hindi, Bengali, Assamese, Odiya, Urdu languages is concerned, the writings of this region although reflect and represent the Indian mentality and temperament but are diversely different from the

Vietnamese one. Indian society is the only society in the world that is divided into four castes for thousands of years having nearly no or minimal commensal and matrimonial ties between each other. Obviously, it has its impact over literature too.

In Indian literature we do find high sounding talks about the women-power but (in reality) without granting the women any independence or equal status with the men. In fact, the Indian women are completely subjugated to men. What an irony, an Indian woman does have the right to elect a President or a Prime Minister but is not allowed to choose her own spouse. Marriages in India are mostly arranged by parents, and not by the would be husband and wife.

In Indian literature although there has been a progressive current but despite it, regretfully, even the progressive writers are deeply affected by the class or caste-system. Except few exceptions they arrange marriages among their own community or caste. Sometimes one feels with concern that we write something else while believing in something else. Our writings and behaviour do not match.

So, the people of Vietnam along with the people of other nations do not have a true picture of Indian society. They get entangled in such a spider's web that they are never able to understand the mainstream of India.

Here one comparison is very essential. Vietnam is the front ranking country among the progressing countries but the Vietnamese women are the most liberated ones among the Asian countries. Men and women in Vietnam love first and then marry while in India we marry first, and then love. In recent years even extra marital relations are being recognised. In the urban areas of Vietnam, even illegitimate children are accepted by the society although in the rural areas they are still being looked down upon despite not being discarded by the society.

Indian society, I believe, is a sort of stagnant society, that runs very fast but doesn't leave its ground. In comparison to Indian society, the Vietnamese society has undergone numerous changes during and after the liberation war, and this society is constantly proceeding forward although its women folk have their own problems. For instance, women outnumber men in Vietnam and so a small section of women is distressed due to isolation. Another problem relates to the increasing incidents of divorce, where the men refuse the responsibility to raise the children and the women are left with no option than to take care of the children after divorce.

So, it is very obvious that the quantum of responsibility of the women in Vietnam is far more than the men.

In India we have to face a problem of corruption and at the same time we have double standard both in speaking and writing. So is in Vietnam too but comparatively little less than India. In Vietnam there are two types of literature, one is patronised by the government, while the other has to stand on its own feet without any government patronage. Both these streams are running parallel to each other in Vietnam.

Despite extreme distinctions between India and Vietnam, one thing that is common is that the poet fraternity of both the countries have a deep down urge of writing poetry and getting it published in book form. People of both the countries who have some attachment with literature aspire that at least one title of collection of his/her poetry must be published. On their own expenses even they get their books published and then distribute free copies among the literary people.

As mentioned earlier that there are numerous points of differences between Indian and Vietnamese literature yet it is utmost essential to know about each other's literature, because as mentioned earlier that it is literature that unites people and leaves an everlasting impact. It brings literatures and their readers closer to each other. Regretfully, however, most minimal endeavour in this direction has been made.

We know that this joint endeavour of ours is on a very small scale, yet we believe, people with literary leaning, as also the common men would appreciate our initiative and would align themselves with this and such endeavours so that the people of both our nations may come close to each other.

In this collection we have also published English translations of poems and short stories published in Hindi and are dedicating the same to Vietnam Writer's Union with this hope and belief that they would translate it into Vietnamese language for the benefit of Vietnamese readers.

- Geetesh Sharma

Vietnamese Poems

Singing Voice in the Jungle

Huu Thinh

Huu Thinh, a freedom fighter, was born in1942.The President of Vietnam Writers' Association. He wrote "The way to the city" (long anthem,1979). Won a prize in the poetry competition held by Literature Newspaper in 1975 – 1976.

Music made in the jungle, you sing in the middle of Trường Sơn
One with malaria singing for one with malaria
Roads are upturned, dirt roads still scorched
The trees cool people, people cool each other

The music is inside the instrument, the instrument has nothing
The jungle sways suddenly before the flimsy strings
People are excited, thriving, stirring
Hands, still our hands, yet we think we're holding someone else's

You sing about the jungle, you sing about trees
You sing about the ones listening to you sing
I suddenly forget my fever has just broken
The jungle suddenly forgets the pain of fresh bombings
I hold myself up with this singing voice to triumph over hardship
The years in Trường Sơn, our friendships clear, pure
The singing voice is gone, the bomb shelter is left—
It turns into a music box deep inside the earth

Trường Sơn Range, 1974
(Translated by Nguyen Phan Que Mai)

A Song of My Native Village

Nguyen Quang Thieu

Nguyen Quang Thieu was born in 1957. A member of the Vietnam Writers Association. Awarded the National Prize for arts and literature.

(or my declaration about my Chua village)

I sing a song of my native village
When everyone is deep in sleep
Under wet stars, under wild winds
Finding their way home.

Somewhere a man speaks in his sleep
Beside a woman's treaming hair
Somewhere the smell of a mother's milk
Flows into the night
Somewhere the breasts of girls of fifteen
Rise from the land like shoots
And somewhere the coughs of old villagers
Like ripe fruits fall from the branches
While grass stays awake all night in the garden

I sing a song of my nitive village
In the light of oil lamp
Left by my ancestors,
The loveliest and sadest of lamps
When I was born my mother placed it
Before me that I might look and learn
To be sad, to love and to cry

I sing a song of my native village
I sing through my navel cord
Which was buried there
And became an earthworm
Crawling under the water jar
Crawling by the edge of the pond
Crawling through my ancestors' graves
Crawling through the paupers' graves
Pushing up red earth in its path like blood

I sing, I sing a song of my native village
Bones lying in terra-cotta coffins
Where mine will lie someday
In this life I am human
In the next I may be an animal
I will ask to be a little dog
To defend the sadness,
The jewel of my native village.

(Translated by author and Martha Collins)

Feed the Cat

Tran Quang Dao

Born in 1957. "Grass hug", "copy and paste dreams", "Flying in the dream" - volumes of poems. Won the Poem Prize by Vietnam Writers' Association in 2020.

He has been living here for ten years, may be more
I love him, but half as much as my wife and daughter.

At times I was angry with him
Wanted to throw the cotton ball out of the window
After he took a pee on a poem I was writing
When his fur clinged to my clothes, what a cat magnet!

When my wife went to Korea
She said, feed the cat on time
So… what about me?

I was surprised
I could do it like a machine
Suddenly I loved him
as much as I loved my wife and daughter...

Hey, cat
Stay with me for a long time
Pee on my fine poem, which I am going to write
It won't matter
Make your fur cling to my clothes
Beautiful girls will look, I don't care
On the streets, I will wear them still

I'm no longer a robot
You just keep going meow meow...

July, 2018

(Translated by JiKhanh. Edited by Bob Chee)

Private Delhi

Ham Anh

"Ham Anh poems - dew drops containing profound sediment waves of human conditions: True, Good and Passionate." – by Trinh Lu. After Natural Color, published in 2008, Calling my March is her second book, published in 2016. She received numerous awards for her writings. This poem was written during Ham Anh's stay in India working at the Vietnam Embassy in New Delhi.

Dazzling void
with too much sunlight
the holy cows sleep-walk
slowly
crossing large boulevards.

An old beggar tends an ant colony
Under the shade of a Bodhi tree
Twinkled with sunshine spots…

Drifting out of Tagore's verses
Bare-footed women,
Walk towards the river, pots swaying on heads…

A desire suddenly flares up
For just a drop of cool water
To quench a secret longing deep in the heart.

New Delhi, 22 July 2009
(From her collection CALLING MY MARCH)

The Poem I can't yet name

Nguyễn Phan Quế Mai

Born in 1973, Nguyễn Phan Quế Mai is the author of eleven books of fiction, poetry and non-fiction published in Vietnamese and English. She has been honoured with many awards including the Poetry of the Year 2010 Award from the Hà Nội Writers Association, the Capital's Literature & Arts Award, and First Prize - the Poetry Competition About 1,000 Years Hà Nội.

My hands lift high a bowl of rice, the seeds harvested
In the field where my grandmother was laid to rest.
Each rice seed tastes sweet as the sound of lullaby
from the grandmother I never knew.
I imagine her soft face as they laid her down into the
earth,
Her clothes battered, her skin stuck to her bones;
In the Great Hunger of 1945 *, my village
Was starved for graves to bury all the dead.
Nobody could find my grandmother's grave,
So my father tasted bitter rice for sixty-five years.

After sixty-five years of searching,
Spirits of my ancestors led my father and me
to my grandmother's grave.
I heard my father call "Mum," for the first time;
the rice field behind his back trembled.

My two feet cling to the mud.
I listen to the burning incense of my grandmother's
soul spread,
joining the earth, taking root in the field,
Where she quietly sings lullabies, calling the rice plants to
blossom.

Lifting the bowl of rice in my hands, I count every seed,
Each one glistening with the sweat of my ancestors,
Their backs bent in the rice fields,
The fragrance of my grandmother's lullaby alive on each one.

Translated from Vietnamese into English by the author and Bruce Weigl

** The Vietnamese Famine of 1945 occurred in northern Vietnam from October 1944 to May 1945, during the Japanese occupation of French Indochina in. Between 400,000 and 2 million people are estimated to have starved to death during this time.*

Oblivion

Tran Anh Thai

Poet Tran Anh Thai, born in 1953. He wrote the long anthem "Shadow the Sun". Won the Poem Prize by Weekly Literature Newspaper.

I

He has been sitting there for a very long time
Ten years
            twenty years
                        like thousand years passing by?
The worn-out chair at the house's corner is covered with moss
Faces are passing by
                        blurred faces
                                    forgotten dates
His children's memories are also forgotten…

He is sitting there like time
Recalling troop columns
                        recalling bombardments
                                    screams and curses

Floating in the air the smell of sweats mixed with burning blood
Quiet battlefields
                        quiet piles of corpses
Hatred is over…
                        Is it over… and is he dead?...

Equivocal gusts of wind
            equivocal incense smoke on hastily buried graves
Mourning and groaning cover battlefields
Endless
            Endless …

II

Nobody says his name
                        no calls
                                    no voices!

The silent shadow pins on the worn-out wall
The sound of house mice seeking for food at night
The weak sound of his aging throat
All seem like they're waiting
Like echoes from the ancient time
Sometimes…
The faraway and wild land was not habituated
From the soil and dark hell…

III

Out there, throngs of people are floating
Where are they heading for?
He forgot the road
    forgot his existence
    forgot old faces…

The wind comes and goes
    the light comes and goes
        his eyes stop looking for things
Even the sadness of being defeated does not bother!...

The forgotten throngs of people
Bitterly cold and motionless
The uniform sticking to the dry skin is decomposing
Flowers in the vase withered
Quietly falling amidst no human presence!…

(Translated by Nguyen Ngoc Hung)

Halloween

Nguyen Thi Anh Huynh

Nguyen Thi Anh Huynh born in 1955. Volume of poems "The sudden rain". She won Ho Chi Minh city Poetry Award in 2006, Military Literary magazine poetry award in 2010.

It's very boring to be a human
why not being a ghost?
Do it
Why not being a devil?
Do it
Why not being a witch?
Do it…

Just make one only!
Let me be a ghost

Thanks for the carnival
Long live a mask
More fun than New Year
Everyone turns out to be a tiger, a panther
Everyone becomes a devil
It's sad to be a human being
It's laughing to be an ogre

Being a ghost might not be compatible
Why being a ghost
But still looks like a human being?

Why attending Halloween
 - the only person without a mask
Just a mask
Under the eyes of others

Someone has forever a mask

That's Halloween

It's when the heart could speak the language of love

Le Thanh My

Le Thnh My. Born in 1966. Poetry volume : Dreaming Of Flowers (1992), Poetry book *For An Always Distant Person* (2000), Poetry book LEAF FATE (2002), Poetry book *In The House of Memories* (2005), Poetry book Floating (2007), Poetry book *The Voice of Silence* (2011), Poetry book *Picking Up* (2015), Epic *From River To Ocean* (2017), Poetry book *The Loving Persons Leading Each Other* (2018).

only when the heart should be able to say the words
of love
Happiness will accompany us through our own lives

When the man bent down to pick up a stone
that blocked
His own path so it has got the door
Before he uttered his words to promise
The brighten yellow moon had made the hand
warm up
It may already have been late
it might be changed
But if we wouldn't catch up with the sunrise
The dawn will become the past
Don't hesitate when the love come!

The moon that was seen from Cherry Springs
State Park
No reason to be bigger than for a man's heart
A woman's smile is far worthier than the world
He would take the moon
He would pick dry yellow leaves up
He would warm the winter up with his breaths
and his hands
Definitely
Have to strong grip!

only when the heart should be able to say the words of love
happiness will accompany us through our own lives.

From Our Home

Mai Văn Phấn

You gather things according to their seasons
A bunch of grapefruit flowers for autumn
plums for spring

We are the pulse of air, deep abyss, breasts of soil
We choose warm places to set our furniture
Uncluttered places to put our tables and chairs

We drop our worries at the dinner table
With chopsticks we pick vegetables from the field afar
The fish bites on the bait inside our clay pot

We love the footprints near the rice stubble
Deep wells, streams and rivers, ponds and puddles

Don't sit in the room too long
Go out into the field, out to the riverbank
Where leaves grow green and fish wriggle

Bite on fresh pineapple or sweet orange
And let juice drop on brown soil.

(Translated by Nhat-Lang Le. Edited by Susan Blanshard)

Mai Van Phấn. Born in 1955. He has won a number of Vietnamese and international literary awards, including The Vietnam Writers' Association Award in 2010, The Cikada Literary Prize of Sweden in 2017, The Award of Serbian Academy of Sciences and Arts in 2019 and The Literary award from Association of Literary Translators of Montenegro in 2020. He has published 16 poetry books and 1 book "Critiques - Essays" in Vietnam. 19 poetry books of his are published and released in foreign countries.

Night in My Native Village

Tran Quang Quy

Tran Quang Quy Was born on January 2, 1955 at Xuân Lộc commune, Tam Thanh district, Phú Thọ. A member of the Vietnam Writers Association. Awarded the National Prize for arts and literature.

I return to the mossy mildewed roof of my dream
Passing through gardens expectant with fruits
In an old farmer's sleep, buffalo hooves still hobble
The field pants with a young woman's sagging
breasts
Weary, the village takes itself into the darkness
The night takes itself back a thousand years

Lonesome bamboo fans sense the changing watch
The wind stays by the river, the lonely waves
Restless in me: a late cockcrow, pale firelight at the
end of the road
My aspiration is still green, like a young fruit
Mother lights the lamp and makes her way to
the grain basket
The field is anxious, waiting for late grain

Darkness moves freely under the sky
Distraught, bamboo hedges shed their hair
Loving the earth, a fruit hurriedly ripens
And falls, stunned, in the garden late at night
I sleep with the cicadas' diminished song in late summer
Tossing and turning, village sweat flows through me

But mother still sits there building a fire
At daybreak, forever, lively footsteps echo.

(Translated by Nguyen Ba Chung, with Martha Collins)

The Faces, the Patches of Sky

Bang Viet

Bang Viet was born in 1941. A member of the Vietnam Writers Association. Awarded the National Prize for arts and literature.

The familiar battlefield back then, but now far away
The blowing wind follows me to many areas of
the sky
Youthful soldiers who promised to see me again
Many ordinary faces, as ordinary as justice
Each face born to welcome a patch of the sky!

Wherever we are, we owe a debt to life
Troops at the outposts who cooked rice underground
The eyes of the Vân Kiều children, as fresh as a song
And gazing through a hundred black fires
Suddenly turned deep blue under a safe sky
Remember the Truong Son mother, deep in the forest night
Cooked a maranta gruel, then let her child have it
Remember the Thừa Thiên girl who was killed, and silenced
They forever left me a vivid region of the sky
I closed her eyes, they remained clear and bright

Silent before the pain, and crying before the joy
O I remember the night we attacked the Quảng Trị fort
Amazing, the thousands of our shells shot into the sky
How bright the blue-yellow cascade that poured down onto the enemy
At the moment of attack, my eyes filled with tears.

I have lived all my life being so moved, O my battlefield, my country!
Every face I know, even just one look, I cherish it forever…
So many innocent children, so many experienced mothers
Soldiers who passed through so many regions, so many trenches,
Those ordinary faces, after a thousand times facing death
Shine a light down on me, and on many high patches of the sky!

1970
(Co-translated by Nguyen Ba Chung and Fred Marchant)

Sailor's Love Song

Tran Dang Khoa

Tran Dang khoa was born on April 26, 1958 at Điền Trì hamlet, Quốc Tuấn commune, Nam Thanh district, Hải Dương. A member of the Vietnam Writers Association. Awarded the National Prize for arts and literature.

On the day you are to sail,
The clouds in the sky unfurl.
You pace the length of the pier,
The sea on one side, and she on the other.

She is calm, says a few words,
And then nothing. You turn
To face the worst of all weathers,
The sea on one side, and she on the other.

Tomorrow, as the lights come on,
The ship at anchor under distant stars,
You don't feel lonely, despite the wide
Sea on one side, and she there on the other.

No peace ever for our native land.
The wind tears at the widows' white headbands.
All night on a bleak island, you stand guard,
The sea on one side, and she on the other.

The heavens might cease to hold her,
The sea disappear, you and the grass
Be all that is left. Still, the memory lasts,
The sea on one side, and she on the other...

1981

(Co-translated by Fred Marchant and Nguyen Ba Chung)

Secret Scent

Phan Thi Thanh Nhan

Phan Thi Thanh Nhan was born in 1943 in Hanoi. A member of the Vietnam Writers Association. Awarded the National Prize for arts and literature.

The windows of the two houses at the end of the street
Always stayed open for no reason.
Two old friends who used to be classmates.
A grapefruit tree behind one house floats its scent to
the other.

She hid a bunch of flowers in her handkerchief
And hesitantly, crossed to her neighbour's house.
Someone there would leave the next day for the front.

In silence they sat, lost for words.
Their eyes met, then turned away.
Who could dare say the first words?
The scent of grapefruit blossoms made them more shy.
The young man didn't dare ask for the blossoms;
The young girl didn't dare give them,
But the warm and refined fragrance
Could not hide itself…
And floated faintly by.

Like the blossoms, the young girl was silent.
She let their fragrance speak for her love:
How distant you seem; you still don't know.
Don't see I come to you?
The fragrance will fill your chest.
When you leave
The fragrance will follow you, everywhere.

Leaving each other
They still didn't speak.
Yet the fragrance sweetens the young man's journey.

1969

(Translated by Nguyen Ba Chung, Nguyen Quang Thieu, and Bruce Weigl)

He Who Returns

Vu Quan Phuong

Vu Quan Phuong was born in 1940. A member of the Vietnam Writers Association. Awarded the National Prize for arts and literature.

To Zen master TNH

Close, very close, yet far, very far
Buddha's the green sky slanting onto the roof
The village field where our parents walked:
On that very path, Buddha passed
The bell, the rattle struck—for whom, where?
Waves at night are cold under the bridge
In the blink of an eye, our life is dazed with change
There's only moon-bright love, back then, and now

Stream runs to river, river to sea
At the end of a person's heart, we meet our hearts
Three thousand worlds are dim with smoke and dust
The radiant moon keeps watch outside the door

(Translated by Nguyen Ba Chung and Martha Collins)

The Cong Tube Song

Thanh Thảo

Thanh Thao was born in 1946. A member of the Vietnam Writers Association. Awarded the National Prize for arts and literature.

The old heroic songs
Are still sung but only in books.
Swords and saddles
Now as old as they can be.

Our own song
Is the *Cong* tube song
About the liberation troops gear,
The simplest in the world.

Cooked rice just finished,
Then the taro broth.
The forest tea a bit tart
But all drink and say good.

From an aluminium can
We work a hundred tasks.
The difficult open up the smart.
Our soldiers are very quick.

Those with malaria
Could not swat a fly,
Yet through a few stations,
The fever over, they leave immediately.

With the *Cong* tube across the backs,
It's *Thach Sanh* pot of today.
Many heroes become giants,
Eating rice from this container.

Months and years will pass,
With many graceful songs
But I know from here,
As if carved into rocks,
As if cut into trees.

Today's song
Is simple and brilliant
And carry the simplest lessons of life
Bitter and sweet.

Translated by Nguyen Ba Chung and Bruce Weigl

Cong tube : a tube usually made out of bamboo, with bamboo knots at the two ends, and a bored hole in between.

Thach Sanh : according to an old legend, Thach Sanh's small earthern pot coud feed thousands of soldiers without running out of rice.

Forest with a Swarm of Butterflies

Nguyen Due Mau

Nguyen Duc Mau was born in 1948 in Nam Ninh, Nam Hà. His native village is Nam Điền village, Nam Trực, Nam Định. A member of the Vietnam Writers Association. Awarded the National Prize for arts and literature.

Night. The unit stopped deep in the forest. There was a well someone had dug near the dried up stream; we scooped up the water and drank with a thirst that could burn our throats. The sweet water cooled our sterile bodies. We hardly noticed that in the well was a body. The night was pitch black, the forest shimmered with many fireflies, the slender thread flickered as if in a hallucination.

I left the hammock, carried my rifle over my shoulder to begin the watch. Walking among the row of black trees, I stumbled over something soft; a nauseating and rotten smell came up. Weary, I wondered if a deer that had been bombed. After the watch I slept heavily on the hammock. Fireflies fell all over my dream. Or was it a dream? And was I really sleeping? How could I know that all night long the maggots were hollowing out dead bodies?

Morning. The cooking crew scooped water to cook the rice, realized in a panic that there were the bodies of two young women in the well. My squad searched deep in the rock hollows, trees and bushes, and came up with the bodies of three young men. We built five graves without birth or dead days, no names, no native villages. I looked at the rolls of wire, the silent walkie-talkie. We realized they had been communication soldiers, caught up short by the enemy.

The war recedes; when I will return to the worn path of Truong Son? Where is the well that's mixed with human blood, where in a great thirst I drank, or the tree root with thousand of maggots that worked through the night? Where are the nameless graves built with pain and tears? In a forest, full of fireflies.

(Translated by Nguyen Ba Chung and Bruce Weigl)

Vietnamese Short Stories

A moonlit market under a secular mulberry tree

Y Ban

Writer Y Ban, born in 1961. Author of the story "The woman born in the darkness". Recipient of 1st Prize in the contest of poems and short stories by Military Literature Magazine in 1990.

Once there lived, at the furthest end of Sủi Village, a widow and her daughter. The mother, in her early forties, was small-waisted and buxom. She had charming lips and dimpled cheeks. Her large, black eyes were like bottomless wells. Local gossips said they must have been the cause of her early widowhood. For ten full years, the beautiful woman's honour remained intact, although there was no lack of men seeking to take liberties with her.

The daughter was in her sixteenth year, an age when a girl's hair acquires a special sheen and her skin bursts with a robust glow. She was almost the mirror image of her mother; only her eyes were not so entrancing.

It was the middle of the fifth lunar month. The full moon cast a silvery light on the broad banana leaves. Lụa, the girl, noted that her mother had been restless since the afternoon. She had hastened to the garden to cut down a cluster of green bananas before hurrying out to buy several bricks of tobacco, which she had set at the bottom of a basket and carefully covered with a round rush mat. She had asked for an early dinner and had advised her daughter not to stay up late.

But try as she might, Lụa could not sleep. Looking out at the moonlit night through the window, she felt herself all aflutter inside and her cheeks ablaze. She wanted to sing aloud. She recalled her encounter with a young man in the afternoon, when she was watering the paddies. He had said "You're so very beautiful! Marry me and you'll not become a widow," and she had hurled the bucket at him.

Lụa was roused from her day dream by a noise from her mother's room. She closed her eyes and tried to breathe evenly. Then she heard the footsteps of her mother, who came to the bed, peered into the mosquito netting, and turned away. Lụa opened her eyes. Her mother had just lifted the basket to her head and was squeezing her way out through the half-open bamboo door. Suspicious, Lụa got up and followed.

The mother walked swiftly along the village lane and Lụa was some twenty steps behind. Outside the village, the mother turned to the road leading towards a field overgrown with large, old mulberry trees. Children liked to play there despite warnings from their parents about possible abduction by elves said to be dwelling in those secular, gnarled giants.

From afar, Lụa heard voices and other sounds characteristic of a market. She saw her mother quicken her pace and she did likewise so as not to get lost. As she drew nearer, she saw people coming out from small lanes and converging on the old mulberry trees.

Lụa's mother stopped by an unoccupied tree, displayed the bananas and other articles on the ground, next to a bowl of water. So, it's the market she's come for, Lụa assured herself and started looking around. In the brilliant moonlight, voices were clear, but all movements were eerily indistinct. In the shade of the aged trees, people were talking with great animation, their faces shining with joy. Some, however, were sad; they embraced one another in silence, their eyes full of mutual reproach.

Someone was playing with flute. Captivated by the lively tune, Lụa hopped lightly on her nimble feet and again felt that her cheeks were burning. She traced the music to its source and found the player sitting at the base of a mulbrerry tree. On the ground before him was a stack of bamboo flutes. Lụa picked one up and gazed at it with curiosity.

" You like it?" asked the flute player.

" Yes."

" This one is better."

" How much do I owe you?" Lụa looked at the man for the first time. He was young, with a finely carved face.

"One quan."

Lụa dug into her pocket and realised with embarrassment that she had forgotten to bring any money.

"It doesn't matter," the flute player said affably. "You can pay me the next time. Do you want to try your flute now?"

"I'm afraid I don't know how."

"It's easy. Look, cover these holes with your fingers and blow into this hole."

"I can learn later. Play another tune, please."

Music filled the air again, sad music and gay music. Lụa was caught in it like in a vortex and was filled with sensations she had never experienced before.

The moon was dipping low over the horizon. The young man stopped playing. "The market's almost over," he said. "Take your flute and pay me the next time."

"What's the use of a flute to me now? I don't know how to pay it yet."

"Will you come again? I'll be waiting for you and I'll show you how."

"I'll come. See you again." Lụa hurried off. Without waiting for her mother, who was preparing to leave her place at the foot of the tree, Lụa went home, washed her feet in the pond, got under the mosquito net, lay down and tried to regulate her breathing. Moments later, she fell asleep.

Both Lụa and her mother got up late the next morning. The hungry pigs were kicking up a racket in the sty. "What happened to you, girl?" the mother asked gruffly, but her radiant face belied her tone.

Lụa was no longer her former serene self. Her mind kept returning to the night of the full moon and she thought of the young flute player with pleasure and yearning.

The moon was full again. Lụa knew what to do this time. After her mother had gone, she combed her hair carefully, coiled it around her head and kept it in place with a horn comb, in the style current among the girls in the village. She extracted from a bamboo trunk what money she had saved and started off at a leisurely pace.

The night was full of the fragrance of freshly planted rice. Lụa searched for the flute vendor, but he had not come yet. She made a tour of the market and realised with a start that it was unlike any she had been to. Fruits were the only produce available. There was no fish, no rice, and no salt. Even the customary blacksmith's shop was missing, so were the vendors of figurines.

Instead, there was a calligraphy stall where scrolls were sold like at New Year Festivals.

Lụa was pondering this anomaly when she heard the sound of a flute.

"Oh, here you are," the young man said with obvious relief. "I was afraid I would not see you again."

"I've money now. I'll buy one of those flutes."

Your presence gives me great pleasure. Sit down and I'll show how to play. By the way, my name is Thắng."

"I'm Lụa."

Lụa had no desire to learn; she only wanted to listen. So Thắng played to her, only gay music this time, so gay that at one moment she sprang up on her feet, stretched her arms and whirled.

"Did you like it?" Thắng asked at last.

"I've never enjoyed myself so much."

"How old are you?"

"Sixteen."

"Call me big brother then. I'm twenty."

"Are you here every time?"

"Yes."

"Business is not very good, is it?"

"No, it isn't. But I couldn't care less. I'm here only for the pleasure of people's company. What brought you here?"

"I was keeping watch on mother."

"You shouldn't have come." Thắng's voice was sad.

"Why? It's fun here."

"I like your comb. Would you lend it to me until the next time?"

"Please, keep it. I'll come again."

The market was unusually animated on the fifteenth of the seventh month. Jostling her way through the unusually large crowd, Lụa noted that many people were conspicuous for their haggard look and shabby clothes.

Thắng took hold of both of Lụa's hands. "I've done some serious thinking," he enthused. "I can't live without you. Be my wife, please. I'll ask my mother to come and see yours."

"I don't know what my mother would say?"

"What about you?"

"My answer is 'yes'."

"Thank you." Thắng said effusively and led Lụa at a run to a sheltered place, where he sat down, pulled Lụa onto his lap, held her in a tight embrace and kissed both her cheeks. At the touch of Thắng's lips, Lụa felt as if her whole being was engulfed in a mass of invigorating air which sent shocks through her and caused her to soar high like a kite. All the while her ears were filled with sounds which were a mixture of the enchanting music from Thắng's flute, her mother's gentle voice, the twittering of birds on the longan tree in her garden, the stridulating of cicadas, and the rustling of rice plants.

Time flew by swiftly and the crowd of market-goers was thinning out. "You should go home now," Thắng said. Lụa ran off, her feet hardly touching the ground.

That night she dreamed Thắng was by her side. His hands roamed over her body, bathing it in pure air, pristine water and lightning.

Both mother and daughter overslept again. The woman. The first to get up, asked the plate-looking girl if she was sick.

"No mother. I'm all right,' Lụa replied. Then remembering the dream, she became confused and hurried off to the well where she splashed cold water on her burning face.

The mother shook her head in puzzlement.

The same dream recurred, night after night, and Lụa began to look unwell.

The moon shone with extra brilliance on the fifteenth of the eighth month. Thắng was waiting for Lụa at the entrance of the marketplace. "I was dying to see you," he whispered into her ear.

"Oh," Lụa exclaimed and checked herself in time. Had they not been together every night?

"You don't feel well?" Thắng asked.

"I'm fine."

"I've told my mother everything. At an auspicious date, she'll call on your mother, bearing presents."

At their customary place, the lovers sat down, Thắng playing on his flute and Lụa leaning against him.

Lụa was pale and exhausted once again the next morning and her mother wanted to know the cause. "Tell me the truth," the mother pleaded. "There're only the two of us. I've raised you single-handedly. If something happened to you, I could never forgive myself. Say, dear, are you in love with someone? Or has someone cast a spell on you?"

Lụa remained silent until tears drenched her mother's face. "Mother," she blurted out. "A man from Vóc has asked for my hand and I've agreed.. His name's Thắng. His mother will bring presents and talk to you."

"So, that's it, hey? You should've told me right away. By the way, why don't you bring him home sometime?"

"We've met only at night."

The mother blanched. With a sense of foreboding, she headed for Vóc as soon as she could. There she made inquiries and was directed to a woman with a kind face and somewhat older than her.

"May I speak to your son, please?" she asked.

The other woman gasped and broke down. "He's dead, bitten by a blue snake while he was cutting bamboo for his flutes."

With the consent of the older woman, Lụa's mother lit three incense sticks and planted them in the holder on the altar. She looked with regret at the picture of a fine young man.

"We are in different worlds and so are incompatible," she prayed. "If you really care for my daughter, use all your power to make her well and help her find a good match."

Back at home, she confronted her daughter. "You've been to the Full Moon Market, haven't you?"

"How did you know?"

"Thắng's dead."

"It can't be true!"

"Yes, it is." And the mother told her daughter all about the strange market. It was held for both the living and the dead. A living person would bring along a bowl of water with which to test any money received: a coin from the living would sink: a coin from the dead would float, but decay within a day.

"I go to the market just for the chance of seeing your father, once a month," she said. "Your father was never happy, though. He came because of his love for me, but he belongs to the other world now."

Lụa tried to picture Thắng in that other world. "I don't believe it!" she protested tearfully.

In the ninth month, the mother took her doubting daughter to the market. It was autumn. The moon was pale and the night was fresh. "Many a time your father has asked me to let him see you, but I always dreaded such an encounter," she confided in the girl on the way.

"Do you remember your father?" she asked when they had arrived at her customary place.

"Very little," the girl said. "It's been a long time."

Lụa heard the familiar flute music again and was itching to go off by herself, but her mother told her to wait. "I've some business to attend to," she said firmly. "Stay here and meet your father. You can see Thắng afterwards."

After a long moment, Lụa saw a man coming towards her. It was her father. She wanted to hold out her arms to him as she used to do as a child, but as a bashful young maiden, she greeted him with reserve.

"How you've grown!" exclaimed the father. "And you're so pretty!"

"Mother said you were sad each time you saw her. Why so?" Lụa asked after a while.

"Because in my present state, I cannot do anything for her any more. I wish she wasn't so attached to me and was willing to find another man for company. I know how lonely she must feel, but there's nothing I can do. A brief visit every month only adds to her memories."

"It's not only memories. Mother's very happy after each visit."

"You mean she's happy because of her dreams? Dreams are just dreams. When you wake up, all that's left is sorrow and longing. In your world, however, people need what they can see when they're wide awake."

Meanwhile, the mother had found her way to the flute vendor.

"I want to buy a flute," she said to Thắng, who was looking around impatiently.

"Can you play?"

"No. I want one for my daughter."

"Can she play?"

"No, but she likes flute music, especially the tune you just played."

"She must be…"

"Lụa's her name."

"She's not coming today, is she?"

"Listen, young man. I've seen your mother and she told me everything. I'm so sorry. I know how you love my daughter and how she loves you. But you exist in different worlds and, therefore, cannot be together. Use your power to help my daughter find a good living man so as she can lead a normal life. I'll set up an altar for you in our home and will remember the date of your passing."

"I cannot object to what you said," Thắng conceded, wiping tears from his eyes. "But is it possible for me to see her from time to time?"

"No. It will do her no good not being able to forget you." Lụa's mother was firm.

"If you say so. Remember me to her, then, and tell her I wish her happiness." Thắng gathered the flutes into a bunch and left.

The mother returned to where she had left her daughter and told Lụa she could go now. Lụa ran off, her heart thumping. However, Thắng was not at his customary place and she found herself alone in the pale moonlight. At the hideout to which they used to withdraw to be alone, there was no sign of her lover either. Utterly heart-broken, she buried her face in her hands and cried bitterly.

When Lụa returned, her parents were talking earnestly, so she stopped within hearing distance.

"This may be our last time," her mother was saying. "I must devote myself to our daughter. Anything can happen to her, now that she's frustrated in her first love."

"You're right," said her father. "Take good care of yourself and our daughter. I'll do what I can for both of you."

"I'll remember you for the rest of my life!"

"No, it'll only make life harder for you. I want you to forget me completely. I want to see you in love with another man, one who can care for you effectively. Only then will I rest in peace."

They both turned at Lụa's approach.

"Did you see Thắng," the mother asked.

"He didn't come."

"Never mind. Come and say goodbye to Father."

"Listen, my daughter," the father said. "You'll meet someone who loves you as much as Thắng did and will care for you in everyday life, not just in your dreams. Pull yourself together and you'll be all right."

Lụa broke into tears. Her father clutched her to his chest, which, strange enough, was inert and cold like solidified air. "See?" he said teasingly. "It's me and yet it's not me!"

Lụa never saw Thắng again. A good girl, she sought oblivion in family chores.

And Lụa's mother never saw her husband again. She dedicated herself to raising funds for a pagoda to be built among the secular mulberry trees.

The pagoda, a splendid construction, was named Dâu*. It was said to be a meeting place for the living and the dead to share their memories. Its completion marked the end of strange Full Moon Market

---

* The Vietnamese word for mulberry

The Sparrows Fly Across the Woods

Vo Thi Xuan Ha

Writer Vo Thi Xuan Ha, born in 1959. Author of the story "Final goodbye to sweet dream". Prize for the best book by VWA's publisher in 1998.

A week after Than and I were married I have an argument with his parents. Than's face goes pale, his lips pouting--so disgusting! He is an incarnation of contradictions. When he kisses me he is so violent. But when he is supposed to speak up, he just stutters.

"Than, you must punish that insolent slut," my father-in-law roars like a butcher.

Sitting in my bedroom, I dangle my naked legs, pursing my lips in defiance.

"Please Mom and Dad forgive her," Than's voice says ruefully.

Than's stupid mother grumbles as she carries her basket into the kitchen:

"If your wife argues with me again, I'll send her back to her parents. I can't put up with her anymore, even though she is our first daughter-in-law."

I feel the urge to burst out of the room and jump on her for preaching to me about my duty as their senior daughter-in-law. Though aware of the difficulties, I married Than because I loved him. Every night our bodies are locked into each other like a pair of snakes. Our room, no larger than five square meters, reeks with the acrid odor of Than's sweat, the fragrance of my hair, the breath of two passionate lovers. Now and then a gust of wind wafts into our small bedroom the pungent smell of the lotus pond, the phosphorous river teaming with fish and prawns, and the sleepy town. After our love making we disengage from each other, lying languorously at the edge of our bed, listlessly looking up at the glittering stars through the window slats.

"Please, dear, do not argue with our old mother," Than says.

While Than pleads to me that way in the dark, I count the stars, nakedly. His steady voice sounds like a lullaby sending me to sleep.

"Every rainy season my parents would whip me for losing a couple of ducks," Than drones on. "In July the ducks would raise their bottoms and dip their beaks into the water to catch the phosphorus. In doing so they dropped their eggs into the river. I would dive to its bottom to pick them up. Sometimes I collected a basketful of them. I was so cold and wet my lips turned purplish, my shorts burst open, revealing my balls..."

I burst out laughing, wide-awake. Than is a handsome man, his skin dark and firm, his chest broad and muscular. His hair--thick, healthy, and dark brown--tumbles down his broad forehead, a sure mark of intelligence. Than could have at his disposal dozens of girls but he is crazy about me, worrying that I might run away. How stupid he is! He does not realize that I am also madly in love with him and would not allow any woman to get in my way. For these reasons I have come to hate my in-laws.

There is only one man I do not hate, though. If he were here, my parents-in-law wouldn't beat me because I wouldn't have been their senior daughter-in-law. He is sitting up there on the altar, smiling and sadly looking out of the window onto the garden. There are a few sweetsops and grapefruit trees in the back yard. I often get bruised as I dig the soil with my bare hands. When I see worms squirm all over the ground, I run back into the house, frightened. He is still smiling and gazing out of the window, absent-mindedly. Calling to Than, I point to the back yard.

"Our soil is full of worms!"

My father-in-law sucks in his water pipe, breathing out clouds of smoke and mumbling:

"The slut is insane!"

Only Nam could protect me.

During the holidays Than would take me with him to the woods to shoot sparrows. The birds perched all over the sycamores pointing straight up to the sky. Holding up his rifle, Than explained:

"Shooting sparrows makes you feel better than killing any other kind of animal."

Than's gun, as it was discharged, gave him a jolt. I asked:

"Why?"

The sparrows shot out of the trees, flying thick in the sky. One went down, landed over a bush far beyond, its blood staining whitish thorny blossoms. Than lunged over to grab the little brown bird writhing on the ground. Slightly tugging at Than's sleeve, I repeated my question: "Why did you say that?"

Than looked at the blood stains on the grass and pointed to the sky, replying with a smile:

"Because they are too many!"

I started gathering dry leaves to build a fire. The bird sizzled over the fire, giving off such a fragrant smell as Than turned it over with his knife. Swallowing my saliva, I poked the tip of my knife at the meat, sliced off a piece and put it in my mouth.

"You're reminding me of the fox Emeline in The Adventures of Fox Emeline," Than teased me. We rolled over in the grass, locked in each other's arms, devouring each other's greasy mouth. Unable to understand what was going on inside each other, I was hungry to see and touch for myself the tiny blood cells pulsating in each and every vessel of the body of the man lying on top of me, to understand the mysterious force that binds a man and a woman together.

We killed and ate one sparrow at a time. Evening was drawing near. We were sprawling on the grass, looking up at droves of birds returning to their nests. The setting sun had turned purple; our blood was mixed with that of the sparrows Than had killed.

In our excursions we would occasionally encounter heavy rains which tattered twigs and leaves and beat upon our flesh with its icy drops, quenching the burning desire inside us. I took off my clothes and frolicked in the rain with Than, laughing like crazy. My naked body soaked with water was ivory-white. The rain made my flesh firm and voluptuous, soothing the everlasting pain of being a woman.

After the rain, the forest grew greener. Young buds burst out of jagged bark to receive the late sunlight. Lines of ants were moving with patience over rotting leaves, some of them carrying on their backs a long leaf that had just fallen from its tree. Than observed:

"These must be hungry ants because they have to eat bitter leaves."

I remember that before I got married, my mother used to make funny remarks about life such as "Ants are fated to starve." She should have taught me to respect my parents-in-law, to fill and refill everyone's bowl in my husband's family with rice to the brim, to slave like ants. I looked at Than, thinking sadly: "To think that you are a starving ant!"

A brook was rippling somewhere. The forest's stillness was punctuated by the occasional snorting of deer and the rustling of fallen leaves. Underneath the mossy pebbles hogfish were scurrying about, hunting their prey. Only the tigers are invisible, unless they spring upon us from behind.

"Let's go home, Emeline, " Than said.

I left the woods hesitantly.

One year after we were married I got pregnant. Nine months later I gave birth to a baby girl who looks very much like Than. With a flourish the midwife cut the umbilical cord. I sprawled out, fainting on the delivery table. A man who was bigger and taller than Than was looking down from the ceiling first at my pale face, then at my belly where the umbilical cord just cut off was still hanging over my genitals. I heard my baby's convulsive wailing then saw that man bend over to kiss her and fondle the bloody cord. He kept gazing at me and smiling sadly. I recognized the man as Nam, Than's late brother. When Than took me from the delivery table to my bed I woke up and suddenly found him a total stranger. Being a new father, Than simpered and went about tidying things up with obvious embarrassment. I heard my father-in-law grumble on the porch:

"When will I have a grandson?"

Ah, just wait! I closed my eyes, exhausted. I felt a strong desire to see that man fondle the stalk of the umbilical cord popping out of my vagina. I was crazy about the man as if he had touched and seized all the minute blood vessels in my body that Than was incapable of touching.

"If your father wants to have another son, find him another woman." Fully awake now, I began to attack Than verbally.

"Tut-tut, tut-tut, you shouldn't have said that. Just take it easy, fox Emeline." Than tried to calm me down.

"Take another wife if you want a son that badly," I said, still fuming.

"This is what I anticipated," Than said, dejectedly. "Once you have a baby, you no longer need me."

"You men better watch out!" I blew up. "Or you'll have no descendants. Once you're gone, we'll drink water from the river to impregnate ourselves. You'll see that we're far much better than you men are. Though we're loud-mouthed and quarrelsome, we're not that crazy about blood and guns."

Than sat still, dumbfounded and crestfallen. Relenting, I held his hand in mine, murmuring:

"I've just seen Nam. He kissed our baby and saw me naked."

"Nonsense!" Than said with a start.

"That's true. He acted as if little Mai was his baby, not yours!"

Convinced that I must be delirious, Than did not mind what I was saying. He calmly said:

"The other day I received information about the location of Nam's unit. After you get well, I'll go to look for him."

Nam was Than's elder brother. At age seventeen, he enlisted in the army. My husband's entire village saw him off and sang his praises. Later, though my father-in-law was arrested many times for smuggling, he was not sentenced to jail because his son was a volunteer. Nobody realized that it was his father's cruelty that forced him to leave home by any means. People like Nam were fortunate because at that time there was a war for them to escape to; now during peace time if children do not like their parents, they will surely end up humming. Than told me that his father used to hang Nam on a beam over the ceiling and beat him with a stout staff for not bringing home money. Two months after his enlistment and before he was sent to the battlefield, Nam was permitted to visit his family for one day. He knocked loudly on the door in the middle of that night, causing all the dogs in the village to bark loudly. Thinking that it was a robber, his father wedged his bundle of money into the thatch window, shouting at the top of his lungs. Nam stayed home for the whole day, consumed a castrated rooster, then said good-bye to everybody. Before he left, Nam gave Than, who was ten years old at that time, a brass cartridge the size of a Jalapeno pepper. He also emptied out his pocket and gave his mother what he had saved from his salary. As he was stepping out of the gate, his mother kept looking at him in tears and with amazement. His father raised his voice, saying:

"Humph! Why are you crying? Don't you know a man has to tread the earth and carry heaven over his head?"

Though Nam did tread the earth, he carried the shells instead of heaven over his head. He had been gone a year when his family received his death notification. His remains must be still lying somewhere in Quang Tri. When ransacking the heap of Nam's dirty toys and finding the cartridge, Than polished and hid it away in a secret place. He would take it out and show it to me, saying each time we made love to each other:

"It's a memento of Nam."

When little Mai turned two, a film crew went to Quang Tri to shoot a film about the war and about a couple separated because of the war. The story, which takes place at the old citadel, is about blunders and meanness as well as lofty sentiments. Though Than is a copy editor, he writes for some magazines occasionally. He usually puts his published articles in a drawer and locks them up. As a journalist, Than knows many people, among them Mr.Vinh, head of the film crew, and the film director, whom Than praised in one of his articles. Both men insisted that Than accompany them in their trip so he could write advance reviews of their forthcoming movie. Than agreed but said:

"All right, but you must let me take Diem along."

"Can you just forget about Diem for a moment?" Mr. Vinh nodded with a snicker. "Did it ever occur to you that when you get old, you might not like each other as much as you do now?"

I knew too well Than wanted me to go with him because he was afraid that in his absence I would cuckold him. Phuong, Than's younger sister, a twenty-five year old girl with flat breasts, whose face was pale when she didn't wear makeup, had a boyfriend that Than had seen devour me with his eyes. Each time Tu came to visit Phuong, she looked embarrassed and awkward, and often spilled tea when serving it to him. Taking advantage of this, I went over to clean up the mess, showing Tu the upper parts of my breasts. When hearing Tu swallow his saliva and seeing Phuong pale with anger, I smiled and walked out of the house.

Than was angry and did not speak to me. If he had not been, I would have relented. I crawled into bed, facing the wall and imagining Tu and Phuong making love to each other and Tu's eyes caressing the length of my body. I started sweating, feeling chilled to the bone when thinking of Nam's sad eyes gazing at me.

The film crew worked hard in the stifling heat of Central Vietnam's summertime. Monsoon after monsoon swooped upon the old citadel, condensing everything into vapor. The lead actress laughingly bragged about losing two kilos and worried that her dog might not recognize her when she came home because of the deep tan on her face. A well-known but unemployed actress, she was spending her time at parties when she was chosen to play a peasant's humble wife.

Against the background of Quang Tri's old citadel the film makers re-created the bloody battles where soldiers tumbled down in the barrage of bullets. There was an acrid smell of gunpowder in the red dust. I was frightened. The war seemed to be happening in front of me. Mr. Vinh yelled to my ears:

"This represents only ten percent of the horrors and brutalities---"

Ten percent or one percent? I don't care to know. At the bottom of my purse full of make-up things I found Nam's smeared letter which says:

". . . too quiet. We crave the crowing of roosters, the cry of children . . ."

Is there any portion of the film that can depict adequately the horror of quiet moments during the war?

Who can tell where Nam's remains are in these clumps of tall grass surrounding the old citadel?

Than and I wandered all over the area. It was so hot nothing could grow here except fronds, reeds, and tussock grass. Glistening under the sun was the dead's white city. I stumbled and paused occasionally. Casting his glance all the way to the end of the cemetery, Than murmured sadly:

"So we couldn't find ----"

An old woman passing by remarked casually:

"People don't seem to stop coming -----"

"Please ma'am, may I ask you a question?" I asked boldly.

"About the dead or the living? I can only answer questions about the dead. The living are all gone."

"About the dead."

"I know it."

We followed her into an unsteady house with a corrugated roof. Inside were a divan made of palm leaves and a wooden table with a couple of broken cups. On the altar was the picture of a young man with a dim face, squinting vacantly. The old woman touched the bottom of the cups to check for dregs, then poured tea from a thermos into the cups.

"Have some tea. When did he die?" she asked.

Than was stunned for a moment, but then he told her the story as clearly as he had done before to so many people we had visited. She listened to Than attentively but shook her head:

"Based on your story I know it's hard to find your brother's remains. I tell you what: Find the woman who loved him, and ask her to speak to him for you. After a person dies, he gives his flesh and skin back to his blood relatives, and only his spirit belongs to the woman he was destined to love ---
-" The old woman explained, her voice thick and harsh.

"That's my son," she said, pointing to the altar. "I couldn't find a single bone of his. In that battle he led a commando squad. He was blown up by a mortar, mixed with sand and dirt."

She started to cough. We divided a bundle of incense and putting its sticks everywhere on the cracked burners.

Lying in our hotel that night, I saw innumerable glow worms glittering and fluttering outside the windowpanes. Stealthily I got up and opened wide the windows. Some of them staggered into our room. Than was squatting on the floor, gazing at them with intense attention.

"In my dream I saw Nam wear a reddish insignia on his lapel, two of his buttons broken, another one almost falling off," I reminded Than of the man I saw in my labor.

"When Nam left home, he was only seventeen, too young to have a girlfriend ---" Than murmured absently.

Unable to find Nam's remains, Than spent all day writing for his newspaper in the hotel. I was asked to substitute for an actor who quit because her mother was gravely ill. My role was very simple--I did not have to say a word, but just watched the birds fly past the old citadel while strong winds were blowing.

On hearing the mention of birds, Than put his pen down, grabbed his rifle, and rushed to the hill. Droves of sparrows perched all over the white reeds. Than spoke softly to the director.

"Promise that you will let me shoot the birds when we finish this scene."

I crawled stealthily to the location indicated by the director and stood up all of a sudden. Frightened, the birds flew away. I looked up at the boundless sky, hearing Than's voice wafted to me from afar, because they are innumerable. The camera clicked and stopped. Than shot his gun in the air. I shook slightly. A sparrow flapped unsteadily then went down. The smell of the roasting meat and Than's body odor suddenly made me feel nauseated.

Lying on the hill, we ate the roasted sparrows. When I finished, Than began:

"You love Nam, don't you?"

"You're insane," I said, stunned by what I heard. "Are you jealous of him?"

Than flung me down on the grass. I fought back, screaming:

"I hate all your family."

"Then who helped you become a woman and have children?"

"We will drink at the river to impregnate ourselves."

Than let go of me, turning his face away. There were tears in his eyes.

"I'm not jealous of the dead," he said. "Please ask Nam's spirit to come back."

I burst into tears. "Dear Nam, I am Than's wife and lover forever. Though we live in two different worlds, I want to be your friend. I promise I'll bear all the hardship to care for your family. Come back and stay with us, let us know where your remains are."

The water on Thach Han River still flows on impatiently, depositing its alluvia, the color of blood, on its banks. Have the remains of so many young men who fell during the war become these alluvia? Amidst the immensity of heaven and earth, which speck of sand do Nam's bones shine?

"My dear Emeline," Than whispered.

Two years after the futile trip, I was pregnant again. My pregnancy this time was much more important to both Than and me, for I knew that Nam would come back to visit us.

After an excruciating labor I gave birth to two cute boys. My God, two baby boys with two umbilical cords dangling. Oldsters, you got what you want! Two grandsons with two umbilical cords dangling. You'll have plenty of time to clean up their shit! I fainted with the desire to see an appearance...

I woke up, exhausted. Than stood by me. There were deep wrinkles on his weather-beaten face. Nam still sits up there, his sad eyes gazing out the windows. One day when Phuong was rude to me, I pointed to the altar and threatened her:

"Behave yourself, or I'll tell Nam."

She cringed.

As for Than, whenever the children asked him about Nam, he said:

"Uncle Nam has turned into a star, up there."

The children looked at the night sky full of stars. I thought about the nights we spent in Quang Tri when the glow worms were just as innumerable and the stars were as red as blood, not this green.

Now and then Than takes the children and me to the woods. Instead of firing single shots as he did years ago, he waits until the birds alight on the low branches and shoots repeatedly. The sparrows that are hit fall to the ground. The two boys help their father pick up the dead birds, frolicking.

Only little Mai stands quietly at a corner. Instead of helping me build a fire, she shades her eyes with her hand, gazing at the blue sky, at the flock of sparrows flying past the woods, upward, higher and higher.

And she smiles.

Rain

Le Minh Khue

Writer Le Minh Khue, born in 1949. Author of the story "The distant stars". Won the Prize of Vietnam Writers'Association.

In the early '80s, the construction site expanded across the river, making the whole area bustle. Vehicles from all over converged here. There were crowds of people, crowds of beautiful girls. Every day, the guest house received one wave of guests after another. Each of the women selected to work as an attendant was as beautiful as a dream, but even among them Ngan stood out.

Ngan had had serious training at the school of dance and had become a dancer for the provincial troupe. Because dancing these days didn't earn much in the way of money, she had asked an uncle to help her find work as an attendant at the construction site guest house. She didn't have to wear an *ao dai*, but merely the uniform of the guest house. The short aquamarine skirt came to just above her knees. The long-sleeved, buttoned-up white shirt was accented by a small black bow tie. This outfit wasn't much but it was enough to cause a stir among members of the opposite sex. Although it hid almost everything on that body, which was fragrant as ripe fruit, it revealed her long, slender legs, shining in her transparent skin-colored stockings. The members of the opposite sex—from dignified ministers who came to the construction site on missions, to engineers, to those who'd earned gaudy doctorates from abroad, to seventeen-year-olds who had just begun their careers—all of these people watched Ngan as she walked by.

Under the circumstances, the gazes of the men were very different from those of the women. The women compared themselves to her jealously while the men gazed with tenderness and desire and speculated on the sweetness of that ripe, unpeeled apple.

Maybe Ngan was aware of all of this. But Ngan's mother was a provincial teacher who had taught her daughter since childhood how to behave around a man. She knew how to keep a safe distance and, though always cheerful, she stopped there. She didn't lose herself and go too far. The members of the opposite sex only advanced as far as they were allowed.

But Ngan wasn't able to keep her guard up around Quoc, who, though only an electrical engineer, had a pull stronger than electricity. Quoc was one meter seventy-eight and weighed 69 kilos. He had the just-ripe body of a thirty-year-old. His face had an arrogance which was matched by the coldness in his beautiful eyes. Although Quoc often came in for coffee, he never paid any attention to Ngan, which is the reason why she began to like him. That's the fatal flaw of women, all through the ages, and Ngan was no exception. A worthy man was the one who paid no attention. Ngan vaguely understood this tactic, but still became crazy when, even in her brilliant white shirt and beautiful new shoes, she attracted no more of Quoc's attention than a brick would. After work, Quoc often sat by himself with his glass of coffee, looking aimlessly at the mountains and hills that stretched into the distance outside the window. Ngan didn't understand that Quoc also lusted after those shiny legs. But he knew that women chased after mystery and so his eyes became even colder, even more indifferent. Night after night, Ngan cried quietly over that gaze that intentionally ignored her.

This situation lasted for so long that Ngan's acquaintances began to see clearly the signs of her physical and emotional deterioration. Ngan put on her makeup more carefully but couldn't conceal her pale complexion and her sunken, sleep-deprived eyes. Her wristwatch, which had once fit so perfectly, now became loose and threatened to slide off. Quoc, who also noticed this, held back for a few more days so that the glass of water would become even more full. Then one afternoon, he turned around and, looking toward the refreshment counter, replaced his once-lofty gaze with something new. The rainy season was approaching, causing work at the construction site to taper off, and fewer guests were coming in to drink or dine. Ngan was sitting by herself behind the money drawer when Quoc stood up from his familiar table and approached her. Feeling as if a mountain was weighing down on her fragile heart, Ngan stared down at the book of checks, unable to look up. Her cheeks flushed and she felt light-headed, as if she might faint. Quoc knew this very clearly because such things were not strange to him at all. Quoc was in no hurry to begin the affair. He tenderly picked up the delicate hand. The electric current that emitted from him had the destructive power of dynamite. The girl's heart exploded and tears streamed down her face. This was the end of several months of pain and hopeless waiting. Her nightly torments. Her questions without answers. Her inability to breathe when he was near.

"Don't worry," he said. "I'll always be beside you, my little sweetheart."

A beginning like that was so sweet. Which woman wouldn't melt like water upon receiving such an offer of protection? Which woman—whether her life was as rare as crystal or as common as the trees—wouldn't exchange that life for those few words "my little sweetheart"?

Quoc lived in the building set aside for engineers. It was built precariously at the edge of the stream, in keeping with the wishes of the engineers when they first came to the construction site. His room was like any other temporary room at a construction site. Quoc shared it with a civil engineer who was currently at a meeting in Europe, putting together contracts for the building of roads. The room was simply furnished with two single beds, several suitcases, and two desks covered with papers. As a matter of fact, though, Quoc was rather wealthy. He was the son of a rich farmer in the South. Although he was working in the North, he could afford to spend money like water. His VCR and piles of videotapes had a dizzying effect on Ngan. Outside, it began to rain, the first of the long August rains that soaked the trees and made Ngan feel content now that her dream had come true. She was now beside him, the man who had never courted her but still attracted her as if by some magic she couldn't resist.

"Ngan, do you agree that from now on we'll live together?" he asked.

That Southern accent was so seductive and that question was so simple. Ngan rested against his broad chest like a small ship that had put down anchor. The child-like way that she lifted her arm around his neck and pressed her cheek against his served as her answer: "I'll give my life to you!"

But Quoc was a man with an overabundance of libido, and he didn't notice the tenderness and sacrifice of her offering. He rushed his lovemaking like an athlete racing toward the finish line, never stopping to admire her smooth skin or the romantic curves of her body, not even noticing the subtle fragrance on the white breasts of this virgin. He devoured her quickly, deeply, greedily. Night after night. Ngan was astonished that what she had held precious seemed merely the prize in a contest to Quoc. Was this love or a strenuous form of exercise, a kind of mountain climbing? How could love be like that? Sometimes Ngan let her spirit fly toward something more romantic. In some rare moments while they were having sex, she wanted to ask him sweetly that question which is a woman's luxury in such circumstances: “Do you love me?” But her hands only touched the sweat on his back, her body nearly breaking from his weight and lust. Romance seemed like the greatest luxury then and she didn't even bother to ask.

At the same time, the television next to the bed would be showing a video of naked bodies. It was a very mediocre film, but it contained one extremely interesting message: “Men only need to have a place but women always need a reason.”

And the eyes of the girl filled with tears when Quoc, sated, lay fast asleep beside her.

This continued for a month, a month of long rains and a roommate still absent in Europe. Night after night, the wind howled as it came down from the mountains and blew across the valley. Ngan had never felt such loss, so vulgarized and used. Now, she understood everything clearly, but she had nothing left to save. All she wished for now was to make a small family. Quoc, had never promised anything, had never even said, “I love you.” However, despite all that, he treated her like a wife, didn't he? And, if she were a wife, then why should she take precautions?

Around midnight, Ngan would get up by herself, her feet feeling around for her flip-flops beneath the bed, her body covered with goose bumps from the sound of Quoc's snores. Only a pig would sleep like that. Ngan went back to her room in the guest house attendants' quarters. Every night she bathed and washed out her clothes but when she finally climbed under her blanket, she always felt that something wasn't right, that she wasn't worthy of her body. She burst into tears. She always wished that tomorrow Quoc would announce to everybody that he would marry her. She would try to envision their wedding.

After the roommate returned, Ngan and Quoc rarely saw each other. Ngan's hatred for Quoc began to equal her passion. Making love without a bed was degrading. Quoc was ready to climb on top of Ngan anywhere that he could find the space, regardless of the smell, the inconvenience, the dinginess, and even the curious eyes. He began to sense Ngan's detachment and discomfort and so he began to make promises about a family and children. Ngan believed him and became more passionate for him after he made those promises. But a short while later, Quoc received a transfer to a construction site in the South. As it happened, Quoc's father had pulled this off so that the son could be near his parents.

"I'll go first, then send for you later," he told Ngan.

Ngan's tearful farewell took place in that familiar room about which she knew every detail. It was the room in which, while her nude body was being ravaged, she had stared at the landscape. Quoc's roommate had hung over the head of his bed. She looked at it as if she were pleading for help, as if she were searching for something within that small forest, bright beneath a spring rain, and she wished that others could have the same sentiments about beauty as those of a woman in love.

Quoc left the construction site on the same day that the long rains stopped. The site became busier because all the contracted engineers were reporting for work. At the vehicle unit and the construction unit, people were swamped with work. As for Ngan, she faced no consequences from her nights with Quoc; maybe, she thought, because he was so experienced about such things. She continued to work in the guest house, waiting for the time when she could go South and marry Quoc, as the two of them had discussed before they parted. Ngan continued to wear the attendant's uniform with its long-sleeved white shirt buttoned to the neck, the small black bow tie, and the aquamarine skirt that reached to her knees. But the dignified ministers who came to the construction site now nodded their greeting to her in the same way that they nodded to everyone else. The educated young men walked by her as if they were walking by a wall. Even the workers who drove the earth movers, who had the habit of making crude passes, no longer even tried to get her attention. Was she like an apple with its skin peeled off? Ngan felt abandoned. Maybe she had magnified her problems somewhat, but her heart was still tormented. What she didn't realize was that the light of happiness had drained from her face. With that light missing, her magnificent expression became as mediocre as any portrait of an anonymous girl on a third-rate calendar. Tired, Ngan walked back and forth carrying trays of glasses among the noisy customers. Night after night she pulled her blanket up to her chin and dozed off. She never recalled those sessions during which Quoc had done his exercises on her body. It was too crude, too insulting. She didn't remember and she didn't bear a grudge but she wasn't able to recover her balance either.

After a very long time, Quoc wrote Ngan a noncommittal letter. Expressions in the letter like "I miss you" and "me and you" were as dry as stones. Quoc said that if Ngan wanted to come down then she should come down. His new construction site also needed attendants of her caliber. She could beat out the rest of them because, while those girls had good legs, their faces couldn't compare to that of a Northern girl like Ngan. They exchanged a few letters and then Ngan quit her job and took her suitcases back to Hanoi. She bought a ticket for a sleeper on the North-South Express, which left at eight in the morning. Everything was going as planned, except that the sound of the train whistle frightened her. It signalled something faraway and dangerous. Most frightening of all was the fact that she would see Quoc again. If only Quoc had never known her body. If only he had never labored on the fertile field that he had so desired. If only her body were still a secret, then she would rush to him and put down her anchor at his port. But now some strange awkwardness prevented her from stepping onto the train which would take her on the longest journey of her life.

Instead Ngan went back to her province to visit her parents. Seeing her daughter so pale and sad, Ngan's mother wouldn't allow her to return to the construction site. Instead, she told Ngan to stay home, where she had just opened a small storefront selling cosmetics. Day after day, Ngan sat behind the glass case reading a book, occasionally chatting with the young women who came to buy the products. She developed the strange habit of looking at these women with intense curiosity. Has she been peeled yet? Has she known what a man with a broad chest and a sweaty back is like yet?

The rainy season arrived, making the town mud-covered and dismal. A doctor in the local hospital often came to drink tea with Ngan's father. He often leaned against the glass case making small talk. The doctor was rather good-looking and, even though they were friends, he was much younger than Ngan's father. At the end of the year, he didn't come by any longer, perhaps because he didn't want to fall into an awkward situation. Ngan cried silently because she knew she could no longer attract anyone. But she was still young and every day she tried to forget what had happened. Every day she still thought about the landscape that had hung in Quoc's room. She remembered the forest that brightened in the rain, remembered her tears, the desire for happiness she'd felt during those days.

And Ngan sat looking out at the rainy street, waiting.

1991

The Red Trace

Nguyen Thi Phuoc

Nguyen Thi Phuoc, born in 1963. Stories: "The train in July", "Words by the field". Awarded A Nguyen Du Literature and Art Prize. Military Literary Magazine's Prize.

Hong seems strangely worried as she sees me preparing for my trip to the Southern writing camp. At first I thought it's because she wants me to help her buy something pricey she can't afford yet. On second thought, maybe that's not it. We are not awkward when it comes to money. During my sleepover at her house, I notice her turning back and forth, thus ask:

-What's the matter? You okay?

-Nothing.

After a pregnant silence, she whispers:

-You remember Hoang, the postal Southern guy, who took asylum at our house?

-The Hoang who was dating you that we would sneak up on every noon?

-Yeah. Good memory there! He's a PhD now, Dean of the IT department for a university there.

-How do you know?

-Last year I saw him assisting his students in some competition. On TV.

I have no recollection of Hoang's facial features, the only thing stuck on my mind was his masculine figure embracing my sister in the West room. Before getting bombarded with B52, my house was the biggest 5-room wooden mansion in town, a potluck my parents hit when the government reallocated the properties of a landlord from a village in Nho Lam, known for producing excellent students as well as carpentry. Located at the two ends were two rooms partitioned by two intricately carved wood pictures, which my father called the East room and the West room respectively. I told what I saw to not only my parents but also other kids in the village. And so some of them, aged 13 or 14, got together and spied on Hong through her room's window every noon. My mother called me stupid. My father, meanwhile, grabbed Hong by her hair, gave her back-to-back slaps, and gave me compliments to feed my ego. He called Hoang in. I remember his low yet clear voice still:

-She still has her studies. Whatever you are up to, wait until she finishes college and give her a proper wedding. Our family does not raise whores.

Then he called Hoang's boss, demanding that he be transferred to another household.

Soon after, Hoang was called to go to B battle field. I had no idea what happened afterwards. That's the grown-ups' affair, and an old, old one at that.

-When you arrive at the South, help me look for Hoang?

-For what? To rekindle your ancient romance?

-No. But I want Hoang to remember me, for once. I refuse to believe I left no trace in his life. Meet him, tell him you're my sister, then leave, that's it!

I feel ridiculous. And surprised. Something is wrong with this old woman. She gets all dramatic all of a sudden. Close to her retirement yet acts like a teenage girl, what kind of disaster is this? Or is she taking after her seventy-something father-in-law, who insisted on going to the South to visit his ex, and died one week after his return without any illness?

I start to panic. I have seen two of my sisters die young. Maybe it was not because fate was mean to our family. This is absurd. Insane and silly. Everything is perfectly ordered for her, with a kind and loving husband- whose retirement does not hinder his great shape, mentality and manners, and she is asking for more! For years I thought she has settled down to be a wife and a mother, and now she is messing everything up.

Side effect of reading too many books maybe? Only if she would get herself together and live a quiet retired life for the sake of her children. Men are quite similar. Why would she torment herself over an old, grumpy one?...But no, she has not been over Hoang, for once. She could never fall as hard in love with anyone else. No regrets nor accusations. She spent sleepless nights crying onto her pillow. Despite looking happily at peace...She yearns for a man who stole her innocence, only to instantly vanish into thin air? Who is alive yet has never attempted to find her. Who is she to him? And what kind of man is he? Straight up a jerk. Don't buy into anything men whisper to your ears. No! He is one genuine soul. She, surprisingly, still believes he did not lie. He failed to come back for a reason. She waited for over ten years after Independence day, turning down every single man, for she feared that her heart would not be able to welcome him back ardently. You have taken me aback, sis. Maybe I am not as good when it comes to giving love. I have yet to meet a man to make me love him in admiration, desire and longing for decades, or I may have simply lost my neuron for romance?

I suddenly feel terrible for Tu, her husband, like people would pity Thuy Van for her fifteen years as Kim Trong's wife. He has been her tower of strength for years. But she now turns out to have been leaning on a blurred and distorted silhouette of another man from the past. "As soon as we got married, I told him everything. I have not done anything wrong to him ever since." "Yeah, but you live with him while your soul is elsewhere. Who needs a wife like that?"I got real mad at her. As if I'm Tu's sister, not Hong's.

I put my first footstep onto Sai Gon's land after thirteen years. Thirteen years. Sounds pretty long doesn't it? I wonder how many thirteen years' can a person live through their whole life. The strangest part is, I don't feel particularly emotional about this reunion. I'm simply dumbfounded with slight sadness.

I'm stepping incredibly close to the past, the young me, filled with passion, idealistic intentions and desires to make changes. The past with my students whose faces brimmed with excitement...

I, too, was once just as pure as the river water people here would use to quench their new guests' thirst, with all its sandy impurities sinking down to the bottom of the good old buckets. I am terrified over the idea of coming back here only to be welcomed by an unfamiliar land: a school changed over time, without my old friends, the old lake, the trees whose flower petals perished and scattered all over the campus, the classroom wherein I spent my eight Lunar New Year's Eve with my beloved students, whose door faced an apricot tree which never failed to bloom in bright gold each year-there I learned how to make the trees bloom just in time for the Eve. I would always tell the kids to leave a few leaves on so that when the new year arrived, the tree would be adorned with not only golden blossoms but also the green shade of the buds and the young leaves... Now I may come back and see only strangers. Or reunite with my former students, whose glowing freshness may have turned into grumpiness and fatigue, just like mine. I am scared thinking about how the Tien river may have swept away the flower village I would not stop rambling about after moving back to the North, or the floating flower market where I would always, all on my own, elbow my way into a crowd of strangers, wander until late night, submerge myself into a sea of colors and petals, and would not return until the salesmen stopped bringing in new stock from their boats. They would have no idea how hard I fell for them, for their passion, talent and their devotion to mother nature, how I turned them into my muse and wrote lines that would bring people, including me, to the verge of tears, without personally knowing anyone from the Hong village.

Without their land and their village, where could they have gone to plant their trees and flowers?

I am not the only one in grief. Some guys from my crew have just returned here for the first time ever since the Independence Day. People with decades carrying guns, wounds and scars around, having defeated our enemies and the death, yet are seeing Sai Gon for themselves, only now. The long journey has been filled with jokes and laughters that could break the train windows. But the moment we step into the said land, everyone becomes quiet. During the ride from Sai Gon to the Vung Tau Writing camp, there is seemingly not one conversation.

After the camp grand opening, everyone locks themselves away to focus on their writing for the whole first week. We would only meet during meals and ruffle our hair in frustration:"So damn hard! People have words flowing out of their mind without any pressure and I would be here feeling so forced to churn out anything." As a rule of thumb, if you go to a writing camp, you have to submit some work, even though it is not compulsory, one should have enough common sense and self-respect to do so when they're living off other citizen's tax. "Hey, we are torn just from enjoying a few meals from the State. How could some people sleep at night stealing money in billions?""Well, then their headaches are a billion times worse than ours! Those dirty money makers will have their children pay for their sins."

"Well, all writers complain about being poor yet any guy exposed to writing would want to do it for a living, don't they?""That's where all the mess comes from. And there are poor guys. Some others would use the writer label to feed off some other businesses, they make super easy money without a tiny bit of effort.""There are jerks in any occupation. But if a jerk starts writing he becomes...less of a douchebag. That's decent enough!""You can't be sure about that!"

A friend of mine who is a poet, drags me to a corner and says:

-I am gonna tell you a story you can use for your writing, can't do it with my poetry that's why. I was thinking, if your story would reunite this man with his sons, it would be brilliant. The one who told me this story is a friend of the guy, who lives in Sai Gon. We work in the same field and both used to stay in Dong Thap Muoi for a while and hence became acquainted. He did not tell me his friend's name, who was only referred to as "he".

Sounds challenging! No matter how thrilling or touching a story may be, it does not always become good literature. Some would be a tear-jerker when told in real life, yet a borer when written down the books. Some luck would be essential for one to write a story with soul and substance. I was only there listening to the story for fun. Or maybe blend some of its elements into a few lines of my work later on. That would be good enough for me!

It was the flood season of 1973, when Dong Thap Muoi was an endless pool of water. The trees in the woods would have half their bodies submerged in water. The rice fields were whipped clean, while a few rice buds remained barely visible as they were wavering way below the new surface. Once in a while, there would be giant rafts of water hyacinth or morning glory, each could be miles in length. They would serve as milestones leading to the canal's center. As you rode your whaleboat into the center, you would see more and more of tree tents built by the local residents along the two banks. There would, without fail, be a packet of salt and water, a few of dried rice, or a basket of snails right down the tent's base, for us. My unit was allocated to a rainforest filled with coconut, palm and apricot trees. During the day, we would sleep on hammocks tied onto apricot trees and when the night came, we would retrieve to the boat, not wanting to face the snakes. It was the land of freedom for the frogs, the fish and the snakes. Whenever there was any sign of the enemy's ship, boat or helicopter, we would sink our whaleboat down the water surface, along with the hammock. As they got out of sight, we would bring them back up. Sometimes they would wander around, back and forth, and we would have to sink ourselves into the water until our whole bodies became deadly pale, our fingers and toes disfigured with creases.

A day long walk from our location would lead us to an unit of underwater agents, a well-beloved team of "Northern boys", as affectionately claimed by the locals.

"They left behind their houses, families and their civilization to come here and fight for ours, they of course deserve our love!" Even the office workers got more love than we did. An old man caught nine kilos of puffer fish to welcome "the Northern boys", leaving us with a few tiny leftovers. Two Nghe An guys from my unit seemed extra excited to meet a new fellow Nghe An boy...They fearlessly rode themselves along countless forests, under a sky of bombs and smoke, only to find a mere compatriot, which touched me as well. I got bored after mumbling the old folk songs times and times over, and thus rode the whaleboat to find my friend, who I heard had just finished his studies at a postal training school in the North and was called in for the central core team. Navigating him was not an easy task. The radio, which was a 15W type, was installed far away from the central camp. Letting it fall under the enemy's radar would mean an instant bomb attack. His daily task consisted of not only monitoring the radio, but also guarding and contacting the central camp since the one originally in charge is in his recovery from a snake bite. He didn't die, fortunately, thanks to a few self-taught first aid tricks he learned somewhere. But apparently the bite was badly swollen and purple, to the point his flesh became rotten, showing part of his leg bone.

In the same core team as him were two girls from the North. Well, not exactly the North, but Nghe An. They were about 6, 7 years older than me. Yet they would become sentimental with tears every time the rainy season arrived. Poor girls. Drowning in water for four to five hours a day can exhaust any healthy man, let alone woman. Yet they feared not the gore, nor the Death, but the sadness, and the homesickness. He told me how bad he felt for them. There was nothing he could do but give them water lotus, freshly caught fish, snakes and turtles. He had a girlfriend back in his hometown, Nghe An, who had just been admitted to Teacher Training University, a pretty and kind girl who he only stopped missing terribly after a long time since he reached the South, for he had learned the taste of the said woman. What a boy. He was indeed not as green as he appeared to be. Even I was jealous of him.

The other day, I saw two Nghe An guys with all their cash, clothing and grocery packed, urging other fellow Nghe An men to donate. One of them got mad when hearing my question about my friend:

-That jerk from your town? If we ever see him again we will take him down with our guns!

-But why?

-He knocked up two girls of the core team, both from our town! Such a douchebag. Two of them, at the same time!

I widened my eyes in disbelief. I decided to donate a few things myself and ride a boat along the shortcut, to teach that friend of mine a lesson and tell him to run away.

He, however, got transferred to another camp, under a new name, not to my knowledge, until recently.

Both girls gave birth to baby boys, fed with the money fundraised by other Nghe An residents in the camp. After the liberalization of Sai Gon, both were brought back to the North...

The poet guy tells me:

-One girl was from another district and the other was from our village. She returned with her husband and two kids. Decades have gone by and both sides of their family don't have a clue, all thinking both kids were the husband's. The latter is quite decent. As for the said guy, I've heard his career is great, but he has stayed single until now, desperate to see his children. Last year, my friend, the one who told me of this story, tried to send her a letter through me.

She tore it apart as soon as she read the last word. Recently I met her again and asked once more, but she insisted on saying no. She's a civil servant for female affairs. The kid has graduated from a foreign language university and is now working in Sai Gon. In your honest opinion, how should this end?

I don't reply. I flinch as if a lightning crossed my head, before asking:

-The guy, is he a PhD, Dean of IT department at K University?

The poet seems even more surprised than me:

-I have never told anyone about this. How did you know?

-If that's indeed true then his name is Hoang, who used to date my sister.

-I don't know about the name, my friend never mentioned it. But the guy's address is exactly so.

I don't have a clue what I should tell Hong. And so I decide to see Hoang first and foremost.

The man facing me is dressed in formal attire, his hair grey and his straight face exhibits slight touches of sadness. A masculine type of handsomeness.

There was nothing unfathomable when two girls living thousands of miles away from their families, in the middle of violent waves of the rainforests gave themselves up to such a guy. Who knew if they'd live to see themselves coming home or not? Why not simply drown themselves into the pleasures every woman deserves, and the tight embrace of a real man? And Hong, is she the one to blame? Had my father known about this, he would have murdered her in seconds. Yet he died holding the pride of a well-mannered family.

Hoang freezes at my mention of Hong at Si village. He trembles:

-I need your sister and everyone there to see me as dead! Had I been dead, I would not have suffered for so many years.

I pretend to not know about his affairs and ask:

-Why did you get your name changed? Why did you now come back and find my sister? Something terrible happened? Did you betray her?

-Worse than that, much worse. I can't say it. I don't deserve to see Hong again.

Hoang's cell phone rings with a tango tune, which slight surprises me. He waits until the end of the track before turning off the phone.

-Hong loved the tango dance, does she still?-Hoang asks with a voice that makes me flinch.

-Hong doesn't know the dance, but she freezes whenever she sees someone dancing to it, which is weird.

-That's not it! Hong was an excellent dancer, trained by me. His voice filled with excitement. A friend of mine who returned from France taught me the dance in secret. Just like I did Hong.

Yet for years she has not danced the Tango, not at all. Only now has it dawned on me a bit. My sister's wish of leaving some trace in Hoang's life, has been fulfilled. But does Hoang's, which is to see his kids, deserve to be fulfilled? Who has the right to give an answer to that? And how will I respond to the longing look Hong will give me at the train station-for sure-because I know she will be there waiting for me? I was not heartless enough to let Hoang know I have learned his secret, how can I carve a new wound on my own sister's heart? Hoang has paid too big of a price. I only want him to have a chance to see his own children, to know he should not feel guilty to anyone else but Hong, to keep his head held high, to take pride in fathering not one, but two men raised in the land of Nghe An. Grown men in their 30s, that is!

(Translated by Prem Kapoor)

Flying Red Arrow

Kieu Bich Hau

Kieu Bich Hau. Born in 1972.Stories "Orphaned waves", "Pub of mice"...Won Award in The short story contest organized by Literature Newspaper in 2007.

Just seeing off an autistic child and her mother leaving after the intervention to restore pronunciation function, Ha pulled the iron door, tried to lock it when she heard the phone ringing. She rushed into the room in search of the smart phone, probably it was on her desk.

A stranger, claiming to be the father of an autistic child, heard that Ha intervened in many cases of successful autistic children, restored the linguistic function of the children, so he called to ask for an appointment on the next Sunday. Ha agreed to meet him at 3 pm on Sunday.

Since Ha finished her master program of educating children with autism, and her successful case in educating her own autistic son, who was able to communicate and control up to 70% of all his personal activities. Many autistic children have been taken to her for treatment. Over the past five years, Ha confidently set up a home-based center for treating her son and some other autistic children. This job turned out to give her a relatively good revenue, something that she did not expect when she decided to pursue a Master degree of education in Autism. At that time, she just thought that she studied at a high level, and carefully in this major, to please herself in recovering some basic functions for her child. Perhaps, in the end, she also needed to thank Minh, her autistic son, who once brought her unbelievable pain, but also brought her a career, an unexpected value...

Thinking about that, Ha suddenly startled. Where was Minh? It looked like she forgot to lock the door. She let go of the phone and ran outside. The sliding door widened to one side. So the son did not overlook his mother's mistake. He jumped out already. This ten-year-old boy was nicknamed "the arrow" by their neighbours because he never took a normal step, without any control he rushed like an arrow leaving the bow, despite the danger... Many times he had rushed out into the street, bumped into a running motorbike, fell swollen head, ripped off the skin of his knees, elbows, and bleed so much but he still stood up laughing. In order to prevent an accident for her child, and to make it easier for her to find the child in the middle of the crowd, she often put a red T-shirt on him.

Ha looked along the small street, trying to find the color of a red T-shirt. Her head was struck in with unlucky predictions, catastrophic images. She ran on the street, grabbed anyone she saw and asked if they had seen a boy at age ten, wearing a red T-shirt. They all shook their heads, she crossed the street and ran along the other side of it to find her son.

Ms. Ha suddenly stopped, was stunned when she saw the scene of an accident. A car stopped in the middle of the road, some people gathered there. Ha tried to calm down, rushed to the crowd and pushed someone out. Her son - Minh, lying unconscious, in the middle of the blood, right at the head of the car. She was dazed by her child.

***

People who are too fond of something often die of it. After that accident, little boy Minh did not die by the car he crashed into, but also broke his left leg and had five stitches on his forehead, three near his elbow. That was the second biggest accident in his life. When he was seven years old, he had already an accident by a car, but in that case the car was backing into the garage at a slow speed, so he was slightly injured in the car accident. Minh really liked cars, in case just seeing the car rushing by, he would try to twist the car mirror, smash the mirror or scratch the body with anything in his hand, or he was hit badly by the car. Ha had to pay to the car owners many times for her son's damaging hobby.

Over the past six years, Ha has learnt and researched methods of educating children with autism and self-therapy for her son. She has achieved the success that the media hailed it as "respectable". Minh, her son, until four years old just lying, drinking milk and crying, but could not know how to walk, talk, and eat like normal child. Ms. Ha quit a job at a university library to stay at home to take care of her child, bought many books on how to teach autistic children for reading, applying on her child, but she did not succeed. Finally, she discussed with Huy -her husband – and they decided to loan an amount of money for Ha to go to school for studying about the autistic care, and hired maids to look after the child. After learning methodically the autistic care at the school, learning more skills of this matter from domestic and foreign teachers, Ha changed the treatment method for her child. Gradually, she helped her son recover his function of talking, eating rice, vegetables, fish, meat... When she shared her joy about her child's progress on facebook, some reporters came to interview her, wrote many articles in newspaper about her amazing success. Then many people knew her, took their children to her and asked her to intervene their autistic children. She also had success with other autistic children. Since then, she has been considered an expert with achievements in the therapy of autistic children.

But after Minh's second accident, Ms. Ha was tormented by the question, did her son's progress slow down? For about a year now, Minh has not gained any new skills, although she tried her best to teach her son how to read, write and do the mathematics. Minh could only read each word separately, but not matching rhymes and sentences, and doing math just in the range of 10. But more worrying, the stronger Minh was, the more he refused to take normal steps, he just rushed away like an arrow out of the bow. Ha and her husband always had to lock the sliding doors to prevent their son from rushing out into the street. But locking up a kid inside is not a good solution. Seeing her son uneasy in his arms and legs, darting back and forth between the two walls, his eyes sometimes flashed with strange rays, Ha felt extremely insecure. Her son, who contained a strange source of energy that she did not know how to control, there was no solution for that energy to be released on right target. Increasingly, her son became more and more like a barrel of gunpowder waiting to explode.

- How about sending him to a normal school? - Huy discussed with his wife after many days of thinking, because he knew that his wife definitely opposed this idea.
- Are you crazy? - Ha lifted her eyes. - Hundreds of times we tried to send our son to a normal school, and hundreds of times the teachers

apologized for not accepting him. I'm too afraid of the shaking and sorry heads of teachers at normal schools. I had to invest in entering an autistic children education course in order to be able to teach our son, but now you made that proposal. I don't understand what you think.

- I think of nothing but the thought that my son must improve. I acknowledge that you have helped Minh to improve a lot. But from last year, he stopped, even regressed. Did you not wake up after the accident? - Huy said, his voice annoyed.
- What do you think I have to do now? - Ha was also angry - I have tried my best.
- You have to change your education method! - Huy replied.
- How to change it? Could you please clarify that for me?
- You have to think by yourself because you are an expert in educating autistic children, not me. We agreed from the beginning, that I am responsible for earning our family's living, you devote your wholeheartedly, full-time, to researching how to teach our son. Now your teaching method does not help our son to improve any more, you have to brainstorm hard to change! You cannot let Minh be like this. If not improve, then he loses.
- I am not a saint! - Ha sulked.

But her husband was right. If not improve, then he loses. Minh's last accident was a serious warning for Ha. If she could not find new ways to develop her son, then she would lose this child. The effort, dedication, love, including the fame she just gained, all would be burned down when her son completely failed in living normally. But what is the new method? Ha could not find out anything. Perhaps she needs to follow a higher level of education for autistic children, to raise her own level to be able to continue to treat her son. She shivered when thinking of the past 10 years. What is the way to continue, it seems in a blindness. If her son has not any proper future, what does she have?

Ha shook her head, trying not to let bad thoughts drown her.

***

Ha rushed over, hastily pulling Minh's left hand out of his mouth. She watched painfully at his ten fingers which were badly gnawed, swollen and bloody with the infection.

- Hoa, I told you before about this matter, why don't you hold him tight, but let him free to bite all ten fingers like this? - Uncontrollable, Ha shouted at the maid.

- I have kept him like your indication. I just left him there alone a little bit to warm his meal. - The maid explained.

With her left hand she held Minh's two hands, and used her right hand to hit his back.

- Bad boy! Do you dare to bite your hands one more time?
- No. - Minh said, laughing.

He did not feel the pain in his hands, and other parts of his body. Because if it hurt, he would not have bitten his ten fingers like that. Ha's head whirled.

Just then, a friend of Ha who worked in high school came to visit her, listened to her complaining about her son's problem, and immediately introduced her a survival skills course.

The word "Survival" sowed in Ha's brain, and pinned up there. That's right, her son needs this skill the most. He needs to be aware of what is dangerous for him, to avoid it and to overcome it. He needs to live after his parents' death...

Not promptly telling her husband about the survival skills course, Ha contacted the organizer of the course, registered for Minh to join it. The intensive course lasted one month in Hai Phong city. Ha did not dare to tell them that her son was autistic, because she was still worried that Minh would not be accepted to join the course if she told the truth. Ngoc, the key teacher and the person in charge of the survival skills training program, happily accepted Minh into the course. The fee for the course was quite expensive, but Ha did not mind. Most importantly, her son was admitted. Ha was quite reassured when Ngoc said that during the course, the children would stay in an army barrack. That meant, Minh would not find the opportunity to escape from that barrack, he would not be in danger.

Leaving Minh for teacher Ngoc to care, Ha went back home. On the following day, she often felt a bit worry. Every few minutes she checked her phone, she was afraid that teacher Ngoc would call her in order to push Minh to return home. But nearly the whole day passed smoothly without any warning calls.

Until 6 pm on that day, teacher Ngoc's phone call came around. Ha picked up the phone, her heart immediately beat up. But Ms Ngoc's voice over the phone sounded quite calm:

- I know this seems a bit difficult for me to tell you. - Ms Ngoc got to the topic - But I think you and I are both working in the education field, and above all, we are mothers, I need to know more clearly about Minh, so we can help him to have good results in the course. What are the different characteristics of Minh, just please let me know.

- I'm so sorry, teacher, for not telling you clearly before about Minh, because I was afraid you would not accept Minh if you knew the truth - Ha hesitated - My son is autistic, too hyperactive. He can not stand still, can not walk normally, just jumps away if he is not restrained...

Ha meticulously recounted the strange disabilities and behaviors of her son. For some reasons, the woman on the other end of the line was just silent, but she was able to make Ha believe so much, that she poured out all the defects of the child, without hesitation or hiding.

- I asked you about this matter, just to understand Minh better, and to prevent any risk due to lack of information. And you, no need to worry, because I have no intention of sending Minh back home. I am sure Minh will progress.

Ha offered to pay for the extra fees for Minh's special case, but Ngoc refused to get it.

The call ended, but Ha remained still for some time. What Ms Ngoc did mean when saying: "I am sure Minh will progress". Did she understand what autism was, when she could assert his progress? Ha would see if the teacher could control Minh for three days or not?

But anyway, clinging to a fragile hope is better than just suspicion and anxiety. Ha tried to focus her energy on teaching other autistic children.

***

One month of not being able to visit her child, not to call and ask any questions like a commitment between the organizers of the "Survival skills" course with the parents of the trainees, was a challenge for both children and parents. For Ha and her husband, the challenge was even harder, because their son bore a weird disease. So many questions have arisen in her mind, what teacher Ngoc did to control Minh? Would she tie him up, or even beat him, because of his bizarre behavior kept repeating? Being biological parents, they could try to endure their child, but it was too difficult for outsiders, even teachers.

The night before the day to pick up the child, the couple could hardly sleep because of impatience. When they came to Ngoc's life skills training facility and met Minh, both of them were stunned. Minh was thinner, and his bluish-white skin because of long-time locking indoors at home before, then turned healthy suntanned here. Ha held his hands. Strangely, his ten fingers have healed.

- He almost got rid of the habit of biting his fingers - Ms. Ngoc explained about Minh's better change. - Basically, he has removed

90% of old bad habits.

- What did you do? - Ha asked in shock.
- Hey, Minh, can you show your parents what you can do with tennis balls. - Instead of answering Ha, Ms Ngoc gave Minh three green tennis balls.
- Yes - Minh replied obediently and stood in front of his parents, juggling three balls in one minute without dropping any of them.
- "By that way," - Ngoc said. "When he refused to give up biting his finger, one of our teachers came up with this method, keeping his hands busy, not putting the fingers to his mouth to bite anymore."

Ha stayed quiet, happy, admiring and grateful. How could Ms Ngoc and some other teachers, who she did not know yet, could do this, while she lived with her child for more than 10 years but could not find out that method? She just threatened him, hit his hand, sometimes tied his hands helplessly. Why she was so evil! Indeed, in education, it was impossible to do everything alone, even though she has devoted all her love and wisdom to her child.

- Your son is very smart - Ms Ngoc emphasized - I suggest you to let Minh stay at our facility to be educated, taught, trained to improve the juggling balls skill, and from this skill, he will develop other skills, and restore thinking.
- Are you sure about this? - Ha was surprised. - Are there any certification by the professional organizations for your training centre?
- We assert that result for your son - Ngoc confirmed - There is no official certification for us by any professional organization, but you know, we can not wait for the right recognition long after our death. We only have actual proofs for the results. Please trust us.

Ha quietly confused. But at that moment Huy moved forward, his eyes were sparkling in hope:

- I trust you, teacher, thank you very much. Seeing that Minh could sit still up till now without rushing away and seeing his hands with healed fingers, I believe in you at once. It was a miraculous result. We are so grateful and many thanks for the teachers. Although I miss him very much, but for Minh's future, we beg you, the teacher to accept our child in boarding school here. I will let him be here as long as he makes progress.

***

Since then, Minh has been studying as a boarding student in Ms Ngoc's training centre. Under the new commitment with the establishment, Ha and Huy visited their child at the training centre once a month and picked up Minh home for two days of the weekend. Ha and her husband have gradually gotten used to being away from their child, and were relieved to see that their child has made visible progress. Minh could read and write as well as a normal child, except that his studying in maths has still not improved. After a year, Minh was no longer the "rushing arrow", he was able to walk normally. Huy was too much happy and fond of Ms Ngoc's method, that he kept praising her as a saint. He went so far as to spend time searching for parents who had the same situation, persuading them to take their children to Ms Ngoc for training like Minh. He also persuaded parents of autistic children who were following the roadmap of intervention by his wife at home to change to Ms Ngoc's method. Ha did not say anything, but she was not satisfied with her husband in believing Ms Ngoc too much. She was suspicious that Ms Ngoc was lucky only with Minh's case. In fact, in the intervention profession of children with autism, Ms Ngoc had no official degree, no certification from any educational organizations...

That day, Ha and her husband were quite surprised when they received a call from Ms Ngoc, informed that the next night, they would go to the Opera House to attend the ceremony of awarding the Vietnamese record to Minh.

- I'm sorry but are you serious? - Ha ventured to ask - What did Minh do to be awarded the Vietnamese record?
- You just need to come to the Opera House, our staff will wait at the control gate to give you an invitation. - Ms. Ngoc said briefly and hung up.

Half being suspicious, half trust the information from Ms Ngoc, Ha and her husband searched online and asked many people, to know if there was an event of awarding the national records of the year for some talented people at the following night, and the list of people who won. The record is not published.

The day had come, Ha and her husband sat in the audience, they still did not believe in what Ms Ngoc informed them, they felt restless, they could hardly concentrate on the performances and the first record awarding. Ha thought about not buying a bouquet of flowers. She was afraid of being shy on stage. Suddenly her husband hit her knee:

- Honey, look! Is that our "arrow boy"?

Ha adjusted her glasses, a short-haired teenage boy with a white satin circus outfit and green duck-necked pants went to the stage. The boy looked familiar and at the same time strange for them. Ha removed her eye glasses, rubbed her eyes, and put on her glasses again.

The boy bowed to the audience. Four assistants dressed in black came out, and they put a wooden board upon five rollers. The boy approached, holding one hand on the wooden board, one hand on the shoulder of the assistant beside him. The audience held their breaths. Her heart at that moment just wanted to jump out. Oh my God! Is that Minh? Her son? He is going to stand on those 5 rollers? He would fall down! Why did they dare to risk her son like that!

But Minh had kept balance while standing on the board lying on 5 rollers. And yet, they even gave him 8 tennis balls, and a bottle of water putting on his forehead. His body swayed, he juggled the balls, faced up to balance the water bottle. Ha held her breath and looked at her son's feet on the wooden board. God, please keep the board balanced. She could not see what that kid was doing with the balls and bottles of water anymore, the fear that made her face faint.

Applause rang out in the audience made Ha awake. It seemed that the boy had jumped down onto the stage floor and was smiling, people did wear him wreaths of laurel wreaths, his hands raised up the record symbol. And people called his name:

- Hoang Binh Minh – A Vietnamese Guinness in 2017, the youngest boy on balance with 5 rollers, putting a bottle of water on his forehead, juggling 8 balls in the longest time!

Ha felt like she could not hear anything. She felt her husband quietly holding tight her hand. It looked like he was crying. People rushed up to give flowers to their son. A television reporter interviewed him:

- In this moment of glory, what does Minh want to say the most?
- I... want to thank... to my mom, my dad, and teacher Ngoc!

Ha burst into tears, her throat choked. In the end, after so much bitternesses and trials, the couple and their son had this beautiful moment. She kept sitting and crying like that, unable to step on the stage and hugging her son, who has now become the idol of so many people. She was just afraid this moment was a dream only.

***

Mom, please drink some water! - Minh smiled with his mother.

- Oh, but where is my water? - Ha was surprised to see that her son's hands were not holding anything.
- Here! - Minh shrugged in front of his mother, letting his mother see the glass of water on his head.
- Ah, thank you! - Ha was both happy, surprised at her son's unique

way of offering water. He did not take the glass of water by his hand as usual but put the glass of water on his head. He was too smart! What a true circus actor.

- In circus language, Minh has a talented skill called "clone" - teacher Ngoc said proudly - from the waist up, he has the flexibility and ingenuity. That is why after a long time of training, he can combine three difficult skills and overcome even the best professional circus performers as you saw on the ceremony of awarding the Vietnamese record.
- We want to express the heartiest thanks to the merits of Ms Ngoc and all the teachers of the training centre - Ha said - As discussed with you on the phone in advance, today my husband and I want to take Minh home. We have just invested in expanding Binh Minh's autism intervention center, with his progress now, he will support me to help many autistic children to make the same progress.
- Actually, our training centre also wants Minh to stay here. He is a star, a role model and a motivation for others to strive. - Ms. Ngoc suddenly lowered her voice - But the right to pick him up is yours. Later, if there are any difficult cases, you can coordinate with us.

Ha and Huy took their son home. They should be happy, but then their hearts seemed being heavy. It felt like they just brushed off Minh's teacher. In the taxi running on the road, their son just kept looking back to his teacher – Ms Ngoc – being litle by litle left far away. It looked like Minh wanted to cry but tried to suppress it.

Because that teacher was the mother who has born a national record holder.

(Translated by JiKhanh)

Twilight

H'Linh Niê

Writer H'Linh Niê. Born in 1948. Story "The blue snake", "The red wind". Won the B Prize of the Unions of Art and Literature.

Dusk

It was time that Mother Earth started to draw a picture of the day.

First, faint pink appeared on the sky. Cu Yang Sin mountain range with dark blue emerged remarkably and firmly in the huge faint pink sky. Accordingly, on the left of the circle top of the mountain occurred a yellow patch. Then, a streak of darker pink appeared on the right side of the mountain, gradually spreading and spreading out on the horizon. In addition, patches of gray and blue robes of the fairies just waking up bloomed. Sparrows got up early, hurried, rushed, and flew frantically in the pinker and clearer sky. It seemed that they prepared for a long day to find food and they tried to stretch their wings and legs to relax after a night sleeping on greeny leaves or gables of long houses.

A giant golden tray jumped out of the mountaintop. Dazzling sunshine harmonized gloriously all over the sky and dispelled every sad streak recently twilight. Cool spaces in the morning would soon disappear with the sunshine. Y Trut breathed out quite deeply. Bamboo leaves in front of him vibrating seemed to welcome someone. Today was another hard day. In holiday season, full of tourists, groups by groups crossing the lake, other groups impatiently moving back and forth were waiting for their turns in the long house. Taking a look towards YaPom's house, Y Trut wanted to check whether his wife had woken up. Though he gave himself a leg up, he could not see her because of being interfered by the roof of the long house. He breathed deeply again. Y Trut did not want to bother Y Dham who was still sleepy in the next bamboo bush.

It was a long time ago and unsure about how many rice harvesting seasons had been passing. Y Trut was born about several moon seasons. The family lived happily in the forest and whenever they went somewhere, his mother always led the family, followed by his siblings and his dad was the last one to protect them from the danger. It was that morning that his mother took the family to an area with plenty of young fresh wild bananas and suddenly appearing a school of elephants with strange two legged creatures, similar to but larger than cra (monkey) jumping on the backs of the elephants, from the leaves ran towards and caught the family. At that moment, his parents had just screamed out to send a signal that his siblings had to run away fast and then they were separated far away from them by four biggest elephants from a school of new coming groups. Y Trut listened to his mother and ran and ran for his life without recognizing how many forests, streams he had passed but he still had been chased by the three elephants. When he was too exhausted, he gradually ran slowly and a throwing rope caught him on his back legs. The more he ran, the more he felt like running around a giant tree. He ran until the rope became shorter and he could not make a move. He had to stop running.

Oh oh! Since then, Y Trut had never seen his parents and siblings. It was tens of rise harvesting seasons. Where did they get lost in this huge jungle with full of deciduous trees like this?

His name, Trut was not named by his parents but later by the people who were on the back of big elephants. At that time, Trut was too small, just as tall as the people's twist. They gave him a leg bracelet and dragged him to a large area with a few trees and tied him firmly there. Eating no things for several days and missing his mother's scent made him so angry, struggle regularly, and scream but he could not escape from a rope as small as a tree he used to break easily for food. Coming out of his eyes were two big bitter drops. Lately, becoming the leader of a herd of ten war elephants in the village and Y Tlo's family, Trut knew that humans called the ropes as chains, bracelets with sharp objects which they used to train baby elephants caught from the forests. The twisted rope they threw and tied firmly on Trut's back legs was made from dried buffalo skin. It was highly durable.

Y Nang, the youngest son in Y Tlo's family, who brought Trut a first bunch of grasses after being starved for several days. He was a little boy. Trut was the smallest one in the school but Y Nang was as tall as half of Trut's trunk. He looked at Trut with his black bright eyes so Trut felt that he was reliable. Trut picked up the fresh grass with his trunk. After a month, Trut came home with Y Nang by holding Y Nang's hand. There, in Y Tlo's house, there were already seven wine jars tied firmly along the long house and a tray with a pig head, tail, and other things. Firstly, mjao (a shaman) wished family health and then worshipped "NguachNgual" god to inform him that the family had a new member. Finally, it was a naming ceremony (Y Trut was given to him on this ceremony). Worshiping Y Trut that " Don't escape because of fear. Eating bamboo in the village comfortably. Living in the village a hundred years and becoming a good hunting elephant to hunt baby elephants.

Since then, the family considered Trut as a sibling of Y Nang. They were always together. They became even closer. That was right because Nang had not had a health worship as Trut. When going hunting or having a new baby elephant come home from the forest, giving birth, or getting sick, all of these things happening were offered a worship. The two grew up together, Nang took Trut to the forest to transport woods home to build a long house with about tens of Trut's steps long. Following Y Nang's father to carry rice, weapons for soldiers fighting boom boom. Due to his help, it was a day that there were a lot of people coming to offer Trut a worship. This time was not as regular worship for his health but for a medal: "having contributions to soldiers". Y Nang said that because Trut did not know about that. He did whatever Y Nang and his father asked him to do. The medal was hung in the long house for fun and Trut was happy to have more bunches of sugar canes and bananas. He was allowed to have his wife eating with him.

No one counted how many seasons that the deciduous forest had been chaning its red clothes. Nostalgia for his parents calmed down because of the affection of Gru Y Tlo's family. Especially Y Nang, Trut loved him much. He always added some salt to grasses for Trut to have better meals (forest leaves did not have salt in) so Trut always remembered his food and he had his meals all the time).

Nang got married and Trut married H Biat. Y Nang had helped Trut get married with Biat because he saw them always get together when they were in fields and at that time Trut got angry easily. Sweat from both sides of his temple was flowing and it was smell of his sweat made H Biat realize him from far away. H Biat was very beautiful. Compared with other girls in the village, she was the most beautiful one. Her ivory just came out and when she smiled at Trut, she looked so pretty. She also had green dots like alstoniascholaris flowers in her back ears. That March, Djam Tang (a native plant in the Central Highlands of Vietnam) was blooming pinky along the river. There were only Trut and H Biat in the field. It was rarely for elephants to stay in the same bathing area but the young man and lady loved each other inseparably. They panted, screamed, and trampled a young bamboo bush nearby... Accidentally, Nang knew that H Biat was pregnant. The two families had organized a wedding ceremony for Trut and H Biat. In the wedding day, there was a range of wine jars and tasty roasted pig. The village had fun for several days. Mjao - shaman called it a wedding ceremony but it had a ceremony called a punishment one for the girl's family so there was a duck and a dog to get rid of unluck. The duck and dog were from H'Biat' owner, the girl's family offering to villagers. People often did not like having baby elephants because it was really hard to train them. H'Biat' child, she was later sold to people in Lang Bian mountain. After marriage, they lived separately with his or her owner but in the TrongLoaih (a type of eggplant) blooming season, the wind bringing the smell of Trut's sweat had helped the couple find each other, their owners would not be fined because of their meeting.

In recent years, the village had suddenly been different from the past. There was only once each year in the flower blooming season and there was an elephant racing festival in the village, people from elsewhere came to the village as many as trees in the forest. In such races, Trut had always been trying his best to win the race because of Y Nang and his father though it was a running, tug of war, or soccer. However, Trut had not led the group of elephants to hunt baby elephants in the forest. The forest gradually became so smaller that Trut was no longer alone in the grazing area as before and he was tied at the bamboo bush. H'Biat was there. It was about several flower blooming seasons had passed but they did not have time together. When missing the scent of wild plants in the forest, Trut moved his head and trunk up high screaming out loud to release his stressful mind. Instead of being free wandering in the forest, there were about five to six elephants together riding visitors across lakes and rivers. Trut always led the group to cross the lakes safely and he used his trunk to check the depth of the lakes (why did not human know? Leading the group always was a elephant mother. Everything had changed inversely). Sometimes, looking back, H'Biat was in the middle and just Y Thi and Y Dham in between but she seemed too far away!

Occasionally, Trut's head was hot severely and the whole body was shaken, especially when the yellow Phi flowers swinging in the wind and seeing H'Biat standing there but he could not move towards her. When a woman in their period sat (in an arm chair) on his back, it gave him goosebumps immediately. However, though he struggled, his mahout also used Creo hitting on his neck painfully so he had to listen to him. Gradually, he got used to this boring job. It was because he loved Ea Thom very much so he did not want to make troubles like the "guy' Y Thih in Krong Na, killed his mahout last March. The reason was that the guy wanted to meet his wife badly in the flower blooming season scented in the wind and he was forced to serve the tourists. He was shot as a punishment. Thih!

Trut's beloved one, Y Nang those days, became Ae Thom (Thom's grandfather). He was too old, no more health, from morning till midnight with a bended back and his two knees higher than his ears, sitting by the fire smoking with a bong.

Y Thom, Y Nang's grandson, was after money weirdly. He was a mahout who used the power of the kreo (a tool to command elephants) to repress the elephant. He just cared about riding the more visitors the better. Many times, Trut felt tired! According to the human, Trut was about 100 years. His health was exhausted. Because of Ae Thom's bread and butter, Trut had tried his best. Recently, some men with unfriendly faces came and asked to rent all flocks of elephants in the village to transport woods at night. Ae Thom did not agree and said:"Trut was as old as me and let him rest at night. However, Y Thom did not listen to his grandpa and he scolded at him "you were old, you knew nothing. Let me own money to buy a motorbike to ride some girls". Talking about money made his eyes brighten like fire. Yang (god)! Seeing his grandpa's tears coming out from deep eye sockets made Trut really hurt. However, if he had hit Y Thom with his trunk, it would have made him sadder. Trut did not want Y Nang's head hurt any more.

Thus, the herd of elephants rode tourists in the day and pulled the woods from the deep forest to an isolated place near Srepk river. Then, the people just dropped these woods into the river, the raft, and pushed them to be flown. The forest was very far away, starting their journey at about late afternoon in strobe and reaching the forest at midnight. Being worn ropes on the neck (each one wore two to three long ropes), the mahouts forced the elephants to go fast and reaching the wood gathering place was also the time that the Mother Earth painted the sky. Coming back home, they just rested until the sun raised. Then, they just had some bananas, sugar canes for breakfast. After that, Trut again led the herd and checked the path to ride tourists across the lake... This afternoon, Trut was too exhausted, his pairs of legs seeming to be out of his body, and could not stand any more. His big ears like deciduous leaves, his tail with several hairs left at the top of it, hanging down tiredly (greedy guys plucking the herd's hairs as thieves nearly leading the herd looking like hairless, these thieves sold the stolen hairs to people who believed that if they wore a elephant hair ring, it would bring them luck). However, Trut still wished he had a chance to touch on H'Biat's back with his trunk or leaned on his wife's cool blue skin. If only the two of them could jump and run in the woods to the stream, drink a pool of water, lovingly yield to the young trees like when they first loved each other ...?

Trut had been trying all day to lead the group of elephants across the lake and find a way to be with his wife, sometimes lingering on the bamboo bush, picking up the wet leaves and putting in the mouth, waiting for H'Biat to come. Several times later, Trut deliberately slowed down, walking his feet in his wife's warm feet (H'Biat's left front foot had a broken nail, so it was easy to recognize). However, Y Thom did not agree with that. There were two or three groups of visitors waiting for the their turn so you had to hurry and return. When he saw Trut stop, he poked the kreo strongly into the neck so bloodyly and painfully, Trut took a slow step forward.

Looking up high, leaning up to look through the long roof again, not seeing his wife, Trut quietly rushed towards the source of the Srepokriver. There, there was a deep pool. There were many crocodiles below. During his trips through the forest, Trut had led the herd through it. It would be a place where Trut chose to leave his body coming home with Mother Earth, Mother Water.

The village was gradually becoming far away behind him, Trut's steps lifted up and down getting slower and heavier...far away it seemed to be a painful scream from H'Biat.

Twilight slowing... slowing ... falling...falling!

The Cat Ghost

Phong Diep

Phong Diep was born in 1976. Published 25 books. Won the Prize for the the best short stories about women after the war held by the Military Literary Magazine in 2014.

The smiles on the lips of the children disappeared immediately as they heard their father call urgently. The two wheelchairs, bumper to bumper, ran along the narrow and dark corridor. The old cat was groaning at the narrow turn to the storehouse. Two immovable dark blue beams opened widely at them.

"What's matter do you think? Daddy came home earlier than usual".

"The sound of the bell seems to be angry".

"Do you …"

The two wheelchairs both turned toward the side room. All the light bulbs have been turned on unusually. The floor shines up. The door is widely opened. Besides the big pair of shoes of their father, there was a small pair of sandals.

Perhaps their owners stepped in a hurry that the mat on the threshold was pushed a little bit out of its proper place.

"Do you think that daddy wants us to go in? It's a long time..." The bell rings again, shortly and sharply.

The two children waveringly pushed their wheelchairs to the door. A woman was standing upright in the middle of the room, waiting just to see them. Her face was cold and sad. Her complexion turned faint in the too bright neon light.

The father was sitting quietly in the armchair. The ashtray on the coffee table was full of cigarette butts.

"From now on, Ms. Boi will teach you," the father kept quiet for a while and looked at them strictly.

"No one is allowed to answer her back. Are you clear? Now, go back to your room."

The woman tiredly waved goodbye to them. Her hand was long with skinny fingers.

"We will see each other again tomorrow morning".

The two wheelchairs turned back to the narrow and long corridor. The old cat was still sitting at the narrow turn to the storehouse with two immovable dark blue beams. The clumps of trees in the garden fluctuated as the wind was blowing impetuously.

"Brother, I am scared".

"Daddy will leave tomorrow morning. Still long-day business trip".

"At with lots of presents".

"But daddy never talks with us".

"Because he is busy. He comes home to relax".

"I sympathise with him. Is there time when he becomes tired of looking after us?"

"You are talking nineteen to dozen".

The alarm went off loudly and woke the children up at seven o'clock. They rushed to get their clothes on and dragged themselves to the wheelchairs placing next to their beds. They could hear the sound of Ms. Boi's sandals clacked on the marble floor. The door of their room opened immediately. The children did not even think of locking the door when they were in.

In the daylight, Ms. Boi looked thinner and sicker than they thought. Her two deep orbits looked at them coldly. The thick dress glued to her skinny figure. Women at her age usually do not wear clothes like that.

"Good morning Ms. Boi". The children hesitantly said.

Ms. Boi seemed not to reply to them. She went straight to the beds. The messy blankets and mosquito nets were folded up in a moment. The bed sheets were straightened up.

"Ms. Boi, did you sleep well last night?" The girl inhaled a deep breathe and made the acquaintance as her brother started to roll the wheelchair to the door.

"Where are you going?" Ms. Boi turned around quickly and asked in a piercing voice.

"I want to go to the garden".

"No. Go to wash your face and sit at the table to have breakfast. Then, we'll study".

The girl looked anxiously at her brother struggling on the wheelchair.

"What's the matter with you?"

Ms. Boi silently pushed each of the wheelchairs out of the room and closed the door. The breakfast started in silence. Ms. Boi ate very fast and did not make any noise. The children chewed and swallowed slowly and reluctantly. Ms. Boi had to sit waiting for more than 10 minutes till they finished their breakfast.

"All are nutritious substance that help nurture a healthy body," she explained as she was cleaning up the table.

"Why didn't you eat up?" Up to one third of the girl's dish was left.

"It is for Ket, Ms."

"It is an old mad cat," the brother explained as he was cleaning his mouth.

"An old mad cat?" Ms. Boi's voice lowered down.

"It screams at night and bites anyone it sees."

"No, it does, Ms. It is too old. It loses a handful of fur. However, it does not go away like other cats."

Ms. Boi kept silent and dropped herself onto the chair. The children quietly left the dining table and went to the next room which was messed up with lots of books and notebooks. A handful of cat fur stuck on the window frame.

Ms. Boi started a new lesson with a strict face.

"The cat ghosts usually come up and scream at midnight. They call each other compassionately and walk in groups…"

The girl glanced at her brother anxiously. However, they kept listening and did not say a word.

The lesson ended when Ms. Boi became fainted. Her face turned emotionally white.

***

The cat did not turn up at the following meals. Its gray fur scattered everywhere in the house.

The children were banned from staying up late. When the evening lessons ended, they had to return to their room and switch off the lights to sleep. This made the girl feel uneasy.

"Do you think that it will die?"

"Who? That smelly Ket? It is too old".

"I did not mean that," the girl explained discontentedly.

"Nobody has fed it for days. It does not harm anyone."

"Ms. Boi would keep telling stories about the cat ghosts if you keep saying like that," the brother said to threaten his sister, "Ms. Boi has a lot of stories about them".

"But I don't like them," the girl sighed and covered her face with the blanket.

"It may die".

In fact, the cat has not died because the brother then heard it groaning at the back of the storehouse when he woke up at midnight. He tried to wake his sister up but she was sweating due to a stomachache.

The corridor was dark. The voice of the cat was fading away. The brother got out slowly on the wheelchair. Ms. Boi's room in the front of the storehouse was still bright as nothing had happened. The boy took a deep breathe and called:

"Ms. Boi! Ms. Boi!"

Now he was standing at the door of Ms. Boi's room. The wind was blowing violently at her bed. Nobody was there.

"Ms. Boi! Ms. Boi!" There was sound of stone and soil echoed at the back garden and then it was silent. The boy tried to return as quickly as he can. Suddenly, he was afraid of the sound of the wheels stressing on the marble floor at midnight. When he was at the room, his sister became glassy with full of saliva on the corners of her mouth. The boy took his sister to the wheelchair and pushed it to the garden on a shortcut.

The woman was frightened as she went to open the door for the children. There are discussing voices inside the house. The sound of the footsteps running toward the gate. And the sound of the water flushing. The girl was placed in the bed. There were many people around her. The boy's wheelchair was pushed to a corner. The mosquitoes flied over his face but the boy still slept as he was very tired.

At noon, there were three men and a beautiful woman went to see Ms. Boi. Then, all went away in an old Zeep, whose engine sounded like a grinding machine.

Ba ... continued to come to cook breakfast for the children. When she went to the back garden to get the vegetables, she saw a plot of land crushed. The children were in their room, reading books until they heard the bell informing meal time.

The father returned after a long business trip. His complexion turned dark with a gaunt face.

"What happened at last?"

"I don't know, daddy. But I heard the cat groaning at the back of the storehouse at that time".

The man sighed: "There were stories about mad cats. They bit people and they died because they did not know. Ms. Boi's child was among them".

The children sat quietly. For a while, the girl said:

"Daddy, we want Ms. Boi".

The father stood up tiredly.

"Children, return to your room. From tomorrow, you will go to school".

The two children silently rolled the wheelchairs to the dark corner.

"Brother, Ket was not mad".

"But we said differently".

***

A new school year started and the children had to get up earlier than usual. The bell rang loudly along the narrow corridor full of sunlight. The old woman, who was living next door, was waiting for them at the ground.

"Goodbye daddy!"

The door of the living-room was still closed. The mat was pushed to the corridor, one of its corners was rumpled.

Near the school, there was always a woman whose thick dress glued to her skinny figure, waited to see them passing by and then left.

The day he goes to Battle

Nguyen Thi Ngoc Ha

Nguyen Thi Ngoc Ha, born in 1949. Author of "Send you my lullaby". Won the Literature prize in 2015 by Vietnam Writers' Association and Ministry of Security.

Remembered the hard time

My young brother was afraid that our mother would be worried, so he only told me privately that he had volunteered to go to battle. At that time, I didn't believe what my brother said because there was less than a month left until the graduation exam of his high school, and then the exam of university. If that's right, I still did not believe my brother would be accepted.

That time, at the battlefield, the battle was very fierce, my brother was only seventeen years old, his face was immature, no beard, his limbs were still limp. I said: "When you can carry fifteen kilos of rice that our family bought every month, and run across the street, then I will believe you are a soldier. Go fight the real enemy, not play the fake match, it's serious, not a joke". He laughed. In my eyes, it was still the smile of a mature man.

In the early afternoon my mother knew the news. When she came home from work, she did not go to the kitchen or indoors as usual, but sat down on the steps. Mom was silent. Eyes were wistful to look on indefinitely. Seeing my mother sitting in a daze like that for a long time, I couldn't bear it; "I already know?" "Yes, I know." My mother remained in the same posture. She answered her daughter as if to answer someone in a distant place.

My mother's voice was wildly with the sound of wind rattling via the ragged banana leaves in the thunderstorm of night before. I sat down slowly beside her, gently stroked her white hair that fell across the forehead. I wanted to say something to reassure my mother, also to reassure myself, but for some reason all the thoughts stuck together.

After a long silence, my mother said in a very low voice: "I don't think your brother has that much energy. I can't stop this decision of your brother, I just worry that his legs are not hard and the stone won't be soft among the fierce bombs". She used to simile when she taught us, but the simulations about the physical condition of my brother seemed too painful. At that time I just secretly hoped he was eliminated. But my brother was not only not eliminated, but his name was also on the first list of that volunteer campaign.

***

The Youth Union of my school organized a rice harvest to prevent water-logging for the people. I joined a few days before coming home. Looking around, I did not see my brother, I just saw my mother leaning on her back in the iron box containing rice. From the empty box came the sound of my mother's hand scratching and dredging. (Later, whenever I remembered that moment, my chest became heavy)

My mother came out sadly from the house, holding a rack of rice in her hand. Mom looked at me half as announced, half as blaming herself. "Your brother is on the way tomorrow, I want to give him a full meal without padding, but the rice is only this much, there is only daphnia in there ..."

I took a deep breath and then exhaled for my mother's pity about brother: "It's my fault, mom. Every time I took rice and blew rice, I should have increased the padding and reduced the rice, so that can save for having special case or someone was sick and cooked porridge as you told me, but looking the two brothers were too difficult to eat, so I felt so poor for them, and I kept loading rice more than boron seed". My mother said nothing, she just thoughtfully pouted.

Suddenly I remembered. My best friend – Thao's family just bought rice. In this period, it can eat wheat fillings, not dry cassava or daphnia like the previous time. "Mom, I can borrow from the family of Thao, flour can mix with this rice. I will do as you instructed… Sprinkle water into the powder and rub it evenly, when the dough almost like a new grain of rice sprinkled in the rice cooker, it is almost dry, when the rice is cooked, mix well. What a good taste! It tastes like sticky rice, we love to eat it like that… ". I said bluntly, and my mother just chuckled trying to give her daughter an approving smile.

The youngest brother also followed his brother to bid goodbye to neighbors. When the two of them got home, it was time for the rice to come. My family's meal that day was really a banquet. In addition to the pork ribs mixed with chopped dried onions with familiar salt and seeds and a plate of boiled sweet potatoes, there was also a full plate of fried eggs. The brown hen laid nearly a dozen eggs. I know my mother to plan eggs hatch into flocks, raise them to grow up for saving food. But tomorrow her son will go to battle, she had nothing to regret. Both the chicken and the egg nest were made all for meal.

My two younger brothers with this special event suddenly grew up. Usually they were fighting all day, I always had to stand to judge. But that day the two of them kept sticking together, especially the youngest one to pick up the food for the elder brother. Suddenly I turned to my mother and saw that she was eating nothing, just sticking her chopsticks to look at the children, her eyes stopped filled with water.

Mother silently prayed in front of our father's altar. Looking up, I saw that my mother was unusually calm. Mother smiled to warm the heart of the child about to leave home, but I still noticed in that smile as the wind was flowing through. All three children feel the imbalance in their mother.

My brother came to hug mother's shoulder. His voice was trying to speak like a real man: "Don't be sad, mother, if I hear the news in the battlefield that you are sick, I cannot hold the gun ...". Paused for a moment, his voice gradually decreased. "I hope that in the future, the youngest of our family will not know about war anymore.".

I was creepy. My two younger brothers are only two years apart. Naturally, my nose was stinging, I quickly averted my eyes from my mother's eyes.

***

Early morning, the horizon was shining in the color of sunlight. Mother rushed to me and put a few handfuls of without meat noodles in my hand. (That day we used to call boiled noodles without meat.) “This morning he didn't eat anything, you try to force him to eat when comes to the gathering place". "Yes" - I tried to chase him quickly to get rid of wanna-to-crying image of my mother.

The line of phoenix trees that year seemed to bloom earlier than usual. Each phoenix still blooms the color of the pupil's red blossoms in front of the eyes of the boys going to battle. Probably just flooded in the new sun, his cheeks were red. I still moved step by step along my brother, but I felt that each step further and further away. I asked myself silently. "Don't know when the war will end? Don't know when my dear brother will return. "

Around the cars that were camouflaged with green leaves, every man who had not even come out of an immature age, they must be like my younger brother, never knowing the warmth of a girl's lips.

It was past noon that the cars carrying the recruits slowly switched wheels. The last one was over. My brother's waving arms were sucked in the sand that was rolling in the sun in the wind. Only me – standing with dream of hope.

(Translated by Khanh Phuong)

Indian Poems

Still Crying

Nawal

Nawal is a senior poet in Hindi, who left for his heavenly abode last year. He is famous for his love poems. All through his life he avoided limelight yet he is highly popular among his readers.

Unable to trace his house
A five years old child
Is still crying.

Slogan shouting people
Are indulging in arson
Audible are the wails
from the houses
People are running
helter skelter
It's disorder all around
And the crying child
Is in search of his house.

Around seventy years back
Sometimes this child
was on the roads of Lahore
Sometimes on the roads of Amritsar
Sometimes over Jhelum and Jagadhari
Sometimes on the roads of Delhi
Around fifty six years back
He was still looking for his house
On the streets of Calcutta
Amidst carnage and arson.

Those killed had no God
And the gods of those responsible
Were safe and secured
In their own fortresses
Alike their rulers.

That child too had no God
Neither earlier nor now.

The same child is now in search of God,
Who had created this universe
And in whose name
People have opened different shops.

Cut throat competition
Is common in trade.
How else would the shops survive
If they don't cut each other's throat.

No disease in this world
Is as big
As predominance.

(Translated by Prem Kapoor)

No Degeneration Any More

Amitava Chakravorty

Eminent Bengali poet Amitava Chakravorty is a retired banker by profession besides being a well-known socio-cultural activist attached to various socio-cultural organizations. He has four published books of collection of his poetry.

May the songs of mental consciousness
Amass trust and confidence among all today
Among the maddening swing of light and air
May it fill the life with a little love and affection
And enliven the scorched contageous breaths
Burying the terror somewhere
May the unblemished man with free mind
Express himself
Shaking off all the expectations
May he openly reveal from top to bottom
His delight destroying all the embankments.

World is undergoing a labour pain now
Our mother Earth is in a devastating state
From day one of the creation
Having been educated
It has destroyed many killer viruses
As if it was a trend of the past
And would never change now
The man, flowers and the Earth would smile again
There won't be a degeneration any more.

(Translated by : Prem Kapoor)

Attire Hanging On a Hanger

Namita Chaudhuri

Namita Chaudhuri is an eminent poet in Bengali literature. She edits Nandimukha literary magazine and is a recipient of various literary awards. 25 collections of her poems have been published.

It seems I have been hanged
On some hook of a hanger
Budging is no more in my hands
I cannot even move my eyes all around
My body is lying dormant
Like an attire on a hanger
Nothing is left any more
My neck seems to be attached to a hook
I am unable to bend and lift anything
What an existence is this
Neither right nor left, neither here nor there
I am just hanging on a hanger
Like an attire.

(Translated by Prem Kapoor)

The Dry Shadows of March

Sharmila Ray

Born in 1960 Sharmila Ray writes both prose and poetry in English. She has nine collections of poetry to her credit and her poems have been translated into Urdu, Hindi, Bengali, Slovania, Hebrew, Spanish, Uzbeek. She is recepient of various awards.

The dry shadows of March have histories inside it.
God has disappeared down empty streets and shuttered shops.
The whole city is gothic zigzag of grey and more grey.
And sometimes a filigree of yellow superimposes on the pattern
Now the Neem talks to the Banyan ripping apart its petrol smeared gag
And the birds have a field day
But it seems a pity that the real world is virtual crisp and definite
Under some fairy's moon cold spell.

From childhood we have heard about the seven wonders of the world
All man-made. Like me many others have added rockets to their list
By risking everything we have forgot that the stars do not belong to us
The universe penetrates and burns
And we are just fleshy dollops
Sliding and slipping on earth's skin.

I'm Life-long Love-Maid of Ravana

Ruma Bhattacharya

Ruma Bhattacharya is a prominent Assamese poet, who prefers to sail against the Stream. Besides being a police official, she is a social activist too and has received various awards for her poetry.

What's the need of an arena to kill Ravana?
Which epic has Ravana as a villain
And why?
In my eyes Ravana is a super hero
Of the youth in life.
If merits and demerits are both signs of humanity
Why then Ravana is despised?
I wish to become Ravana's beloved.
He is the dream-man of my life-long devotion.
Who wanted to find Sita
In the chains of grandeur.
I am a sita of today, and now
Ravana is my only lover.
No, I am not a Sita of yester-years,
Amphibious, reptile.
I am a goddess of agriculture today,
Who aims to be on top of the world-stage.
And so I wish to be the beloved of Ravana,
Who had been valiant, learned, loving and heroic.
I am prepared to be a rival of ten Mandodaris
And yet I'm ready to be Ravana's beloved for
thousands of lives.
I am the claimant of his vermillion.
Stop now,
Or I will myself shut off
This arena of killing Ravana.

(Translated by Prem Kapoor)

Campfire

Dr. Indu Joshi

Letters dance in circle
I am in the middle
Words move in a circle
I am in the middle
Sentences sing in a circle
I am in the middle

Round and Round in a circle
I am in the middle
I dance in a circle
Letters are in the middle
I move in a circle
Words are in the middle
I sing in a circle
Sentences are in the middle

Round and round in a circle
Fire! letters
Fire! Words
Fire! Sentences
Round and round in a circle.

(Translated by Prem Kapoor)

Dr. Indu Joshi is a prominent academician and renowned Hindi poet. Two collections of her poetry have been published. She has also edited a number books and she is the editor of quaterly journal 'Nari Manch Apoova' besides Swar Samarth, and Sahitya Bulletin.

Dejected Sparrow

Geeta Dubey

Born in 1973, Geeta Dubey is an educationist, well known poet and critic. She has edited a number of books. Her poems, criticism and research papers have been published in various magazines.

The sparrow is extremely dejected today
Perched on a window-sill
It looks around
Searching for some corner
Some pigeon hole
where it may arrange its menage
But finds none.
Sanitationist people
Have blocked all the windows
To prevent dust and sunshine
Where would it build
Its tiny nest?
Where would it go?
There is a network
Of mobile-towers
All around
It feels suffocated
Nobody keeps water in bowls
For the birds anymore
Nobody throws about corns and grains
Any more on the roof-tops
As people living in flats and apartments
Have no time for roof tops
And where are the roof tops now
All have been devoured by the promoters
So, will the sparrow be lost
In this jungle of concrete?
Who will save the sparrow?
All are busy in 'Face book' and 'Whatsapp'
Nobody bothers about the little sparrow
It doesn't have any 'union'
Nor any representative.

Only few environmental freaks
Raise questions
Few crack brained poets
write poems...
So, will the sparrow survive
Only on the pages of books?
Will it chirp in poems alone?
This piercing question is
Churning since morning----
Where would the sparrow go?
It had adorned its little world
Behind the framed photograph
And that has been destroyed
By the unmerciful human hands
The sparrow is extremely dejected
And is crying aloud
It is registering its protest
I am reassured
Having seen its courage
And untiring efforts
The sparrow is not despondent
With added vigour
It has started once again
It would build afresh
It nest
It would spruce up
Its little world
As many times
As we destroy it.

(Translated by Prem Kapoor)

Virility And Woman

Vidya Bhandari

Born in 1945, Vidya Bhandari is an eminent poet in Hindi and has eight titles of poetry and short stories to her credit. She has also edited two books.

Alive are the feet of your virility
As I have rolled up my feet
Like a silk-worm.

Alive are the eyes of your virility
As I have lowered my eyes
Like a modest bride.

Alive is your virility
As I have concealed my identity
With the hem of my shawl.

You've held your head with pride like Himalaya
As I am having a sense of dedication
In my heart.

The pages of your dictionary didn't flutter
As I myself am a dictionary.

High sound of your virility continued
As I adopted the language of silence
Lime an ascetic.

I did not befriend protest
So your virility is alive.

I myself have become your breath
To keep the breaths of your virility running.

Better you perceive me.

(Translated by Prem Kapoor)

Sufferings of A Poet

Sushil Panja

Sushil Panja is a proletariat poet of Bengali language. Once he was a Jute Mill Worker, who is now out of job for years. He writes what he has experienced in life. About eight collections of his poems have been published.

Destructive game is being played
with the livelihood of a poor poet
By the mill-owners,
The mill is under lock-out for three years.

No wage, no provident fund
Puja bonus is also due for two years
It is known to all the political parties
Even the government is not unaware
Far more aware are
The cunning and clicky trade union leaders

The poet and his family are
Passing days under hunger, poverty, misery
No, he is not alone
There are thousands of workers
Of hundreds of closed mills
Who are suffering along with the poet

Lonely poet with infirm body
is lying desolate in a dark corner
While the flowers are swinging
Over the dilapidated wall outside.

(Translated by Prem Kapoor)

In the Name of Sun

Jitendra Dheer

Born in 1954, Jitendra Dheer is a well known Hindi Poet and critic. His poetic work has been published in more than 20 collections. Collections of his poems titled 'Indradhanushi Rangon Ka Sach' earned him a wide acclaim. He was awarded Geet Gandharva Award in 1998.

You could give
Nothing but hollowed words
    kept on writing history
    of concocted achievements
    In language of statistics
Pen, paper, ink
and writers
Are all yours
    Kept on changing administrative machinery
    In the name of system
    used us in incidents of
    Riots and violence
    In the name of non-violence
In search of light
The aging eyes, teethless mouth
Rusted lantern with broken glasses
Hanging in the cottage
    This is what you have gifted us
    In the name of Sun.

(Translated by Prem Kapoor)

A Verse

Shahid Hussain 'Shahid'

Born in 1948, Shahid Hussain 'Shahid' is one of the prominent poets in Urdu language , and is ceaselessly writing poems since 1970. For his literary works he has received many awards from various organizations.

The time would be troublesome
The scene would be blood smeared
There would be a stone over the body of glass
Every house would be sheathed with fire

There would be a dagger in your hands
While pain would be our camp

There would be hiccuping blue water
While the ocean would turn bloody-red
Why are you worried about the world
You would face this scenario very often

People would be showing off blandishment
while keeping a dagger under belt

To whom would you open your heart
Everybody would have a changed posture

'Shahid' being a dutiful person
Is bound to be homeless one day.

(Translated by Prem Kapoor)

A Poem

Ruchhita Kazaria

Born in 1982, Ruchhita Kazaria is a poet who writes political poems. She is a prominent peace activist and a journalist and has edited about 20 books.

No, it's not a border, it's a thorn
It's a tree of the barrenness
Someday such a storm would rage
And would fly away with the border

There would be such an earthquake
That would bury all the wounds
On that fateful day we would meet...
Oh dear friend!
And would write an autobiography
Of the vagrant border.

Just How!

Anita Sharma

Born in 1968.
Collection of poem 'Inner Landscape'
Articles and poems published in leading English magazines.

Just how my small town became larger than life,
just how the narrow streets swelled up
with sea of memories
on that one unexpected trip
Just how hard I tried to adhere to the links
to break the barrier and the link
Curiously peeping out of the window,
I sniffed the air, sensed the dust
re- winded, to break the gap crust
formed by the years
that slipped too soon
in a manner unjust.
Just how the gigantic lorries fetched tons of coal
from the land of mafias
where we had fearlessly strolled
sometimes in search of diamonds
that hid in those mines,
to get them studded
into rings of gold.
Just how the neem had grown manifolds
demonstrating warmth,
by reciting prose from the days
when we were just learning to stand on our toes,
played mind games
and gradually rose.
Just how all known appearances
merged along to reunite,
with expressions of hope
of tearful delight
and a more developed insight.
Just how the school teacher failed this time
to suppress the lump
caused by the time leap,

by the jump too long,
erasing my myth
of mentors being exceptionally strong.
Cacophony by the timepiece distracts
signaling retreat..
I obeyed
Silently prayed
Grateful and indebted
for a set of fresh memories in clusters,
time had again bestowed
And, just how!

Anguish of the Innocent

Dilnasheen Zarreen

Magnificent flowers bloom
Reaching for the stars, trees dance
This world has plenty of treasure
To make a room for others to groom.

Yet these sublime flowers are uprooted
Harassers leave no chance to bruise the innocent
The flower is gathered until it submits
Our soul quivers when we
hear about such incidents.

The agonizing beings are shackled
Nonetheless, all the brutes are regular
Once again someone withers another flower
Once again another rose devastates
leaving ahead in life only pain.

Every now and then
A life is ruined
Injured, wounded, thrashed
Humanity is ashamed
Humanity is ashamed!

Dilnasheen Zarreen is a student of Higher Secondary (final) in Jewish Girls' School. Her poetry compilation titled 'Lalazar' was published in 2020 by Bharti Parishad, Prayag. Her short story titled 'Misunderstood' was published in the prestigious bi-monthly magazine 'Indian Literature' of Sahitya Academy.

A Sparse Smile

Kusum Jain

Born in 1952, Kusum Jain is a well known Hindi poet. She has two collections of her poems to her credit besides translation of many of her poems in Vietnamese, Islandic, Swedish, English and various Indian languages. She has also edited many books.

Something always remains in our memories
And that keeps us alive
Something always remains in oblivion
There always remains a passage in between
For marching
Even after breaking
Something still remains unbroken
Report of sentiments full of depriviations
Bustling heart restive to measure the depth
Waits with expectations at the lobby of twilight
For a tired and unmindful age
A sparse-smile is scattered
On the ramp of fiery setting Sun
And has filled many crevasses
Like a sentence between two comas.

(Translated by Prem Kapoor)

God ?...Oh No

Geetesh Sharma

89 years old Geetesh Sharma had recently wrote this poem, that was highly appreciated by the readers.

Far from near and dear ones
There's a deep silence all around
And a solitude
One craves to hear
Even the croak of a crow
That sounded bitter earlier
Now sounds sweeter
The shreik of cuckoo
Sounds still sweet.
The dogs barking
That disturbed sleep earlier
Now sounds like a lullaby
And doesn't disturb any more
The birds' twitter
Sound like the bells of a temple
Who did this miracle?
God?
Oh no...
It's done by nature
Through its virtue
Corona...Corona!

Indian Short Stories

Morning Tea

Siddhesh

Siddhesh is a senior most short story writer in Hindi. He has also translated a number of books from Bengali to Hindi and received numerous awards.

Getting up in the morning Prava opens the windows of the drawing room. Fresh air enters the room. After arranging the curtains, she picks up the newspaper from the balcony, casts a glace over it and gets busy in her other works. She has to wait for Samir to get up, freshen up and then take his seat at the sofa near the window. Meanwhile she prepares tea and toast.

Outside the window in the small garden of the adjacent building, air keeps itself busy flowing in between the trees and plants. Playful birds hop over the branches of the trees. Their twitter sounds so sweet to the ears. Prava comes with tea and toasts and takes her seat near the window. Meanwhile Samir also comes to join her. They both are here in this building since last thirty or may be thirty two years. After retirement they crave to share these moments together. Nodody knows when the time clock would stop ticking. They both suffer the pain of loneliness even before being lonely.

A shade of despondency is always evident over the face of Prava. She recollects the building in the small town, the roof of which was casted after a longtime. The building was earlier a thatched one yet it was quite lovely where little Prava had once played with her bothers and sisters. She used to climb over the trees to pluck fruits, pull water from the well, have a long bath. While going to school she used to run even bare foot. She was number one in all these activities. When she grew up a little she had faced the scoldings from elder brother for learning dance. Yet it all continued. When she joined college, she could not escape the sight of Samir. The ocean of delight, fascination towards nature and pleasant dreams for future, all faded while arriving at this age.

Now at the age of seventy Prava looks dejected always. All these years she could understand the essence of life. She faced , till now the ups and downs of life without any regret but now all the time she feels dejected. Suddenly, the courage to hold and shape up the future slips from her hand.

When during the childhood she used to see the mountain range from the roof top of her small house; when she used to see the fire burning between the mountain range and forest, she used to ask her mother--"Mama, what is this light for?"

"That light is from the households of the tribal people, who inhabit in the forests and on the mountains. It is far from here and that is why it looks like that," said her mother.

But the same burning fire was as good as a fairy tale for her. She used to think--may be there is a fairy, who is running all around holding a torch. Charmed by that idea Prava used to go to the roof top silently in the night. During those moments she felt herself like fairy who is hiding in the forest having a torch in her hand while her mother, brothers and sisters were all worried for her. When she used to come down, she was welcomed with scoldings, "why did you go upstairs in this cold?"

Father always kept quiet as he was aware that Prava was little different from her siblings. He used to think that she would cause something to happen in her life. Her father used to worry a lot about her although he used to keep quiet. And yes, finally she did cause a great thing happen. Without infoming anyone she entered into the life of Samir, for ever.

Now neither Prava is a fairy any more nor there is any roof top of a small town. The charm of the past has faded now and dejection has taken its place.

Samir got up with the sound of opening windows. Surely Prava might have opened the windows to make sure that he gets up. But these were the windows of his bedroom. Sunlight entered and spread all over his bed. He got up. He thought of lying down for a while more but then he would miss the moments of sipping tea in the company of Prava.

Prava spent nearly forty years of her life in work. She built her own house, raised the children. How did the time pass, she did not know. Now she has no charm left in anything. She did not say anything to any one. Not even to Samir. Samir, however, knows that Prava is not made of raw clay but of terracotta and so she is strong enough. Why then the sign of dejection over her face?

Samir got up, washed his hands and mouth and then came to the drawing room. Keeping aside her tea and toasts Prava got busy in going through the newspaper. No conversation between the two. Her tea was getting cold and Prava was unmindful of it. Samir looked towards her and asked, "what happened?"

–I was just thinking, what would happen if one among us is no more...

Samir went on with his sips of tea quietly. Strong wind was blowing outside.

"You know, who will go first?" asked Samir.

–God forbid, it should not be me.

–Why?

–If you are alone, who will take care of you?

Prava kept quiet having said that. The children had grown up and were engrossed in their own world. The daughter was quite happy in her in-laws' house. The son stays in the upper floor of the house and is busy in his own world. He has almost no time for parents. He may not be far but not near either as he takes a little care of his parents.

Prava is unable to go upstairs any more. Flower pots on the roof top have all dried up. Now neither any mountain range nor any jungle is visible from the roof top, nor ever any fairy with a burning torch.

"One more cup of tea, please," said Samir and pulled the newspaper towards him. It had news of political turmoils, police and people's clashes, advertisements and semi nude photographs of model girls. Prava was engrossed in her own thoughts. Samir kept the newspaper aside and after a little thought said, "Let's go on tour somewhere. May be we can go to the same mountain that was visible from the roof top of your old building.

Even if it is for 3-4 days."

"What purpose will it serve? Now, it is better..."

But Prava and Samir had gone on tour to the same mountain where the fairy of Prava lived. They had visited the old town and had casted a greedy glance over the old roof top. They had also seen the tribals on the mountain, visited their houses and tried to locate the fairy, who carried the burning torch in her hands, but could not. However, they could see the zeal to live life among the tribal men who were carrying bundles of dried leaves to make a living, holding a hatchet in their hands. Prava was lost in the sweet memories of her childhood and in her search for the fairy.

Although she was much relieved after her return from the tour but for how long? Soon, once again she was obsessed with the thought–what would happen if she becomes all alone. To depend on children seemed to her like a search for water in a desert. No, now she wants to live for Samir.

Suddenly a gust of air brought her back to senses and she realised that it was the time for her to go to kitchen. She has to prepare breakfast for Samir. She could hear the sound of utensils from the upper floor, which meant that the maid had come and was busy in cleaning the house.

Prava knew it well that Samir has his own world and so she encouraged him to visit his friends although it kept her all alone in the house for the whole day. Many a time Samir avoided going out. He would say, at this age I don't feel like going out and taking the stress."

Prava would still encourage him saying, "you'll get bored in the house. With friends you would enjoy your time."

Samir wanted to say the same things to Prava but whenever Prava moved out for some reason or the other, he felt himself to be helpless. After retirement Prava had only one reason to go out and that was to attend 'Teachers forum' twice a week to meet her colleagues and to solve their problems related to bonus, gratuity or some internal problems. On request of the Secretary she also participated in their movements. Prava was highly attached with the forum and the school management also used to honour its suggestions.

Even while going for Forum's meeting she used to explain to Samir. "For the evening I have made some snacks for you. Do not forget to have it. I may be a little late."

Usually she used to return home much earlier before the dinner time. She prepared dinner only after her return. In between either she used to read some book or any magazine. At times she would watch some serial over TV in the evening.

Sometimes Prava enjoyed her loneliness too and she had explained it to Samir also– "I don't like moving on the same axis everyday. Sometimes I feel like spending my time all alone. Even the presence of children could not provide me few moments of bliss."

Samir would reply, "your children are busy in their own world. Why would they care for you or your self respect. The time has changed. Those days are no more there when all in the family shared both pleasure and pains together."

"I continued toiling for them for about forty years but now when the time has come for them to look after us, they have side stepped," said Prava.

In fact since her son and daughter-in-law decided to move over to some other city, Prava has become all the more careful for her life. Samir and Prava had never expected this from thier son and so they were all the more distressed.

It rained through out the night. Not being able to guess the exact time Samir continued with his sleep even when it was seven O'clock in the morning. The sky was covered with the clouds and there was no sign of sunshine. Although Prava got up in time but could not go out for a morning walk as she regularly did.

For past several days she was insisting that Samir should also go for a morning walk which was good for him, since he was suffering from diabetes and blood pressure but Samir was avoiding on some pretext or the other.

Last night he did not have a sound sleep and so he was so late in getting up but he still felt it was due to sound sleep that he was late in getting up and said, "at this stage sound sleep denotes good health." Yet he had to gulp down three tablets a day with water.

He shouted from the drawing room, "what happened ? Is the tea ready?"

"Yes, it is ready and that too for long. Now I am warming it up again for you," said Prava and when she finally came with tea it was already 8 a.m.

The rain had stopped. But due to shower the flower plants had bent down. Prava straightens them up with some support. She loves the flower plants a lot and takes care of them. She also remembers the birth dates of

Rabindranath Tagore, Kazi Nazrul Islam etc. but Samir's memory often fails. He doesn't remember his own birthday even. He although tries to remember Prava's birthday but forgets right on the day. Prava, however does not mind it as she all the time feels dejected with the thought of her pain through probable loneliness; how will she be able to cope up with it? How will she be able to pass the mountainous time. Her son's family is ready to move to some other city. Her grandson needs better education elsewhere in some good school of a metropolitan city. She is unaware of Samir's reaction towards it.

Sipping his cup of tea Samir looks towards the pensive face of Prava-- "I may not be able to sit for long time today," he said.

– "So, you would deprive me of this pleasure even."

Samir could not understand. What pleasure was she talking about. However, to please her he said, "O.K. I will sit here for some more time. It is only 8:30 a.m."

–No, today is sunday. Our grandson's school is closed today. So, he would also not come downstairs so early. His parents are also having holiday."

– "Oh yes! Had it not been sunday, he would have come down by now."

– "That's true. On holidays he keeps playing on the roof top."

– "Yeah! How come, you didn't go for the morning walk?"

– "How could? It was raining. From tomorrow onwards even you will go with me."

– "No, no you cannot compell me. I need to sleep."

– I will compell you. You have to care for your health. You have to live till I wish."

– "As if the death will obey your orders."

– "It will."

Meanwhile a sweet sound of somebody's small footsteps is heard. Prava and Samir look towards the main gate with intense eagerness and there emerges the little angel, their beloved grandson.

"Granny! Here I am."

Prava's pensive look disappears and with smiling face she embraces her grandson.

(Translated by Prem Kapoor)

Black Kite

Madhu Kankaria

Madhu Kankaria is one of the most renowned short story writers in Hindi. Besides short stories she has a number of novels also to her credit.

No memory is bigger than life, nor any thought. Certain memories, however, become lively and warm feeling and sting all through life.

I had read a story of Chekov—Death of a Clerk—in which there is a clerk. Once he was viewing a play. Suddenly he sneezed hard and few droplets of his saliva fell on the bead held of another viewer, who glared back with rage. The clerk was stunned to find that the person was no other than his boss. The boss did not say a word but his probable displeasure pierced deep into the bones of the clerk. He could not sit in peace any more and thought that his boss might fire him from the service. The terror of his boss was sitting like a vulture over his sholder and was smearing blood all over with its piercing beak. He could not sit in the theatre hall any more and returned even before the show was over, and went straight to the house of his boss. After a long wait the boss came and he whined before him—'boss, I am sorry, I countn't hold my sneeze. Please forgive me. 'The boss says nothing and only casts an indifferent look. The clerk got even more scared and thought that the boss was highly displeased with him. He came back home but could not sleep. He felt that he had committed a greatest crime on the earth. Finally, in the middle of night he once again went to the house of his boss and said, 'Sir, please forgive me. I did not sneeze willingly.' This time the boss was furious and shouted at him-- 'Get out.'

In the morning, the clerk was found dead in his room.

The question is, why do I remember this story off and on?

Is it because it relates to some deep down pain or sense of guilt in the subconscious state of mind?

Probably yes.

Because guilty conscience is like a black kite flying in the sky, that dives to swipe upon you.

So what to do? Should we have a postmortem of our own past?

What's wrong in it!

To make the long story short, those were the days of 86-87, when the telecommunication revolution was at its initial stage. Small desk top computers had arrived on the scene and were slowly becoming necessity of small offices because the time was running at a faster pace and computers were replacing the red coloured account books. Computer centres were opening up at every nook and corner and even our dreams had aligned with computers. The sky was the limit for those who knew to operate computers. The older generation felt its blood pressure shooting up as it had the least knowledge of computer and its operation and as they had no energy left to learn computer operation afresh.

During those days I had been appointed as a computer programmer at a renowned tea export house. My job was to computerise the said export house. Till then all the reports of the export house were printed on the typewriters by the typists and now all the reports were to be processed and printed through computers and I had to make sure of it. So half of the typists lost their employment while the rest were absorbed in other petty jobs of the office. So, computer was a villain for the typist community, that was highly impressed by the perfectness, clarity and speed of the computerised reports. Sometimes when some error in operation resulted in some faulty statistics, the old lot of typists had their moments of laughter and they wishfully hoped to drive out computers someday.

Being indifferent from their reactions, while enjoying their helplessness I kept busy with my work of system computerizing. During those experimental days, one day my hard disc crashed. My export house had to send its rates to the representatives of countries like Russia,

Germany, Japan etc. next day as the auction was scheduled on that day. Our export house used to purchase tea leaves from the local market and after blending, testing and grading it, exported the same to various countries, at a substantial profit. Anyway, I got an order from the top that the total report should be ready and filed the next day. Before I join the export house, one slender guy named Phani Babu used to look after all these affairs. He was the most experienced typist cum clerk of the export house. Had it been some other day, he would have been the happiest person for computer's failure. May be he would have arranged a 'Party' for his friends because computer was his biggest enemy. However, that was a fateful day. All the reports of the export department were under his charge. He cast a distressed glance towards me as if asking how the 230 pages report would be typed till next morning? Can another computer be arranged? Do you have back-up floppy with you?

I shrugged my shoulders and asked him to get in touch with the management. He smiled in despair and said, Boss is most ill tempered. I can't dare to talk to him. He asked me to talk to the boss for he would listen to me with patience.

For me it was not at all a difficult task. I looked at my wrist watch and then towards him. Phani Babu asked me with lot of expectations, 'will you please talk to the boss.'

'I will', I said in reply.

Next day when I reached office, I came across a very strange scene. The fifty two years old Phani Babu was being escorted by the peon towards a taxi, whereas the old man was trying to wriggle out of the grab of the peon and he was saying, 'there are still forty pages left.'

I could not make out what was happening. I asked another clerk, who was standing nearby. 'What's the matter?'

I was told that Phani babu had been typing the report all through night. He did not reach his house. Next morning his son came to the office by first train only to find his father busy over typewriter least knowing that the night was over and another day had dawned. For him the only thing that mattered was his service, his employment, his typewriter and the 230 page's report...

(Translated by Prem Kapoor)

The Two Women

Uma Jhunjhunwala

Uma Jhunjhunwala is a poet, short story writer, playwright, dramatist. She has also translated a number of plays from different languages into Hindi. She has earned numerous awards for her stage productions.

Two women were together yet cut off from each other, not for any particular big reason, yet there was some big reason. One had the right to pass orders while the other had to obey it being her subordinate. Both served each other's purpose, worked for each other yet one could hardly tolerate the other. Despite their likes and dislikes both gazed each other's face, dropped like autumn leaves.

Once the commanding woman was arranging her nails. By filing and giving them a proper shape she was applying nail polish at it while the other one was looking towards her with curious eyes. The commanding woman looked towards her nails, who responded with complaining eyes-- "How unarranged you are? So awkwardly you have applied henna over us... while applying henna over your hair you do not even ask us if we are prepared for it or not. You do not even take due care of ourselves. The woman immediately closed her fist so that the nails may not complain any further.

The subordinate woman was thinking. "The commanding woman says that I am useless. Is she right?"

The commanding woman could understand somewhat the racing expressions over the face of the subordinate one. Her black eyes smiled. She had terrible attracting power in her eyes and could attract anyone, who looked even once towards her eyes. Whenever salty tears rolled down through her eyes, it refreshed the wounds of many. The eyeliner of her eyes served as an ointment to the wounds of many hearts. The eyes of the subordinate woman were dry and stale. It neither had dreams in them nor even courage to have dreams. Her eyes had no past and no present as well that could beget the sprout of future...She had most simple and flat eyes.

Alike nails, the eyes were also considering the subordinate woman guilty of carelessness and stupidity for the lack of beauty of the eyes. The commanding woman expressed her superiority by caressing the cheeks of the subordinate one and said "Even five fingers are not of the same size. The distinction is eternal and divine. So don't regret being an ordinary one. Keep on obeying the orders. All cannot be the same."

The tree outside the window was well acquainted with the smell of every breath that passed through the window. It had pulled the smell of irritation in it through its strong trunk. That is why for once the colour of the leaves had turned purple... The commanding woman was greatly astonished having seen such a peculiar colour of the leaves. She mentioned about it to the other woman and asked, "the sun is on the other side, why then there is the shade of this colour over our face...what's the matter?

"How would I know madam! It is you who is seeing all this. My eyes, skin, nose, ear, tongue--all understand and follow your instructions. How then could I say anything...!"

The colour of the subordinate woman was fading while the floor of the mistress's room was turning purple and was spreading all around like some smell. Nose and eyes had stopped functioning for a while and then everything vanished.

The colourful dreams kept on strolling over sparking sky, whose string was held by the woman with dark red nails. In the company of man the commanding woman felt proud of her assembly of colourful laughters. The taste of different colours pleased the vains of man through his nostril.

Once the smell of the purple colour entered his nostril. When the breaths of the master and mistress were clinging to each other and spreading over navel through lips and neck, suddenly it formed a ring of purple colour and the pride got cracked. Disconcerted nostrils devastated over the slander of sense organs. The navel of the commanding woman got shrunk.

Years before man had created such a bright and dazzling corner in the universe for the commanding woman that her pride was regularly on the increase. Her chin was always shining with pride. Suddenly another corner dazzled... but when and how...? The commanding woman became restless of the dazzled another corner. Her hatred kept on increasing in her eyes, and her breaths even while attending nature's call. While bathing also the commanding woman could never free herself from the shadow of hatred. She rubbed soap after soap, spent hours under shower yet she could feel the spread of the purple smell from her head to toes. Now whenever the breaths of the man and woman were to unite, the woman started vomiting. And then the dazzle of another corner increased.

Long back, once some left over food was lying on the table. Nobody was willing to eat it. Its smell was irritating the nostrils. The utensils of the subordinate woman always had plain and simple food. So, the smell was beyond control for her. With the permission of the commanding woman she satisfied her sensory nerves, nostrils and tongue. Now, she derived some pleasure even over occasional left overs. Earlier, to dispose off the left overs was like saving it from being thrown into dustbin for one, while for the other it was used to satisfy both tongue and stomach. So, the left overs slowly turned into a medium of obligation. One was obliging while the other was obliged. But during this process of granting and accepting favours started turning into webs on the tree outside the window. Even inside the house walls the webs formed various shapes and faces that frightened and aroused a sense of insecurity. The subordinate faces in various forms battered the heart of the commanding woman.

Now, whenever four eyes met one pair had queries in it while the other had shamelessness. Most of the times the commanding woman felt the warmth of the back of the subordinate one on her throne. Answers to queries were given covering it with sheet of lies. Sharp eyes however, could yet note the naked truth and naturally, therefore, the harshness of the commanding woman increased more and more. Suspicion became so intense that the haze got cleared. Now while dressing up when she fixed flowers in her hair, know not why the commanding woman felt a fowl smell; while applying eye-liner she felt its darkness was spreading over her face; the lipstick seemed to be full of puss.

One day, having seen the picture of her bed in the sticky eyes of the subordinate woman, the commanding one was so raged that the bed got burnt and reduced to ashes. Even the tree got burnt. "why me? I had always warned you, why then I became a victim to your fire?"

–"My body is burning. Why didn't you soak up everything? Why did you plant its shape in my mind. Your coolness is for everybody .... and what belongs to all is not mine...what is mine should not belong to anybody..."

– "No, no. Don't get annoyed...you need a little coolness. Come out of your room, come out of your courtyard and pacify your inflammation with my coolness..."

And then the tree started humming some very sweet song to pacify the pains of the commanding woman. It hummed–wet nights/smelling gifts/cool...soft/sinking in oneself.../forest.../grove.../loud cries.../ stairways of beauty.../gem of heart.../sound of creation.../you and me...

Listening to this melodious song the woman rested her head on the shoulder of the tree and slept for a while. It turned green all around. The tree smelled sweet. Body turned bodyless; melted and turned into soil; became fragrance and got assimilated with the tree and all of its branches... Suddenly the dream got shattered and the commanding woman found herself burried till neck in a mound of salt. She could locate two ends–one of darkness and the other one of light... both the ends were beyond her reach... She saw that the subordinate woman and man along with few more forms were all proceeding towards darkness. The darkness had a great attraction... it was beyond gravitation... all the desires were eager to get absorbed in the attraction of the black-hole of the space. Speedy incidents took place in the ocean; the incidents got engaged in the process of turning into cloud; particles of light started spreading in the moisture; the commanding woman started gulping down those particles; the gravity of those eyes was quite soft and it filled the pores of the subordinate woman. A struggle about the commanding woman was going on in the subordinate woman regarding the desire for meeting of darkness and light; the commanding woman turned that meeting into a blue line; in a beautiful aversive poisonous blueline where manly blue light started dancing on the attractive tunes of darkness with the soft desire for rough body, like waves.

And the commanding woman sitting near the tree keeping her head over its shoulder kept on seeing the embrace of cracked heals and flashing tongue and being salt.

Moved by the pains of the woman who was to become salt the tree sucked the greenness hoping that the heart of the sky would be attracted towards it; the sun would shower its rays over it; there would be a blast in the colours; golden clouds would collect the echo of expectation and would create some charismatic rain, the drops of which would turn into a bunch of flowers and would perfume the hopes of this loving woman.

Both the women kept on not tolerating each other. Despite likes and dislikes they continued gazing at the face of each other. To hate every pore of each other became a regular rule for them. Man was used to move his knight two and a half places. And the tree kept on praying to have the life of a human being so that he could raise dark red flowers on the mound of salt that was created by the salt flowing through its shoulder.

(Translated by Prem Kapoor)

Identity

Dr. Karuna Pandey

Dr. Karuna Pandey born in 1962 is an eminent writer in Hindi having eighteen titles to her credit that include four collection of short stories, three novels besides collections of poems and research books. She has various national, international awards to her credit.

Shankar, Sumit, Ajay, Rajan, Rakesh and myself, we all were discussing, how to remove aversion and hatred that was germinating among the people, as today itself a bomb blast had taken place in our locality, which had left numerous people infused. We all were deeply distressed to see the excessively wounded people, some of whom were released after first-aid by the hospitals people, some lost their lives. We could not understand how such a blast occured and who was behind it. Was it caused by some terrorist? We were unable to arrive at any conclusion. Even my hand was plastered. In the evening we had all assembled to discuss about the incident and to visit those families to express our shock and grief, who had lost their near and dear ones in the blast, when police raided the area and arrested all the young boys of our locality. We all were stunned and within no time we all were lodged in the police lock-up, where we were being tortured and probed about our family, place of birth and profession etc.

What could we tell? Originally we belonged to Sindh province, that became Pakistan after partition of India. In 1972 when Bangladesh came into existence, we moved over to Bangladesh and became Bangladeshis. Longing for bread and butter, later we sought shelter in India as a refugee. We were born here. Our parents were happy that their place of birth was India and that finally they were back home.

We all were proud that we took our birth in India. To help our parents in managing the family, for livelihood we decided to go to Mumbai. We had a strong feeling that whole India was ours and that we belonged to whole India. However, we were considered and treated as outsiders. Yet we had to silently bear all the ill treatment with a sense of belief that India was our motherland.

Today when we have stabilised our lives a little bit, we are being viewed as a suspect of the bomb blast incident. We ask it to ourselves, where do we belong? Do we belong to Pakistan, Bangladesh or India? If India, to which of its province do we belong? It is an irony that even today an ordinary Indian has to search for his place of origin.

The division of India had taken place to fulfil the ambitions of certain leaders. When the country was divided and the nation was taking shape, religion was the centre for divisive activities and it was in the name of religion that the nation was divided into India and Pakistan. Subsequently, however, caste, province and language replaced religion and on its basis Bangladesh was formed. Today casteism, provincialism and language are the basis of every divisive movement. A person belongs to the place where he resides. If a Bihari resides in Bengal since his birth, his place of origin should be Bengal, yet he is termed as an 'outsider'. India today is divided in many provinces and every province wishes to be separate.

While I was thinking all this, a police sergeant came to me and curtly asked, 'where do you belong? Who do you work for?'

Sir, I am a salesman. I work here to earn a livelihood for myself and my family,' I replied.

He shouted, 'you are telling a lie. You all come from other provinces to loot and create problems here. On whose instructions do you work, or do you have your own gang?'

'Sir, trust me, we are innocent. We do not know how the blast occurred in our locality. Even we are highly distressed, I replied with abject entreaty.

We kept on whimpering but to no effect. Mumbai police charged us for being involved in the bomb blast case, as we belonged to some other province. The police received admiration for its quick action while we were sentenced to prison.

We are behind bars. What for? We don't know. Probably for being an outsider belonging to a different province.

My friend Shankar said, "Earlier it was a crime being a Muslim but now it's crime being whatever we are."

"What do you mean by whatever."

It means a series of identity. A man has various identities—religious, linguistic, regional and gender identities, with which one gets attached to a national identity.

Today, under the garb of globalisation the agents of the capitalists and those in political power are out creating a paralleled nationality. I have realised that while I was serving my prison term my Marathi neighbours used to visit us and take care of our families, while certain leaders make these Marathis an issue to spread enmity and division among the society.

It is certain political leaders and the capitalists, who are spreading the divisive tendency among the people because the violence was spread in the name of snatching the rights of the Mumbaikars (inhabitants of Mumbai) by the outsiders, although those Mumbaikars were the one who helped 'Bhaiyas' (the people from Uttar Pradesh).

Myself and my friends have served our sentence and still have a pertinent question— "Where do we belong to; to which province? Are we not Indians? We only share a little air, a little water, a little earth and manage with a small earning. Still people like us wander from place to place in search of their identity.

Today, capitalists and political leaders are free to set up their business or political lives anywhere they feel like and they are welcomed. Nobody asks them, which province they belong to. Will ever a day would dawn when a person's identity would be beyond any caste, religion, economic status and provincialism; when a person would be recognised with his identity as an Indian alone? Will ever this question be answered? I least know.

Today, numerous people like me are in search of their identity. They crave to know their identity, where they belong to?

We are leading a pathetic life, worse than animals.

Will anyone tell me my identity?

(Translated by Prem Kapoor)

Semi Displaced People

Nupur Ashok

Poet and author Nupur Ashok has written a number of novels in Hindi. She is also a women's activist. Besides writing she is also involved in business.

One experiences a different type of excitement while returning back to one's own city. Possibly the acquainted area provides some sort of peace. We had not been out for a long time. It was only about three months yet we were feeling nice while returning. Even the three months that we spent in foreign were also nice, far from dust and smoke. A complete peace all around, so beautiful buildings, difficult to see people. Whereas here, crowd is all around. I tried to lower the window glass of the car, Amar obstructed, "A.C. is on buddy."

–yes, I know but what's harm in experiencing the air of our own place.

–Better experience the air at home. It is so polluted here.

I abstained and raised back the glass. I felt, besides pollution there was too much noise also.

"It is too much traffic here, said Parag. Parag is although my nephew but

I always considered him alike my son Samir. Their age difference was hardly one year. When Samir went away to foreign, we never felt a void, that usually parents feel in absence of their children and it was due to the presence of Parag.

Joint families do have certain merits. You may get lost in the crowd but would never feel loneliness. While in foreign, I felt pity for the old people, who collected provisions from the malls, paid bills and pushed trollies, all by themselves towards the parking lot. Amar used to comment, "see, how independent these people are, whereas at our place people above fifty become senior citizens and for every little thing they become dependent on others. Fetch for them tea, water, everything and still they have complaints. They have only abuses for their sons and daughter-in-laws that they have been left on the mercy of servants..."

I replied, "they are forced to be independent due to compulsions. If you don't have a helping hand, what option do you have? You will have to work for yourself. You will have to purchase breads and toilet rolls all by yourself. Anyway, I have taken two breads. What about toilet papers? Using paper... oh lord! I think our system of using water is far better."

I got a jerk due to sudden break in the car as an auto had suddenly appeared before it. Parag shouted over the auto-keeper. The condition of the traffic was really very bad. Half of the space was occupied by the hawkers and the rest was left for vehicles like cars, cycles, tempos, rickshaws, buses and pedestrians. Everything seemed to be in disorder. One wondered that there were places on this earth where everything was in order and discipline; where pedestrians waited for the traffic signal to turn green; where drivers halted their cars to allow pedestrians to cross the roads; but here everything was in disarray. Finally, we reached near our house. As soon as the car turned right I was startled to see the grand old banyan tree, that always greeted us as a watchman, had fallen on ground.

"What happened to this banyan tree?" I asked.

–It has fallen due to cyclone and heavy rain fall.

–But It was a very old tree having very deep roots. How could it fall?–I just wondered.

The fragnance of tea in the house was quite pleasing and it is all the more pleasant if someone else prepares tea for you.

–Yor may not find anywhere else, the pleasure that is there in India. I said while taking a sip of tea.

“Have you got bored of washing the utensils,” asked my brother-in-law.

–Not at all. Now I have to live there only. So can’t help.

–Have you applied for P. R. (permanent residency)?

–Yes, On Samir’s insistance I have applied. Let’s see when the approval arrives.

–That’s nice. It’s not good here anymore. We are still struggling here for basic things like water and electricity. Last night there was no electricity and on top of it the mosquito bites made life a hell.

Meanwhile hot Kachauris arrived over the dining table. I picked up few and said, ‘where else would you find these and that too without any labour.’

“Would you like to have jalebis?” asked Parag, “I may bring within ten minutes.”

–“Let me accompany you.”

Having come out of the house, once again we passed through that fallen banyan tree. Once again it opted to my mind, how this huge tree got uprooted? It was creating obstacle on the road.

I asked Parag, “Now that this tree has fallen, why is it not being removed?”

–There are lots of problems. The tree is not fully uprooted. Some of its roots are still in the earth. So, it being a live tree, the municipal corporation cannot remove it. They will have to take permission from the forest department.

–So, the forest department should remove it.

–But the forest department says that it was the duty of the municipal corporation to remove the uprooted tree.

His simple answer forced me to think–what a fate this tree has got. It is semi uprooted. Half of it has left the ground while the rest half is still attached to the ground. A tree that had endured so many rains and typhoons for years could...

Next evening I once again went near the uprooted tree. Earlier there had been a small garden near it where few multistoreyed buildings have come up pruning its huge branches.

While passing by it I witnessed this pathetic site on a number of occasions. The banyan tree was lying on the road and we were all passive on lookers.

Now according to their respective needs people were cutting its various parts and were taking it away.

The excitement of returning to India had faded now. While moving across the streets, the jostling crowd, the rugged roads, reminded us of the foreign malls and departmental stores where all the provisions were neatly displayed.

Amar seemed to be fed up here and wished to return. Sooner the better. We were scheduled to return after four months, yet Amar reacted as if it was too late.

As soon as the air-ticket was confirmed Amar started preparing a list for shopping. We were going back to our son and so we had a lot of shopping to do–Sonpapri, laddu, Dalmoth, (all Indian snacks) and black shoe-polish that costed four dollars equal to about 200 rupees there.

Once again we were proceeding towards the airport. On our way I noticed that the fallen banyan tree had now totally disappered from the road leaving behind only a big ditch.

(Translated by Prem Kapoor)

Native House

Nandita Acharyya

Nandita Acharya is a popular novelist and short story writer in Bengali. Her writings are published in various literary magazines.

Slightly reddish light was spreading all around thraugh the wall over which few large oil-paintings were hanging. The atmosphere was filled with tempting smell of biryani. Iqbal Bhai said, "Firni of this restaurant is also very famous."

I was, however, silently looking all around. Although I was obliged to Iqbal bhai, still I was feeling a bit uneasy.

"You may taste the brain-curry of this restaurant, which is also very famous, said Iqbal bhai's friend Asif Raza, while I was going to say–you know, Jeevanananda also used to visit here.

"I hope you won't mind beef brain-curry?" asked Asif

"Oh no, I don't eat beef," I replied.

"Oh yes, it's prohibited in your religious texts," said Asif and started browsing the menu card.

"No, it's not because of religious texts," I replied with a bit of hesitation," in fact, in my maternal grand father's place we had many pet cows, with whom I had spent my childhood and developed an affinity. That's why I don't like to have it. Even an year back, i did not eat any meat whatsoever . I was very fond of ducks, chicks, kids... So, I never opted to eat their meat..."

"OK, I do appreciate, you are quite a sensitive person," said Iqbal bhai with a wide grin.

—Mistu Mona, has the screw of your brain loosened yet again?

Knocking down my feet in irritation I said, "Even you would say so? Only for going there I had got my passport prepared long back."

"Oh then why did you not go till now? Now you would be all alone here... after a few days even I would be out..."

–Dad didn't allow me. When he had flown from there during riots, he was too young. The terror and fright of the riots always haunted him... then he suddenly left us for his heavenly abode. Since then only my native house is drawing me towards it. I always visualise all those rivers, ponds and gardens in its vicinity. I have heard a lot about my native house from dad and grandpa....

Vaibhav bent down to kiss my forehead in Rabindra Sadan station itself and said, "I know Mona. You badly miss your dad and your native house baby!

–What do you know!

–I know you. OK I would take two days leave and would go along with you.... but you don't have the definite address of your native house.

–I would have been pleased had you accompanied me but you yourself have to go to Denmark...

–We may plan it a little later...after I return from Denmark.

–No, no, I can't wait. I have to go. In fact I am being drawn towards Barishal...and cause no obstruction please. I have already applied for my visa. I would leave within two-three days as I have to return before you leave for Denmark. I have already asked a very senior journalist there to find out the definite address of my native house....Dad was too young when he had come from there. My paternal aunts were a little older to him, but even they are unable to tell the exact address. Never mind, I will find out myself. Even I am a journalist.

–So far so good, but I was unaware that you have already applied for your visa.

–Don't get annoyed. I did not tell you because you had to plan your visit to Denmark. You had your preoccupations. Had I told you, you would have got engaged in my problems. Come on, let us cross the road. Tea Junction is on the other side. Isn't it?

Vaibhav pulled out his handkerchief to wipe out my perspiring forehead and asked, "were you all zamindars there... having huge estate... ponds, gardens, wooden house and what not?"

–Oh yes, i had told you, we had everything, a big pond, a wooden house... We were not zamindars but were quite rich. Dad's grandpa was a very big trader. He had earned a lot and used to lend money even to kings and zamindars.

–Really? What did he trade in?

–I won't tell. You'll consider him bad, if I tell.

–Whom? To your dad's grandpa? ... OK don't tell...

–No, no, I am telling. I feel shy. In fact my dad's grandpa and his brothers were well educated but they were money lenders. One king did not repay a substantial amount he had taken on loan and due to that shock my dad's grandpa died. My grandpa had once told, when I was quite young, that it was due to the sin of moneylending business that they had to abandon everything, all the wealth, property, a good job in college and had to flee in a pair of clothes...

–Which tea would you like to have? Should I order your favourite special tea? Mistu, although it is painful to hear all this, yet I wish to hear everything about your native house. Will you tell me?

—You are saying so just to appease me. You have your origin here only. You may not realise the pain of leaving your native house. My dad, grandpa could never return to their native house. I wish I could go there. May be I could fulfil their intense desire through my eyes.

–See, how attentively I am listening to you. Tell me Mistu more about your native house, about the rivers, ponds, gardens, wooden house around it.

Meanwhile, tea was served in big tumblers along with french fry. On the 4th floor of our native house there was a big hall and its walls had beautiful carvings. It had a tin roof. When it rained, the falling raindrops on the tin roof produced a wonderful music. Dad had lost his mother in childhood, so he loved his grandma the most. During rainy days his grandma used to open the pandora's box of her various stories before her grand children. When young, my grandpa used to return on cycle after teaching at the college. On way he used to stop over at our book-shop. He had got a teaching job at the famous Brajamohan College at Barishal. On his way back home on both sides of the street there were numerous trees and rivulets that had earlier been a river. In fact, Barishal is an island surrounded by water, where people had to struggle hard for survival. People of Barishal are known as struggling people.

–Great. I can imagine, how lovely a place it would have been...I wish to visit such a lovely place, Mistu!

–We had a very big pond there having quite big fishes. Children used to swim and row boats in that pond. During the Annaprashan (first rice feeding) ceremony of dad, two big fishes were fished out from the same pond each weighing about 30 or 40 kgs. My grandpa used to use the privacy of the pond to chat with his newly wed bride. Even I have a desire to hold your hand and stand on the edge of that pond...

–Why not? Next time I would accompany you to your native house... but you have yet not told me anything about the river, that had a strange name.

–Oh yes Kirtankhola is the name of that river, which was not very far from our house. During rainy season, the river had so many hilsa fishes that even we could eat one full fried Hilsa fish. There was an annual sports competition, in which grandpa won on several occasions. I was quite young then when grandpa told me a lot about all these...that I could hardly comprehend.... but it made me happy to note the sparkle in my grandpa's eyes. Most of the time I identified him with Bhishma, but at certain times he seemed to me as bright as Arjuna.

–Mistu, tell me whom do I look alike?

–like Lord Krishna....naughty, playful and unstable... you leave me to roam about here and there...

–Ha, ha, ha...even you choose to stay afar from me. For instance right now you are planning to leave me here and visit your native house...

–Oh yes, right at the entrance of our native house there was a temple of Lord Krishna. On its both sides there were two ponds through which the path-way led to the main gate. In the house itself there was a primary school, where children from far and near used to visit for studies. Possibly the illustrious personality had opened the school and Krishna temple to counter the sins committed through money-lending business. I wonder what I would witness there now...now people believing in different religion live there. Although my grandpa was atheist still at times he used to tell me about the temple....strange!

–Mistu, there are several things that are beyond our comprehension. For example, you belong to the new generation here. Your parents as well as you were brought up here in Calcutta...still you are so obsessed to visit your native house.

While taking a sip of the tea, I was just thinking am I really obsessed? ... Who knows....

Having crossed Buri-Ganga our ship was proceeding over Meghna towards Barishal. Iqbal bhai from Dhaka, before boarding the ship, had passed on good news that he had finally traced out our native house. He also had some trace of our book-shop. The wind on the deck of the ship was strong enough and it seemed as though I was flying in that wind. Tomorrow morning I would be standing right in front of the house, where dad played ball throwing, where he used to catch fish from the pond. After observing the lovely sight of the river till midnight I proceeded towards my single cabin to sleep. I was however, too excited to sleep. The four storied ship was proceeding towards Barishal...where Kirtankhola river had extended its empire.

While wandering over the deck of the ship I had befriended a number of people, who were all too eager to extend their hospitality to 'a solitary girl from India.' Even the captain of the ship Mr. Sarang had too many details about the river to share with me. He also took a very good care of the girl from India, who had come to visit his country. He invited me to have dinner with him and said that he would awaken me in early morning when the ship arrives at Chandradweep.

I was overwhelmed...so much of love and affection...my dad and grandpa failed to witness.

Having slept for a while I hurriedly got up in the dead of the night...I was dreaming that sitting in the courtyard of our native house, I was eating puffed rice and coconut. Sitting next to me grandpa was explaining to me about the trees....Night was about to end. I got up in a haste and came back to the deck at the fourth storey next to the cabin of Captain Sarang. After a while he called me and said, "Look sister, there it is Chandradweep over Kirtankhola, that you were asking about."

It seemed that the island had awoken despite a little dark. It was the king of this island, who had displaced one generation of our family and had left it helpless.

The day break was nearing. There was water all around along with a smell of greenery. A little while thereafter the ship anchored at a wharf. Iqbal Bhai was there to receive me. I felt like embracing him in delight, as it was he, who would take me to my native house, that I was craving for...

Do we first go to Brajamohan College, where your grandfather used to teach? I have already talked to the Principal...the way to your native house is also in the same direction.

I nodded my head —It's OK but would I be able to see the house properly? I have to return by the evening ship.

–Oh sure...look, that one is Jeevanananda's house...he was a friend of your grandfather, isn't it?...

–No, age wise, he was quite elder to my grandpa, but yes, he used to visit our book-shop. Many big personalities used to visit there...but where are those rivulets? I had heard a lot about them from dad and grandpa.

–Yes, those are there only on both sides of the road but those are not as had been earlier and have been narrower now.

–I could already see the stream on both sides. The car was proceeding towards the college and from there towards our native house.

In college I located the name plate of grandpa. After that I was astonished to see the huge lawn where grandpa used to play football with his students. The Principal insisted that I should have fish and rice with him. So unique was my native place.

The car was proceeding slowly on the neat and clean road having trees on both sides. The place looked like a tourist city. One could clearly hear the crickets even during the day time. I was extremely delighted .... so finally I am about to reach my native house.

The car stopped. I could see the ponds with crystal clear water on both sides of the pathway lined with coconut, betelnut and rain trees and I was moving on my dream path. Yes, this is it, the entrance to my native house about which I knew and had heard... but what's that? A very ordinary two storied middle class building at the end of the road. I was taken aback and I retreated. No, no, this is not my native house. This can't be. Where is that four storied building...walls with lovely carvings...where is all that?

Iqbal bhai smiled and said, "According to the details that you had provided, this is your house. Look, here is the temple...

I turned around and saw that on the side of the road there was an old and dilapidated temple. Meanwhile, some of the residents of the building started peeping from behind the windows. The women had covered their heads and the men were wearing 'lungis'. The faces of the men seemed a bit annoyed, as they were closing their gates on my face.

Iqbal bhai rushed towards me and said, "Please don't get upset...let me see..."

Some people were approaching towards me from both the sides, while I was standing still in the courtyard.

When asked, one of the residents confirmed, "oh yes, this was the house of Charkrabortys and here only there was a primary school. Long back they had all gone to India...."

From inside the house some more residents had come out and were approaching towards me.

Iqbal bhai murmered in my ears, "In fact they are all scared since it is an enemy property."

After a little while some lungi clad men and women with covered heads came to me and said affectionately, "Please do come, take your seat here and have some refreshment."

"No, thank you. I only want to look around the house," I said.

Please come in, they said and ushered me in.

Following them, I entered the house. Everything seemed quite unknown to me. I was offered the water of a green coconut, which was very sweet. The lady, who had brought the coconut water smiled and said, "The coconut is from a very old tree, that may have been planted by your grandfather.

I proceeded further and stood beside the pond, next to which there had been our garden full of various trees. I whispered slowly. I would have a look around the garden.

The lungi clad people said, "but there is no garden here.

I turned towards Iqbal Bhai and insisted, "No, there had been several gardens and a four storied wooden house, on the fourth storey of which there was a large hall. Believe me..."

The tongue of the person, who was cutting green coconut for us, was as sharp as sickle. He said, "we are also not telling lie. So many years have passed. Everything cannot remain same. It might have changed."

"...Let's make a move", I said. I dipped my hand in the water of the pond. I felt as if the pond was asking. "You have found time now, after so many years?"A water bird meanwhile shrieked.

I slowly retreated from the path-way of my dreamland... I peeped into the dilapidated temple where the idol of the deity was standing still and lonely...

The ship would make a move after sometime...so, at last I paid a visit to our bookshop, that my grandfather had gifted to his dear student Qadir. Prof. Qadir is now a renowned person, who stays mostly in foreign. The book shop has now turned into a famous and aristocratic restaurant of Barishal, sitting where Asif was asking me to taste the famous brain curry, while I wanted to tell him with throat choked with emotion that this was the place where Jeevanananda and many literary luminaries once visited and had their adda sessions.

Asif was paying all his attention towards the hospitality that he was offering to me rather than listening to my words. He said, "If not the brain curry, you better have Mutton Biryani. you may not forget the taste of Barishal's Mutton Biryani...

It was the same ship in which I had come. Iqbal Bhai had placed my luggage in the cabin, when the ship sounded its hooter, as its first signal. Iqbal looked towards me and smiled, "Please do come again. This time you could not properly see the river of Barishal.

I nodded, "Oh sure."

...The ship slowly made a move. Standing on the deck I saw Iqbal Bhai waving his hands. The tears that I had checked so long, slowly dropped from my eyes.

(Translated by Prem Kapoor)

Identifying Who Is One's Own

Aarti Singh

Born in 1969, Aarti Singh is a popular Hindi poet and short story writer. She is also the Secretary of Bengal branch of Ladies Poetry Forum.

When Mahesh got up from sleep, he heard Yashoda fuming. Still lying on bed he asked, "What's the matter? So early in the morning you have already started. Can't you be quiet at least in the morning?" He had said so in a teasing mood.

Yashoda shot back, "What's it to you? It's me, who has to face everything. All the utensils are yet to be washed. The maid Sudha has absented even today. She takes seven hundred per month but absents at her sweet will. Singularly how do I manage everything? Should I prepare tiffin for the children or your meal and tiffin? Mother (in-law) is busy with her worship. She doesn't even care to lend a helping hand."

–"Yashoda, you should not expect all this from mother. She is an old woman and needs a little rest. Don't you forget that it was she, who has raised Priti and Ramesh. Remember, how she had taken care of even yourself after your delivery." Mahesh said trying to explain and console Yashoda and proceeded towards the washroom.

Yashoda intercepted and said, "Look, I don't complain against your mother. I am simply saying that it is not justified that one would keep on working all the while whereas the other would be resting."

Mahesh flared up in anger. "You mean to say that at this age mother should clean up the kitchen and utensils? It's not fair."

"I am not saying that, you are making a mount out of a molehill", said Yashoda.

Without answering Mahesh entered the washroom and fuming Yashoda got busy with her work.

Mother-in-law Parvati could hear all the conversations while performing her worship. It was nothing new to her. She was used to such acronomy regularly but it was her love for her son and his family that she quietly endured the harsh words with a smile. Know not why she could not tolerate it today. She decided to talk to Mahesh about it, as she did not want any affliction in the house due to her. In fact, she loved her son Mahesh very much. She still remembered the day when Mahesh's father had died in an accident. Mahesh was only 12 years old then and was studying in sixth standard. After the accident all the relatives started avoiding her. For somedays Parvati managed to tackle her economic problems with the savings of her husband. Soon it became difficult for her to manage but she also did not want to discontinue the study of her son. So she decided to do some kind of work for earning and succeeded too.

Through her acquaintances she started getting sufficient sewing and needle-work. She worked hard to make sure that her son completed his studies and get some honourable job. The toil of both mother and son finally fetched results and Mahesh got a job in the Sales Tax office and soon he became a high ranking officer there.

Parvati was extremely pleased with her son, who did not want his mother to do any job any more. He took extreme care for her comforts. So, on his wedding night he had clearly told his wife Yashoda to take a very good care of his mother and that she should ensure to keep his mother happy.

Earlier Yashoda too paid sincere attention towards the comforts of her mother-in-law but as her responsibilities in the household increased, her attention towards her mother-in-law gradually decreased. Subsequently the mother-in-law turned to be a burden to her.

Parvati could understand all these, but kept her cool, as she realised that the time for her retirement had come.

Today was holiday. The children were busy in their games. Yashoda had gone to the neighbourhood for some work. Mahesh was reclining on bed and was reading the newspaper. Parvati was reading some religious text. Suddenly she thought that it was the appropriate time. She looked towards Mahesh and said, "should I say something?"

–Oh sure.

–Hope, you will not mind.

Mahesh got up, placed the newspaper aside and said, "come on mother. Why are you saying so. What's the matter? Don't you trust me any more? Or you find some fault in me?"

–No, no, it's not that son!...

–Then what's it that you have to ask for my permission?

–Son! I have talked to an old-age home. I wish to live there now.

–Why mother? Is there any problem here?

–No, there is no problem as such, but it is very difficult for me to pass time here. There it would be easier for me to pass time among the people of my own age through easy interaction.

–It is painful for me to hear this from you. Had you raised me for this day? I wish I had died before hearing it all.

–Don't utter such inauspicious words my son.

Tears rolled down Parvati's eyes.

"Has Yashoda said something to you?" asked Mahesh.

–No, nobody has said anything to me.

–Then swear on me and tell why have you taken such a decision? Do you feel that I have changed or you don't wish to see my face anymore..." Mahesh could not complete the sentence and burst into tears.

Even Parvati could not control her motions. She embraced her son and said, "No, my son. I only wish to see you all happy." And even she burst into tears.

"No son, fault is there in me only that I could not properly understand my own people. In the meantime both the grand children entered. Parvati immediately wiped out her tears and took both the children in her lap.

Parvati could well understand that her son would not allow her to go anywhere so easily. Gradually they both forgot the incident.

One day, suddenly Mahesh had to go out for a week for some office work. Due to additional load of work Yashoda became a bit more vocal. Parvati could not tolerate her garrulousness so she left a letter for Mahesh and proceeded for the old-age home. When somebody knocked on the door, Yashoda asked, "Who is it?"

"It's me" said Mahesh.

Yashoda immediatly opened the door. While opening the shoe laces Mahesh asked. "where are the children? Have they yet not come back from their school?"

– "No, the school authority has taken them to some excursion. So, it will take some more time for them to return."

– "Where is mother? I don't see her."

Yashoda opened the almirah and handed over a letter to Mahesh which he instantly started reading–

Dear Son Mahesh,

Be happy always. May God bless you with a long life.

Son, you need not worry about me. I am going to old-age home. I know, I should not have, but in your presence it wouldn't have been possible. I wouldn't have been able to leave the house. You should not scold Yashoda, as she is not responsible for it. Oh yes, during my last moments I would certainly try to meet you. Never feel sorry or dejected. This is my last wish. May you succeed in every sphere of your life. With this wish I conclude.

Yours Mother

Holding his head Mahesh sat down over couch. Meanwhile the children arrived but they both looked a bit worried. Yashoda asked many questions but they did not answer any and kept quiet. Suddenly Ramesh looked towards Yashoda and asked, "Mom, may I ask you something?"

"Yes, why not?" said Yashoda trying to be cheerful.

"Mom, where is granny?" asked Ramesh.

Yashoda felt nervous and perplexed, yet she tried to balance herself and said, "how many times should I tell you?"

Ramesh still insisted, "No mom, granny has not gone to Kashi. I know, you are telling a lie. Today on excursion, we had visited an old-age home where there were many women like granny. Teacher told us that they all had their families but their own people had turned them out of their houses. Granny has not gone to Kashi, she has gone to the old-age home. When I become a young man, I would send you too to an old-age home."

Little Priti also sided with her brother and joining him she said, "even I would turn you out from the house."

Yashoda was stunned to hear it. She thought in herself, "when did the children reach the age of discretion? When have they become adult?"

Mahesh embraced his children and said, "Don't worry children, I would go to the old-age home today itself to bring your granny home."

The children became happy. Mahesh paid an annoying glance towards his wife. Yashoda felt perplexed.

(Translated by Prem Kapoor)

My Home

Dr. Fatma Khatoon

Dr. Fatma Khatoon is a well-known short story writer in Urdu and a Ph.D scholar in Urdu Short Stories and their social texture.

Rupa, the lovely and innocent daughter of Shiela and Ramesh was spreading the fragrance of flowers all over the house through her sweet talks, "Baba, our village house is so beautiful. We should visit it this time happily and enjoy."

Rupa was highly emotional despite being a child of only 10 years of age. She was intensely attached to her small ancestral house and the village. She loved its greenery and enjoyed playing in the open atmosphere of the village besides having a dip in its pond along with her friends. Ramesh, however, had to proceed to Mumbai to earn a livelihood leaving behind the charm of the ancestral house and the village. After sometime he brought his wife Shiela and daughter Rupa also to live with him in a small room in a narrow street of the city.

Having no other option, Shiela and Ramesh adjusted with the city life in no time, but it was not all that easy for a child like Rupa, who did not like to live a captive life. She wished to live like a free bird. Every now and then she remembered her ancestral house, but time is a big healer. Soon, even she learned to live a city life.

A time came when Ramesh lost his job due to lockdown and he could not manage a new one. At times all in the family had to face hunger and poverty. Even the government aid could not reach the jobless workers. One day Ramesh's old friend Kailash confided in him and said that he had no choice than to go back to his native village.

"But due to lock down, the trains are not running," said Ramesh.

--- "So what? We are ten-fifteen people and we are all planning to go on foot. If we stay here, we may not be able to survive hunger. If we are to die, its better that we die at our own village" raplied Kailash with determination.

Kailash's point of view was quite convincing. Ramesh consulted with wife Shiela and decided to go back to his village. Rupa was overjoyed to learn that finally they were going back to their ancestral home. Next morning Ramesh along with his family joined other workers, who had decided to travel to their native places on foot. Ramesh had taken small luggage with him that was carried by both the husband and wife while holding the silken finger of their beloved daughter Rupa.

They had travelled on foot for about a fortnight and were too tired to walk any more. Rupa was unable to move and had fallen a few times despite her mother's consolations and encouragements.

They all were damn tired besides being hungry, thirsty and exhausted. Yet the lone hope of reaching their home kept on motivating and encouraging them. Even Rupa encouraged her mother Shiela---"come on mother we are about to reach our place, it would be a great fun playing with Guddu and other children." Rupa, was unable to move any further and fell down once more.

This time Shiela encouraged her daughter, "you must be hungry. Radha aunty must be waiting with bread and porridge for you. There would be plenty of ripe mangoes in our courtyard." All these temptations made her move again.

Rupa was overjoyed when she could see her home from a distance of about 50 metres. She exclaimed in joy-- "Mama, my home!" and fell down. Efforts to revive her could not succeed and she breathed her last. She was relieved of all her miseries.

(Translated by Prem Kapoor)

Corpses Speak

Dr. Pravamayee Samantaray

Dr. Pravamayee Samantaray is a lecturer of English in Odisha, a painter, translator, cultural and social activist, the Secretary of Indo-Vietnam Solidarity Committee, Kolkata. Formerly she was working in Diplomatic Academy of Vietnam, Hanoi. She has four books of poetry collections to her credit.

The eyes are opening slowly. Oh, the pain is unbearable. It's like all the muscles of my body are struggling hard just to open the eyes. But why can't I see anything? It's only darkness visible. Have I gone blind or the world? I have no idea. Somewhere the darkness is deep and some where it is dim. It's too cold here, in fact, I am shivering. Even I don't realize whether my hands and legs are intact as I don't feel any movement in them. The whole body is aching. Something is stinking from inside, from around and from far distance. It's deep silence here, only I can hear the ripples of the waves and the sound of the flowing water. The silence is so deep that my own sound is echoing like a scream.

Till now, I was sensing myself and the world around me. The girl who was scared of darkness even inside the house was lying in a newly turned graveyard. Now, I looked for my family members but did not see them.

Where did they go leaving me behind? Did they leave me behind or I? The cold was so much that it was pinching. My whole body was wet. I was not aware of my clothes. The girl who was always covered with the dupatta (scarf) was almost unaware of her clothes. I wanted to see my family members but was unable to move; neither my head was moving nor the hands and legs, not even my body. With great pain if anything was moving, it was only eyelids.

I was scared of being alone. I was suffering finding no one around. Perhaps, the darkness of my mind was more intense than the darkness outside. Still, I was scared of a tree lying nearby and a stone stuck at the rock which were appearing some scary figures. A graveyard appears like a town in an unknown city, but when a city turns into a graveyard before the eyes, one gets scared of everything.

The pain inside was strangling. The memory of my loved ones was haunting every moment. Where would everyone be? Whether alive or.... I was shaken up thinking ahead. No no..... Everybody must be alive. they must be looking for me. How will I meet them all? Somebody help me, please!

Why is this night so long and deep? As if the whole life has been immersed in this night! Only water water water. But the skin of my body was much dry like the cracks on earth surface in famine. I had come here to visit. I, with my family members, had come here to worship Lord Shiva. I think it's a lie that He removes the sorrows of all His devotees who come under His shelter. I wished we had not come here! Life would have been too beautiful if there had not been this flood. I looked at the temple from a distance. The temple premises had been swept away. Many people like me were dispersed here. How will He bless us? Rather He is killing people who have come to His shelter. How will He be declared as God if He can't protect us? If He does not protect us in spite of His capability, He does not deserve to be called as God. If everything happens at His indication then this mishap must have happened at His indication too. I felt disgusted for whom people call as 'God'. My mind was getting blurred. Someone came floating towards me that forced me to look at it.

Mommy......Mommy......Mommy. She was a little child. I consoled her not to cry and asked her to come to me. What's your name? There was no answer, only crying. Her cries melted into silence when she got tired of crying. There remained only the sound of sobbing. She was still calling her mother while sobbing. Where would be her mother? The little girl was weeping recollecting her mother. I got thrilled looking at her face. Is this a human or a ghost? The colour of her body had merged with the colour of her hair. She was unable to narrate her misery, but her eyes were very much expressive of what she had experienced. The sound of her sobbing was shaking my soul. I forgot my own misery for a moment. I felt like my pain was melting in comparison to her. Suddenly, I felt of getting back my strength. My dead hands felt like moving and I caressed her head with affection. She hugged me. Who is this girl? Where did she come from? She seemed very close to me for a moment.

The fear inside me was melting away just like the darkness of night was confining with the rays of dawn. I never waited for the morning with such a passion. But it was too dull because the shadow of dark clouds was wide spread for miles. It's strange that I got scared of witnessing the morning that I was passionately waiting for. The more the day was unfolding, the more the fear was increasing. The day-light was scarier than the dark night. I was watching and feeling the pain of everyone. The eyelids fell down. Which desolate city is this? I wished this morning had never come! I reopened my eyes after a few moments, assuming that the scene was a nightmare. But the reality was in front of me. Nothing was at its place there, neither the house, nor the trees, the stones, the mountains, nor even the humans. Everything was scattered. Where there was life jingling till yesterday, there was a deep wide silence today. The ruins were screaming out the havoc of last night. The eyes got closed when they got tired of watching the wilderness. The happenings of past few days flashed before eyes like the scenes of a movie. I had come along with my parents and elder brother to visit Chardham namely, Gangotri, Yamunotri, Kedarnath and Badrinath in the vacation. We were very happy and excited. We could not believe our eyes to see the Himalayan mountain just before our eyes that we had read only in books. We were rather surrounded by the Himalayan mountain ranges. The holy Ganga water that I had only seen in a small bottle in our Puja Ghar was flowing swiftly ripping the chest of the mountains. The sound of the river was resounding among the mountains. I was admiring human brain and was praising its intelligence looking at the buildings houses and long road at such height among the clouds. I thought, if man desires, nothing is impossible for him; nothing is there that he cannot make bow down. However, in the way of beating nature, he himself was being beaten by it. Tampering with nature more than necessity had already proved to be a harm to his healthy life. On the mountainous road when we were rolling ahead on a rented cab, fright was also increasing along with pleasure. The heart was beating as fast as we were going up from the ground. There were breath taking curved turns. Eyes were getting closed of impending danger while passing the vehicles from the front. I was more excited to witness the holy river Ganga, mountains, clouds, houses and colonies in such height than worshipping God. In the mountainous road, my mother exclaimed,—'Oh my god!' We were proceeding while having conversation among each other. To witnessing the clash of the clouds on the mountains, to clicking photos, to relishing steamed sweetcorn etc. everything was emerging from the past. Even the dull weather was unable to hamper our zeal. Clouds, rainfall and sleets; everything was beautiful amid the mountains. We were scared, but were more excited than scared and that did not let the fear dominate.

Finally, we reached Kedarnath. It was unbelievable. I had imagined that Kedarnath Temple must be higher than Jagannath Temple. But Kedarnath Temple was much smaller and was surrounded by Himalayan mountain ranges with a few buildings and hotels. I remembered our rented room where we stayed and the window through which I was watching the evening view of the nature. And all of a sudden, the screams of people, running of the people in chaos and the flood. We were united till then, but don't remember when did we get separated. I was swept away in the sharp stream of the water screaming 'mommy, daddy please save me.' I was choking. There was a feeling of uneasiness when the water went into the nose and the head. My body which was drowned earlier, was now becoming light and was floating on the water. Water slammed me here when it got tired of washing me away.

My pain revived. I pressed the girl more tightly into my chest. Probably I wanted to console myself that I was not alone. Someone else was coming towards us with throbbing groans. I looked up and it was a stout young man who had lost his strength in the fight with nature. I grabbed his hand. One of his legs was missing from the knee and the carcasses of the flesh were swinging. After sometime his eyes opened; till then I was staring him. He looked at me with blank half-closed eyes. All of a sudden, he started crying. A strong and stout man crying before a girl must have been a surprising thing in any normal situation, but at this moment I also joined him and cried because it's easy to lose our control and cry before an elder. He was crying for his wife and son. Probably, he was trying to scream and cry aloud, so that his voice could reach to his wife and son. I allowed him to cry until being relaxed, so that he would be light. After a while, I asked, 'what's your name?'

I am Nihar and I had come to Uttarakhand from Bihar with my family. We were very happy. My son...and he started crying. He was speaking with teary eyes. My son kept on asking through out the way, 'when will we reach Kedarnath?' Finally, we reached Kedarnath comforting him throughout the way. We worshipped Lord Shiva and by that time it was already raining. We returned to Gaurikund and from there we went to Rampur via Sitapur. We spent the night there. It was still raining heavily on 16th. Good number of people, horses and vehicles were there at Rampur. We got the news in the afternoon that Gaurikund and Sonprayag were completely washed away. We thanked God for being alive. The same day we set out for Haridwar in a small car. The roads were broken. We spent four days in that car with much difficulty, then we managed, somehow, with the help from the government. We again moved ahead when the roads opened, but we did not know that the catastrophe was waiting for us ahead. Hardly we had moved five kilometers that there befell the landslide. It felt like the whole mountain had fallen on our car. I was sitting at one side in the car. The door of the car broke with the pressure of the falling rock and I fell out of the car and with the rolling stones I rolled down. Before I could realize pain, it left me inert and I came here with the rapid flow of the water. What would have happened to my son and wife? He could not speak a word any more. Perhaps, his lips were trembling to say anything. After a few moments he described his story. I was not in favour of bringing our son, Rohan with us. I thought if anything happens to us in this journey, he would be skipped of the mishap. But he did not listen to me. His stubborn nature resembles to his mother. He came with us. Hopefully, I would not have brought him with us! Hopefully, we would not have come here!

I wanted to comfort him, but my hands and legs were already numb. Tears only dropped out of my eyes with utter helplessness. Then there was a deep silence. Did not realize how much time passed. Perhaps, we all were thinking, what if we had not come here or there would not have been this deadly deluge!

Then suddenly two people came with a sturdy stream of water. We all moved a bit so that they could settle down their scattered bodies. One of them will probably be as old as my father, that means he will be in his early fifties. Their bodies were scorched with water stone injuries. Perhaps they were suffering of joint pain. And the other one was an old woman. There were only petticoat and blouse on her body. This was the symbol that she must be from a well-to-do family because in my village women of her age don't wear petticoat and blouse under saree. They only wear thick cotton saree. After weeping for a while, both of them narrated heir stories.

May be that woman was suffering too much, on one hand, the deep wound and on the other of the old age. With much pain and broken words, she told her story. I had come from Jharkhand with my son, daughter-in-law, daughter, son-in-law and grand children to pay our homage to Lord Kedarnath. Chamoli, a place of a few kilometers before Yamunotri was totally ruined when we reached there. The roads were washed away from both the sides. We got stuck there. My children were crying watching the devastation. I was shivering inside. I also wanted to express my fear, but if I break down, who will handle them? I was just dying inside. We lived this fear for about ten hours. Then that place got, washed away in a big torrent. I was holding my grand son's hand, but the water took him away from me. The flood took my family away from me which was the source of my life. I don't know, how will they be? But I hope everyone must be alive. God is there, He can't be that cruel...Everyone must be alive. She murmured.

Then we looked at the man. I along with my wife, two daughters and relatives had come to Kedarnath from Odisha. We reached Gaurikund on 15th and from there we walked to the temple. After paying our homage to Lord Kedarnath we returned to Gaurikund on the same day via Rambada. From there we went to Sonprayag on foot as no vehicle was available there. Finally, we arranged to stay in a guest house of Forest Dept., Govt. of India. We remained locked there for two days and when we opened the door on 17th morning, there was nothing intact. Everything was washed away and we were marooned. As we had no other way, we remained locked that day. But the next day the watchman of the guest house wanted to lock the guest house to go to his family members. As all the roads were washed away, we chose the mountainous way. I was in the front as a guide and while stepping on a rock to check whether it's solid, that slipped. And I also got carried away with the same stone just before the eyes of my family members. My body got hurt a lot and at one place my head bumped on a stone and everything blacked out before my eyes.

Our talk was not over yet, when two more people came flowing to fill the space that was left among us. One of them was a young man and he was, in fact, a half-burnt body. And the second one was a monk. We gave them space too in our nature-made abode.

We looked at the half-burnt body and could not understand where his legs and head were. It was a burnt flesh, but he spoke fearlessly. I am Praveen, the pilot of MI-17-B-5 Aeroplane. We were returning after rescuing the trapped people in Guptkashi and Kedarnath. On the way back our aeroplane crashed in an accident and we all got burnt alive. We were watching his style more than listening to him. There was no regret, no pain on his face, he was lying fearlessly.

The second one who was looking like a monk from his face started his story. I was in the temple when the flood came. In order to protect myself, I swang from the temple bell and spent one day and one night swinging from the bell. I landed down when the water level decreased. There was a pile of dead bodies including children, older ones, younger and women. My eyes fell on the jewelry of the dead bodies. I collected all the jewelry from their hands, legs and necks because I had a dream to build an ashram. I sheltered in a mountain and remained there for three days without food and water. My strength and courage were dying. On the fourth day, life left my hand and did not know how far the water washed me away. He then became silent. But I got angry and for the first time I felt so much hatred for any unknown person. Suddenly, I felt more pain than him and looked at somewhere else. I wanted to divert my mind. I did not like to think about that monk who was not worthy to be called even a human in any way.

I thought heavy rain was always there, but why was nature bestowing wrath upon its loved ones this time? This disaster was not at all natural, rather it was man-made. Building up too many hydro projects, cutting up the trees from the forest, building up too many sky-scrappers on the river bank, defying laws and regulation, stealing huge amount of sand from the river bank, blasting of mountains using dynamite, not protecting trees on loose mountain, spreading pollution etc. are, in fact, reasons for this disaster. Money mindedness of a few people is the reason of the death of thousands of people like us. We all had come to hang out and pay our homage to Lord Shiva. We did not know that we would have to pay for the crimes of others. We are among those thousands of people who lost their lives in this disaster. This accident took our lives and left our families to cry behind us. Here are only rotten bodies and bad order. There is still a spark of hope left in us in utter helplessness that our loved ones would find us. Well, they do not know our where about. Still, we are waiting; what if some day somebody comes in search of us and our wandering souls reach their ultimatum.

(Translated by the author)

साहित्य-संगम
भारत-वियतनाम

साहित्य-संगम भारत-वियतनाम

सम्पादक
गीतेश शर्मा

सह-सम्पादक
प्रेम कपूर
कुसुम जैन
डॉ. प्रभामयी सामंतराय

राजकमल प्रकाशन

ISBN : 978-93-93768-26-1

मूल्य : ₹1495

पहला संस्करण : 2022

प्रकाशक : राजकमल प्रकाशन प्रा. लि.
1-बी, नेताजी सुभाष मार्ग, दरियागंज
नई दिल्ली-110 002

शाखाएँ : अशोक राजपथ, साइंस कॉलेज के सामने, पटना-800 006
पहली मंजिल, दरबारी बिल्डिंग, महात्मा गांधी मार्ग, प्रयागराज-211 001
36-ए, शेक्सपियर सरणी, कोलकाता-700 017

वेबसाइट : www.rajkamalprakashan.com
ई-मेल : info@rajkamalprakashan.com

मुद्रक : बी.के. ऑफसेट
नवीन शाहदरा, दिल्ली-110 032

आवरण : अशोक वर्मा

SAHITYA SANGAM : BHARAT-VIETNAM
Edited by Geetesh Sharma

गीतेश शर्मा

(6अगस्त, 1932 - 2मई, 2021)

भारत-वियतनाम कूटनीतिक संबंधों की 50 वीं वर्षगाँठ के अवसर पर प्रकाशित प्रस्तुत संकलन समर्पित है

गीतेश शर्मा को

जो हमारे पथ-प्रदर्शक विशिष्ट लेखक ही नहीं थे वरन् जिन्होंने अपने जीवन का एक बड़ा हिस्सा भारत-वियतनाम संबंधों के विकास के लिए अर्पित किया।

आभार

मैं हृदय से आभारी हूँ, सुप्रसिद्ध कवि एवं वियतनाम लेखक संघ के पूर्व अध्यक्ष भाई हू थिन्ह का जिनके अप्रतिम सहयोग बिना इस संग्रह का प्रकाशन संभव न हो पाता।

मैं अंतरहृदय से ऋणी हूँ, भारत के प्रमुखतम प्रकाशन राजकमल प्रकाशन समूह के प्रबंध निदेशक श्री अशोक महेश्वरी का जिनके महत्त्वपूर्ण योगदान से यह संग्रह प्रकाशित हो पाया।

मैं हमारे घनिष्ठ सहयोगी श्री प्रेम कपूर, श्रीमती कुसुम जैन एवं सुश्री प्रभामयी सामंतराय राय के प्रति विशेष रूप से आभारी हूँ जिनका संपादन में सतत् सक्रिय सहयोग मिला।

मैं हृदय से कृतज्ञ हूँ, श्री अंजन बोराल का, जिनका इस संग्रह-प्रकाशन में बहुमूल्य सहयोग मिला।

अनुक्रम

संपादक की कलम से

पंद्रहवीं शताब्दी तक मध्य और दक्षिण वियतनाम के कुछ हिस्से पर भारतीय संस्कृति और साहित्य का जबर्दस्त प्रभाव रहा। जब हम लोक-कथा और लोक-काव्य पर नज़र डालते हैं तो जबर्दस्त समानता पाते हैं। पर इसके साथ ही एक मूलभूत अंतर भी रहा है। हालांकि वियतनाम एक बौद्ध देश कहलाता है, पर वहां की संस्कृति हमेशा ही धर्म निरपेक्ष रही है। वहां का सबसे बड़ा त्यौहार 'टेट त्यौहार' है। पर इसके पीछे धर्म का संबंध लेश मात्र भी नहीं है। जहां तक मेरी जानकारी है, इस मामले में यह दुनिया में अपने ढंग का अकेला देश है।

वियतनाम में जब मुक्तियुद्ध की शुरुआत हुई फ्रांसीसी उपनिवेशवादियों के विरुद्ध, तो वहां के साहित्य संस्कृति पर इसका जबर्दस्त प्रभाव पड़ा। विचारों में, लेखन में और व्यवहार में आधारभूत परिवर्तन हुआ। इसकी शुरुआत प्रोपेगंडा साहित्य से होती है। हो-चि-मिन्ह गर्व से कहते थे कि हां यह प्रोपेगंडा साहित्य है, जो शिक्षित-अशिक्षित, आम जनता से गहरे रूप से जुड़ा है। साहित्य में ऐसी भाषा का प्रयोग किया जाने लगा, जो अशिक्षित व्यक्ति को भी आसानी से समझ में आ सके।

पहले भी लिखा जा चुका है, स्वयं हो-चि-मिन्ह न केवल जनसाहित्य के प्रेरक थे बल्कि स्वयं कवि, कथाकार, नाट्यकार, गीतकार (एक सिम्फनी के वे खुद संचालक थे), इसके अलावा युद्ध कौशल में तो पारंगत थे ही। उन्होंने स्वयं युद्ध के मोर्चे पर न केवल युद्ध का संचालन किया बल्कि मोर्चे पर उपस्थित रह

कर कविताएं और कहानियां भी लिखीं।

कवि हू थिन्ह, जिनका मैं सहोदर भाई की तरह सम्मान करता हूं, ने मुझे बताया कि वे एक हाथ में बंदूक और दूसरे में कलम रखते थे। अमेरिकी साम्राज्यवादियों के कई बमवर्षक विमानों को उन्होंने अपनी बंदूक से गिराया और वे रात के समय कविताएं लिखते थे।

1945 से 1975 तक निरंतर चले मुक्तियुद्ध के दौरान जो जनप्रिय साहित्य लिखा गया उसमें केवल युद्ध का ही वर्णन नहीं होता था, मानवीय संवेदनाओं से जुड़ी कविता-कहानियां-उपन्यास भी लिखे जाते थे।

वियतनाम के एकीकरण के बाद साहित्य में एक और बदलाव आया। यह बदलाव था मैत्री, शांति और विकास का और इसके साथ ही लोगों में जो खुशहाली आई, जो स्वतंत्रता का मज़ा चखा तो लोगों ने प्रेम और सेक्स संबंधित रचनाओं का सृजन किया।

प्रस्तुत संकलन में वियतनाम की 15 कविताएं और आठ कहानियां शामिल हैं, जिनका चयन वियतनाम रायटर्स यूनियन के अध्यक्ष महाकवि हू-थिन्ह ने किया। मेरी समझ के अनुसार उन्होंने उन्मुक्त प्रेम और सेक्स संबंधी साहित्य को एकदम बाद दे दिया। उन्हें लगा होगा कि इससे गलत संदेश जा सकता है। किंतु उन्होंने जिन रचनाओं का चयन किया उनके रचनाकार वरिष्ठ और नई पीढ़ी के श्रेष्ठतम रचनाकार हैं।

भारतीय पाठकों के लिए वियतनामी साहित्य को जानने का यह पहला सुअवसर है, क्योंकि इससे पहले इस तरह का कोई प्रयास सरकारी या गैरसरकारी स्तर पर कभी किया ही नहीं गया। इसके लिए निश्चित रूप से वियतनाम रायटर्स यूनियन और इण्डो-वियतनाम सौलिडैरिटी कमिटी को श्रेय जाता है।

'पीपुल टु पीपुल डिप्लोमेसी' की बात तो की जाती है, पर दोनों देशों के बीच सौहार्दपूर्ण घनिष्ठ संबंधों के बावजूद लगभग नहीं के बराबर चेष्टा की गई है।

इन संबंधों को गाढ़ा बनाने की नितांत आवश्यकता है क्योंकि इस प्रकार के प्रयास दिलों को जोड़ते हैं, जिसका प्रभाव स्थायी होता है।

संकलन की वियतनामी रचनाओं को पढ़कर हम न केवल वियतनामी साहित्य से परिचित होते हैं बल्कि वियतनामी समाज से भी परिचित होते हैं।

जहां तक कलकत्ता और पार्श्ववर्ती अंचल केंद्रित हिन्दी, बांग्ला, असमिया, ओडिया, उर्दू के साहित्य का प्रश्न है, यह रचनाएं भारतीय मानसिकता को परिलक्षित तो करती हैं किंतु वियतनामी समाज तथा वहां की मनोदशा से बिल्कुल भिन्न हैं। दुनिया में भारतीय समाज एकमात्र समाज है जो हजारों वर्षों से चार वर्णों में विभाजित है, इनमें आपस में रोटी-बेटी का रिश्ता नहीं के बराबर है। जाहिर है, इसका असर साहित्य पर तो पड़ता ही है।

भारतीय रचनाओं में नारी शक्ति की बात तो की जाती है पर नारी को किसी प्रकार की स्वतंत्रता दिये बगैर। भारतीय नारी पूरी तरह पुरुषों के अधीन है। क्या विडम्बना है कि संविधान के अनुसार भारत में औरत प्रधानमंत्री तो चुन सकती है, पर अपना पति नहीं। वैवाहिक संबंध मां-बाप तय करते हैं न कि होने वाले पति-पत्नी।

भारतीय साहित्य में प्रगतिशील धारा रही है, पर यह देखा गया है कि व्यवहार में प्रगतिशील लेखक-लेखिकाएं भी जातीयता से बुरी तरह ग्रस्त हैं और अपवाद को छोड़ कर ये अपनी जाति में ही वैवाहिक संबंध करते हैं।

कभी-कभी ऐसा लगता है कि हम लिखते कुछ और हैं और करते कुछ और हैं।

इसलिए वियतनाम सहित अन्य देशों के लोगों को साहित्य के माध्यम से भारतीय समाज का सही चित्र नहीं मिलता। वे मकड़जाल में इस तरह भटक जाते हैं कि इस देश की मूल धारा को समझ ही नहीं पाते।

यहां एक तुलना बहुत आवश्यक है। वियतनाम उन्नतिशील देशों की अग्रिम पंक्ति में है, पर वियतनामी महिलाएं एशियाई देशों में सबसे अधिक स्वतंत्र हैं। विवाह स्त्री-पुरुष प्रेम के बाद करते हैं न कि विवाह के बाद प्रेम। हाल के कुछ वर्षों से वियतनाम में विवाहेतर संबंधों को भी मान्यता मिलने लगी है। वहां शहरों में जो विवाहेतर सबंधों से बच्चे पैदा होते हैं, समाज उनको मान्यता देता है। हां, गांवों में अभी भी उन्हें हेय दृष्टि से देखा जाता है। पर इनका सामाजिक वहिष्कार नहीं होता।

भारतीय समाज एक तरह से ठहरा हुआ समाज है, वह दौड़ता तो बहुत तेज है पर अपनी धुरी को नहीं छोड़ता। भारतीय समाज की तुलना में मुक्ति युद्ध और उसके बाद वियतनामी समाज में निरंतर परिवर्तन होते रहे हैं और यह समाज हर

पल, हर क्षण आगे की ओर बढ़ता रहा है, बावजूद इसके कि वहां नारी जाति की अपनी समस्याएं भी हैं। मसलन, चूंकि पुरुषों की तुलना में स्त्रियों की संख्या अधिक है, इसलिए एक छोटी आबादी को एकाकीपन सालता है।

दूसरी समस्या बढ़ते हुए तलाक की है। बच्चों को औरत संभालती है क्योंकि पुरुष उनकी जिम्मेदारी नहीं लेता।

जाहिर है, वियतनामी समाज में नारी जाति की जिम्मेदारी पुरुषों से अधिक है।

भारत में भ्रष्टाचार है तथा बोलने व लिखने में दोहरापन है। ऐसा वियतनाम में भी है किंतु भारत की तुलना में बहुत कम। वियतनाम में दो तरह का साहित्य है। एक जिसे सरकारी प्रश्रय प्राप्त है, दूसरा अपने बल-बूते पर अपने पैरों पर खड़ा है, बिना किसी सरकारी आश्रय के। किंतु साहित्य की ये दोनों विधाएं एक-दूसरे के समानांतर चल रही हैं। भारत और वियतनाम में घोर असमानताओं के बावजूद एक बात बहुत ही समान है और वह है कविता लिखना और कविता की पुस्तकें छपाना। दोनों ही देशों के लोगों की, जिनका साहित्य के प्रति जरा भी जुड़ाव है, उनकी एक ही महत्वाकांक्षा होती है कि उनकी कम से कम एक कविता की पुस्तक छप जाए। अपने खर्च से पुस्तकें छपवाते हैं और मुफ्त में बांटते हैं।

मिला-जुलाकर यह कहा जा सकता है कि असमानता के बावजूद एक-दूसरे के साहित्य को जानने की नितांत आवश्यकता है। जैसा कि जिक्र किया जा चुका है, साहित्य दिलों को जोड़ता है और इसका स्थायी प्रभाव होता है। साहित्यकार और पाठक एक-दूसरे के करीब आते हैं। इस दिशा में जितना प्रयास होना चाहिए, लगभग नहीं के बराबर हुआ है।

हालांकि हमारा यह संयुक्त प्रयास बहुत छोटे पैमाने पर है, पर हमें यह विश्वास है कि साहित्य से जुड़े लोग और आम पाठक स्वयं को इससे जोड़ेंगे ताकि दोनों देशों के लोग एक-दूसरे के करीब और करीबतर आ सकें।

इस संकलन में हमने हिंदी में प्रकाशित कहानियों व कविताओं का अंग्रेजी अनुवाद भी किया है, जो वियतनाम रायटर्स यूनियन को समर्पित कर रहे हैं ताकि वे वियतनामी भाषा में इनका अनुवाद करा कर वहां के पाठकों तक पहुंचाएं।

-गीतेश शर्मा

वियतनामी कविताएँ

जंगल में गाती हुई आवाज़

हू थिन्ह

जन्म 1942, वियतनाम राइटर्स एसोसियेशन के अध्यक्ष, कई संग्रह प्रकाशित, 'शहर को जाता रास्ता' (एक लम्बा गान, 1979) 'लिट्रेचर न्यूज़पेपर' द्वारा आयोजित कविता प्रतियोगिता 1975-1976 में पुरस्कृत।

त्रांग सोन के जंगलों के बीचोंबीच गाते हुए तुमने
सारे जंगल को संगीत में बदल दिया
मलेरिया से ग्रस्त गा रहे हो गीत, उसके लिए जो ग्रस्त है मलेरिया से
ऊपर जाती हुई सड़क धूल से भरी और झुलसी है
वृक्ष करते हैं लोगों को शीतल और लोग एक-दूसरे को करते हैं शीतल

वाद्ययंत्र के भीतर भरा है संगीत, फ़िलहाल शांत है वाद्ययंत्र
अचानक झंकृत हो उठता है जंगल झीने तारों से
लोग उत्साहित, बढ़ने को बेताब, हलचल से भरपूर हैं
हाथ, हमारे ही हाथ हैं, फिर भी हम सोचते हैं, पकड़े हुए हैं किसी और का।

तुम जंगल के गीत गाओ, तुम वृक्षों के गीत गाओ
तुम उसके बारे में गाओ जो तुम्हें गाते हुए सुन रहा है
मैं अचानक भूल गया हूँ अपने ज्वर के बारे में जो अभी ही टूटा है

जंगल अचानक भूल गया है, अभी हुई बमबारी के दर्द को
कठिनाइयों पर क़ाबू पाने के लिए मैं गीत की आवाज़ के सहारे सँभालता हूँ अपने आप को
त्रांग सोन के जंगलों से मित्रता सालों पुरानी सच्ची और बेदाग़ है
गाने की आवाज़ गायब हो गई है, बमों से रक्षा के लिए बचे हैं बंकर
आवाज़ धरती के भीतर गहरे संगीत के बक्से में रूपांतरित हो गई है।

(अनुवाद : कुसुम जैन)

मेरे गाँव का गीत

न्गुएन क्वांग थिउ

जन्म : 1957।
वियतनाम राइटर्स एसोसिएशन के सदस्य एवं नेशनल प्राइज़ फ़ॉर आर्ट्स एंड लिट्रेचर से सम्मानित

मैं गाता हूँ अपने गाँव का गीत
जब सोये होते हैं सब गहरी नींद में
आर्द्र सितारों के नीचे, उन्मत्त झोंकों के बीच
घर की राह खोजता

कहीं कोई आदमी नींद में बोलता है
औरत के खुले बालों के पार्श्व में
कहीं रात में बहती है
माँ के दूध की सुगंध
कहीं पंद्रह वर्षीय बालिका के स्तन
गोलियों की तरह धरती से उठे हैं
और कहीं बूढ़े ग्रामीणों की खांसी
गिरती है शाखाओं से पके फलों की तरह
वहाँ बगीचे में जगी रहती है दूब सारी रात

मैं गाता हूँ अपने गाँव का गीत
तेल से जलते दीपक की रोशनी में
जो मिला है पूर्वजों से
सब दीपकों में सबसे प्यारा और सबसे दुखदायी है
जब मैं पैदा हुआ था, मेरी माँ ने रखा था
मेरे सामने ताकि मैं देखूँ और सीख सकूँ
उदास होना, प्यार करना और रोना

मैं गाता हूँ अपने गाँव का गीत
मैं गाता हूँ अपने गर्भनाल के द्वारा

जिसे गाड़ दिया गया था वहाँ
और बन गया था एक केंचुआ
जो रेंग रहा है पानी के घड़े के नीचे
जो रेंग रहा है पोखर के किनारे
जो रेंग रहा है मेरे पूर्वजों की कब्र के नीचे
जो रेंग रहा है भिखारी की कब्र के नीचे
लाल धरती को देते हुए धक्का जैसे हो रक्तसना रास्ता

मैं गाता हूँ, मैं गाता हूँ अपने गाँव का गीत
मिट्टी के ताबूत में पड़ी हैं जहाँ हड्डियाँ
जहाँ मेरी भी होंगी एक दिन
इस जन्म में मैं एक मानव हूँ
अगले जन्म में मैं जानवर हो सकता हूँ
मैं चाहूँगा कि बनूँ एक श्वान
अपने गाँव को उदासी से बचाने के लिए
मेरे अपने गाँव के लिए जो अनमोल है।

(अनुवाद : कुसुम जैन)

बिलाव को खाना खिलाना

चान क्वांग दाओ

जन्म 1957। ग्रास हग, कॉपी एन्ड पेस्ट, फ्लाइंग इन द ड्रीम्स- कविता संग्रह। वियतनाम राइटर्स एसोसिएशन 2020 के कविता पुरस्कार से सम्मानित।

वह दस साल से, उससे कही ज़्यादा वर्षों से यहाँ रह रहा है
मैं उसे प्यार करता हूँ, लेकिन अपनी पत्नी और बेटी से आधा

जब कभी उस पर गुस्सा होता हूं
उस रूई की बॉल को खिड़की से बाहर फेंक देना चाहता हूँ
वह मेरी कविता, जो मैं लिख रहा होता हूँ, पर पेशाब कर देता है
जब उसका रोयां मेरे कपड़े पर चिपक जाता है, कहता हूँ 'क्या ही चुंबकीय है !'

मेरी पत्नी जब कोरिया गई
जाने से पहले उसने कहा , बिलाव को समय पर खाना देते रहना
लेकिन...... मेरे बारे में ?

मुझे आश्चर्य हुआ
बिलाव को मैं मशीनवत खाना दे सकता था
लेकिन अचानक ही मैं उसे प्यार करने लगा
उतना ही जितना प्यार अपनी पत्नी और बेटी को करता हूँ

ए बिलाव,
मेरे साथ लम्बे समय तक रहो
मेरी सुंदर कविता, जो मैं लिखने जा रहा हूँ,
पर पेशाब करना
मुझे नहीं आएगा गुस्सा
अपने रोयें मेरे कपड़े पर चिपका देना
रास्ते भर भले ही देखें खूबसूरत लड़कियाँ
कोई फ़र्क़ नहीं पड़ेगा मुझे

मैं अब नहीं रह गया हूँ रोबोट
तुम बस करते रहो म्याऊँ म्याऊँ ।

(अनुवाद : कुसुम जैन)

आदिम प्यास

हाम आन्ह

चकाचौंध शून्यता कड़ी चुभती धूप
अलसाई सी एक गाय
कर रही है चौड़ी सड़क पार

चींटी के बिल की रक्षा करता एक आदि भिक्षु
बोधि-बृक्ष की छाया के नीचे
झिलमिल धूप के टुकड़े...

टैगोर की कविता से निकलती
एक स्त्री नंगे पांव
जा रही है नदी की ओर सिर पर घड़ा रखे

अचानक उद्दीप्त हो उठती है
बस एक बूंद शीतल जल की कामना
हृदय में छिपी आदिम प्यास बुझाने के लिए।

(अनुवाद : कुसुम जैन)

कवि हाम आन्ह की कविताएँ ओस की बूँदें हैं जो मानवीय जीवन के गहरे अवसाद को अपने भीतर समेटे हुए है। सच्चाई और आवेग से भरी अच्छी और ख़ूबसूरत हैं । कवि हाम आन्ह मैक्सिम गोर्की स्कूल ऑफ क्रियेटिव राइटिं, मॉस्को से स्नातक हैं। अन्ना आख्मातोवा के अनुवाद पर वियतनाम एसोसिएशन ऑफ राइडर्स एवं लिट्रेचर एंड आर्ट्स वीकली द्वारा द्वितीय पुरस्कार मिला (प्रथम पुरस्कार किसी को नहीं मिला) दो कविता संग्रह 'नेचुरलनेस कलर्स' (2008) और 'कॉलिंग माइ मार्च' (2016) में प्रकाशित। प्रस्तुत कविता उन्होंने भारत प्रवास के दौरान लिखी थीं।

कविता : जिसे अब तक नहीं दे सकी नाम

नुएन फान क्यूइ माई

1973 में जन्मी कवि नुएन फान क्यूइ माई की कविता, गद्य और कहानियों की दस पुस्तकें वियतनामी और अंग्रेज़ी दोनों भाषाओं में प्रकाशित हो चुकीं हैं । कई महत्त्वपूर्ण पुरस्कारों से वह सम्मानित हो चुकी हैं जिनमें प्रमुख हैं हनोई लेखक संघ द्वारा प्रदत्त वर्ष 2010 का कविता पुरस्कार, द कैपिटल्स साहित्य एवं कला सम्मान, हनोई के एक हज़ार वर्ष पूरे होने के अवसर पर आयोजित कविता प्रतियोगिता में प्रथम पुरस्कार आदि आदि।

मेरे हाथ धान से भरा कटोरा उठाते हैं,
कटे धान से भरा खेत
जहाँ दफ़नाया गया था मेरी दादी को
धान के हर दाने में मिठास है दादी की लोरियों
की
जिसे मैंने देखा नहीं कभी
मैं कल्पना करती हूँ धरती के भीतर समाए
उसके कोमल चेहरे की,
उसके फटे पुराने कपड़ों की, त्वचा से चिपकी
हड्डियों की;
1945 में पड़े अकाल में मेरा गाँव बन गया था
क़ब्रिस्तान
और मेरे पिता खोज नहीं सके थे मेरी दादी की
कब्र,
उनके चावल का स्वाद पैंसठ वर्षों तक कड़वा
बना रहा था।

पैंसठ वर्षों की खोज के बाद,
हमारे पूर्वजों की आत्माओं ने पिता और मुझको
सुझाया दादी की कब्र का रास्ता।
अपने पिता को पहली बार माँ पुकारते हुए
सुना;

और उसकी पीठ के पीछे फैला धान का खेत
काँप उठा था।

मेरे दोनों पाँव मिट्टी में धँस गए थे।
मैं सूंघ रही थी दादी की आत्मा की जलती धूप की
सुगंध को
जो धरती में मिल खेतों में फैल गई थी,
जहाँ वह चुपचाप गीत सुनाते हुए
धान की बालियों के खिलने का आह्वान कर रही थी।

धान के कटोरे को अपने हाथ में उठाते हुए हर दाने
को गिना
हर दाने में मेरे पूर्वजों के पसीने की चमक थी,
जिनकी पीठ धान के खेतों में झुकी हुई थी,
और हर एक दाने पर दादी की ख़ुशबू जीवित थी।

(अनुवाद : कुसुम जैन)

विस्मृति

चान आन्ह थाई

जन्म 1953। कवि चान आन्ह थाई की लंबी कविता 'आच्छादित सूर्य' साप्ताहिक साहित्य पत्र द्वारा कविता पुरस्कार से पुरस्कृत हुई ।

वह वहाँ बहुत समय से बैठा है
दस बरसों से
बीस बरसों से
जैसे बीत गए हों हज़ारों बरस ?
घर के कोने में पड़ी पुरानी जर्जर कुर्सी ढंकी है काई से

बगल से गुज़रते चेहरे
धुँधलाए चेहरे
बिसरी तारीख़ें
अपने बच्चों की यादें तक भूल गया......

वह वहाँ समय की मानिंद बैठा है
फ़ौज की क़तार को याद करते हुए
बमों की बरसात को याद करते हुए
चीख़ता है श्राप देता है

हवा में तैर रही है स्वेद मिश्रित दग्ध रक्त की गंध
शांत हैं युद्ध के मैदान
शांत हैं एक पर एक पड़े कंकाल
नफ़रत समाप्त हो चुकी है
क्या सचमुच समाप्त हो
गई.....और क्या वह मर गया है ?

गोल गोल घूमती प्रचंड हवा
जल्द जल्द दफ़नायी क़ब्रों पर जलाई गई धूप का गोल
गोल धुँआ
करुण विलाप और सिसकियों से भरा युद्ध का मैदान
अंतहीन.......,,
अंतहीन........

कोई नहीं लेता उसका नाम
न कोई बुलाहट
न कोई आवाज़
जर्जर दीवार पर चिपकी एक मूक परछाईं
भोजन की खोज में दौड़ती चुहिया की आवाज़
उसके बूढ़े गले की कमजोर आवाज़
लगता है जैसे प्रतीक्षा कर रहे हैं सब
जैसे हों प्राचीन समय की प्रतिध्वनियाँ
कभी-कभी......,
दूर बहुत दूर एक वीरान जंगल
जैसे हो अंधेरे नर्क की ज़मीन

वहाँ लोगों का एक सैलाब उमड़ रहा है
कहाँ जा रहे हैं वे सब
वह भूल गया है रास्ता
भूल गया है अपना अस्तित्व
भूल गया है पुराने चेहरे

हवा आती है, जाती है
रोशनी आती है, जाती है
उसकी आँखों ने देखना बंद कर दिया है
अब तो पराजय की वेदना भी परेशान नहीं करती !...
भूले हुए लोगों का सैलाब
एकदम ठंडा और गतिहीन
सूखी त्वचा पर चिपकी वर्दी गल गई है
गुलदस्ते में सजे फूल मुरझा गए हैं
निशब्द गिर रहे हैं बिना इंसान की उपस्थिति में।

(अनुवाद : कुसुम जैन)

हैलोवीन

नुएन थि आन्ह ह्युयान्ह

जन्म 1955 -
'अचानक बरसात'
काव्य संग्रह। 2006
में हो चि मिन्ह
सिटी कविता
पुरस्कार एवं 2010
में मिलिटरी लिटरेरी
पुरस्कार से
सम्मानित।

इंसान होना बहुत उबाऊ है
क्यों न बन जाएँ भूत ?
चलो बनो
क्यों न बन जाएँ शैतान ?
चलो बनो
क्यों न बन जाएँ डायन ?
चलो बनो

चलो बनते हैं बस एक !
बनने दो मुझे एक भूत

भला हो मेला उत्सवों का
दीर्घजीवी हों मुखौटे
नए वर्ष से भी ज़्यादा मज़ेदार हैं
कोई बाघ बनता है तो कोई अजगर
कोई बनता है शैतान
उदासी से भरा होता है एक इंसान होना
हंसी से भरा होता है एक दानव होना

भूत होना उपयुक्त नहीं भी हो सकता है
भूत होना क्यों
लेकिन अभी भी इंसान की तरह दिखता है ?

क्यों उपस्थित हैं हैलोवीन उत्सव में
अकेला व्यक्ति बिना मुखौटे के
बस है मुखौटा

दूसरों की आँखों के भीतर

जिस किसी के पास चिरकालिक मुखौटा है

वह ही है हैलोवीन

(अनुवाद : कुसुम जैन)

हृदय जब प्रेम की भाषा नहीं बोल पाता

जन्म : 1966। प्रकाशित कविता संग्रह-ड्रीमिंग ऑफ फ्लावर्स(1992), फ़ोर एन ऑलवेज डिसटेंट पर्सन (2000), लीफ़ फ़ेट (2002), इन द हाउस ऑफ मेमोरीज (2005), द वायस ऑफ साइलेंस(2011), पिकिंग अप (2015), फ़्रॉम रिवर टू ओशन (2018).

ले थान्ह माई

हृदय जब प्रेम के शब्द बोलने में समर्थ होगा
ख़ुशी हमारे साथ आएगी हमारे जीवन में

आदमी पत्थर उठाने के लिए झुकता है
जिसने अवरुद्ध किया हुआ है
उसका अपना ही पथ ताकि पहुँच सके वह दरवाज़े तक
इससे पहले कि वह वादा करने के लिए शब्द बोले
चाँद की सुनहरी चाँदनी ने उसके हाथों में भर दी है
गरमाहट
हालाँकि देर हो चुकी है
फिर भी शायद बदल जाए
लेकिन अगर हम उगते हुए सूर्य को नहीं पकड़ पाते
और भोर वेला गुज़र जाती है
तब भी प्रेम मिले तो मत करना संकोच लेने में

चेरी स्प्रिंग्स स्टेट पार्क से दिखा था जो चाँद
ज़्यादा बड़ा होने का कोई कारण नहीं
एक पुरुष के हृदय से
एक स्त्री की मुस्कान इस दुनिया से कहीं बहुमूल्य है
वह पकड़ेगा चाँद
वह उठाएगा पीली सूखी पत्तियाँ
वह अपनी श्वासों से गर्म करेगा सर्दी का मौसम
उसके हाथों की पकड़ को
निश्चित रूप से
मज़बूत होना होगा

हृदय जब प्रेम के शब्द बोलने में समर्थ होगा
ख़ुशी हमारे साथ आएगी हमारे जीवन में

(अनुवाद : कुसुम जैन)

अपने घर से

माइ वान फान

वस्तुओं को ऋतुओं के अनुसार एकत्रित करते हो
पतझड़ में चकोतरा के फूलों का गुच्छा, बसंत में आलूबुख़ारे

हम हवा की धड़कन हैं, ज़मीन में गहरे धँसे, मिट्टी के स्तन
हम चुनते हैं अपने फ़र्नीचर को व्यवस्थित करने के लिए गर्म स्थल
अपनी टेबुल और कुर्सियों को रखने के लिए बड़ी ख़ाली जगह

हम खाने की टेबल पर छोड़ देते हैं अपनी चिंताएँ
चोप्स्टिक से उठाते हुए सब्ज़ियाँ, आती हैं दूर खेतों से
मटके के भीतर मछली चुगती है कीट पतंगों को
हम ख़ुश होते हैं देख कर अपने पदचिह्न
चावल के भूसे के समीप
गहरे कुएँ, झरनों और नदियों, ताल-तलैयों के आस पास

घर के भीतर मत बैठो बहुत देर तक
बाहर जाओ खेतों पर, जाओ नदी के किनारे
जहाँ पत्तियाँ उगती हैं हरी और मछलियाँ फ़र्राटे भरती हैं

ताज़ा अनानास या मीठे संतरे को दांतों से काटते हुए खाओ
और उनके रस की बूँदों को भूरी मिट्टी पर टपकने दो।

जन्म 1955। माइ वान फान कई राष्ट्रीय और अंतरराष्ट्रीय साहित्यिक पुरस्कारों से सम्मानित हो चुके हैं जिनमें प्रमुख हैं - वियतनाम राइटर्स एसोसिएशन 2010, स्वीडन का सिकाडा पुरस्कार 2017, सर्बियन एकेडमी ऑफ साइंस एंड आर्ट्स 2019, एसोसिएशन ऑफ लिटरेरी ट्रांसलेटर ऑफ मोंटेनेग्रो 2020। सोलह कविता संग्रह प्रकाशित और एक पुस्तक आलोचनात्मक निबंध की प्रकाशित। विदेशों में 19 काव्य संग्रहों का प्रकाशन एवं लोकार्पण ।

अपने गाँव में एक रात

चांग क्वांग क्युई

जन्म 2 जनवरी 1955। वियतनाम राइटर्स एसोसिएशन के सदस्य एवं नेशनल प्राइज़ फ़ॉर आर्ट्स एंड लिटरेचर पुरस्कार से सम्मानित ।

मैं काई-फूफंद लगी अपने सपने की छत पर लौट आता हूँ
फलों से भरे बाग़ीचों से गुजरते हुए
एक बूढ़े किसान की नींद में, अभी भी भैंस के खुर लंगड़ाते हैं
खेत युवा औरत की ढीली लटकी हुई छातियों से पड़े हैं
थका हारा गाँव अपने आप को अंधेरे में ढक लेता है
रात अपने आप को एक हज़ार साल पीछे ले जाती है

एकाकी बांस के पेड़ों से निकलती बयार समझती है
बदलती घड़ी का रुख़
हवा ठहरती है नदी के किनारे, एकाकी लहरें
मुझमें छटपटाती हैं : देर से होती भोर, सड़क के छोर पर
मद्धिम होती आग की कमजोर रोशनी
मेरी आकांक्षाएँ अभी भी हरी हैं, कच्चे फलों की तरह
माँ जलाती है चिराग़ और जाती है अन्न के भंडार की ओर
खेत चिंतित हैं, प्रतीक्षारत हैं अन्न के दानों के लिए

अंधकार आज़ादी से घूमता है आसमान के नीचे
बेचैन बाँस की बाड़ गिराती है अपने फूस
धरती को करते हुए प्यार, हड़बड़ी में पका फल
गिरता है, हैरान, निस्तब्ध बाग़ीचे में देर रात को
जाती हुई गर्मी में मैं 'सिकाडा' के मद्धिम होते गीत के साथ सो जाता हूँ
करवटें बदलते हुए मेरे एक छोर से दूसरी छोर तक बहता है गाँव का पसीना
लेकिन माँ अभी भी वहाँ बैठ चूल्हा जलाती है
हर सुबह गूँजती उसकी पदचाप से जीवंत है पूरा घर।

(अनुवाद : कुसुम जैन)

चेहरे, आसमान, धब्बे

बांग विएत

जन्म 1941।
वियतनाम राइटर्स एसोसिएशन के सदस्य एवं नेशनल प्राइज़ फ़ॉर आर्ट्स एंड लिटरेचर से सम्मानित।

जाना पहचाना युद्ध का मैदान अब पीछे, बहुत दूर छूट गया है
हवा बहाते हुए ले आई है मुझे अनंत आकाश में
युवा सैनिक जिन्होंने फिर मिलने का वादा किया था
साधारण से वे, जैसे साधारण होता है न्याय
जन्मा हो जैसे हर चेहरा बादल के एक टुकड़े के स्वागत के लिए

हम जहाँ कहीं भी हैं, हम ऋणी हैं जीवन के
सीमा की चौकी पर तैनात सेना जिसने पकाया था भात भूमिगत
'वान किउ' बच्चों की आँखें थीं जैसे हो कोई गीत ताज़ा
एकटक देखती रही थीं सैकड़ों बारूदी काले धुएँ को
अचानक हो गई थीं नीली सुरक्षित आसमान के तले

याद है घने जंगल की वह रात, 'त्रांग सोन' माँ!
जब पकाया था 'मारंता पौधे' का भोजन अपने बच्चों के लिए
याद है 'थुआ थियेन' प्रांत की लड़की जो मारी गई और शांत हो गई थी
मुझे हमेशा के लिए छोड़ कर चली गई थी चमकते आसमान में
मैंने बंद किया था उसकी आँखों को, जिनकी चमक अब तक मेरी यादों में जीवित है

दुख के पहले की नीरवता, और ख़ुशी के पहले का क्रंदन
याद है मुझे वह रात, जब हमने 'क्वांग टेकि' क़िले पर आक्रमण
किया था
विस्मित थे जब दागे गए हज़ारों गोलों से भर गया था आसमान
कितनी चमकीली थी नीली पीली लपटें जो दुश्मनों के ठिकाने पर
बरसी थीं
आक्रमण के उस एक क्षण में, मेरी आँखें आंसुओं से भर गई थीं

सारी ज़िंदगी मैं उन्हें जीते हुए दुखी परेशान रहा,
ओ मेरी युद्धभूमि, ओ मेरे देश !
हर वह चेहरा जिसे मैं जानता हूँ या देखा हो बस एक नज़र,
याद रहता है हमेशा
कितने सारे मासूम बच्चे, कितनी ही अनुभवी माताएँ
बहुत से सैनिक कई प्रदेशों, कई खाइयों को पार करते हुए
वे सारे साधारण चेहरे, हज़ारों बार सामना करने के बाद किया
होगा मृत्यु का वरण
नीचे मुझ पर और आसमान की ऊँची सतह पर उड़ते धब्बों पर
रोशनी चमकाओ।

(अनुवाद : कुसुम जैन)

माँझी का प्रेम गीत

चान डांग खोआ

दिओन त्रि हैमलेट, क्वोक तुओंश कम्यन, नामथान्ह डिस्ट्रिक्ट, होइ दुओंग में 26 अप्रैल 1958 में जन्मे चांग डांग खोआ वियतनाम राइटर्स एसोसिएशन के सदस्य हैं तु कला व साहित्य के राष्ट्रीय पुरस्कार से सम्मानित हो चुके हैं।

यात्रा के लिए रवाना होना है
आकाश से बादल छँट गए हैं
तुम घाट तक चल कर आए हो
एक किनारे पर फैला है समुद्र
दूसरे किनारे पर खड़ी है वह
वह शांत है, थोड़ा कुछ कहती है
फिर चुप हो जाती है, तुम चली गई हो
सब से ख़राब मौसम का सामना करने के लिए
एक किनारे पर फैला है समुद्र
दूसरे किनारे पर खड़ी है वह

कल जब जलेगी रोशनी
दूर तारों के नीचे लंगर डाले खड़ा होगा जहाज़
तुम अकेला महसूस मत करना, दूरी के बावजूद
एक किनारे पर फैला है समुद्र
दूसरे किनारे पर खड़ी है वह

कभी नहीं होगी शांति हमारी जन्मभूमि पर
हवा रोती है विधवाओं के माथे पर बंधी सफ़ेद पट्टियों पर
सारी रात एक उजाड़ द्वीप पर तुम प्रहरी बन खड़े रहते हो
एक किनारे पर फैला है समुद्र
दूसरे किनारे पर खड़ी है वह

आसमान भले ही उसे न रख सके
समुद्र विलुप्त हो जाए, तुम और दूब
बचे हैं बस, अब भी बची हैं स्मृतियाँ
एक किनारे पर फैला है समुद्र
दूसरे किनारे पर खड़ी है वह।

(अनुवाद : कुसुम जैन)

रहस्यमयी ख़ुशबू

फान थि थान्ह न्हान

जन्म : 1943। वियतनाम राइटर्स एसोसिएशन की सदस्य, नेशनल प्राइज़ फ़ॉर आर्ट्स एंड लिट्रेचर से सम्मानित।

गली के अंत में स्थित दो मकानों की खिड़कियाँ
हमेशा खुली रहती थीं बिना किसी कारण।
वे पुराने दोस्त जो सहपाठी भी होते थे
एक घर के पिछवाड़े में लगे चकोतरा के वृक्ष की ख़ुशबू
दूसरे के घर तक महकती रहती थी।

अपने रूमाल में फूलों का गुच्छा छिपाए झिझकते हुए
उसने रास्ता पार किया अपने पड़ोसी के घर के लिए ।
जहाँ कोई अगले दिन जाने वाला था मोर्चे पर।

वे निशब्द बैठे थे जैसे शब्द खो गए हों
उनकी नज़रें मिलीं, फिर घूम गईं
कौन पहला शब्द बोलने की हिम्मत करेगा ?
खिले फूलों की ख़ुशबू में वे और शरमा रहे थे।
लड़का हिम्मत नहीं कर पा रहा था फूलों के बारे में पूछने की;
लड़की फूलों को देने की हिम्मत नहीं समेट पा रही थी,
लेकिन वह गर्म एहसास से भरी निर्मल ख़ुशबू
अपने आप को छिपा नहीं पा रही थी
मंद मंद महक रही थी।

खिले फूलों की तरह वह लड़की भी चुपचाप थी
उसकी ख़ुशबू उसके प्यार का इज़हार कर रही थी

तुम कितने दूर दीखते हो ; क्या अब भी नहीं जानते तुम
क्या दिखाई नहीं देता तुम्हें कि मिलने आई हूँ तुमसे
मेरी ख़ुशबू तुम्हारे हृदय को भर देगी
जब तुम चले जाओगे
यह ख़ुशबू तुम्हारा पीछा करेगी, हर कहीं।

एक दूसरे से विदा लेते समय भी
वे नहीं बोलते कुछ
तथापि लड़के की यात्रा को ख़ुशबू मीठे एहसास से भरती है।

(अनुवाद : कुसुम जैन)

लौट आया है जो

वु क्युआन फुओंग

जन्म : 1940। वियतनाम राइटर्स एसोसिएशन के सदस्य एवं नेशनल प्राइज़ फ़ॉर आर्ट्स एंड लिट्रेचर से सम्मानित।

पास, बहुत पास, फिर भी, बहुत दूर
छत पर तिरछा पड़ता बुद्ध का हरा आकाश
गाँव का मैदान जहां हमारे माता-पिता चला करते थे
उसी रास्ते से गए थे बुद्ध

घनघनाती घंटी की आवाज़-किसके लिए और कहाँ से?
रात में पुल के नीचे की लहरें ठंडी हैं
पलक झपकने भर से ज़िंदगी में आए परिवर्तन से स्तब्ध हैं
मात्र चाँद सा चमकता प्रेम, तब भी और आज भी है

झरने नदी की ओर, नदी समुद्र की ओर बहती है
अंततः एक व्यक्ति का हृदय, हमारे हृदयों से मिलता है
तीन हज़ार ग्रह धुएँ और धूल से मलिन हो गए हैं
दरवाज़े के बाहर ऊपर चमकता चाँद रखता है नज़र।

(अनुवाद : कुसुम जैन)

कोंग ट्यूब गीत

थान्ह थाओ

जन्म : 1946।
वियतनाम राइटर्स एसोसिएशन के सदस्य तथा नेशनल प्राइज़ फ़ॉर आर्ट्स एंड लिट्रेचर से सम्मानित।

पुरानी वीरों की गाथाएँ
अब भी गाई जाती हैं, लेकिन बस किताबों में
तलवार और घोड़ों की जीन
हो गए हैं अब अतीत

हमारे अपने गीत
मुक्तिवाहिनी सेना के मनोबल को बढ़ाता
कोंग ट्यूब का गीत
दुनिया में सबसे आसान है

बस अभी ख़त्म हुआ है भात
इसके बाद टारो पेड़ की जड़ों से बना सूप
फिर थोड़ी कड़ी जंगली चाय
लेकिन पीते सब हैं और कहते हैं अच्छी

अल्युमिनियम के एक पतीले से
हम सैकड़ों काम करते हैं
मुश्किलें होशियार करती हैं
हमारे सैनिक अत्यंत फुर्तीले हैं

मलेरिया से ग्रस्त जो सैनिक थे
मुँह तोड़ जवाब नहीं दे सके
कुछ आराम के बाद
जब बुख़ार उतर गया, वे तुरंत प्रस्थान कर गए

कोंग ट्यूब से बना पतीला हमेशा पीठ पर रहता है
वह उनके लिए आज का 'थैच सान्ह' है
बहुत से नायक महानायक हो गए
इस पतीले से भात खाते हुए

महीने और साल गुज़र जाएँगे
बहुत सारे मधुर गीतों के साथ
लेकिन मैं जानता हूँ भलीभाँति
जैसे इन्हें चट्टानों पर तराश दिया हो
जैसे इन्हें वृक्षों में रूपांतरित कर दिया हो

आज का गीत
सरल और उत्कृष्ट है
जीवन के सरलतम अनुभवों से परिपूर्ण
कड़वा और मीठा।

(अनुवाद : कुसुम जैन)

जुगनुओं के झुण्ड वाला जंगल

न्गुएन डुक माउ

न्गुएन डुक माउ का जन्म 1948 में नाम निन्ह, नाम हा, वियतनाम में हुआ था। मूलतः उनका पैतृक गांव है नाम दिएन। आप वियतनाम लेखक संघ के सदस्य हैं तथा कला व साहित्य के लिए आपको नेशनल प्राइज़ फॉर आर्ट्स एण्ड लिटरेचर से पुरस्कृत भी किया जा चुका है।

रात का समय था। घने जंगल में जाकर दस्ता रुका। वहां सूखे नाले के पास किसी ने एक कुआं खोद रखा था। प्यास के कारण गला सूखा जा रहा था, सो हमने कुएं से पानी निकाल कर पीया। ठण्डे मीठे पानी से हमारे शरीरों को कुछ राहत मिली। हमने उस वक्त ध्यान ही नहीं दिया कि कुएं में एक लाश पड़ी थी। रात घुप्प अंधेरी थी पर जंगल में जुगनू जगमगा रहे थे।

चौकसी शुरू करने के लिए मैंने अपनी रायफल को कंधे पर रख लिया। काले वृक्षों की कतार से हो कर गुज़रते हुए मुझे नर्म सी किसी चीज से ठोकर लगी जिससे सड़ांध की ऐसी दुर्गंध उठी कि उबकाई आ गई। थकावट में मुझे लगा कि शायद कोई हिरण होगा, जो बम लगने से मर गया होगा। बहरहाल, निगरानी के बाद मैं खटोले पर आकर गहरी नींद में सो गया। मेरे स्वप्नों पर जुगनू मंडराते रहे। पर क्या वे मेरे स्वप्न थे? क्या सचमुच मैं सो रहा था? मुझे क्या पता था कि रात भर मुर्दा शरीरों को कीड़े खोखला कर रहे थे।

सुबह हुई। खाना बनाने के लिए जब कुएं से पानी निकाला गया तो यह देख कर हलचल मच गई कि कुएं में दो युवतियों की लाशें थीं। हमारे दस्ते ने जब चट्टानों, पेड़ों, झाड़ियों में सघन खोज शुरू की तो और तीन युवकों की लाशें मिलीं। हमने पांच कब्रें खोद कर उन्हें दफ़ना दिया। कब्रों पर न उनके नाम का कोई जिक्र था, न उनके पैतृक गांव का और न ही उनकी जन्म व मृत्यु तिथि का। जब हमने तारों के गुच्छों और

नीरव 'वाकी-टाकी' को देखा तो हमें समझते देर न लगी कि वे संचार-व्यवस्था से जुड़े सैनिक थे जो दुश्मन के हत्थे चढ़ गए।

युद्ध समाप्त हो गया है। पता नहीं कब मैं त्रुओंग सोन के जाने-पहचाने रास्तों पर लौटूंगा। पता नहीं तब वह कुआं कहां होगा, जिसके रक्त-मिश्रित जल से हमने अपनी प्यास बुझाई थी। पता नहीं कहां होंगे वे वृक्ष, उनके तने और जड़ें जहां हजारों कीड़े रात भर लाशें कुतरते रहे। जाने कहां होंगी वे नाम रहित कब्रें जो भारी हृदय और आंसुओं से भरी आंखें ले कर हमने खोदी थीं जुगनुओं के झुण्डों वाले जंगल में।

(अनुवाद : प्रेम कपूर)

वियतनामी कहानियाँ

शहतूत के पेड़ तले एक लौकिक चांदनी बाज़ार

वाइ बान

वाइ बान का जन्म 1961 में हुआ। अपनी कहानी 'अंधेरे में जन्मी औरत' के लिए आपको कहानी प्रतियोगिता में मिलिटरी लिट्रेचर मैगजीन से 1990 में प्रथम पुरस्कार प्राप्त हुआ।

सुई ग्राम के सुदूर कोने में एक विधवा और उसकी बेटी रहते थे। भरे-पूरे शरीर वाली माँ की उम्र रही होगी यही कोई चालीस के आस-पास। उसके प्यारे से होंठ थे और गालों में गड्ढे पड़ते थे। उसकी बड़ी-बड़ी आंखें थीं और लोगों का कहना था कि उसके अकाल वैधव्य का कारण भी वही थीं। पूरे दस साल तक उस खूबसूरत महिला ने अपनी इज़्ज़त पर आंच नहीं आने दी, हालाँकि ऐसे लोगों का अभाव न था जो उसकी इज़्ज़त से खेलना चाहते थे।

उसकी बेटी का सोलहवाँ साल चल रहा था। यह ऐसी उम्र होती है जब किसी लड़की का यौवन फूटना शुरू होता है। यों तो वह अपनी माँ की प्रतिमूर्ति थी किंतु उसकी आंखें अपनी मां के समान दिलकश न थीं।

पाँचवें चंद्र मास के बीच का समय था, जब पूर्णमासी की चाँदनी केले के

चौड़े पत्तों पर चाँदी सी चमक रही थी। बेटी लुआ ने देखा कि माँ दोपहर के बाद से ही कुछ बेचैन थी। वह तेज़ी से बगीचे में जाकर कच्चे केलों का एक गुच्छा तोड़ लाई थी और फिर तम्बाकू की कुछ पत्तियों को लाकर उसने सावधानीपूर्वक एक डलिया के नीचे ढँक कर रख दिया। उसने रात्रि का भोजन भी शीघ्र कर लिया था और बेटी से कह दिया था कि वह देर रात तक न जागे।

किंतु चाह कर भी लुआ को नींद न आई। खिड़की के बाहर छिटकी चाँदनी को देख कर उसे अपने भीतर कुछ कसमसाहट सी महसूस हुई, गाल दहक से उठे। वह ऊँचे स्वर में गाना चाहती थी। उसे याद आया कि दोपहर बाद जब वह धान के पौधों को सींच रही थी तो उसकी भेंट एक युवक से हुई थी, जिसने उससे कहा था, ''तुम बहुत खूबसूरत हो। मुझसे विवाह कर लो तो तुम्हें विधवा होना नहीं पड़ेगा।'' यह सुन कर उसने अपनी बाल्टी उस पर दे मारी थी।

इसी बीच मां के कमरे से कुछ आवाज़ सी आई जिसने लुआ की तंद्रा भंग कर दी। उसने आँखें मींच लीं। तभी उसे मां के कदमों की आहट सुनाई दी। मां उसके बिस्तर तक आई और मसहरी में एक बार झाँककर देखा, फिर लौट चली। लुआ ने आँखें खोली तो देखा कि माँ सिर पर टोकरी रखे बांस के अधखुले द्वार से बाहर जा रही थी। लुआ को कुछ संशय हुआ, वह उठी और पीछे चल पड़ी।

मां तेज़ी से गांव की गली में बढ़ी जा रही थी और लुआ उससे बीसेक कदम पीछे थी। गाँव से बाहर निकल कर माँ उस सड़क की ओर बढ़ी जो उस मैदान की ओर जाती है जहाँ विशाल शहतूत के पेड़ों की बहुतायत है, जहाँ जाने से माँ-बाप अपने बच्चों को यह कह कर मना करते हैं कि वहाँ से कल्पित बौने उन्हें उठा कर ले जाएँगे, पर फिर भी बच्चे वहीं जाकर खेलना पसंद करते।

दूर से लुआ को कुछ ऐसी आवाज़ें सुनाई दीं, जैसी अमूमन बाजारों में सुनाई देती हैं। उसने देखा, माँ के कदमों में कुछ और तेज़ी आ गई थी। उसने भी अपनी रफ्तार तेज कर दी ताकि माँ उसकी नज़रों से ओझल न हो जाए। दूरी जब कुछ कम हुई तो उसने लोगों को छोटी गलियों से निकल कर पुराने शहतूत के पेड़ों तले एकत्र होते देखा।

लुआ ने देखा कि एक पेड़ के नीचे खाली जगह देख कर माँ रुकी तथा कच्चे केले व अन्य वस्तुओं को पानी के एक कटोरे के पास सजाकर रखा। लुआ ने सोचा - तो यह है वह बाज़ार जिसके लिए माँ आई है। उसने चारों ओर नज़र दौड़ाई, देखा चारों ओर चांदनी फैली थी, आवाज़ें तो स्पष्ट थीं किंतु गतिविधियाँ

कुछ डरी-सहमी अस्पष्ट सी थीं। पुराने वृक्षों की छाँव तले लोग अत्यंत उत्साह से बातें कर रहे थे। खुशी से उनके चेहरे चमक रहे थे। कुछ लोग उदास भी थे और चुपचाप एक-दूसरे से गले लग रहे थे। उनकी आंखों में पारस्परिक तिरस्कार भरा था।

कोई बाँसुरी बजा रहा था, उसकी बाँसुरी की धुन में सम्मोहित होकर लुआ अपने चुस्त पैरों पर थिरकने लगी और एक बार फिर उसे लगा जैसे उसके गाल दहक रहे हों। संगीत के स्रोत को जब उसने ढूँढा तो देखा कि बाँसुरी बजाने वाला एक शहतूत के पेड़ के तने के सहारे बैठा था और उसके सामने बाँसुरियों का ढेर था। उत्सुकतावश लुआ ने एक बाँसुरी उठा ली।

''तुम्हें पसंद है ये?'' बाँसुरी वाले ने पूछा।

''हाँ।''

''ये बहुत अच्छी हैं।''

''कितने की है?'' लुआ ने पहली बार बाँसुरी वाले को देखा। वह युवा था। सुघड़ था उसका चेहरा।

''एक क्रान।''

लुआ ने अपनी जेब तलाशी, पर वह पैसे लाना तो भूल ही गई थी।

''कोई बात नहीं'', बाँसुरी वाले ने कहा, ''पैसे बाद में दे देना। पर पहले बजा कर तो देखो।''

''बजाना तो मुझे आता ही नहीं।''

''बहुत आसान है। देखो, इन छेदों को उंगलियों से ढको और इस छेद में फूँक मारो।''

''मैं बाद में सीख लूँगी। तुम कोई और धुन बजाओ न।''

एक बार फिर हवा में खुशगवार और दर्द भरे सुर गूँज उठे। बाँसुरी की धुन में लुआ कहीं खो सी गई। उसे एक ऐसी उत्तेजना का अहसास हुआ जैसा इससे पहले कभी नहीं हुआ था।

क्षितिज में चाँद धीरे-धीरे नीचे उतर रहा था। बाँसुरी वाले युवक ने बाँसुरी बजाना बंद कर दिया और कहा ''बाज़ार उठ रहा है। यह लो अपनी बाँसुरी, अगली बार आओ तो पैसे दे देना।''

''पर बाँसुरी ले कर मैं करूँगी क्या? बजाना तो मुझे आता ही नहीं।''

जंगलों में उड़ती गौरैया चिड़िया

वो थि शुआन हा

1959 में जन्मी वो थि शुआन हा वियतनाम की एक लब्धप्रतिष्ठ कथाकार हैं, जिनकी मशहूर लोकप्रिय कहानी ''फाइनल गुडबाय टु स्वीट ड्रीम'' (मधुस्वप्न की अंतिम विदाई) को 1998 में वियतनाम लेखक संघ द्वारा सर्वश्रेष्ठ पुस्तक का पुरस्कार प्रदान किया गया।

थान के साथ विवाह के हफ्ते भर बाद मेरी उसके माता-पिता से कुछ कहासुनी हो गई। थान का चेहरा पीला पड़ गया। उसके उभरे हुए होंठ घिनौने से लगने लगे। दरअसल वह विरोधाभासों का पुलिंदा है। मुझे चूमते वक्त तो हिंसक सा हो जाता है, पर जब उसे कुछ कहना होता है तो हकलाने लगता है।

''थान, इस फूहड़ औरत को तुम्हें सजा देनी चाहिए'', मेरे ससुर एक कसाई की तरह चीखे।

अपने कमरे में बैठी मैं अवज्ञा में अपने होंठ दबाए, नंगी टांगें झुलाती रही।

''मां-बाबूजी, कृपया उसे माफ कर दें'', उदास स्वर में थान ने मिन्नत की।

थान की बेअक्ल मां टोकरी उठा कर भुनभुनाती हुई रसोईघर में चली गई।

''तेरी बीवी ने यदि फिर मुझसे बहस की तो मैं उसे उसके मायके भेज दूंगी।

अब और मैं उसके साथ नहीं रह सकती, हालांकि वह हमारी पहली पुत्रवधु है।''

मेरी इच्छा तो हुई कि मैं कमरे से निकल कर उन पर कूद पड़ूं जो मुझे पुत्रवधु के कर्तव्य समझा रहे थे। पारिवारिक दिक्कतों का ज्ञान मुझे था, फिर भी मैंने थान से विवाह इसलिए किया था क्योंकि मुझे उससे प्यार था। हर रात हमारे शरीर सांप के जोड़े की तरह एक-दूसरे में गुंथकर एकाकार हो जाते। पांच वर्गमीटर का हमारा कमरा थान के पसीने की गंध, मेरे बालों की सुगंध तथा दो आवेशपूर्ण प्रेमियों की सांसों की गर्मी से सराबोर हो उठता। बीच-बीच में हवा का झोंका हमारे छोटे से कमरे को कमलताल की सुगंध से भर जाता। प्रेम-क्रिया के पश्चात् बिस्तर के किनारे पर निढाल हो कर पड़े-पड़े हम खिड़की के पल्लों से आसमान में झिलमिलाते सितारों को निरुत्साही ढंग से निहारते रहते।

और तब थान कहता, ''प्रिये, तुम हमारी बूढ़ी मां से हुज्जत मत किया करो।'''

अंधेरे में थान जब मुझसे यह सब निवेदन करता तो मैं तारे गिनती रहती। उसके शब्द मुझ पर लोरी का-सा उपचार कर मुझे सुला देते।

''हर बरसाती मौसम में एक जोड़ी बत्तखें गंवाने के लिए मुझे मां-बाबूजी की डांट सुननी पड़ती है'', थान कहता। ''जुलाई के महीने में बत्तखें तालाब में अपना पिछवाड़ा ऊंचा कर पानी में अपनी चोंच डुबा जब मछली या घोंघा पकड़ती हैं तो इस प्रक्रिया में वे पानी में ही अंडा दे देती हैं। कभी-कभी तो मैं डलिया भर अंडे संग्रह कर लेता और ऐसा करने में ठंड के कारण मेरे होंठ नीले पड़ जाते..., जांघिया से खुलकर अंडकोष बाहर आ जाता...''

उसकी बातें सुन मेरा हंसते-हंसते बुरा हाल हो जाता। थान एक रूपवान इंसान है। रंग सांवला, चौड़ी छाती और सुपुष्ट देह है। घने काले बाल और चौड़ा ललाट बताता था कि वह निश्चय ही बुद्धिमान है। दर्जनों लड़कियां उसकी दीवानी हो सकती थीं, पर वह तो मेरा दीवाना था और उसे यही चिंता सताती थी कि कहीं मैं उसे छोड़ न दूं। कैसा मूरख था वह! उसे इस बात का अहसास ही नहीं था कि मुझे भी उससे बेइंतहा मुहब्बत थी, पागलपन की हद तक, और मैं नहीं चाहती थी कि हमारे प्यार के बीच कोई आए। शायद इसीलिए मुझे अपने सास-ससुर से घृणा थी।

केवल एक ही आदमी था जिससे मैं घृणा नहीं करती थी। वह रहता तो मेरे

सास-ससुर मुझ पर हाथ उठाने की हिम्मत नहीं करते, क्योंकि यदि वह रहता तो मैं उनकी ज्येष्ठ पुत्रवधु न रहती। वह वेदी पर बैठा मुस्कुराता और खिड़की से बाहर बगीचे में देखता रहता। बगीचे के पीछे की तरफ कुछ अंगूर के पेड़ हैं। कई बार जब बगीचे की मिट्टी को मैं हाथों से खोदती तो हाथों में खरोंच लग जाती। कीड़ों को मिट्टी में जब कुलबुलाते देखती तो मैं डरकर घर में दौड़ आती। वह फिर भी अन्यमनस्क सा मुस्कुराता बाहर की ओर देखता रहता। थान को बुलाकर मैं कहती, ''हमारी मिट्टी में कीड़े पड़े हैं।''

तब मेरे ससुर पाइप गुड़गुड़ाते हुए मुंह से धुएं का गुबार छोड़ते हुए कहते- ''पागल है यह फूहड़ स्त्री।''

यह केवल नाम ही था जो मेरी रक्षा कर सकता था।

छुट्टियों के दिन थान मुझे अपने साथ गौरैया चिड़ियों का शिकार करने जंगल में ले जाता। चिनार के पेड़ों पर बैठी गौरैया चिड़ियों पर आसमान की ओर अपनी रायफल तानकर वह कहता, ''गौरैया चिड़ियों को मारना किसी अन्य जानवर को मारने से अच्छा लगता है।''

थान की रायफल से गोली छूटने पर उसे एक झटका लगा। ''पर क्यों ?'' मैंने पूछा।

गोली छूटते ही गौरैया चिड़ियां पेड़ की डालों से ऊपर आसमान की ओर उड़ गईं। एक कहीं दूर झाड़ियों पर जा गिरी। थान ने उस छटपटाती चिड़िया को उठा लिया। मैंने अपना प्रश्न दोहराया, ''तुमने ऐसा क्यों कहा कि गौरैया को मारना अच्छा लगता है ?''

''वो इसलिए क्योंकि वे बहुत सारी हैं।''

आग जलाने के लिए मैंने पत्तियों को इकट्ठा करना शुरू किया। चिड़िया आग पर झुलसती रही और थान बीच-बीच में उसे अपनी छड़ी से पलटता रहा। कुछ देर बाद छड़ी की नोक से कुरेद कर मांस का एक टुकड़ा मैंने अपने मुंह में डाला।

''तुम्हें देखकर मुझे 'द एडवेंचर्स ऑफ फॉक्स एमेलीन' की लोमड़ी एमेलीन की याद आ गई'', थान ने मुझे चिढ़ाते हुए कहा। एक-दूसरे की बाहों में बंधे, एक-दूसरे का चिकना मुंह चूमते हुए हम धरती पर लुढ़कते रहे। मैं समझ नहीं पा रही थी कि हम दोनों को क्या हो गया था। मेरे ऊपर जो इंसान था उसकी रक्त-कोशिकाओं को छू कर मैं जानना चाहती थी कि वह कौन सी रहस्यमय

शक्ति है, जो एक पुरुष व स्त्री को आपस में बांध कर रखती है।

हमने एक बार में एक गौरैया का भक्षण किया। हम घास पर लेट रहे थे और आसमान में चिड़ियों के झुंड को अपने घोंसलों की ओर लौटता देख रहे थे। सूरज का रंग जामुनी हो गया था।

अपने जंगल के सैर-सपाटों में कभी-कभी हमें तेज बारिश का भी सामना करना पड़ता। उस बारिश में पत्तों और डालियों के साथ हम भी भीजते और बर्फीली बारिश की बूंदों से अपने भीतर की ज्वलंत कामनाओं को शांत करते। मैं अपने कपड़े उतार कर बारिश में शान के साथ नहाती। बारिश की बूंदों में नहाई मेरी नग्न देह हाथी-दांत सी चमक उठती।

बारिश के बाद जंगल कुछ और हरा हो उठता। धूप ग्रहण करने को नई कलियां खिल उठतीं। चींटियों की कतारें पेड़ों से गिरी सड़ी पत्तियों को अपनी पीठ पर ढो रही हैं, यह थान ने देखा।

''ये चींटियां जरूर भूखी होंगी, तभी तो खाने के लिए कड़वी पत्तियां ले जा रही हैं।''

मुझे याद है, मेरे विवाह से पहले मां कुछ मजेदार टिप्पणियां करती थी जीवन के बारे में, जैसे ''चींटियों की तो तकदीर ही है भूखों मरना''। उसे तो मुझे सास-ससुर की इज्ज़त करने की सीख देनी चाहिए थी ताकि अपने पति के परिवार में मुझे भरपेट भात मयस्सर हो।

पास ही कहीं झरना बह रहा था। जंगल की निस्तब्धता को बीच-बीच में भंग कर रही थी यदाकदा हिरनों की फटफटाहट और पेड़ों से गिरे पत्तों की सरसराहट।

''चलो एमेलीन, अब घर चलें'', थान ने कहा।

अनिच्छा से मैंने जंगल छोड़ा।

विवाह के साल भर बाद मैं गर्भवती हो गई। नौ महीने बाद मैंने एक बेटी को जन्म दिया, जो देखने में काफी कुछ थान जैसी लगती है। जच्चा-चौकी पर मैं हाथ-पैर फैलाए बेहोश पड़ी थी, जब दाई ने गर्भनाल काटी। एक आदमी,जो थान से कुछ बड़ा और लम्बा था, छत से नीचे पहले मेरे पीत चेहरे और फिर सद्य काटी गई गर्भनाल, जो मेरे जननांग पर लटक रही थी, की ओर देख रहा था। फिर मुझे अपने बच्चे का रुदन सुनाई दिया और उसके बाद देखा कि वह

व्यक्ति मेरे बच्चे को चूम रहा था। वह अपनी उदास मुस्कुराहट के साथ मुझे देख रहा था। मैं उसे पहचान गई। वह नाम था, थान का स्वर्गीय भाई। जब जच्चा चौकी से थान ने मुझे उठा कर बिस्तर पर लेटाया तो अचानक मुझे होश आया और वह मुझे बिल्कुल अजनबी सा लगा। नया-नया बाप जो बना था। थान मुस्कुराते हुए सफाई में लगा था। मैंने ड्योढ़ी में अपने ससुर को भुनभुनाते सुना:

''मुझे पोता कब होगा?''

थकान से मैंने आंखें मूंद लीं।

''तुम्हारे पिता को यदि पोता चाहिए तो कहो कि वे तुम्हारे लिए कोई और औरत ले आयें'', मैं अब पूरे होश में थी और थान पर अपने शब्द-वाण छोड़ रही थी।

मैं अभी भी तुनक रही थी, ''बेटा चाहिए तो दूसरी बीवी ले आओ।''

''मुझे यही अपेक्षा थी'', हताश स्वर में थान ने कहा, ''बच्चा होते ही तुम्हें मेरी जरूरत नहीं महसूस होगी।''

''तुम पुरुषों को यह ध्यान रखना चाहिए कि हम न हों तो तुम्हारा कोई वंशज ही नहीं होगा'', गुस्से से उबलते हुए मैंने कहा, ''जबकि हम नदी का पानी पीकर भी गर्भधारण कर सकती हैं। तुम पुरुषों से तो हम स्त्रियां कहीं बेहतर हैं। हां, हम थोड़ी झगड़ालू होती हैं।''

थान बेचारा चुपचाप सब कुछ सुनता रहा। फिर कुछ नरम पड़ते हुए उसका हाथ अपने हाथ में लेते हुए मैंने कहा, ''अभी कुछ देर पहले मैंने नाम को देखा था। प्रजनन के वक्त वह वहां था। उसने मुझे निर्वस्त्र देखा, हमारी बच्ची को प्यार भी किया।''

''बकवास'', थान ने कहा।

''नहीं, यह सच है। बल्कि उसने तो इस प्रकार व्यवहार किया मानो माइ तुम्हारी नहीं उसकी बच्ची हो।''

यह मानकर कि मैं सन्निपात की स्थिति में वह सब कह रही थी, थान ने बुरा नहीं माना और शांतचित्त हो उत्तर दिया, ''मुझे नाम के जत्थे की सूचना मिल गई है। तुम ठीक हो जाओ तो मैं उसकी खोज में निकलूंगा।''

नाम, थान का बड़ा भाई था। सत्रह साल की उम्र में फौज में भर्ती हो गया था। जब वह फौज में जाने लगा तो मेरे पति के पूरे गांव ने उसे विदा किया,

उसकी प्रशंसा की। बाद में, मेरे ससुर कई बार तस्करी के अभियोग में गिरफ्तार हुए किंतु उन्हें सिर्फ इसलिए जेल नहीं भेजा गया क्योंकि उनका बेटा एक स्वेच्छासेवी फौजी था। किसी को भी इस बात का भान नहीं था कि पिता की निर्दयता के कारण बेटे ने घर छोड़ा था। नाम जैसे लोग खुशकिस्मत थे कि उन दिनों युद्ध चल रहा था, जहां वे घर से पलायन कर भाग ले सकते थे। अब शांति के ज़माने में बच्चों को यदि मां-बाप के साथ रहना पसंद न हो तो उनके पास जाने के लिए दूसरा कोई ठिकाना ही नहीं। थान ने मुझे बताया था कि उसका पिता नाम को, यदि वह कुछ कमा कर न लाये तो, छत से उल्टा लटका कर मोटे डंडे से पीटता था। फौज में भर्ती के दो महीने बाद लड़ाई के मोर्चे पर जाने से पहले नाम को घर जाने के लिए एक दिन की छुट्टी मिली। आधी रात को जब वह घर पहुंचा और दरवाज़े पर दस्तक दी, तो उसके पिता ने यह सोच कर कि डकैत होंगे, दरवाज़ा ही नहीं खोला और खिड़की के ऊपर छप्पर में अपना धन छिपाने में लगा रहा। अगले दिन सारा दिन नाम घर पर रहा पर उसे एक बधिया मुर्गी के अलावा खाने को कुछ नहीं मिला। जब वह घर से विदा होने लगा, तो उसने थान को, जिसकी उम्र उस वक्त दस साल थी, एक पीतल का कारतूस दिया और अपनी पगार से बचाया सारा पैसा अपनी मां को दे दिया। जब वह विदा हुआ तो आंखों में आंसू लिये मां उसे जाते हुए उदास नजरों से देखती रही। इस पर पिता ने ऊंची आवाज़ में कहा, ''तुम रो क्यों रही हो? क्या तुम नहीं जानती कि मर्द को आसमान सिर पर ढोते हुए धरती को नापना पड़ता है।''

नाम ने धरती नापी तो सही, पर सिर पर आसमान नहीं गोला-बारूद ढोते हुए। उसे गये हुए कोई साल भर हुआ होगा जब एक दिन उसके परिवार को उसकी मौत की खबर मिली। उसके अवशेष अभी भी क्वांगत्री में कहीं पड़े होंगे। नाम के गंदे पुराने खिलौनों के ढेर को संभालते हुए थान को वो पीतल का कारतूस मिल गया जो उसे नाम ने दिया था। उसने उसे चमकाकर किसी गुप्त स्थान में रख दिया। हर बार जब हम एक-दूसरे को प्यार करते तो वह उस कारतूस को निकाल कर मुझे दिखाता और कहता, ''यह मेरे पास नाम की निशानी है।''

जब नन्हीं माइ दो साल की हो गई तो फिल्म वालों का एक जत्था युद्ध में बिछड़े एक जोड़े और युद्ध के बारे में बन रही एक फिल्म की शूटिंग के सिलसिले

में क्वांगत्री गया। फिल्म की कहानी एक दुर्ग में घटी भारी भूलों, नीचता तथा उदात्त भावनाओं पर आधारित थी। हालांकि थान एक 'कॉपी एडिटर' है, पर वह कभी-कभी कुछ पत्रिकाओं के लिए भी लिखता है। आम तौर पर वह अपने प्रकाशित लेख एक दराज में रख कर ताला लगा देता है। एक पत्रकार के रूप में थान कई लोगों को जानता-पहचानता है, जिनमें एक है मिस्टर विन्ह, जो कि फिल्मी जत्थे के प्रमुख थे और दूसरे हैं फिल्म के निर्देशक स्वयं, जिनकी अपने एक लेख में उसने प्रशंसा की थी। इन दोनों व्यक्तियों ने जोर दे कर थान से आग्रह किया कि यात्रा में थान भी उनके साथ जाए ताकि वह उनकी आगामी फिल्म की अग्रिम समीक्षा कर सके। इसके लिए राजी होते हुए थान ने कहा, ''ठीक है, मैं तभी जाऊंगा जब दिएम को साथ ले जाने देंगे।''

मक्कार हंसी हंसते हुए मिस्टर विन्ह ने कहा, ''तुम एक पल के लिए भी दिएम को भूलते नहीं? बूढ़े हो जाओगे तब क्या करोगे, तब तो आज जैसी चाहत रहेगी नहीं।''

मैं जानती थी कि वे सभी चाहते थे कि मैं भी उसके साथ जाऊं क्योंकि उसे डर था कि उसकी गैरहाजिरी में मैं किसी और से न फंस जाऊं। थान की एक पच्चीस वर्षीय छोटी बहन थी फुओंग, जिसकी छातियां सपाट और मेकअप नहीं लगाने पर जिसका चेहरा पीला सा था। उसके प्रेमी लू को थान ने देखा था मुझे भूखी आंखों से घूरते हुए। लू जब भी फुओंग से मिलने आता तो वह कुछ परेशान व असहज हो उठती और उसे जब पीने को चाय देती तो अक्सर छलका देती। छलकी हुई चाय को जब मैं पोंछने जाती तो वह मेरी उभरी छातियों का ऊपरी हिस्सा ताकता रहता। ऐसे में फुओंग का चेहरा गुस्से में कुछ लाल हो उठता तो मैं मुस्कुरा कर घर से बाहर निकल जाती।

यह सब देख कर थान गुस्सा हो जाता और मुझसे बात न करता, तो मैं नरम पड़ जाती और दीवार की ओर मुंह कर बिस्तर में घुस जाती और कल्पना करती कि लू और फुओंग एक-दूसरे से प्रेम कर रहे थे। कभी-कभी मैं सोचती कि नाम की उदास आंखें मेरी देह को घूर रही हैं तो हड्डियों तक एक ठंडक सी पहुंचती महसूस होती।

फिल्मी जत्थे ने मध्य वियतनाम की उमसदार गर्मियों में कड़ी मेहनत की। फिल्म की प्रमुख अभिनेत्री ने मुस्कुराते हुए डींग हांकी कि उसका वजन दो किलो

कम हो गया था और उसे चिंता थी कि कहीं उसका कुत्ता उसे पहचानने से इनकार न कर दे। वह अभिनेत्री थी तो मशहूर पर उसे जब फिल्म के लिए चुना गया तब वह बेकार थी और घरेलू पार्टियों में अपना समय बिता रही थी। उसे एक किसान की विनम्र पत्नी की भूमिका के लिए चुना गया था।

क्वांगत्री के पुराने दुर्ग की पृष्ठभूमि में फिल्म-निर्माताओं ने खूनी युद्ध के दृश्यों को फिल्माया जिसमें सैनिकों को गोलियों की बौछार झेलते और गिरते दिखाया गया। लाल धूल में बारूद की तीखी गंध थी। मैं डर गई थी। मुझे युद्ध अपनी आंखों के सामने होता हुआ लग रहा था। मिस्टर विन्ह ने चीखकर मेरे कानों में कहा - ''युद्ध की भयावहता और नृशंसता का यह तो मात्र दस प्रतिशत था...''

दस प्रतिशत हो या एक प्रतिशत, मुझे जानकर क्या करना है? पर्स में मेकअप के सामान के नीचे से मैंने नाम का मलिन पत्र निकाला जिसमें उसने लिखा था :

''... अत्यधिक शांति है। हम मुर्गेकी बांग और बच्चों का रुदन सुनने को तरस गए हैं...''

फिल्म का क्या कोई ऐसा हिस्सा है जो युद्ध की भयावहता में नीरवता के क्षणों को पर्याप्त रूप से दर्शाता हो।

पुराने दुर्ग के चारों ओर फैली ऊंची घास के झुरमुट में नाम के अवशेष किस स्थान पर हैं, यह कौन बताए?

थान और मैं उस पूरे क्षेत्र में घूमे। गर्मी इतनी थी कि वहां घास के अतिरिक्त कुछ उग ही नहीं सकता था। हमने पूरे कब्रिस्तान का चक्कर लगा लिया। आखिर में थान बुदबुदाया : ''तो फिर हम नहीं ढूंढ पाए...''

दूर से गुजर रही एक बुजुर्ग स्त्री अनायास बोली ''पर फिर भी लोग आते हैं...''

मैंने साहसपूर्वक पूछा, ''आपसे एक सवाल कर सकती हूं?''

''जिंदा के बारे में या मुर्दा के बारे में? मैं केवल मुर्दों से संबंधित सवालों के जवाब दे सकती हूं। जो ज़िंदा थे, वे तो चले गये।''

''मुर्दा के बारे में।''

''जानती हूं।''

उसके पीछे-पीछे हम लहरदार एक टिन की छत वाले घर में आये। भीतर

ताड़ के पत्तों से बना एक दिवान, लकड़ी का एक टेबल और कुछ टूटे हुए कप थे। वेदी पर किसी जवान की तस्वीर थी। महिला ने कप उठा कर थरमस से चाय उड़ेली।

''लो-चाय पिओ।... उसकी मौत कब हुई थी?'' उसने पूछा।

क्षण भर को थान अवाक हो गया, फिर उसने विस्तार से सारी कहानी सुनाई जैसे पहले भी वह कइयों को सुना चुका था। उस महिला ने बड़े ध्यान से थान को सुना, फिर सिर हिलाते हुए बोली, ''तुम्हारी कहानी के आधार पर मैं यह जानती हूं कि तुम्हारे भाई के अवशेषों को ढूंढ़ पाना बहुत कठिन है। मैं तो तुमसे कहूंगी कि उस स्त्री को ढूंढो जिसे वह प्यार करता था और उससे कहो कि वह तुम्हारे लिए उससे बात करे। जब कोई व्यक्ति मरता है तो अपना हाड़मांस व त्वचा अपने परिजनों के लिए छोड़ जाता है, और उसकी आत्मा पर उसकी प्रेयसी का अधिकार होता है...।''

फिर वेदी की ओर इंगित करते हुए उस महिला ने कहा, ''वह मेरे बेटे की तस्वीर है। मुझे उसकी एक हड्डी तक नहीं मिली। वह एक कमांडो जत्थे का नेता था। उसे एक मोर्टार से उड़ा दिया गया था। धूल और मिट्टी में मिल गए थे उसके अवशेष।'' वह खांसने लगी।

हमने तस्वीर के सामने धूपबत्ती जलाई और लौट आये।

उस रात होटल के बिस्तर पर लेटे-लेटे मैंने खिड़की से बाहर असंख्य जुगनुओं को फड़फड़ाते हुए देखा। चुपके-से उठ कर मैंने खिड़कियां खोल दीं। कुछ जुगनू उड़ कर अंदर आ गए। थान फर्श पर बैठा बड़े ध्यान से उन्हें देखता रहा।

''सपने में मैंने नाम को एक लाल सा बिल्ला लगाए हुए देखा था। उसके दो बटन टूटे हुए थे और तीसरा गिरने ही वाला था'', मैंने थान को उस आदमी की याद दिलाई जिसे मैंने अपनी जचगी में देखा था।

''नाम जब घर छोड़ कर गया था, तब वह मात्र सत्रह वर्ष का था। उस उम्र में प्रेयसी नहीं होती'', थान चुपचाप बुदबुदाया।

नाम के अवशेष ढूंढ पाने में असमर्थ होने पर थान सारा दिन अपने समाचार-पत्र के लिए होटल में बैठ कर लिखता रहा। एक अभिनेत्री को शूटिंग छोड़ कर जाना पड़ा क्योंकि उसकी मां बहुत बीमार थी। उसकी जगह उसकी भूमिका

निर्वाह करने के लिए मुझसे आग्रह किया गया। मेरी भूमिका बड़ी सहज थी। मुझे कुछ बोलना नहीं था, केवल तेज हवा में दुर्ग के ऊपर उड़ रही चिड़ियों को देखते रहना था।

चिड़ियों का जिक्र आते ही थान ने अपनी कलम रख दी, झपट कर अपनी रायफल उठाई और पहाड़ी की ओर दौड़ा। गौरैया चिड़ियों के झुंड चारों ओर सफेद सरकंडों पर बैठे थे। थान ने हौले से निर्देशक के कान में कहा - ''वादा करो कि इस दृश्य की शूटिंग के बाद मुझे गौरैया चिड़ियों का शिकार करने दोगे।''

मैं लोकेशन पर छिपकर निर्देशक के बताए अनुसार घिसट कर आगे गई और फिर अचानक उठ खड़ी हुई। डर कर चिड़ियां उड़ गईं। वेदी से थान की आवाज़ आई - ''वे असंख्य हैं'', सुन कर मैंने अनन्त आकाश की ओर देखा। कैमरा क्लिक हुआ फिर रुका। इसी बीच थान ने हवा में गोली दाग दी। मैं हल्के से हिली। एक गौरैया फड़फड़ा कर आ गिरी।... फिर भुने हुए मांस और थान की देहगंध से मुझे उबकाई आ गई।

पहाड़ी पर लेटे-लेटे हमने गौरैया का भुना मांस खाया। जब मैं खा चुकी तो थान ने कहा :

''तुम नाम से प्यार करती हो ना?''

तुम पागल हो?'' थान के प्रश्न से मैं अवाक रह गई थी। ''क्या तुम्हें उससे ईर्ष्या हो रही है?''

थान ने मुझे घास पर पटक दिया। मैं चीखते हुए उससे उलझ गई, ''मुझे नफरत है तुम्हारे पूरे परिवार से।''

''तो फिर औरत बनने और एक बच्चे की मां बनने में तुम्हारी मदद किसने की?''

''वो तो ... नदी का पानी पी कर भी मैं गर्भवती हो सकती थी।''

थान की आंखों में आंसू थे, ''नहीं मुझे उससे ईर्ष्या नहीं थीं। तुम नाम की आत्मा से कहो वह लौट आये।''

मैं भी रो पड़ी। ''प्रिय नाम मैं थान की पत्नी और प्रेमिका हूं। हालांकि हम दोनों की दुनिया अलग है पर मैं तुम्हारी दोस्त बनना चाहती हूं। मैं वादा करती हूं, तुम्हारे परिवार का ध्यान रखूंगी। तुम लौट आओ और हमारे साथ रहो। हमें

बताओ तुम्हारे अवशेष कहां हैं?''

हान नदी अभी भी बेताब सी बह रही है। युद्ध में मारे गए कितने ही युवकों के अवशेष इसकी जलोद मिट्टी में मिल गए हैं। स्वर्ग व मर्त्य की असीमता में जाने किस मिट्टी में नाम के अवशेष हैं।

इस व्यर्थ की यात्रा के दो वर्ष बाद मैं फिर गर्भ से थी। इस बार मेरा गर्भ थान और मेरे, हम दोनों के लिए महत्वपूर्ण था क्योंकि मैं जानती थी कि नाम हमसे मिलने अवश्य आएगा।

जचगी की भयंकर पीड़ा के बाद मैंने दो प्यारे से लड़कों को जन्म दिया।

जब मुझे होश आया तो थान मेरे बगल में खड़ा था। नाम अभी भी वहीं बैठा था और उसकी उदास आंखें खिड़की से बाहर ताक रही थीं। एक दिन जब फुओंग मुझसे रूखेपन से पेश आई तो मैंने उसे वेदी की ओर इशारा कर कहा, ''मैं नाम से शिकायत कर दूंगी।''

सुन कर वह चापलूसी करने लगी।

थान से बच्चे जब भी नाम के बारे में पूछते तो वह कहता, ''चाचा नाम सितारा बन गए हैं।''

थान मुझे और बच्चों को कभी-कभी जंगल लेकर जाता है पर अब वह पहले की तरह एक गौरैया नहीं मारता बल्कि जब गौरैया चिड़ियां निचली शाखों पर आकर बैठतीं, तब वह कई गोलियां चला कर उनमें से कइयों का शिकार करता। फड़फड़ा कर जब गौरैया चिड़ियां नीचे गिरतीं तो दोनों लड़के आनंद मनाते हुए उन्हें उठा कर अपने पिता को देते।

केवल माइ चुपचाप एक किनारे खड़ी आग जलाने में मेरी मदद करने के बजाय नीले आकाश में उड़ती गौरैया चिड़ियों को ऊपर, और ऊपर उड़ते देखती और हंसती रहती।

(अनुवाद : प्रेम कपूर)

बारिश

ले मिन्ह खुए

ले मिन्ह खुए वियतनाम की चर्चित कथाकार हैं, जिनका जन्म 1949 में हुआ तथा जिन्हें श्रेष्ठ कथा 'द डिस्टैंट स्टार्स' (दूरवर्ती सितारे) के लिए वियतनाम लेखक संघ द्वारा पुरस्कृत किया जा चुका है।

अस्सी के दशक की शुरुआत में नदी-किनारे के विस्तृत अंचल में तेजी से निर्माण कार्य चल रहा था, जिसके चलते पूरे जंगल में गाड़ियों के आवागमन के साथ ही लोगों की भीड़ भी जुट रही थी, जिनमें खूबसूरत युवतियां भी थीं। प्रत्येक दिन 'गेस्ट हाउस' अतिथियों से भरे रहते। परिचारिकाओं के काम के लिए जिन युवतियों का चयन होता वे अतीव सुंदरियां होतीं, किंतु उन सब में अपूर्व सुंदरी थी... न्गान।

न्गान ने नृत्य विद्यालय से नृत्य की गम्भीर शिक्षा ग्रहण की थी तथा वह प्रांतीय नृत्य-मंडली की प्रशिक्षित नर्तकी भी थी। नृत्य से चूंकि इन दिनों पर्याप्त आय नहीं हो पाती थी, इसलिए उसने एक परिचित 'अंकल' से आग्रह किया था कि वह उसे 'कंस्ट्रक्शन साइट' के गेस्ट हाउस में परिचारिका का काम दिला दे।

गेस्ट-हाउस में उसे गेस्ट हाउस की पोशाक 'शॉर्ट-स्कर्ट' पहननी पड़ती जो उसके घुटनों के कुछ ऊपर तक आती। स्कर्ट के ऊपर पूरी बांह की सफेद कमीज और काली बो-टाइ पहननी पड़ती। यों तो इस पोशाक में ऐसा कुछ खास नहीं था, फिर भी विपरीत सेक्स यानी पुरुष वर्ग को उकसाने और हलचल मचाने के लिए यह काफी थी। हालांकि इस पोशाक से शरीर का लगभग हर हिस्सा ढका रहता था किंतु काली स्टॉकिंग्स (काले मोजों) के बावजूद उसकी सुडौल टांगें बरबस लोगों का ध्यान आकर्षित कर लेतीं। भले ही वह कोई मर्यादित मंत्री हो, जो निर्माण-कार्य देखने आया हो, या कोई इंजीनियर हो, या शोधार्थी, या कोई किशोर, सभी की निगाहें जब न्गान गुज़रती, तो उस पर स्थिर हो जातीं।

जाहिर है, परिस्थितियों के अनुरूप पुरुषों की दृष्टि स्त्रियों की दृष्टि से बिल्कुल भिन्न होती। स्त्रियां न्गान को ईर्ष्या की दृष्टि से देखतीं जबकि पुरुष वर्ग उसे चाहत की दृष्टि से देखता और पके हुए फल के समान उसका स्वाद चखने की कल्पना करता।

न्गान को इन सब बातों का आभास था, किंतु उसकी मां, जो कि एक प्रांतीय शिक्षिका थी, ने बचपन से ही अपनी बेटी को सिखा रखा था कि वह पुरुषों की उपस्थिति में किस प्रकार का आचरण करे। वह जानती थी कि किस प्रकार उसे सदैव प्रफुल्लित रहना है तथा एक सुरक्षित दूरी बनाए रखना है। वह हमेशा अपनी सीमा में रहती और एक खास हद तक ही पुरुषों को अग्रसर होने देती।

किंतु क्वोक, जो कि एक इलेक्ट्रिकल इंजीनियर था, के वैद्युतिक उपकरण के समक्ष वह स्वयं पर नियंत्रण नहीं रख पाती थी। क्वोक एक तीस वर्षीय जवान था, जिसके चेहरे पर एक अक्खड़पन और खूबसूरत आंखों में एक अजीब सी ठंडक थी। वह अक्सर कॉफी पीने जाता था और न्गान पर कभी कोई खास ध्यान नहीं देता था। शायद यही वह कारण था कि न्गान उसे चाहने लगी थी। अपनी दूधिया सफेद कमीज और नये जूतों में भी जब वह क्वोक का ध्यान आकर्षित न कर पाती तो उसे स्वयं पर झुंझलाहट सी होती। काम के बाद अक्सर क्वोक आ कर काफी का प्याला लिये बैठा रहता और निरुद्देश्य खिड़की से बाहर पर्वतमाला की ओर निहारता रहता। न्गान समझ नहीं पा रही थी कि उसकी चमकदार सुडौल टांगों के प्रति ललक तो क्वोक में भी थी, किंतु वह स्त्रियों की कमजोरी पहचानता था, इसीलिए उसकी आंखों में कुछ अधिक ठंडापन, कुछ अधिक उदासीनता थी।

न्गान रात दर रात क्वोक की साभिप्राय उपेक्षा भरी दृष्टि पर चुपचाप आंसू बहाती रहती।

ऐसा तब तक चलता रहा जब तक न्गान के परिचितों को स्पष्टतः उसके दैहिक भावनात्मक सौंदर्य में ह्रास के चिन्ह दिखाई देने लगे। न्गान ने और अधिक सावधानी से चेहरे पर मेकअप लगाना शुरू किया किंतु वह अपनी पीली पड़ती रंगत और आंखों का उनींदापन छिपा न पाई। उसके हाथ की चूड़ी/घड़ी, जो कभी उसकी कलाई पर फिट बैठती थी, अब बेतरह ढीली हो गई थी। क्वोक ने यह सब लक्ष्य किया पर कुछ दिन और चुप रहा ताकि खाली ग्लास कुछ और भर जाए। फिर एक शाम उसने 'रिफ्रेशमेंट काउंटर' की ओर घूम कर देखते हुए अपनी दृष्टि में परिवर्तन किया। वर्षा ऋतु आने वाली थी, जिसके चलते निर्माण कार्य धीमा पड़ गया था और काफी पीने या भोजन के लिए आने वाले लोगों की संख्या भी कम हो गई थी। न्गान गल्ले पर अकेली बैठी थी। क्वोक अपने टेबल से उठा और उसकी ओर बढ़ चला। न्गान को लगा जैसे उसके नाजुक दिल पर किसी ने भारी पत्थर रख दिया हो। उसने गल्ले में पड़े नोटों की ओर अपनी नजरें झुका लीं। उसके गालों पर लाली दौड़ गई और उसे लगा कि कहीं वह बेहोश न हो जाए। क्वोक यह सब अच्छी तरह जानता था। उसके लिए यह सब कुछ अनजाना नहीं था। अपने प्रेम-संबंध की शुरुआत करने की उसे कोई हड़बड़ी नहीं थी। उसने हल्के से न्गान के मुलायम हाथ को अपने हाथ में लिया तो न्गान के बदन में मानो बिजली सी दौड़ गई। क्वोक की छुअन से उसे बिजली का जो झटका लगा वह किसी डायनामाइट के विस्फोट से कम नहीं था। न्गान को अपने हृदय में एक विस्फोट का सा अहसास हुआ और उसकी आंखों से अश्रुधार बह चली। यह शायद उसकी कई महीनों की प्रतीक्षा का, कई रातों की उसकी पीड़ा का, उसके अनुत्तरित प्रश्नों का उत्तर था। उसे अपनी सांस रुकती हुई सी प्रतीत हुई, जैसा कि उसके साथ अक्सर तब होता, जब वह पास होता।

''घबराओ नहीं'', उसने कहा ''मैं हमेशा तुम्हारे साथ रहूंगा, प्रिये।''

अत्यंत मधुर थी यह शुरुआत। शुरुआत का ऐसा प्रस्ताव पाकर किस स्त्री का हृदय नहीं पिघलेगा? इतना प्यारा शब्द 'प्रिये' सुनने के लिए कौन स्त्री अपना जीवन नहीं वार देगी?

क्वोक इंजीनियरों के लिए नियत एक मकान में रहता था, जो कि बड़े जोखिम

पूर्ण ढंग से नाले के किनारे बना था। जब इस निर्माण क्षेत्र में इंजीनियर आये थे तो उनकी इच्छानुसार यह मकान बना था। क्वोक का कमरा भी निर्माण-क्षेत्र के अस्थायी कमरों जैसा ही था। क्वोक के साथ उसके कमरे में एक सिविल इंजीनियर भी रहता था, जो फिलहाल सड़क निर्माण के ठेके से संबंधित किसी बैठक के सिलसिले में यूरोप गया हुआ था। कमरे में दो बिस्तर, कई सूटकेस तथा दो मेजें थीं, जिन पर कागजात बिखरे थे। सच पूछा जाए तो क्वोक एक धनी व्यक्ति था। दक्षिण में एक धनी किसान का बेटा था वह। उत्तर में काम करने के बावजूद वह पैसा पानी की तरह खर्च कर सकता था। उसका वीसीआर और वीडियो टेप न्गान को बिल्कुल नहीं भाते थे। बाहर बारिश होने लगी थी। अगस्त महीने की लम्बी बरसातों जैसी बरसात में न्गान को यह सोच कर तृप्ति का अहसास हो रहा था कि उसका सपना सच हो रहा था। जिस व्यक्ति ने कभी उसके प्रति अपना प्रेम नहीं जताया, बावजूद इसके वह उसके प्रति हमेशा आकर्षित होती रही, अब वह उसके साथ है। यह तो एक जादुई अहसास था।

''न्गान, क्या तुम चाहती हो कि अब से हम साथ-साथ रहें ?'' उसने पूछा।

दक्षिणी लहजे में पूछे गए उसके सीधे से सवाल में अद्भुत प्रलोभन था। न्गान ने उसके चौड़े सीने पर अपना सिर टिका दिया, ठीक वैसे ही जैसे कोई जहाज लंगर डाल देता है। अपनी बाहों के घेरे में उसकी गरदन को ले कर अपनी गाल उसकी गाल से दबाते हुए उसने उत्तर दिया, ''मेरा तो जीवन ही तुम्हारा है।''

क्वोक किंतु एक अत्यधिक कामुक व्यक्ति था, उसने न्गान के कथन में छिपी त्याग की कोमल भावना पर ध्यान नहीं दिया। उसका ध्यान तो अपनी काम-तृप्ति की ओर था, बिल्कुल उस धावक की तरह जो शीघ्रातिशीघ्र 'फिनिश लाइन' पर पहुंचना चाहता है। उसने न तो न्गान की कोमल त्वचा, न ही उसकी देहयष्टि और न ही उसके धवल वक्ष या उसकी मृदु देहगंध की प्रशंसा की। वह तो एक प्रलुब्ध लोभी की तरह उसकी देह से अपनी वासना शीघ्रातिशीघ्र शांत करने में लगा रहा। रात दर रात। न्गान को आश्चर्य हो रहा था कि जो देह उसके लिए अनमोल थी, वही क्वोक की दृष्टि में किसी प्रतिस्पर्द्धा के पुरस्कार स्वरूप थी। यह क्या प्रेम था या किसी पहाड़ पर चढ़ने का व्यायाम ? भला प्यार ऐसा कैसे हो सकता है ? न्गान को तो चाहत प्रेम की थी, इस यांत्रिकता की नहीं। संभोग के कुछ दुर्लभ क्षणों में वह उससे करना चाहती थी एक सवाल : ''क्या तुम मुझसे

प्रेम करते हो ?'' किंतु उसकी कामुकता और देह-भार के तले प्रेम उसे विलास सा लगा और उक्त सवाल करने की उसकी इच्छा ही नहीं हुई।

ठीक उस वक्त टेलिविजन पर नग्न देहों का एक वीडियो किसी फालतू किस्म की फिल्म का चल रहा था जिसका संदेश बड़ा रोचक था कि पुरुष को तो बस स्थान मिलना चाहिए, जबकि स्त्री हमेशा कारण ढूंढती है।

न्गान की आंखें आंसुओं से भर आईं जबकि क्वोक उसकी बगल में लेटा गहरी नींद में सो गया।

ऐसा महीने भर चलता रहा। महीने भर रुक-रुक कर बारिश होती रही। क्वोक का कमरे में साथ रहने वाला सिविल इंजीनियर अभी भी यूरोप में ही था। रात दर रात पहाड़ पर शोर मचाती हवा पूरी घाटी में गूंजती रहती। न्गान को लगता जैसे उसे इस्तेमाल किया गया हो, बर्बाद कर दिया गया हो। हालांकि अब वह सब कुछ समझ रही थी, पर उसके पास अब सहेजने के लिए कुछ बचा ही न था। अब तो उसकी ख्वाहिश बस इतनी सी थी कि उसका अपना एक परिवार हो छोटा सा। क्वोक ने उससे कभी कोई वादा नहीं किया था। और तो और उसने कभी यह तक नहीं कहा कि ''मैं तुमसे प्यार करता हूं''। बावजूद इसके वह उससे व्यवहार पत्नी के समान करता था। और यदि वह उसकी पत्नी थी, तो एहतियात क्यों बरते ?

आधी रात के आसपास क्वोक के खर्राटों से न्गान की नींद टूट गई। ऐसे तो कोई सूअर ही सो सकता है। न्गान उठ कर गेस्ट हाउस की परिचारिकाओं के क्वार्टर में अपने कमरे में लौट आई। हर रात वह नहाती और अपने कपड़े धोती किंतु अंततः जब वह बिस्तर में लेट कर लिहाफ ओढ़ लेती तो हमेशा उसे लगता कि उसके साथ कुछ गलत हो रहा है, और यह सोच कर वह फूट-फूट कर रो पड़ती। उसे हमेशा लगता कि कल क्वोक सबके सामने घोषणा करेगा कि वह न्गान से विवाह करेगा, और वह विवाह के सपने देखने लगती।

क्वोक का कमरे का साथी जब यूरोप से लौट आया तो उसके बाद न्गान और क्वोक मुश्किल से ही एक-दूसरे से मिल पाते। क्वोक के प्रति न्गान की घृणा बढ़ती जा रही थी क्योंकि बिना बिस्तर के सम्भोग उसे अपमानजनक लगता जबकि क्वोक जगह मिलते ही उस पर कहीं भी चढ़ बैठने को उतावला रहता, बिना किसी गंदगी, दुर्गंध, असुविधा या घूरती नज़रों की परवाह किए। अब उसे

न्गान की असुविधा, अलगाव और असहज भाव समझ में आने लगा था इसलिए उसने न्गान से परिवार और बच्चों के बारे में वादे करना शुरू किया। उसके वादों पर न्गान ने ऐतबार कर फिर से उस पर अपना प्यार उड़ेल दिया। किंतु कुछ समय बाद क्वोक का तबादला दक्षिण के किसी निर्माण क्षेत्र में हो गया। दरअसल यह तबादला क्वोक के पिता ने कराया था क्योंकि वह चाहते थे कि उनका बेटा मां-बाप के पास रहे।

''पहले मैं जाऊंगा, बाद में तुम्हें बुला लूंगा'', उसने न्गान से कहा।

क्वोक ने न्गान से विदाई उसी कमरे में ली, जिसके कोने-कोने से वह परिचित थी। यह वही कमरा था, जहां उसका निर्वस्त्र शरीर रौंदा जा रहा था और वह परिवेश में नज़रें गड़ाए रही थी।

क्वोक ने उसी दिन निर्माण क्षेत्र से विदा ली। बारिश भी कभी की रुक चुकी थी। निर्माण क्षेत्र अब पहले से कुछ अधिक व्यस्त हो गया था, क्योंकि ठेके के सभी इंजीनियर काम के लिए हाजिर हो रहे थे। वाहन इकाई तथा निर्माण इकाई में काम के लिए काफी लोग जुट रहे थे। न्गान इस दरम्यान यथावत गेस्ट-हाउस में काम करती रही और उस वक्त का इंतजार करती रही जब वह दक्षिण में जा कर क्वोक से विवाह कर सके, जैसा कि दोनों ने सोच रखा था। न्गान ने गेस्ट-हाउस की परिचारिका की लम्बी बाहों वाली तथा गले तक बंद बटन वाली कमीज़, छोटी बो-टाइ तथा हरे व नीले रंग वाली घुटनों तक की स्कर्ट पहनना जारी रखा। मर्यादित मंत्रीगण जो निर्माण-क्षेत्र के दौरे पर आते, वे अन्यों की तरह ही उसके अभिवादन का प्रत्युत्तर देते। पढ़ेलिखे युवा उसकी बगल से यों गुज़रते मानो किसी दीवार के करीब से गुजर रहे हों। भारी अर्थमूवर गाड़ियां चलाने वाले मजदूर, जो आम तौर पर स्त्रियों को देख कर भोंडी फब्तियां कसते हैं, भी अब उसकी ओर ध्यान दिये बिना ही निकल जाते। क्या वह अब मुरझाए हुए सेब जैसी हो गई थी? न्गान को लगा जैसे वह कोई परित्यक्त हो। हो सकता है उसने अपनी समस्याओं को बढ़ा-चढ़ा कर देखा हो, किंतु यह तो सच है कि वह हृदय से संतप्त थी। वह समझ नहीं पा रही थी कि उसके चेहरे पर जो खुशी की झलक नज़र आया करती थी, अब कहाँ गुम हो चुकी थी। चेहरे पर एक थकान लिये अब वह गेस्ट-हाउस के ग्राहकों के बीच ट्रे में गिलास लिये आती-जाती रहती और रातों को ठोड़ी तक लिहाफ ओढ़ कर सो जाती। वह उन क्षणों

को कभी याद नहीं करती जिन क्षणों में क्वोक उसकी देह को नोचता-खसोटता। उनको याद करना भी अत्यंत भोंडा और अपमानजनक था। उन क्षणों को न तो वह याद करती थी और न ही असंतोष से कुढ़ती थी, पर उन क्षणों से वह उबर भी नहीं पा रही थी।

एक लम्बे अंतराल के बाद क्वोक ने न्गान को एक पत्र लिखा जिसमें कोई वचनबद्धता नहीं थी और न ही थे "तुम्हारी याद आती है" या "मैं और तुम" अलफ़ाज़। किसी पत्थर सा सूखा-सपाट था पत्र जिसमें क्वोक ने न्गान से कहा था कि यदि वह चाहे तो दक्षिण में आ सकती है क्योंकि उसकी कंस्ट्रक्शन साइट में उसके जैसी परिचारिकाओं की आवश्यकता है। दक्षिण की लड़कियों की टांगें तो अच्छी हैं पर उनका चेहरा उत्तर की न्गान सरीखा सलोना नहीं।

क्वोक और न्गान के बीच कुछ पत्रों का आदान-प्रदान तो हुआ पर फिर न्गान नौकरी छोड़, अपना सूटकेस ले कर हनोई के लिए निकल पड़ी। उसने सुबह आठ बजे छूटने वाली नॉर्थ-साउथ एक्स्प्रेस में स्लीपर बर्थ की एक टिकट खरीदी। सब कुछ ठीक-ठाक था योजनानुसार सिवाय ट्रेन की सीटी की आवाज़ के जिसे सुन कर उसे डर लग रहा था, क्योंकि वह उसे किसी खतरे का आभास सा दे रही थी। सबसे अधिक डर तो उसे इस बात से लग रहा था कि फिर से उसकी मुलाकात क्वोक से होगी। यदि क्वोक उसकी देह से अनजान होता तो शायद वह न डरती। किंतु कुछ अजीब अटपटापन उसे उस ट्रेन में चढ़ने से रोक रहा था, जो ट्रेन उसे जीवन की सबसे लम्बी यात्रा पर ले जा रही थी।

उसने अपना इरादा बदल दिया और अपने माता-पिता के प्रांत की ओर लौट पड़ी। अपनी बेटी का उदास और मुरझाया हुआ चेहरा देख कर न्गान की मां ने कहा कि अब वह उसे 'कंस्ट्रक्शन साइट' पर नहीं जाने देगी। इससे तो बेहतर होगा कि वह घर में रहे जहां उसकी मां ने एक छोटा सा 'कॉस्मेटिक्स स्टोर' खोल रखा है।

अब न्गान 'कॉस्मेटिक्स स्टोर' में बैठ कर किताबें पढ़ती, तेल-फुलेल खरीदने आई महिलाओं से गप्पें लड़ाती। वह उन महिलाओं को अत्यधिक जिज्ञासु दृष्टि से देखती और सोचती कि क्या उन्हें भी वही अनुभव हुआ है, जो उसे हुआ था। क्या उन्हें पता है कि पुरुष का चौड़ा सीना और पसीने से भीजती पीठ कैसी होती है?

बरसात का मौसम आ गया और कादे-कीचड़ ने शहर को बदरंग कर दिया। स्थानीय अस्पताल का एक डॉक्टर अक्सर न्गान के पिता के साथ चाय पीने आया करता। कांच के 'शो-केस' पर झुक कर वह दो-चार बातें न्गान से भी कर लिया करता। डॉक्टर देखने-सुनने में अच्छा था। हालांकि वह न्गान के पिता का दोस्त था किंतु उम्र में उनसे काफी छोटा था। साल के आखिर में उसने आना बंद कर दिया, शायद वह किसी चिंतनीय स्थिति में नहीं पड़ना चाहता था। उसके न आने से न्गान बहुत दुखी हुई। वह समझ गई थी कि अब वह किसी को अपनी ओर आकर्षित नहीं कर सकती। किंतु वह अभी भी जवान थी और उसके साथ जो कुछ भी हुआ था, उसे भूल जाना चाहती थी। प्रत्येक दिन उसे क्वोक के कमरे से नज़र आता बाहर का नज़ारा याद आता। उसे बारिश में झिलमिलाता जंगल याद आता, याद आते अपने आंसू और उन दिनों की अपनी खुशियों की चाहत। और न्गान बैठी बारिश में भीजती सड़क को देखती और इंतजार करती रहती।

(अनुवाद : प्रेम कपूर)

लाल निशान

नुएन थि फुओक

1963 में जन्मी नुएन थि फुओक वियतनाम की लब्धप्रतिष्ठ कथाकारों में एक हैं जिन्हें उनकी अत्यंत चर्चित कहानियों, 'द ट्रेन इन जुलाई' तथा 'वर्ड्स बाइ द फील्ड' के लिए मिलिटरी साहित्यिक पत्रिका के साहित्य व कला पुरस्कार से पुरस्कृत किया जा चुका है। प्रस्तुत कहानी में मुक्ति-युद्ध के दिनों की एक झलक मिलती है।

मुझे दक्षिण के लेखन-शिविर में जाने की तैयारी करते देख, लगता है, हौंग कुछ चिंतित हो गई है। पहले तो मुझे लगा कि वह कहना चाहती है कि मैं वहां से उसके लिए कोई ऐसी महंगी चीज खरीद कर लाऊं जिसे खरीद पाने में वह सक्षम नहीं, पर फिर मैंने सोचा कि शायद ऐसा नहीं है क्योंकि पैसे के मामले में हम बेतकल्लुफ हैं। घर में बेचैनी से उसे आगा-पीछा करते देख मैंने पूछा, ''बात क्या है? तुम ठीक तो हो?''

- नहीं कुछ नहीं।

फिर थोड़ी सी चुप्पी के बाद वह बुदबुदाई, ''तुम्हें होआंग की याद है? दक्षिण का वह व्यक्ति जिसने हमारे घर में आश्रय लिया था?''

- होआंग, वही न जिसके साथ तुम्हारा कुछ चक्कर चला था?

- हां, वही। तुम्हारी याददाश्त अच्छी है। अब वह पीएचडी है तथा वहां की एक युनिवर्सिटी में आई टी विभाग का 'डीन' है।

- तुम्हें कैसे पता?

- पिछले साल टी वी पर मैंने देखा था उसे किसी प्रतियोगिता में अपने सूत्रों की सहायता करते हुए।

होआंग का चेहरा-मोहरा मुझे कुछ याद नहीं। मोटे तौर पर जो तस्वीर मेरे जेहन में थी, वह यह थी कि हमारे पश्चिमी कमरे में किसी मर्दाना आकृति ने मेरी बहन हौंग को अपने आलिंगन में ले रखा था। बी-52 की बमबारी से पहले हमारा घर शहर का सबसे बड़ा काष्ठ-महल था, जिसमें बड़े-बड़े पांच कमरे थे। बाद में सरकार ने न्हो-लाम के एक भूस्वामी की सम्पत्ति का एक अंश हमें आवंटित किया। न्हो-लाम गांव मेधावी छात्रों तथा सुंदर काष्ठ-कला के लिए मशहूर था। हमें आवंटित अंश में दो सिरों पर दो कमरे थे जिन्हें खूबसूरत नक्काशीदार तस्वीरों से 'पार्टिशन' किया हुआ था। पूर्व की ओर अवस्थित कमरे को मेरे पिता पूर्वी कमरा तथा पश्चिम की ओर वाले को पश्चिमी कमरा कहते थे। मैंने जो कुछ देखा था वह न सिर्फ मां-बाबूजी को बल्कि गांव के अन्य बच्चों तक को बता दिया। नतीजा यह हुआ कि हर दोपहर को खिड़की से सभी हौंग के कमरे की जासूसी करने लगे। जाहिर है, इस काम के लिए मां ने मुझे बेवकूफ कह कर डांटा, और बाबूजी ने हौंग के बालों को पकड़ कर खींचते हुए उसे दो चांटे रसीद किए और मुझे शाबाशी दी। मुझे याद है, बाबूजी ने होआंग को बुला कर धीमी किंतु सख्त व स्पष्ट आवाज़ में कहा था ''उसकी अभी पढ़ाई बाकी है। कॉलेज की पढ़ाई पूरी होने तक इंतज़ार करो। उसके बाद उससे यथारीति विवाह करो, फिर जो चाहे सो करना। ध्यान रहे, यह हमारा परिवार है, कोई रंडीखाना नहीं।''

फिर बाबूजी ने होआंग के 'बॉस' को फोन कर कहा कि वह उसका तबादला कहीं अन्यत्र कर दें।

शीघ्र ही युद्ध-क्षेत्र के 'बी' मोर्चेपर जाने के लिए उसका बुलावा आ गया। बाद में उनके प्यार के मामले का क्या हुआ, मुझे पता नहीं। वो बड़े लोगों की बात थी और इस बीच काफी वक्त भी गुजर गया था।

- तुम जब दक्षिण में पहुंच जाओ तो होआंग का पता लगाना।

- किसलिए? तुम्हारा पुराना प्यार फिर से रोशन करने के लिए?

- नहीं, मैं बस इतना जानना चाहती हूं कि उसे क्या मेरी याद भी है या नहीं। मैं यह मान ही नहीं सकती कि उसके जीवन में मेरा कोई चिन्ह तक शेष नहीं। उससे मिलना, मिल कर कहना कि तुम मेरी बहन हो, और फिर चली आना। बस इतना ही।

मुझे यह हास्यास्पद लगा और आश्चर्यजनक भी। मैंने सोचा, क्या हो गया है इस औरत को? क्यों यह इतना नाटकीय हो जाती है? रिटायर होने की उमर हो आई और एक किशोरी की सी बात कर रही है? क्या वह अपने वृद्ध ससुर की बात को गम्भीरता से ले रही है, जिनकी जिद थी कि वह दक्षिण में जा कर उसके पूर्व प्रेमी से मिलेंगे, और वहां से लौट कर आने के हफ्ते भर के अंदर ही बिना किसी बीमारी के चल बसे?

मुझे डर सा लगने लगा। मैंने अपनी दो बहनों को जवानी में मरते देखा है। शायद यह भी हमारे परिवार पर तकदीर की कोई मार हो। हौंग के लिए सब कुछ ठीक-ठाक था। एक बढ़िया प्यार करने वाला पति था, रिटायरमेंट के बावजूद जिसके स्वास्थ्य और व्यवहारकुशलता में कोई कमी नहीं थी और अब वह यह फरमाइश कर रही थी। वर्षों तक मैं सोचती रही थी कि एक पत्नी और मां के रूप में उसका सबकुछ व्यवस्थित हो चुका है, और अब वह सब कुछ गड़बड़ करने जा रही थी। शायद यह सब बहुत ज्यादा किताबें पढ़ने का नतीजा था। काश वह अपने कार्यों को करने के लिए अपना रिहायशी जीवन शांतिपूर्वक बिताती! गलती सब से होती है। एक बुजुर्गवार व्यक्ति के लिए वह क्यों खुद को कष्ट देने जा रही है? पर नहीं... होआंग को उसने जिस गहराई से प्रेम किया उतना गहरा प्रेम उसने और किसी से नहीं किया। और इसका न उसे मलाल है न परवाह। खुश दिखने के बावजूद उसने कई रातें रो-रोकर गुजारी हैं।उसे चाहत है उस एक इंसान की जिसने उसकी मासूमियत चुराई और फिर कहीं गुम हो गया। जिंदा होते हुए भी जिसने कभी उसकी खोज-खबर नहीं ली। कैसा आदमी है वो? मर्दों की बात का यकीन ही नहीं करना चाहिए।... पर नहीं! आश्चर्यजनक रूप से वह आज भी उसे सीधा-सच्चा इंसान मानती है। उसे यकीन है कि उसने उसे झूठ नहीं कहा था। उसके वापस लौट कर न आने के पीछे जरूर कोई कारण रहा होगा। आज़ादी के दस वर्षों बाद तक वह उसका इंतजार करती रही,

विवाह-प्रस्तावों को ठुकराती रही। कहती रही कि वह किसी और को प्यार नहीं कर सकती।...

अचानक मुझे उसके पति 'तू' के लिए बुरा लगा कि वर्षों तक वह उसकी शक्ति का स्रोत रहा और अब यह अतीत के किसी व्यक्ति के पीछे दीवानी है। कहती है, "जब मेरा विवाह हुआ था तो मैंने अपने पति को सब कुछ साफ-साफ बता दिया था। तब से आज तक मैंने उसके साथ कभी कुछ गलत नहीं किया।"

- "हां, पर रहती तुम उसके साथ हो और मन किसी और के पास। ऐसी बीवी कोई चाहता है क्या?" मुझे उस पर इतना गुस्सा आया, मानो मैं हौंग की नहीं तू की बहन हूं।

सैगोन की धरती पर मैंने तेरह वर्षों बाद कदम रखा था। तेरह वर्षों का अर्सा काफी लम्बा अर्सा होता है...। किंतु मैं जिससे मिलने जा रही थी, उसके प्रति मैं भावुक तो बिल्कुल भी नहीं थी, कुछ भौंचक थी और कुछ उदास भी।

अतीत के दिनों को याद करती हूं तो मुझे लगता है कि युवावस्था में मुझमें काफी जोश था, आदर्शवादी इरादे थे और थी बदलाव लाने की प्रबल इच्छा। आज भी जब मैं अतीत के अपने छात्रों के जोशपूर्ण चेहरों को याद करती हूं तो मुझे लगता है कि मैं भी कभी यहां की नदी के उस स्वच्छ पानी की तरह शुद्ध थी, जिसकी अशुद्धियां पुरानी बाल्टियों की तहों में रह जाती थीं और ऊपर का शुद्ध पानी यहां के लोग अपने मेंहमानों को प्यास बुझाने के लिए देते थे। यहां एक अनजान जगह पर अनजान लोगों के बीच लौट कर आने के विचार से ही मुझे डर लगता था। समय के साथ पुराना विद्यालय भी बदल गया है। आज वहां मेरे पुराने दोस्त नहीं हैं, पुरानी झील नहीं है और न ही वे पुराने पेड़ हैं जिनके कुम्हलाए पत्ते स्कूल के आहाते में सर्वत्र बिखरे रहते थे। वे पुरानी कक्षाएं भी तो नहीं हैं, जहां मैंने आठ साल बिताए। खूबानी के पेड़ों के सामने खुलते थे कक्षाओं के दरवाजे। हर साल वृक्षों पर सुनहरे फल लगते और मैं अपने छात्रों को याद दिलाती रहती कि वह पत्तों को इतना न तोड़ें कि जब नया साल आये तो पेड़ों पर पत्ते ही न बचें और उन्हें सुनहरे फलों, कोमल कलियों और नई पत्तियों सहित सजाया ही न जा सके।... अब लौटने पर मुझे वहां अजनबी चेहरे मिलेंगे। पुराने छात्र यदि मिले भी तो उनके चेहरों की ताजगी की जगह रूखापन और

थकन नज़र आएगी, जैसी कि मेरे चेहरे पर नज़र आती है।... मुझे तो यह सोच कर भी डर लगता है कि तिएन नदी उस पुष्प-ग्राम को मेरे उत्तरी अंचल में चले जाने के बाद बहा ले गई होगी। वहां के पुष्प-बाजार में मैं अकेली ही घूमने निकल जाया करती थी और काफी देर रात तक वहां की भीड़ में घूमती रहती। जब विक्रेता अपनी नावों में फूल लाना बंद कर देते, तब मैं लौटती। उन फूल वालों को तो पता भी नहीं था कि प्रकृति के प्रति उनके लगाव को मैं कितनी प्रशंसा से देखती थी। मैंने हौंग नाम के किसी भी व्यक्ति को व्यक्तिगत तौर पर जाने बिना ही वहां के फूलवालों पर ऐसी-ऐसी कविताएं लिखीं, जिन्हें सुनकर मेरे सहित लोगों की आंखें नम हो जाएं।

बिना भूमि और ग्राम के वे फूलवाले अब जाने कहां गये होंगे अपने फूल और पौधे उगाने। दुखी सिर्फ मैं ही नहीं थी, मेरे साथी-सहकर्मियों में भी कुछ ऐसे थे जो स्वाधीनता दिवस के बाद पहली बार यहां लौटे थे। वर्षों कंधे पर बंदूकें ढोते, शरीरों पर घाव खाते-खाते अपने दुश्मनों और मौत पर विजय पाने के बाद लोग सैगोन को अब अपनी आंखों से देख रहे थे। इतनी लम्बी यात्रा हंसी-ठहाकों में पूरी करने के बाद यहां की भूमि पर कदम रखते ही सभी कुछ खामोश से हो गए थे। सैगोन से वुंग-ताउ लेखन-शिविर तक के रास्ते में किसी ने कोई बातचीत तक नहीं की।

लेखन-शिविर के भव्य उद्घाटन के बाद सभी ने पूरा प्रथम सप्ताह अपने लेखन पर ध्यान केंद्रित किया। हम केवल भोजन के वक्त मिलते। मुझे लगता, कितना कठिन काम है लेखन। लोगों के दिमाग में शब्द कितनी आसानी से आ जाते जबकि मुझे इसके लिए मशक्कत करनी पड़ती। नियम तो यह कहता है कि आप जब किसी लेखन-शिविर में जाओ तो आपको अपनी कोई रचना वहां प्रस्तुत करनी होती है। हालांकि यह अनिवार्य नहीं है किंतु आत्मसम्मान के लिए यह अपेक्षित तो है ही। इन आयोजनों पर नागरिकों के टैक्स का इतना पैसा व्यय जो होता है। मैं सोचती, ''क्या हम यहां सरकारी खर्च पर कुछ वक्त का भोजन करने आये हैं? पता नहीं कुछ लोग करोड़ों की चोरी कर रात को आराम से सो कैसे जाते हैं?'' पर फिर सोचती, ''उनका सिरदर्द भी तो हमसे करोड़ गुना अधिक होता होगा। उनके बच्चों को उनके पापों की सजा भुगतनी होगी।''

''सभी लेखक अपनी गरीबी का रोना रोते हैं, पर हर लेखक फिर भी लेखन को ही अपनी जीविका के रूप में चुनता है, नहीं क्या?'' वहीं से तो सारी गड़बड़ शुरू होती है। पर कुछ लोग ऐसे होते हैं जो लेखक का लेबल लगा कर कुछ अन्य व्यवसाय करते हैं और सामान्य से प्रयास से अच्छी कमाई भी कर लेते हैं। ''किंतु झटके तो हर धंधे में लगते रहते हैं।''

मेरा एक कवि मित्र मुझे खींच कर एक किनारे ले गया और बोला :

- मैं एक कहानी बताता हूं जिसका उपयोग तुम अपनी कहानी में कर सकती हो, उसका उपयोग मैं अपनी कविता में नहीं कर सकता। मैं सोच रहा था कि तुम्हारी कहानी यदि इस व्यक्ति को पुनः उसके पुत्रों से मिला दे तो बहुत भला हो। जिसने मुझे यह कहानी सुनाई, वह उस व्यक्ति का मित्र है, जो सैगोन में रहता है। हम एक ही खेत में काम करते थे और कुछ दिन 'डोंग-थाप-मुओइ' में रहे थे, इसलिए हमारा अच्छा परिचय हो गया। उसने मुझे अपने मित्र का नाम नहीं बताया।

मेरे लिए यह एक चुनौतीपूर्ण प्रस्ताव था क्योंकि कहानी कितनी भी रोमांचक और मर्मस्पर्शी क्यों न हो, वह साहित्य की दृष्टि से भी अच्छी हो, यह जरूरी नहीं। वास्तव जीवन में आंखों में आंसू ला देने वाली घटना भी लिखे जाने पर उबाऊ कहानी हो सकती है। एक सफल कहानी के लिए केवल सार-तत्व का होना ही पर्याप्त नहीं होता, उसके लिए कुछ भाग्य का होना भी जरूरी है। मैं तो केवल मज़ा लेने के लिए कहानी सुन रही थी। सोच रही थी कि यदि हुआ तो कहानी के कुछ रोचक तत्वों का समावेश अपनी किसी रचना में कर लूंगी। इतना पर्याप्त था मेरे लिए।

सन् 1973 में उन दिनों बाढ़ का मौसम था जब डोंग-थाप-मुओइ पानी में डूबा था। जंगल में पेड़ आधे पानी में डूबे थे। धान खेतों का तो लगभग सफाया हो गया था। धान की गिनीचुनी कलियां पानी की सतह के नीचे मुश्किल से नज़र आ रही थीं। बीच-बीच में पानी के नीचे उगने वाले पौधों, खरपतवार आदि के विशाल गुच्छ पानी की सतह पर तैरते नज़र आते। नहर के दोनों किनारों पर स्थानीय निवासियों द्वारा निर्मित लकड़ी के तम्बू नज़र आ रहे थे। हमारे यूनिट के लिए जो वर्षा प्रचुर वन आवंटित था वहां नारियल, ताड़ तथा खूबानी के पेड़ भरे

पड़े थे। हमारे तम्बू के मेलाधार पर हमें रोज पानी, नमक, थोड़ा सा सूखा हुआ भात तथा घोंघों की डलिया रखी मिलती। दिन के वक्त दो खूबानी के वृक्षों के बीच एक झूलन-खटोला टांग कर हम लेटते और रात के वक्त सांपों से बचने के लिए नौकाओं में चले जाते क्योंकि बाढ़ के पानी में डूबी धरती पर अबाध विचरण के लिए मेढक, मछलियों और सांपों को आज़ादी थी। जब भी हमें कोई शत्रु-जलयान, नाव या हेलिकॉप्टर नज़र आता तो हम अपने झूलन-खटोले समेत 'व्हेलबोट' (एक प्रकार की नाव) को पानी की सतह के नीचे डुबा लेते और जब शत्रु आंखों से ओझल हो जाता तो हम पुनः अपनी पूर्व स्थिति में आ जाते। कभी जब शत्रु आसपास मंडराता नज़र आता तो हमें लम्बे समय तक स्वयं को पानी की सतह के नीचे डुबाए रखना पड़ता और इस प्रक्रिया में हमारा सारा शरीर पीला पड़ जाता और हाथ-पैर की उंगलियां सिकुड़ कर विकृत हो जातीं।
जहां हम ठहरे थे, वहां से दिन भर पैदल चल कर उस स्थान तक पहुंच सकते थे जहां जल-गर्भ में काम करने वाले लड़कों का जत्था स्थित था। स्थानीय लोग स्नेहवश उन्हें ''उत्तरी लड़के'' कह कर बुलाते। ''वे अपने घर-परिवार और सभ्यता को पीछे छोड कर यहां आये थे हमारी खातिर लड़ाई लड़ने के लिए। जाहिर है, वे हमारे स्नेह के हकदार थे।'' दफ्तरों में काम करने वालों को भी हमसे अधिक स्नेह मिलता था। एक वृद्ध व्यक्ति ने ''उत्तरी लड़कों'' के स्वागत के लिए नौ किलो 'पाफर' मछलियां पकड़ीं, जबकि हमारे हिस्से केवल अवशेष आया। मेरे जत्थे के न्धे-आन के दो व्यक्ति न्धे-आन के दो लड़कों से मिलने के लिए इतने उत्साहित थे कि बमबारी और धुएं की परवाह न करते हुए अपने हमवतनों से मिलने भर के लिए जाने कितने ही जंगलों को पार कर उन तक पहुंचे। उनके इस स्नेह ने मेरे भी मर्म को छुआ। और मैं अपने एक मित्र की खोज में व्हेल-बोट की सवारी तथा एक ही लोकगीत बार-बार गाते-गाते ऊब चुकी थी। मैंने सुना था कि मेरे उस मित्र ने हाल ही में उत्तर स्थित पोस्टल ट्रेनिंग स्कूल में अपनी पढ़ाई पूरी की थी और अब उसे केंद्रीय कोर-टीम में शामिल होने के लिए बुलाया गया है। उसे ढूंढ़ पाना कोई आसान काम नहीं था। 15 डब्लू प्रकार का जो रेडियो था, वह केंद्रीय-शिविर से काफी दूर पर स्थापित था क्योंकि शत्रु के रडार की पहुंच-सीमा के अंतर्गत होने का अर्थ था कि शत्रु-पक्ष तत्काल बम वर्षा कर देता। मेरे मित्र का दैनंदिन कार्य केवल रोडियो की 'मॉनिटरिंग' करना

नहीं था किंतु केद्रीय शिविर का संरक्षण और उससे संपर्क-स्थापन भी था। और यह काम वह सर्प-दंश की व्याधि से स्वस्थ होने के बाद से कर रहा है। दरअसल सर्पदंश से वह मरा नहीं क्योंकि उसने प्राथमिक उपचार की विधि कहीं से सीख रखी थी। वह बच तो गया पर दंश का स्थान अत्यधिक फूल कर पहले-नीला पड़ गया और बाद में वहां से उसकी त्वचा इतनी सड़ गई कि पैर की हड्डी का एक हिस्सा नज़र आने लगा।

उसकी 'कोर' टीम में 'उत्तर' की दो लड़कियां भी थीं। सच पूछा जाए तो वे उत्तर से नहीं न्धे-आन से थीं। उम्र में वे मुझसे 6-7 साल बड़ी थीं। पर फिर भी जब भी बरसाती मौसम होता भावुकता में उनकी आंखों से आंसू बहते। बेचारी लड़कियां। दिन भर में चार-पांच घंटे पानी में डूबकर रहना तो किसी स्वस्थ व्यक्ति तक को थकन से चूर कर दे, फिर ये तो लड़कियां थीं। बावजूद इसके वे मौत से नहीं डरती थीं, वे तो घर से दूर होने के कारण मायूस रहतीं। उसने मुझे बताया कि उनके बारे में सोच कर उसे बुरा लगता। किंतु उन्हें ताजा पकड़ी हुई मछलियां, पानी के कमल, सांप और कछुए देने के अलावा वह कुछ कर भी तो नहीं सकता था। उसके गृहनगर न्धे-आन में उसकी एक प्रेयसी थी, वो अभी हाल ही में शिक्षक प्रशिक्षण विश्वविद्यालय में भर्ती हुई थी। दक्षिण में पहुंचने के बाद उसे उसकी बहुत याद आती। आज उसे उसकी उतनी याद नहीं आती क्योंकि उसे उस महिला का चस्का लग गया था। बड़ा रंगीन मिजाज था वह। मुझे भी उससे ईर्ष्या होती थी।

अभी हाल ही में मैं न्धे-आन के ऐसे दो लोगों से मिला जो अपने नगदी, कपड़े-लत्ते और किराने के सामान की पोटलियां लिये न्धे-आन के अपने हमवतनों से कुछ दान मांग रहे थे। मैंने जब अपने मित्र के बारे में उनसे सवाल किया, तो उनमें से एक बुरी तरह खफा हो गया:

- उसके बारे में कोई बात नहीं। अब वो नज़र आ गया तो गोली मार दूंगा।

- उसने हमारे गृहनगर की दो लड़कियों को एक साथ बर्बाद कर दिया। ऐसा लम्पट है वो।

अविश्वास से मेरी आंखें फटी की फटी रह गईं। मैंने उन दोनों को कुछ दान दिया तथा एक नाव पकड़ कर छोटे रास्ते अपने उस लम्पट दोस्त को सबक सिखाने

और भाग जाने की हिदायत देने चल दिया।

पर उसका अन्य किसी शिविर में तबादला हो गया था, जिसकी मुझे कोई जानकारी नहीं थी। दोनों लड़कियों ने दो शिशुओं को जन्म दिया और शिविर में न्धे-आन के आवासियों द्वारा संग्रह की गई रशि से उनकी देखभाल शुरू की। सैगोन मुक्ति के बाद उन्हें वापस उत्तर ले जाया गया।...

मेरे कवि मित्र ने बताया:

- एक लड़की किसी दूसरे जिले की थी, और दूसरी हमारे गांव की थी। वह अपने पति और दो बच्चों के साथ लौट गई। दशक बीत गये और उनके परिवार के दोनों पक्षों को इस बात का पता ही नहीं चला। सभी का मानना है कि वे बच्चे उसके पति के ही हैं। पति बड़ा भला आदमी है। और जहां तक उस लम्पट व्यक्ति का सवाल है, उसकी अच्छी-खासी आजीविका है। अभी तक वह अविवाहित है और अपने बच्चों से मिलने को बेताब है। पिछले साल, मेरे जिस मित्र ने यह कहानी मुझे बताई, उसने मेरी मार्फत उस लड़की को पत्र भेजने की कोशिश की जिसने पत्र पढ़ कर फाड़ दिया। हाल ही में मैं उस लड़की से फिर मिला और एक बार फिर उससे पूछा, पर उसने साफ 'ना' कह दिया। वह स्त्री मामलों की महिला प्रशासनिक अधिकारी है। उसके पुत्र ने विदेशी भाषा विश्वविद्यालय से स्नातक की उपाधि प्राप्त की है तथा अब वह सैगोन में कार्यरत है। तुम्हारी राय में इस लड़की का अंत कैसे हो ?

मैंने कोई उत्तर नहीं दिया। अचानक मेरे दिमाग में आया और मैं पूछ बैठी:

- वह व्यक्ति एक पी एच डी तथा इस विश्वविद्यालय का.....डीन (विभागाध्यक्ष) है न ?

कवि मित्र मुझसे भी अधिक अचम्भे में था:

-तुम्हें कैसे मालूम ? इस बात का जिक्र तो मैंने किसी से नहीं किया।

- यदि यह सच है, तो उसका नाम ही होआंग है, यदि लड़की तेरी बहन .....

- नाम का तो मुझे पता नहीं, पता बिल्कुल वही है।

मैं समझ नहीं पा रही थी कि मैं हौंग से क्या कहूंगी। इसलिए मैंने पहले ..... होआंग से मिलने का निश्चय किया।

मैं जिस व्यक्ति से मिल रही थी वह औपचारिक पोशाक में था। उसके धूसर और सादगी भरे चेहरे पर कुछ उदासी की छाप थी। एक मर्दाना खूबसूरती थी उसमें। मुझे लगा कि अपने परिवारों से मीलों दूर वर्षा-वनों में हिंसक लहरों के बीच रह रही लड़कियों ने इस पुरुष के प्रति आत्म-समर्पण कर कुछ भी अस्वाभाविक नहीं किया। उन्हें क्या पता था कि वे कभी घर लौट भी पाएंगी या नहीं। ऐसे में यदि उन्होंने किसी पुरुष की बाँहों में पनाह ले कर जीवन-सुख के कुछ पलों का उपभोग किया तो क्या गलत किया? और हौंग? क्या उसके लिए वह जिम्मेवार थी? पिताजी को पता होता तो वह उसका खून ही कर देते। पर वह तो अपने पारिवारिक गर्व के साथ स्वर्ग सिधार गए।

हौंग का उल्लेख करते ही होआंग जम सा गया और थरथराने लगा :

- मैं तो चाहता था कि तुम्हारी बहन हौंग और गांव के अन्य लोगों के लिए मैं मर गया होता। काश, ऐसा होता तो इतने वर्षों तक मुझे कष्ट न सहने पड़ते।

उसके प्रेम-प्रसंगों के प्रति अनजान बनते हुए मैंने पूछा:

- तुमने अपना नाम क्यों बदल लिया? मेरी बहन के पास तुम लौट कर भी तो आ सकते थे? क्या इस बीच कोई भयानक घटना घटी? क्या तुमने हौंग को धोखा दिया?

- भयानक से भी कहीं अधिक भयानक हादसा हुआ। मैं हौंग को मुंह दिखाने के काबिल नहीं रहा।

होआंग के सेल-फोन पर टैंगो-धुन की रिंग-टोन बज उठी, जिसे सुन कर मुझे तनिक आश्चर्य हुआ। धुन की समाप्ति तक वह रुका, फिर फोन बंद कर दिया।

- ''हौंग को टैंगो-नृत्य पसंद था, क्या अब भी है?''

- हौंग को टैंगो-नृत्य नहीं आता, पर किसी को इस धुन पर नाचते देखती है तो जम सी जाती है। अजीब बात है।

- ''यह सही नहीं है। हौंग अच्छी डांसर थी। मैंने उसे सिखाया था।'' उसकी आवाज में कुछ उत्तेजना थी, ''मेरा एक दोस्त, जो फ्रांस से लौटा था, उसने यह नृत्य गुप्त रूप से मुझे सिखाया था, और वैसे ही मैंने हौंग को।''

फिर भी वर्षों से उसने टैंगो-नृत्य किया ही नहीं, बिल्कुल भी नहीं।

अब मुझे कुछ-कुछ समझ में आ रहा था। होआंग के जीवन में अपना कोई

निशान छोड़ने की मेरी बहन की इच्छा तो पूरी हो गई, पर अपने बच्चों से मिल पाने की होआंग की इच्छा क्या कभी पूरी होगी? इस सवाल का जवाब देने का अधिकार आखिर किसको है? और मैं खुद हौंग की चाहत भरी निगाहों को क्या जवाब दूंगी? मैं जानती हूं, मुख्य स्टेशन पर वह मेरी प्रतीक्षा अवश्य कर रही होगी। मैं इतनी हृदयहीन भी नहीं थी कि होआंग को जता देती कि उसका रहस्य मैं जानती हूं। साथ ही मैं अपनी बहन का दिल भी कैसे तोड़ सकती थी। होआंग बहुत बड़ी कीमत अदा कर चुका है। मैं सिर्फ यह चाहती हूं कि उसे अपने बच्चों से मिलने का एक अवसर तो मिलना ही चाहिए ताकि वह हौंग के अलावा अन्य किसी की नज़र में दोषी न हो और सिर उठा कर चल सके तथा न्धे-आन में पले-बढ़े दो-दो ऐसे जवानों का पिता होने पर गर्वित हो सके, जो उम्र के बीस साल पार कर चुके हैं।

(अनुवाद : प्रेम कपूर)

उड़ता हुआ लाल तीर

किउ बिच हाउ

वियतनामी कथाकार किउ बिच हाउ का जन्म 1972 में हुआ था। ''अनाथ लहरें'', ''चूहों की सराय'' जैसी कहानियों की ख्यातिप्राप्त इस कथाकार को साहित्यिक समाचारपत्र द्वारा सन् 2007 में आयोजित लघुकथा प्रतियोगिता में श्रेष्ठ कथाकार के रूप में पुरस्कृत किया जा चुका है।

एक आत्मलीन (ऑटिस्टिक) बच्चे को, जो सही उच्चारण नहीं कर पा रहा था, सही उच्चारण करना सिखला कर, उसे उसकी मां के साथ विदा कर लौटते वक्त जब हा लौह-द्वार बंद कर रही थी, उसे फोन की घंटी सुनाई दी। अपना स्मार्ट-फोन उठाने के लिए वह कमरे की ओर दौड़ी। फोन सम्भवतः डेस्क पर पड़ा था।

किसी अजनबी का फोन था, जिसने सुन रखा था कि हा बच्चों का तोतलापन या उच्चारण की भाषाई अशुद्धियों को सुधारने में माहिर है। वह व्यक्ति हा से आग्रह कर रहा था कि अगले रविवार को वह उसके बच्चे के लिए थोड़ा वक्त निकाले। हा ने उसे रविवार को दोपहर बाद तीन बजे का 'अपॉइंटमेंट' दिया।

'ऑटिस्टिक' बच्चों की उच्चारणगत अशुद्धियों के उपचार-कार्यक्रम में हा ने स्नातकोत्तर डिग्री हासिल कर रखी थी। इसके अलावा अपने आत्मलीन

(ऑटिस्टिक) पुत्र का, जो स्वयं को केवल सत्तर प्रतिशत तक संप्रेषित कर पाता था, का उपचार कर पाने में वह सफल हो पाई थी। इसलिए उपचार के लिए कई 'ऑटिस्टिक' बच्चों को उपचार के लिए उसके पास लाया जाता। इस काम में उसे महारत हासिल हो गई थी। पिछले पांच वर्षों से ऐसे बच्चों के उपचार के लिए हा ने अपने घर में एक उपचार केंद्र खोल लिया था, जिसमें वह अपने पुत्र तथा कुछ अन्य ऑटिस्टिक बच्चों का उपचार करती। इस काम से उसे इतनी आमदनी हो जाती जिसकी उसने स्नातकोत्तर डिग्री हासिल करते वक्त कल्पना भी नहीं की थी। उस वक्त तो उसने बस इतना सोचा था कि उक्त डिग्री प्राप्त कर वह अपने बच्चे के उच्चारणदोषों को सुधार पाएगी, उसके जीवन के कष्टों को कुछ कम कर पाएगी, पर अंततः उसे लगा कि उसे अपने पुत्र मिन्ह को धन्यवाद देना चाहिए, जिसके चलते कभी उसे अविश्वसनीय कष्ट अवश्य हुआ, पर उसी के कारण उसके लिए अप्रत्याशित रूप से आजीविका के द्वार खुले।

यह खयाल आते ही हा अचानक चौंक उठी। मिन्ह कहां है ? उसे लगा कि वह दरवाजा बंद करना भूल गई थी। फोन छोड़ वह बाहर की ओर दौड़ी। स्लाइडिंग-डोर एक ओर से खुला था। जाहिर था कि पुत्र ने मां की गलती को देख लिया था, और वह बाहर कूद गया था। हा के दस वर्षीय बेटे को पड़ोसियों ने उसे ''तीर'' उपनाम दे रखा था क्योंकि वह सामान्य कदम न उठा कर, अनियंत्रित सा तीर की तेजी से दौड़ जाता था, किसी खतरे की परवाह किए बिना। कई बार वह दौड़ता हुआ गली में निकल कर किसी गुजरती हुई मोटरसाइकिल से टकरा जाता था। कभी सिर फूट जाता तो कभी घुटनों या कोहनी की चमड़ी छिल जाती और खून निकलने लगता। पर उसे मानो कोई फर्क ही नहीं पड़ता था, वह फौरन हंसते हुए उठ खड़ा होता। अपने बेटे को किसी दुर्घटना से बचाने तथा भीड़ में उसे आसानी से पहचान पाने के लिए हा उसे लाल टी-शर्ट पहनाती।

हा ने गली में नज़र दौड़ाई। वह गली में दौड़ी और उसने हर आने-जाने वाले से पूछा कि उसने किसी लाल टी-शर्ट पहने हुए दस वर्षीय लड़के को तो नहीं देखा। अपने बेटे को खोजती वह गली में बेतहाशा दौड़ी जा रही थी। तभी उसने देखा गली के बीच एक गाड़ी खड़ी थी और उसे घेरे हुए भीड़ लगी थी। वह उसी ओर दौड़ी। भीड़ हटा कर उसने देखा कि सड़क पर खून फैला था और उसका बेटा मिन्ह बीच सड़क में बेहोश पड़ा था। उसे गाड़ी ने टक्कर मार दी थी।

कहते हैं कि किसी को जो चीज अधिक प्यारी हो, अक्सर उसी से उसकी मौत होती है। बहरहाल, उस कार से मिन्ह की मौत तो नहीं हुई पर उसके बाएं पैर की हड्डी टूट गई, सिर पर पांच तथा कोहनी पर तीन टांके लगे। यह उसके जीवन की दूसरी बड़ी दुर्घटना थी। जब वह सात साल का था, तब भी उसे एक कार ने टक्कर मार दी थी। दरअसल ड्राइवर गैरेज करने के लिए कार को 'बैक' कर रहा था। कार की रफ्तार बहुत धीमी थी, इसलिए उसे हल्की चोटें आई थीं।

वास्तव में मिन्ह को गाड़ियां पसंद थीं। जब भी वह किसी गाड़ी को आते हुए देखता तो उसके 'साइड-मिरर' को उमेठने की कोशिश करता, हाथ में कुछ होता तो वह 'साइड-मिरर' पर दे मारता और इस प्रक्रिया में उसे चोट भी लग जाती। कई बार अपने बेटे की इस आदत की वजह से हा को गाड़ी-मालिकों को हर्जाना भी चुकाना पड़ता।

पिछले छः वर्षों से हा ने 'ऑटिस्टिक' बच्चों को पढ़ाने व प्रशिक्षित करने तथा अपने बेटे की आत्म-चिकित्सा (सेल्फ थेरेपी) के तौर-तरीके सीखे और उन पर अनुसंधान किया। अपने काम में उसे सफलता भी मिली और प्रचार-माध्यमों से 'सम्मान' भी। चार साल की उम्र तक तो उसका बेटा मिन्ह सिर्फ पड़ा रहता था, दूध पीता या सोता रहता। अपने बच्चे की घर में रह कर देखभाल करने के लिए हा को युनिवर्सिटी लाइब्रेरी की अपनी नौकरी छोड़नी पड़ी। आत्मलीन बच्चों की देखभाल कैसे की जाए, उन्हें किस प्रकार पढ़ाया व प्रशिक्षित किया जाए, इस विषय पर उसने कई पुस्तकें खरीदीं और उनमें वर्णित तौर-तरीकों का अपने बेटे पर प्रयोग किया, पर सफलता नहीं मिली। अंततः उसने अपने पति हुइ से इस विषय पर चर्चा की। दोनों ने तय किया कि ऋण लेकर हा उस स्कूल में प्रशिक्षण ले जहां सिखाया जाता है कि ऑटिस्टिक बच्चों की देखभाल कैसे की जाए। अपने बच्चे की देखभाल के लिए उसने एक परिचारिका को रख लिया। ऑटिस्टिक बच्चों की देखभाल की स्कूल में विधिपूर्वक जानकारी हासिल करने के बाद हा ने इस विषय पर घरेलू तथा विदेशी शिक्षकों से जानकारी प्राप्त कर अपने बेटे के इलाज का तरीका बदल दिया। धीरे-धीरे उसके बेटे के बोलने, खाने-पीने आदि में सुधार आने लगा। जब उसने अपने बच्चे की स्थिति में सुधार की खुशी फेसबुक पर शेयर की तो कई समाचार-पत्रों के संवाददाताओं ने उसके साक्षात्कार लिये और अपने-अपने समाचार-पत्रों में उसकी अद्भुत सफलता का

उल्लेख करते हुए कई लेख लिखे। तब लोगों ने उसकी प्रतिभा को पहचाना और अपने-अपने आत्मलीन बच्चों की स्थिति सुधारने के लिए उससे आग्रह किया। हा के सद्प्रयासों से अन्य आत्मलीन बच्चों में भी सुधार आया और तब से आत्मलीन बच्चों के शिक्षण-प्रशिक्षण के क्षेत्र में अपनी उपलब्धियों के लिए हा को ऑटिस्टिक बच्चों की चिकित्सा (थेरेपी) का विशेषज्ञ मान लिया गया।

मिन्ह के दूसरे ऐक्सीडेंट के बाद किंतु हा को बार-बार यह प्रश्न व्यथित करने लगा कि क्या उसके पुत्र की प्रगति की रफतार धीमी पड़ गई है? उसे लगा कि अपने पुत्र को पढ़ाना, लिखाना, गणित के सवाल हल करना सिखाने की आप्राण चेष्टा के बावजूद पिछले साल भर से उसे कोई नई युक्ति या दक्षता हासिल नहीं हुई है। मिन्ह अक्षरों को अलग-अलग तो पढ़ लेता था, पर उन्हें जोड़ कर नहीं पढ़ पाता था। उसी प्रकार वह दहाई तक ही गणित के सवाल हल कर पाता था। सबसे ज्यादा चिंताजनक बात यह थी कि मिन्ह सामान्य कदम उठाना ही नहीं चाहता था। वह तो कमान से छूटे तीर की तरह बस दौड़ना जानता था। हा और उसके पति को इसीलिए हमेशा स्लाइडिंग-डोर पर ताला लगा कर रखना पड़ता था कि कहीं मिन्ह बाहर सड़क पर न दौड़ जाए। पर एक बच्चे को ताले में बंद कर रखना भी तो कोई अच्छी बात नहीं क्योंकि तब वह अपने बच्चे को दो दीवारों के बीच की जगह में अपने हाथ-पैर आगे-पीछे चलाते देखती, तो कभी उसकी आंखों में उसे विचित्र सी चमक दिखाई देती। हा, दरअसल अत्यधिक असुरक्षित महसूस करती। वह समझ नहीं पाती थी कि अपने पुत्र के विचित्र ऊर्जा-स्रोत को वह नियंत्रित करे भी तो किस प्रकार। वह समझ नहीं पा रही थी कि अपने पुत्र की ऊर्जा का सही दिशा में उपयोग वह किस प्रकार करे। उसके पुत्र की ऊर्जा तो किसी बारूद के पीपे की तरह थी, जो कभी भी फट सकता था।

कई दिनों के सोच-विचार के बाद हुई ने पत्नी हा से कहा, ''क्यों न हम मिन्ह का दाखिला किसी साधारण स्कूल में करा दें?'' आंखें तरेरते हुए हा ने कहा ''सैकड़ों बार हम उसका दाखिला किसी साधारण स्कूल में कराने का प्रयास कर चुके हैं और हर बार स्कूल के शिक्षक हमें मना कर चुके हैं। बार-बार के इन्कार से तंग आकर ही तो मैंने 'ऑटिस्टिक चिल्ड्रेन एडुकेशन कोर्स' में शामिल होने का निर्णय लिया था। और अब तुम फिर वही पुराना प्रस्ताव रख रहे हो। पता नहीं इसके पीछे तुम्हारी क्या सोच है?''

''मेरी सोच तो बस इतनी है कि जैसे भी हो हमारे बेटे की स्थिति में सुधार हो। मैं जानता हूँ कि तुम्हारे ही कारण मिन्ह में काफी सुधार आया है, पर पिछले सालभर से सुधार की गाड़ी न सिर्फ थमी है, बल्कि पीछे लौट रही है। दुर्घटना के बाद तो हमारी आंखें खुल जानी चाहिए''। कुछ नाराजगी थी हुइ के स्वर में।

''तो फिर तुम्हीं बताओ कि मुझे क्या करना चाहिए''। नाराज़ तो हा भी थी। ''अपनी तरफ से हर सम्भव कोशिश कर तो रही हूँ'', उसने कहा।

''तुम्हें अपनी पढ़ाने की पद्धति बदलनी चाहिए'', हुइ ने जवाब दिया।

''कैसे बदलूं? जरा खुल कर बताओगे?''

''यह तो तुम खुद सोचो क्योंकि ऑटिस्टिक बच्चों को पढ़ाने में माहिर तुम हो, मैं नहीं। हममें पहले ही यह सहमति हो चुकी है कि मैं अपना पूरा ध्यान परिवार की खातिर धनोपार्जन पर लगाऊंगा और तुम अपना पूरा समय इस खोज पर लगाओगी कि किस विधि से हमारे पुत्र को शिक्षित किया जाए। अब जबकि तुम्हारे पढ़ाने से हमारे बेटे में कोई प्रगति नज़र नहीं आ रही है, तो तुम्हें ही अपने पढ़ाने के तरीके में कुछ बदलाव लाना होगा । हम मिन्ह को यों ही नहीं छोड़ सकते। कुछ न कुछ तो करना ही होगा।''

हा ने महसूस किया कि हुइ का कहना कुछ हद तक सही था। मिन्ह को यों ही भाग्य के भरोसे नहीं छोड़ा जा सकता। मिन्ह का पिछला कार-ऐक्सीडेंट हा के लिए एक गम्भीर चेतावनी था। यदि उसने अपनी शिक्षण विधि में परिवर्तन कर मिन्ह की प्रगति के नए तरीके न ईजाद किए तो कहीं ऐसा न हो कि बेटे से ही हाथ धोना पड़ जाए। यदि उसका बेटा सामान्य जीवन न जी पाया तो किस काम के हैं उसके सारे प्रयास, उसका समर्पण, उसकी शोहरत। पर शिक्षा का वह नया तरीका, नई पद्धति क्या है? हा की समझ में नहीं आ रहा था। ऑटिस्टिक बच्चों को पढ़ाने व प्रशिक्षित करने के लिए शायद शिक्षा के उच्च स्तर की आवश्यकता थी, यानी अपने बेटे के इलाज के काबिल बनने के लिए उसे स्वयं अपने पढ़ाने के स्तर को ऊँचा उठाना होगा। पिछले दस वर्षों के बारे में सोच कर हा कांप उठी। यदि अपने बेटे का भविष्य ही न संवार पाई तो किस काम के हैं सारे प्रयास!

हा ने अपना सिर झटका, नहीं, वह नकारात्मक विचारों को हावी नहीं होने देगी।

हा दौड़ी और शीघ्रतापूर्वक उसने मिन्ह के बायें हाथ को उसके मुंह से निकाला। बहुत कष्ट से हा ने अपने पुत्र की दसों लहूलुहान अंगुलियों को देखा।

—"होआ! मैंने तुमसे पहले भी कहा था कि उसे कस कर पकड़ा करो, पर हाथ आज़ाद रहने दिया करो" हा ने परिचारिका को डांटा।

—"आपने जैसे कहा था, वैसे ही तो पकड़ा था। वह तो मैं खाना गर्म करने गई तो उसे अकेले छोड़ना पड़ा।"परिचारिका होआ ने सफाई दी।

अपने बायें हाथ से उसने मिन्ह के दोनों हाथ पकड़े और दायें हाथ से उसकी पीठ को चपतियाया -"गंदा बच्चा! अब दांत से काटेगा अपने हाथ को?"

—"नहीं।" मिन्ह ने हंसते-हंसते कहा।

जाहिर है, मिन्ह को अपने हाथों में दर्द महसूस ही नहीं हुआ, क्योंकि यदि उसे दर्द की अनुभूति हुई होती तो वह अपनी दसों उंगलियों को इतनी जोर से न काटता। हा का सिर चकरा गया।

ठीक तभी हा का एक मित्र, जो हाई स्कूल में काम करता था, उससे मिलने आया। उसने जब हा के बेटे की समस्या के बारे में सुना तो उसने उसे फौरन एक उत्तरजीविता कौशल पाठ्यक्रम (सर्वाइवल स्किल कोर्स) के बारे में बताया।

"उत्तरजीविता" यानी सर्वाइवल यह शब्द हा के जेहन में जम गया। उसे लगा कि यही वह सही विधि है, जिसकी उसके बेटे को अत्यधिक आवश्यकता थी। हां, उसके बेटे को इस बात से अवगत होना होगा कि उसके लिए क्या खतरनाक है, ताकि उस खतरे से वह स्वयं को बचा सके। उसे तो अभी बहुत जीना है, अपने माता-पिता की मृत्यु के बाद भी...

सर्वाइवल स्किल कोर्स के बारे में हा ने अपने पति को तत्काल कुछ नहीं बताया किंतु स्वयं कोर्स के व्यवस्थापक से सम्पर्क किया और उस कोर्स में शामिल होने के लिए मिन्ह का पंजीकरण कराया। वह सघन पाठ्यक्रम (कोर्स) हाइ फोंग सिटी में महीने भर तक चला। हा ने पाठ्यक्रम के व्यवस्थापकों को अपने बेटे के ऑटिस्टिक (आत्मलीन) होने की बात यह सोच कर नहीं बताई कि कहीं वे उसे कोर्स में शामिल करने से इनकार न कर दें। उत्तरजीविता कौशल प्रशिक्षण कार्यक्रम की प्रमुख शिक्षिका न्गोक ने किंतु खुशी-खुशी मिन्ह को कोर्स में शामिल कर लिया। हालांकि कोर्स का शुल्क बहुत ज्यादा था, पर हा ने इसकी परवाह नहीं की, उसे तो इसी बात का संतोष था कि मिन्ह को कोर्स में दाखिला

मिल गया। प्रमुख शिक्षिका न्गोक ने हा को भरोसा दिलाया कि कोर्स के प्रशिक्षण के दरम्यान बच्चे सेना-निवास में रहेंगे, जिसका तात्पर्य यह हुआ कि बच्चे सेना-निवास से निकल नहीं पाएंगे। अर्थात् मिन्ह को किसी भी प्रकार का कोई खतरा नहीं होगा।

मिन्ह को शिक्षिका न्गोक की निगरानी में छोड़ कर हा घर लौट गई। अगले दिन वह घबराहट में बार-बार फोन के पास जाती रही। उसे यही चिंता सता रही थी कि कहीं शिक्षिका न्गोक, मिन्ह को वापस घर न भेज दे, पर लगभग सारा दिन सुचारु रूप से बीत गया और कोई फोन नहीं आया।

शाम के छः बजे के अंदाज शिक्षिका न्गोक का फोन आया। फोन उठाते ही हा की धड़कनें तेज हो गईं किंतु दूसरी ओर से मिस न्गोक का धीर-शांत स्वर सुनाई दिया :

''मुझे आपसे यह पूछते हुए कुछ अजीब सा लग रहा है, पर मेरे ख्याल से आप और मैं, दोनों शिक्षा के क्षेत्र में कार्यरत हैं, और सर्वोपरि हम माताएं हैं, इसलिए मैं मिन्ह और उसकी समस्याओं के बारे में आपसे स्पष्ट रूप से जानना चाहती हूँ ताकि कोर्स में बेहतर नतीजे के लिए हम उसकी मदद कर सकें। आप कृपया मिन्ह की विभिन्न विशिष्टताओं-संलक्षणों के बारे में मुझे बताएं।''

''मुझे क्षमा करें टीचर कि मैंने आपको मिन्ह के बारे में स्पष्ट रूप से पहले नहीं बताया क्योंकि मुझे डर था कि सच्चाई जान कर कहीं आप मिन्ह को दाखिला देने से इन्कार न कर दें'', हा ने कुछ झिझकते हुए कहा, ''मेरा बेटा मिन्ह ऑटिस्टिक (आत्मलीन) और अत्यधिक सक्रिय व चंचल है। वह स्थिर खड़ा नहीं रह सकता, सामान्य रूप से चल नहीं सकता, बस उछलता-कूदता रहता है, यदि उसे नियंत्रण में न रखा गया...।''

हा ने पूरी बारीकी से अपने बेटे की विचित्र अक्षमताओं और आचरण के बारे में बताया। फोन के दूसरे छोर पर जो महिला थी, वह चुपचाप सुन रही थी। पर उसकी चुप्पी के बावजूद हा को उस पर इतना भरोसा था कि हा ने बिना कुछ भी छिपाए या झिझके अपने बच्चे की सारी कमियों और दोषों को खुल कर बता दिया।

''मैंने आपसे यह सब इसलिए पूछा ताकि मैं मिन्ह को ठीक से समझ सकूं और जानकारी के अभाव में किसी जोखिम से बचा जा सके। आपको चिंता की

कोई जरूरत नहीं क्योंकि मिन्ह को वापस भेजने का मेरा कोई इरादा नहीं। मुझे पूरी उम्मीद है, मिन्ह की स्थिति में सुधार होगा और वह प्रगति करेगा।''

हा ने अतिरिक्त शुल्क देने की पेशकश की, पर न्गोक ने लेने से मना कर दिया। न्गोक ने यह क्यों कहा कि ''मुझे उम्मीद है... मिन्ह प्रगति करेगा?'' क्या वह 'ऑटिज़्म' को जानती है? क्या वह अगले तीन दिनों तक मिन्ह को नियंत्रण में रख भी पाएगी या नहीं?

बहरहाल हा ने सोचा कि संशय और चिंता से बेहतर है कि उम्मीद का दामन थामे रहे। लिहाजा, उसने अपनी ऊर्जा अन्य आत्मलीन बच्चों को पढ़ाने में लगाई।

'सर्वाइवल स्किल्स' कोर्स के आयोजकों और उसमें भाग लेने वाले बच्चों के माता-पिताओं के बीच तय हुआ था कि न तो वे महीने भर अपने बच्चों से मिल पाएंगे, न फोन पर बात कर पाएंगे। यह माता-पिताओं और उनके बच्चों के लिए किसी चुनौती से कम नहीं था। हा और उसके पति हुइ के लिए तो यह चुनौती कुछ और कठिन थी क्योंकि उनका पुत्र एक विलक्षण रोग से ग्रस्त था। हा के दिमाग में कई सवाल उठ रहे थे - न्गोक ने मिन्ह को नियंत्रित करने के लिए क्या किया होगा? क्या उसने उसे बांधा होगा? या कि उसके अजीबोगरीब आचरण के लिए उसे पीटा होगा? पिता-माता होने के कारण वे अपने बच्चे को बर्दाश्त कर सकते थे, किंतु किसी बाहर वाले, यहां तक कि शिक्षक के लिए भी, ऐसा कर पाना बहुत मुश्किल था।

जिस दिन न्गोक के प्रशिक्षण विद्यालय से मिन्ह को वापस लाना था, उसकी पूर्व रात को बेचैनी के कारण हा व हुइ, दोनों को नींद नहीं आई। जब वे न्गोक के प्रशिक्षण-केंद्र में मिन्ह से मिले तो अवाक रह गए। मिन्ह पहले से कुछ दुबला हो गया था। अब उसकी लंबे समय तक घर में बंद रहने के कारण नीलाभ गोरी त्वचा धूप के कारण कुछ ताम्रवर्णी हो गई थी। उसकी उंगलियों के घाव भी अब आश्चर्यजनक रूप से ठीक हो गए थे।

''अब मिन्ह ने दांतों से उंगलियां काटने की आदत से छुटकारा पा लिया है'', मिस न्गोक ने मिन्ह में आये बदलाव के बारे में बताते हुए कहा, ''अब यह अपनी नब्बे प्रतिशत पुरानी बुरी आदतों को छोड़ चुका है।''

हा ने एक झटके से पूछा, ''आपने ऐसा क्या कर दिया?''

हा के सवाल का जवाब न देकर न्गोक ने मिन्ह से मुखातिब हो कर कहा, ''मिन्ह! अपनी ममा-पापा को दिखाओ कि तुम टेनिस बॉल से क्या कर सकते हो।''

न्गोक ने मिन्ह को तीन टेनिस-बॉल दीं। आज्ञाकारी बच्चे की तरह मिन्ह ने कहा - ''जी।'' और तीनों गेंदों को मिन्ह ने बड़ी खुबसूरती से 'जगल' करना शुरू किया, बिना किसी गेंद को गिराए।

न्गोक ने कहा, ''जब यह अपनी उंगलियों को काटना नहीं छोड़ पा रहा था तो हमारे एक शिक्षक को उसके हाथों को व्यस्त रखने की युक्ति सुझी जिससे उसके हाथ व्यस्त रहें और वह उंगलियां मुंह में न रख पाए।''

हा चुपचाप प्रसन्न, सराहना व आभारयुक्त दृष्टि से बस देखती रही और सोचती रही कि न्गोक और उसके साथी शिक्षक जिन्हें वह जानती भी नहीं थी, कैसे यह सब कुछ कर पाए और अपने बच्चे के साथ दस साल रह कर भी वह यह सब क्यों नहीं कर पाई? क्यों वह कोई ऐसी युक्ति नहीं खोज पाई? वह तो उसे केवल डराती रही, हाथों को चपतियाती और कभी-कभी बांधती भर रही। वह इतनी असहाय क्यों थी? वास्तव में, शिक्षा में, प्यार और बुद्धिमत्ता के बावजूद सब कुछ अकेले कर पाना असंभव है।

''आपका बेटा बड़ा होशियार है'', मिस न्गोक ने कहा, ''मेरा सुझाव है कि आप मिन्ह को हमारे केंद्र में रहने दें। यहां वह पढ़ेगा भी और बॉल-जगलिंग का कौशल भी सीख जाएगा और आगे चलकर वह और भी कई युक्तियां सीख जाएगा, उसकी सोच विकसित होगी।''

''ऐसा आप दावे से कह सकती हैं?'' हा आश्चर्यचकित थी ''आपका प्रशिक्षण केंद्र क्या अन्य पेशेवर संगठनों से मान्यता प्राप्त है?''

''नहीं, हमें कोई आधिकारिक मान्यता प्राप्त नहीं है'', न्गोक ने पुष्टि करते हुए कहा, ''आपके पुत्र में सुधार ही हमारी प्रामाणिकता है। हम मान्यताओं की प्रतीक्षा में नहीं रह सकते। हमारा काम ही हमारी अनुशंसा है।''

हा को किंकर्तव्यविमूढ़ देख कर हुइ ने आगे आकर कहा, ''आप पर हमें पूरा भरोसा है टीचर! आपको बहुत-बहुत धन्यवाद। मिन्ह को इतनी देर शांति से बैठा देख कर, उसकी घायल उंगलियों को स्वस्थ देखते ही मुझे आप पर यकीन हो गया था। आपने तो एक करिश्मा कर दिखाया। हम आपके तथा अन्य शिक्षकों

के हृदय से आभारी हैं। हालांकि हमें उसकी कमी खलेगी, फिर भी मिन्ह के भविष्य को देखते हुए हम चाहेंगे कि आप उसे अपने आवासीय (बोर्डिंग) स्कूल में स्थान दें। जब तक उसकी स्थिति में सुधार आता रहेगा, तब तक मैं चाहूँगा कि वह आपकी देखरेख में रहे।''

तब से मिस न्गोक के प्रशिक्षण केंद्र में मिन्ह एक आवासी छात्र की तरह रहने लगा। केंद्र के साथ नये करार के मुताबिक हा और हुई महीने में एक बार प्रशिक्षण केंद्र में अपने बेटे से मिलने जाते और सप्ताहांत के दो दिनों के लिए उसे अपने साथ घर ले आते। हा और हुई दोनों को अब अपने बेटे से दूर रहने की आदत सी हो गई थी। मिन्ह की प्रत्यक्ष प्रगति देखकर उन्हें बड़ी राहत मिलती। मिन्ह अब सामान्य बच्चों की तरह पढ़-लिख तो सकता था, पर उसकी गणित में सुधार नहीं हुआ था। साल भर बाद मिन्ह एक ''धावक तीर'' नहीं रहा। अब वह सामान्य चाल से चल पाता था। हुइ अब मिस न्गोक की प्रशिक्षण पद्धति से काफी खुश था और उसकी एक संत के रूप में प्रशंसा करता था। यही नहीं, अब तो वह ऑटिस्टिक बच्चों के माता-पिता को खोज कर उन्हें रजामंद तक करता कि वे अपने बच्चों को मिस न्गोक के केंद्र में दाखिल करें। हा कुछ कहती तो नहीं थी किंतु न्गोक पर अत्यधिक भरोसा करने के मामले में वह अपने पति से सहमत नहीं थी। उसे संदेह था कि मिन्ह की प्रगति के मामले में भाग्य ने न्गोक का साथ दिया था क्योंकि न्गोक के पास न तो उसकी योग्यता की कोई आधिकारिक डिग्री थी और न ही किसी शिक्षण संस्थान का प्रमाण्-पत्र।

उस दिन हा और उसके पति को बहुत आश्चर्य हुआ जब न्गोक ने फोन पर उन्हें सूचित किया कि अगले दिन रात को वे ओपेरा हाउस के कार्यक्रम में अवश्य पधारें, जहां मिन्ह को 'वियतनामीज़ रिकॉर्ड' से पुरस्कृत किया जाएगा।

''आप मज़ाक तो नहीं कर रही हैं?'' हा ने पूछा, ''ऐसा क्या कर दिया मिन्ह ने कि उसे इस राष्ट्रीय पुरस्कार से नवाज़ा जा रहा है?''

''आप ओपेरा हाउस में आइए तो सही, हमारे लोग द्वार पर आपको आमंत्रण-पत्र दे देंगे।'' न्गोक ने संक्षिप्त उत्तर दिया और फोन रख दिया।

न्गोक की बात पर न तो पूर्णत: विश्वास हो पा रहा था, न अविश्वास। हा और उसके पति ने इंटरनेट पर सर्च किया, कई लोगों से पूछा भी कि क्या अगली शाम ऐसा कोई कार्यक्रम होने जा रहा है जिसमें कुछ प्रतिभावान लोगों को राष्ट्रीय

पुरस्कार से सम्मानित किया जाएगा? कार्यक्रम तो था, किंतु पुरस्कार प्राप्त करने वालों की सूची प्रकाशित नहीं हुई थी।

नियत दिन हा और उसका पति हुइ कार्यक्रम में पहुँचे और दर्शकों के बीच बैठे। उन्हें अभी भी न्गोक की सूचना पर यकीन नहीं हो रहा था। उन्हें इतनी बेचैनी हो रही थी कि वे कार्यक्रम पर ध्यान केंद्रित नहीं कर पा रहे थे। अचानक हा के कान में हुइ फुसफुसाया, ''देखो, वो मंच पर अपना 'तीर' बेटा है न?''

हा ने अपना चश्मा साफ कर देखा। मंच पर सर्कस की पोशाक में एक लड़का था, जो उन्हें कुछ-कुछ जाना-पहचाना और कुछ-कुछ अजनबी सा लग रहा था। हा ने फिर चश्मा ठीक किया।

मंच पर लड़के ने दर्शकों का अभिवादन किया। काली पोशाक पहने चार सहयोगी आये और मंच पर पांच रोलरों पर एक लकड़ी का तख्ता रख दिया। अब लड़का आगे बढ़ा, एक हाथ से लकड़ी के तख्ते को पकड़ कर, दूसरा हाथ अपनी बगल में खड़े सहयोगी के कंधे पर रखा और उचक कर तख्ते पर चढ़ गया। हा को धड़कन रुकती हुई सी महसूस हुई। ''हे भगवान! क्या ये मेरा बेटा मिन्ह है? पांच रोलरों पर संतुलन बना कर खड़ा है? कहीं गिर न जाए!''

नहीं वह गिरा नहीं, लुढ़कते रोलरों पर वह संतुलन बनाए खड़ा रहा। अब उसके माथे पर एक पानी की बोतल रख उसके हाथों में टेनिस की आठ गेंदें दे दी गईं। अब उसने गेंदों को 'जगल' करना शुरू किया। उसने कुछ इस प्रकार संतुलन बना रखा था कि न तो वह खुद गिरा, न उसके हाथों में उछलती गेंदें और न ही माथे पर रखी पानी की बोतल गिरी। अत्यधिक घबराहट में हा अपने बेटे की बाजीगरी नहीं देख पा रही थी। हर क्षण उसे डर लग रहा था, कहीं वह गिर न जाए। उसने अपनी आंखें मूंद ली। दर्शक दीर्घा जब तालियों की गड़गड़ाहट से गूंज उठी, तब उसने आंखें खोलीं।

अब मिन्ह रोलरों पर के तख्ते से कूद कर फर्श पर खड़ा मुस्कुरा रहा था, हाथ उठा कर लोगों का अभिवादन स्वीकार कर रहा था, तभी मंच से घोषणा हुई:

''वियतनाम के एक छोटे से बच्चे होआंक मिन्ह ने पांच रोलर्स पर संतुलन बनाने के साथ-साथ माथे पर पानी की बोतल रख कर काफी लम्बे समय तक आठ गेंदों को जगल करने का गिनीज़ बुक रिकॉर्ड बनाया है।''

हा को अपने देखे और सुने पर यकीन ही नहीं हो रहा था। हुइ ने उसका हाथ

कस कर अपने हाथ में ले रखा था, ऐसा लगा जैसे वह रो रहा था। लोगों ने मिन्ह को घेर रखा था। कोई उससे हाथ मिला रहा था तो कोई उसे फूल भेंट कर रहा था। एक टेलिविजन रिपोर्टर ने उसका साक्षात्कार लेते हुए पूछा : ''गौरव के इन क्षणों में मिन्ह क्या कहना चाहता है ?''

''मैं... धन्यवाद देना चाहता हूँ... अपनी मां को, पिताजी को तथा शिक्षिका न्गोक को !''

हा का गला रुंध गया, आंखों से आंसू बह निकले कि इतने कष्टों और संघर्षों के बाद उनके बेटे मिन्ह के जीवन में ऐसा खूबसूरत क्षण आया। वह मंच पर जा कर अपने पुत्र को गले से न लगा पाई और अपनी सीट पर बैठी रोती रही। आज उसकी आंख का तारा दर्शकों का दुलारा था। सब कुछ उसे एक सपने जैसा लग रहा था।

''मां ! लो थोड़ा पानी पी लो !'' मिन्ह हा के सामने खड़ा मुस्कुरा रहा था।

''ओह हां, पर पानी है कहां ?'' हा को मिन्ह के हाथ खाली दिखे।

''यह रहा पानी।'' उसने उचक कर मां को अपने सिर पर रखा गिलास दिखाया।

''हां, हां, थैंक यू बेटे !'' पानी पेश करने की अपने बेटे की अदा पर हा खुश थी और आश्चर्यचकित भी। उसका बेटा एक सच्चा और होशियार सर्कस अभिनेता लग रहा था।

''मिन्ह एक अपूर्व प्रतिभा का धनी है जिसे सर्कस की भाषा में 'क्लोन' कहते हैं'', शिक्षिका न्गोक ने गर्व से कहा, ''कमर से ऊपर मिन्ह में अद्भुत लचीलापन और कुशलता है। इसीलिए सुदीर्घ प्रशिक्षण और अभ्यास से वह एक साथ तीन-तीन कठिन बाजीगरियों को न सिर्फ अंजाम दे पाया बल्कि सर्कस के प्रवीण पेशेवर कलाकारों तक को इसने पछाड़ दिया, जैसा कि आज के कार्यक्रम में हमने देखा।''

''हम मिस न्गोक के गुणग्राहक हैं तथा तहे दिल से उनका शुक्रिया अदा करते हैं। हम उनके केंद्र के अन्य शिक्षकों के भी आभारी हैं'', भरे गले से हा ने कहा, ''जैसा कि टेलिफोन पर आपसे हुई बातचीत में हमने पहले ही तय किया था, आज मैं और मेरे पति हुइ,मिन्ह को अपने साथ घर ले जाना चाहते हैं, जहां हम बिन्ह मिन्ह ऑटिज़्म सेंटर को और अधिक विस्तार देकर ऑटिस्टिक बच्चों में

सुधार के लिए काम करेंगे ताकि वे भी सामान्य जीवन जी सकें। और इस काम में मिन्ह मेरी मदद करेगा ताकि जो प्रगति इसने की है, अन्य ऑटिस्टिक बच्चे भी उस प्रगति के स्तर को हासिल कर सकें।''

''दरअसल हमारा प्रशिक्षण केंद्र भी चाहता है कि मिन्ह हमारे साथ रहे। आज वह एक स्टार है, प्रसिद्ध व्यक्ति है, दूसरों को प्रेरित कर सकता है'', न्गोक ने अपना स्वर धीमा करते हुए कहा, ''किन्तु मिन्ह पर पहला हक आपका है। बाद में यदि कोई कठिन 'केस' आया तो आप हमारे साथ समन्वय स्थापित कर सकती हैं। इस महत् काम में साथ मिल कर काम करना हमारे लिए खुशी की बात होगी।''

मिन्ह को ले कर जब हा और हुइ घर लौट रहे थे तो स्वाभाविक तौर पर उन्हें खुश होना चाहिए था, किंतु उनका मन भारी था। लग रहा था जैसे वे मिन्ह को उसकी शिक्षिका से छीन कर ले जा रहे हों। टैक्सी से मिन्ह पीछे की ओर अपनी शिक्षिका न्गोक को देख रहा था, जो धीरे-धीरे दूर होती जा रही थीं।

मिन्ह की आंखें भर आईं क्योंकि उसके लिए उसकी शिक्षिका भी मां से किसी भी मायने में कम नहीं थीं। उसी ने तो एक राष्ट्रीय रिकॉर्ड होल्डर के रूप में उसे जन्म दिया था।

(हिंदी रूपांतर : प्रेम कपूर)

सांझ

लिन्ह न्गा ली क्डम

सन् 1948 में जन्मी लिन्ह न्गा ली क्डम वियतनाम की प्रख्यात कथाकारों में एक हैं। आपको अपनी कथाओं - ''नीला सर्प'' तथा ''लाल हवा'' के लिए वियतनाम के कला व साहित्य संघों का सुप्रतिष्ठित पुरस्कार भी प्राप्त हो चुका है।

यह वह वक्त था जब धरती माता ने दिन का चित्र उकेरना शुरू ही किया था।

सर्वप्रथम आसमान पर हल्की गुलाबी आभा उभरी। आसमान पर उस विशाल हल्की आभा में कुशन सिंग पर्वतमाला अद्भुत व स्पष्ट रूप से उभर कर सामने आई, जिसके आखिरी बायें कोने पर एक हिस्सा कुछ पीलापन लिये हुए था। फिर पर्वतमाला के दाहिने सिरे पर एक गहरी गुलाबी लकीर सी उभरी जो धीरे-धीरे सारे क्षितिज पर छा गई। फिर इसके साथ-साथ सद्यजागृत परियों की पोशाक के कुछ धूसर व नीले हिस्से खिल उठे। चिड़ियां शीघ्रतापूर्वक कुछ क्षितिज के निर्मल गुलाबी से आसमान की ओर उड़ीं। लगा जैसे वे भोजन की तलाश के लिए, रात भर के आराम के बाद अपने पैर व डैने फैला कर स्वयं को तैयार कर रही थीं।

एक विशाल सुनहरी तश्तरी पर्वत चूड़ा पर उदय हुई। चुंधियाती रोशनी धुंधलके को दूर भगाती सारे आसमान पर छा गई। अब सुबह की ठंडक धूप के कारण शीघ्र ही गुम हो जाएगी। वाइ त्रुत ने एक लम्बी सांस छोड़ी। उसके सामने हिलती हुई बांस-पत्तियां मानो किसी का स्वागत कर रही थीं। आज एक और मशक्कत का दिन था। छुट्टियों के मौसम में झील पर पर्यटकों की भीड़ लगी रहती है। एक दल आता है तो एक जाता है। सभी को या-पोम के लम्बे से घर के परिदर्शन का बेसब्री से इंतजार रहता है। वाइ त्रुत यह निश्चित करना चाहता था कि उसकी पत्नी जगी भी है या नहीं। उसने अपने पैरों को कष्ट भी दिया पर वह उसे दिखी नहीं। उसने फिर लम्बी सांस ली। वाइ त्रुत, वाइ धाम को परेशान नहीं करना चाहता था। वह अभी भी बांस की झाड़ियों में सो रही थी।

बहुत समय पहले की बात है, तब से जाने कितनी बार धान की फसल कट चुकी है, जब वाइ त्रुत का जन्म हुआ था। पूरा परिवार सुख से जंगल में रहता था। जब भी उन्हें कहीं जाना होता तो हमेशा परिवार का नेतृत्व मां करती। उसके पीछे सभी भाई-बहन होते और अंत में किसी भी संकट से उनकी रक्षा के लिए पिता रहते। यह उस सुबह की बात है जब मां पूरे परिवार को एक ऐसी जगह ले कर गयी थी जहां ताज़े जंगली केलों की बहुतायत थी। अचानक जाने कहां से कुछ विचित्र दो पैरों वाले प्राणियों के साथ एक हाथियों का झुंड आ पहुंचा। दो पैरों वाले विचित्र प्राणी बंदरों की 'क्रा' प्रजाति से कुछ बड़े थे और हाथियों की पीठ पर उछल-कूद रहे थे। वे सभी दौड़ते हुए पूरे परिवार की ओर आ रहे थे। उसी क्षण माता-पिता दोनों चीखे — 'भागो'। और वे सभी इतनी तेजी से दौड़े कि एक-दूसरे से बिछड़ गए। वाइ त्रुत ने अपनी मां का निर्देश सुना था और वह जान बचा कर इतनी तेजी से भागा कि उसे पता ही नहीं चला कि उसने कितने चैनल और कितनी जलधाराएं पार कीं, पर तीन हाथी तब भी उसका पीछा कर रहे थे। जब वह बहुत थक गया तो कुछ धीमे दौड़ने लगा। तभी पीछे से फेंकी गई एक रस्सी में उसका पैर जकड़ गया। अब वह एक विशाल वृक्ष के चारों ओर गोल घेरे में दौड़ने लगा। रस्सी छोटी होती गई और फिर इतनी छोटी हो गई कि वह दौड़ न पाया और उसे रुकना पड़ा।

तब से दसियों फसल के मौसम बीत गए और वाइ त्रुत ने अपने मां-बाप, भाई-बहन, किसी को भी नहीं देखा। पता नहीं इस पतझड़ी वृक्षों भरे विशाल

जंगल में वे सब कहां खो गए थे।

त्रुत नाम उसे उसके माता-पिता ने नहीं बल्कि उन लोगों ने दिया था, जो विशाल हाथियों की पीठ पर थे। त्रुत उस वक्त बहुत छोटा था। उन्होंने उसे पैरों का कंगन पहनाया, खींच कर एक विशाल जंगल में लाये, जहां कई पेड़ थे और एक पेड़ से उसे कस कर बांध दिया। कई दिनों तक उसने कुछ नहीं खाया। उसे अपनी मां की गंध की याद आ रही थी। वह क्रोधित होकर चीखने-चिल्लाने और संघर्ष करने लगा, पर वह एक रस्सी से मुक्त न हो पाया जबकि कभी वह भोजन के लिए छोटे वृक्षों को तोड़ डालता था। उसकी आंखों से आंसुओं की दो बूंदें ढुलक पड़ीं।

हाल ही में वह वाइ दलों के परिवार दस युद्धक हाथियों के झुंड का नेता बन गया था। त्रुत जानता था कि जंगल से पकड़े गए हाथियों को सधाने के लिए जिन रस्सियों और कंगनों का प्रयोग होता था, मनुष्य उन्हें जंजीर कहते थे। त्रुत के पिछले पैरों को जिस रस्सी से कस कर बांधा गया था, वह भैंस के चमड़े से बनी थी और जिसे तोड़ना आसान नहीं था।

वाइ त्लो के परिवार का सबसे छोटा बेटा था वाइ नांग, जिसने कई दिनों के भूखे त्रुत को ला कर ताजी घास का पहला गुच्छा दिया, वह एक छोटा सा लड़का था। त्रुत हाथियों में सबसे छोटा था किंतु वाइ नांग तो उस की आधी सूंड़ बराबर लम्बा था। त्रुत ने जब नांग की काली चमकीली आंखों को देखा तो उसे लगा कि उस पर भरोसा किया जा सकता है। त्रुत ने सूंड़ से ताजा घास उठा ली। एक महीने बाद वाइ नांग का हाथ थाम कर त्रुत घर आया। वाइ त्लो के घर में पहले से ही सात शराब के बड़े-बड़े मर्तबान थे और सूअर के सिर, पूंछ तथा अन्य वस्तुओं सहित एक थाल था। सबसे पहले जाओ (एक जादूगर) ने परिवार को स्वास्थ्य की शुभकामना दी फिर भगवान ''न्गुआक न्गुआल'' की पूजा कर उन्हें सूचित किया कि परिवार में एक नया सदस्य शामिल हुआ है। और फिर अंत में नामकरण संस्कार हुआ (इसी नामकरण संस्कार में उसे वाइ त्रुत नाम दिया गया)। पूजा में त्रुत को सीख दी गई, ''डर कर भागना नहीं, गांव में खाओ-पियो, सौ साल जियो तथा शिशु हाथियों का शिकार करने वाले अच्छे हाथी बनो।''

चूंकि तब से त्लो परिवार ने त्रुत को वाइ नांग का भाई मान लिया तो वे और अधिक घनिष्ट हो गए तथा हमेशा साथ में रहते। त्रुत की तरह नांग का किंतु स्वास्थ्य-पूजन नहीं हुआ था, जो कि शिकार पर जाने पर या नये शिशु हाथी के जंगल से घर लौटने पर, जन्म होने पर या बीमार होने पर हुआ करता है। दोनों साथ-साथ बड़े हुए। नांग त्रुत को एक इतना बड़ा घर बनाने के लिए लकड़ियां लाने के लिए जंगल ले जाता, जिसमें त्रुत कम से कम दस कदम चल सके। त्रुत युद्धरत सैनिकों के लिए हथियार और चावल ढोने के लिए भी नांग के पिता के पीछे-पीछे जाता। उसी की मदद के कारण बहुतेरे लोग त्रुत को पूजने आते। नहीं यह कोई सामान्य पूजा उसके सुस्वास्थ्य के लिए नहीं बल्कि सैनिकों के प्रति उसकी सेवाओं के लिए उसे पदक प्रदान करने के लिए थी। नांग का कहना था कि त्रुत को चूंकि इन सब का पता नहीं था, इसलिए त्रुत वही करता जो नांग या उसके पिता उसे करने को कहते। पदक घर में सजावट के लिए टांग दिया जाता, त्रुत तो गन्ने की अधिक झाड़ियों और केलों से ही खुश था। उसे अनुमति थी कि अपनी पत्नी के साथ वह इनका भक्षण कर सके।

इस प्रकार कितने मौसम बीत गए किसी को पता नहीं। वाइ त्लो परिवार और खास तौर पर वाइ नांग से त्रुत को इतना प्यार मिला कि उसे अब अपने माता-पिता की याद उतना नहीं सताती थी। नांग त्रुत से बहुत प्यार करता। वह हमेशा उसकी घास में कुछ नमक मिला देता ताकिउसे भोजन रुचिकर लगे।

नांग का इसी बीच विवाह हो गया तो त्रुत ने बियात से विवाह कर लिया। दरअसल त्रुत के बियात से विवाह में नांग ने ही मदद की थी क्योंकि उसने लक्ष्य किया था कि त्रुत और बियात मैदान में अक्सर साथ रहते थे। त्रुत के पसीने की गंध को बियात दूर से ही पहचान लेती थी। बियात दरअसल बहुत अधिक सुंदर थी। जब वह हंसती तो उसके हाथी दांत चमक उठते। कुछ विशिष्ट फूलों की तरह उसके कान के पीछे की ओर कुछ हरी बिंदियां थीं, जो बड़ी खूबसूरत लगती थीं। उस मार्ग के महीने में दिअम बांग (वियतनाम के केंद्रीय पहाड़ी इलाकों में पाये जाने वाले फूल) के गुलाबी फूल नदी के किनारे खिले हुए थे। हालांकि हाथी एक ही स्थान पर साथ-साथ नहीं नहाते किंतु त्रुत और बियात तो एक दूसरे से अलग रह ही नहीं सकते थे। वे अपनी प्रेम केलि में हांफ रहे थे,

चिंघाड़ रहे थे, पास की बांस की छोटी झाड़ियों को पैरों तले कुचल रहे थे...

अकस्मात् नांग को पता चला कि बियात गर्भवती है तो दोनों परिवारों ने त्रुत और बियात के विवाहोत्सव का आयोजन किया। कई दिनों तक गांव में आनन्दोत्सव मनाया गया। कहने के लिए दंडस्वरूप एक बत्तख और एक कुत्ता था दुर्भाग्य से छुटकारे के लिए। बत्तख और कुत्ता कन्या पक्ष की ओर से गांव वालों के लिए भेंटस्वरूप थे। लोगों को आम तौर पर शिशु हाथी रखना पसंद नहीं था क्योंकि उन्हें प्रशिक्षित करना अत्यंत कठिन काम था। इसलिए बियात के शिशु को बाद में लांग बियान पर्वत के लोगों को बेच दिया गया। विवाहोपरांत त्रुत और बियात अपने-अपने मालिकों के साथ अलग-अलग रहने लगे। परन्तु त्रोंग लाआइ (भंटे का पौधा) के प्रस्फुटन के मौसम में जब हवा में त्रुत के पसीने की गंध उड़ कर आती तो त्रुत और बियात आपस में मिलते और उनके इस मिलन के लिए उनके मालिकों को कोई जुर्माना नहीं देना पड़ता।

हाल के वर्षों में गांव वैसा नहीं रहा जैसा अतीत में हुआ करता था। हर साल एक बार, फूलों के खिलने के मौसम में गांव में हाथियों की दौड़ का एक उत्सव होता था। उस वक्त बाहर के इतने सारे लोग गांव में आते थे, जितने कि जंगल में वृक्ष थे। इन दौड़ों में त्रुत जीतने की जी जान से कोशिश करता, और वह भी नांग और उसके पिता की खातिर, परन्तु यह दौड़ किसी रस्साकसी या फुटबॉल के खेल जैसी होती। तथापि शिशु-हाथियों का जंगल में शिकार करने वाले किसी जत्थे का नेतृत्व त्रुत ने कभी नहीं किया। धीरे-धीरे जंगल इतना छोटा हो गया था कि अब त्रुत पहले की तरह जंगल के चरागाह क्षेत्र में अकेला नहीं होता था। उसे बांस की झाड़ियों से बांध दिया गया। उस वक्त बियात वहां थी। फूलों के खिलने के कई मौसम बीत गए थे, पर उन्हें आपस में मिलने का समय ही नहीं मिला था। जंगल में जंगली पौधों की गंध न मिलती तो त्रुत अपना सिर और सूंड़ उठा कर अपना तनाव दूर करने के लिए चिंघाड़ता, और जंगल में मुक्त भ्रमण तो दूर उसे आगंतुकों को नदी व झील की सैर कराते पांच-छः हाथी नज़र आते। त्रुत हमेशा झील को पार करते जत्थे का नेतृत्व करता और यात्रियों की सुरक्षा के मद्देनज़र झील की गहराई का अंदाज अपनी सूंड़ डुबा कर लगा लेता था। पहले जत्थे का नेतृत्व हमेशा माता हथिनी किया करती थी। अब किंतु सब उल्टा

हो गया था। बियात अब वाइ धाम के साथ बीच में थी, पर काफी पीछे।

कभी-कभी त्रुत का सिर गर्मा जाता और पूरा शरीर हिल उठता, खास कर तब जब बियात को वहां खड़े देखता हवा में हिलते पीले की-फूलों के करीब, किन्तु वह उसकी ओर उसके पास न जा पाता। महावत उसकी गर्दन पर अंकुश चुभा देता, तो दर्द से बचने के लिए उसे उसका निर्देश मानना पड़ता। धीरे-धीरे वह इस उबाऊ काम का आदी हो गया। यह तो उसका अपने महावत के प्रति प्रेम था जो उसे कोई भी गड़बड़ी करने से रोकता था, वर्ना वह भी त्रोंग ना के वाइ थिन्ह की तरह अपने महावत को मार डालता, जो उसके और उसकी पत्नी के मिलन में रोड़े अटका रहा था। बाद में उसकी करतूत के कारण दंडस्वरूप उसे गोली मार दी गई थी।

त्रुत का प्रिय नांग अब ऐ-थोम का दादा बन गया था और बहुत बूढ़ा हो चुका था। अब वह स्वस्थ नहीं रहता था। दिन-रात झुकी कमर लिये, घुटनों को मोड़े आग के पास बैठा हुक्का गुड़गुड़ाता रहता। उसका पोता वाइ थोम किंतु अत्यंत धनलोलुप था। वह एक ऐसा महावत था, जो हाथियों को अपने अधिकार में लाने के लिए उन्हें हांकने के लिए, उन पर अंकुश की चोट करता था। उसे तो अधिक से अधिक लोगों को हाथी की पीठ पर बैठा कर सैर कराना था ताकि उसे अधिक से अधिक आमदनी हो सके। त्रुत अब मनुष्यों के मानदंड के अनुसार लगभग सौ साल का हो गया था। स्वास्थ्य अब पहले की तरह उसका साथ नहीं देता था। वह थक जाता था, किंतु फिर भी वह वाइ थोम को संतुष्ट करने की यथासाध्य कोशिश करता।

हाल ही में कुछ मनुष्य, जो चेहरों से अमित्रवत लग रहे थे, आये। वे रात के वक्त जंगल से लकड़ियां ढो कर लाने के लिए हाथियों के झुण्ड को किराए पर लेना चाहते थे। से थोम किंतु राजी नहीं हुआ और बोला, ''त्रुत अब मेरे ही समान बूढ़ा हो गया है, रात के वक्त उसे विश्राम चाहिए।'' परन्तु अपने दादा की बात अनसुनी करते हुए वाइ थोमने उन्हें डाटा और कहा, ''आप को कुछ नहीं पता, आप बूढ़े हो गए हैं, पर मुझे धन चाहिए। मुझे मोटरबाइक खरीदने के लिए पैसे चाहिए।'' यह सोच कर कि रात में हाथियों के इस्तेमाल से अतिरिक्त आमदनी हो सकती है, उसकी आंखें चमक उठीं। किंतु उसके विपरीत बूढ़े दादा

की आंखों से आंसू छलक पड़े, जिन्हें देख कर त्रुत को कष्ट हुआ। वह चाहता तो वाइ थोम पर अपनी सूंड़ से प्रहार कर सकता था, किंतु उसने यह सोच कर ऐसा नहीं किया क्योंकि तब ऐ-थोम को और कष्ट होता।

अब हाथियों का झुण्ड दिन में पर्यटकों को सैर कराता और रात को जंगल से लकड़ी के बड़े-बड़े कुंदे ढो कर लाता। लोग उन कुंदों को अपने गंतव्य के लिए नदी में बहा देते। जंगल काफी दूर था। हाथी दोपहर बाद अपनी यात्रा शुरू करते तो आधी रात तक जंगल पहुंचते। महावत अंकुश गोद-गोद कर हाथियों को शीघ्रातिशीघ्र जंगल पहुंचने का संकेत करते। और लकड़ियां इकट्ठा कर उनके लौटते-लौटते पौ-फटने लगती और आसमान की रंगत बदलने लगती। घर लौट कर सूर्य के उदय होने तक हाथी कुछ विश्राम करते, फिर केलों और गन्ने का नाश्ता करते। उसके बाद त्रुत के नेतृत्व में हाथियों का जत्था फिर निकल पड़ता सैलानियों को सैर कराने झील के किनारे...।

आज की सांझ त्रुत बुरी तरह थका हुआ था। उसे लग रहा था जैसे पैर उसके शरीर में थे ही नहीं। वह खड़ा तक नहीं हो पा रहा था, फिर भी वह चाहता था कि सूंड़ से अपनी पत्नी बियात को छू पाए, उसकी नीली त्वचा को सहला पाए। वह सोच रहा था, काश वह पहले की तरह अपनी पत्नी के साथ जंगल में दौड़ लगा पाता, नदी के पानी में जल-क्रीड़ा कर पाता, प्रेम से युवा वृक्षों को ठीक वैसे ही सहला पाता जैसा कि वे पहले आपस में एक-दूसरे से प्यार करते वक्त करते थे।

त्रुत सारा दिन झील के पास हाथियों का नेतृत्व करते हुए जाने का प्रयास करता रहा ताकि वह बियात तक पहुंच सके, किंतु उसकी सारी चेष्टा व्यर्थ गई। आलस्य में बांस की झाड़ियों की टेक लगाए गीली पत्तियों को अपने मुंह में रख कर बियात के आने की प्रतीक्षा करता रहा।

फिर धीरे-धीरे उठ कर उसने कोशिश की कि वह अपनी पत्नी के पैरों के निशान पर ही अपने पैर टिका कर साध मिटा ले। वह बियात के पदचिन्ह पहचानता था। उसके बायें पैर का एक नाखून टूटा हुआ था, इसलिए पैरों के निशान पहचानना आसान था। किंतु वाइ थोम को यह मंजूर नहीं था। सैलानियों के दो-तीन जत्थे अभी भी हाथी की पीठ पर झील का चक्कर लगाने के लिए

अपनी बारी का इंतजार कर रहे थे। त्रुत पर जब थोम की नज़र पड़ी तो उसने पीठ पर सैलानियों के एक जत्थे को झील का चक्कर लगाने के लिए त्रुत की गर्दन पर कुछ जोर से अंकुश चुभाया। दर्द से त्रुत कराह उठा। लड़खड़ाते हुए उसने एक धीमा कदम सामने की ओर रखा।

त्रुत ने ऊपर आसमान की ओर देखते हुए चारों ओर निगाह दौड़ाई, पर उसे अपनी पत्नी बियात कहीं दिखाई नहीं दी। त्रुत चुपचाप नदी की ओर दौड़ा जिसके करीब ही एक छोटा सा किंतु गहरा तालाब था, जिसमें नीचे की ओर कई मगरमच्छ थे। त्रुत ने वहीं अपनी देह त्यागने का निर्णय लिया ताकि उसे एक साथ धरती माता और जल की गोद प्राप्त हो।...

... गांव अब काफी पीछे छूट चुका था। त्रुत के पैर धीमे-धीमे उठ रहे थे। धीमे व भारी कदमों से बढ़ा जा रहा था।... दूर कहीं बहुत दूर से उसे बियात का दर्द भरा चीत्कार सुनाई दिया।

धीरे-धीरे सांझ का धुंधलका फैल रहा था चारों ओर।

(अनुवाद : प्रेम कपूर)

बिलाव-भूत

फोंग दिएप

फोंग दिएप वियतनाम की एक प्रतिष्ठित कथाकार हैं, जिनका जन्म 1976 में हुआ था, तथा जिनकी 25 पुस्तकें प्रकाशित हो चुकी हैं। युद्धोत्तर स्त्रियों के बारे में लिखी आपकी लघुकथाओं के लिए मिलिटरी लिटरेरी मैगजीन द्वारा आपको पुरस्कृत भी किया जा चुका है।

बच्चों के होठों की मुस्कुराहट तत्काल गुम हो गई जैसे ही उन्होंने सुना कि उनके पिताजी ने उन्हें फौरन बुलाया है। दो-दो व्हीलचेयर्स एक के बाद एक संकरे अंधियारे गलियारे से होती हुई मुख्य द्वार की ओर दौड़ीं।

''क्या हुआ होगा? पिताजी आज रोज से जल्दी घर आ गए?''

''घंटी की आवाज से लगता है, गुस्से में हैं।''

''क्या तुम ...''

स्टोर हाउस के मोड़ पर बूढ़ा बिलाव कराह उठा। दोनों व्हीलचेयर बगल वाले कमरे की ओर मुड़ गईं। असामान्य रूप से सारी बत्तियां जल रही थीं, जिनसे फर्श चमचमा रहा था। दरवाजा पूरा खुला था। पिताजी के बड़े जूतों के बगल में

एक जोड़ी छोटी चप्पलें भी पड़ी थीं। जिसकी चप्पलें थीं, उसने शायद असावधानी में उन्हें उतारा था क्योंकि पैरपोश अपने स्थान से कुछ खिसका हुआ था।

''तुम्हें क्या लगता है, क्या हमें अंदर जाना चाहिए? काफी देर हो चुकी है...''

घंटी फिर बज उठी, इस बार कुछ और तीखेपन से।

दोनों बच्चों ने लड़खड़ाते हुए व्हीलचेयरों को दरवाजे की ओर धकेला। कमरे के बीचोंबीच एक महिला सीधी खड़ी थी, बच्चों की प्रतीक्षा में। उसके चेहरे पर एक ठंडापन और उदासी थी। कमरे की तेज़ नियोन-लाइट में उसकी रंगत कुछ फीकी सी पड़ गई थी।

पिताजी चुपचाप एक हत्थेवाली कुर्सी पर बैठे थे। कॉफी-टेबल पर पड़ा ऐशट्रे सिगरेट के टोटों से भरा पड़ा था।

''अब से मिस बोइ तुम लोगों को पढ़ाएंगी'', कुछ देर चुप रह कर पिताजी ने उनकी ओर देखते हुए सख्ती से कहा।

''किसी को भी उनके मुंह पर जवाब देने की अनुमति नहीं है। आया समझ में ? अब जाओ अपने कमरे में।''

महिला ने थकन भरी आवाज में उन्हें 'गुडबाय'- कहा। उसके हाथ लम्बे और उंगलियां पतली-पतली थीं। ''हम कल सुबह फिर मिलेंगे'', उसने कहा।

दोनों व्हीलचेयर्स फिर से लम्बे व संकरे गलियारे की ओर मुड़ गईं। बूढ़ा बिलाव अभी भी स्टोरहाउस के मोड़ पर दो अचल शहतीरों के पास बैठा था। हवा तेज चल रही थी। बगीचे में वृक्षों के झुरमुट डोल रहे थे।

''भाई, मुझे डर लग रहा है।''

''पिताजी कल सुबह लम्बी 'बिजनेस ट्रिप' पर निकल जाएंगे।''

''कितने सारे उपहार भी तो लाते हैं।''

''पर पिताजी हम से कभी बातें नहीं करते।''

''वे व्यस्त रहते हैं। घर तो वे आराम करने आते हैं।''

''मुझे उनसे सहानुभूति होती है। हमारी देखभाल करते-करते उनके पास थकावट का समय ही कहां बचता है ?''

सुबह सात बजे अलार्म की घंटी जोरों से बजी तो बच्चे उठे और शीघ्रतापूर्वक अपने कपड़े बदलने दौड़े। व्हीलचेयरों को उन्होंने बिस्तर के बगल में रख दिया। मार्बल के फर्श पर उन्हें मिस बोइ की चप्पलों की आवाज सुनाई दी और फिर उनके कमरे का दरवाजा फौरन खुल गया। रात को वे दरवाजा भीतर से बंद करना भूल गए थे।

दिन के उजाले में मिस बोई और भी दुबली-पतली तथा बीमार सी लग रही थीं। उनकी मोटी पोशाक उनके सींकिया बदन पर चिपकी हुई सी लग रही थी। उनकी उम्र की औरतें आम तौर पर इस तरह के कपड़े नहीं पहनतीं।

''गुड मॉर्निंग मिस बोइ'', बच्चों ने झिझकते हुए उनका अभिवादन किया।

मिस बोइ ने कोई उत्तर नहीं दिया। सीधे बिस्तर तक जा कर उन्होंने अस्त-व्यस्त चादर और लिहाफ को ठीक कर मसहरी को तहाया।

लड़की ने भाई को व्हीलचेयर दरवाजे की ओर ले जाते देखा तो एक गहरी सांस लेते हुए मिस बोई से पूछा, ''आपको रात में नींद अच्छे से आई मिस बोइ?''

''तुम किधर जा रहे हो?'' मिस बोइ फौरन लड़के की ओर घूमीं और तीखे स्वर में पूछा।

''मैं बगीचे में जा रहा हूं।''

''नहीं, पहले हाथ-मुंह धोओ और टेबल पर बैठकर नाश्ता करो। फिर हम पढ़ने बैठेंगे'', मिस बोइ ने कहा। फिर लड़की की ओर देखते हुए पूछा ''तुम क्या कर रही हो?''

मिस बोइ ने दोनों व्हीलचेयर्स को कमरे से बाहर कर दरवाजा बंद कर दिया। फिर सब चुपचाप नाश्ता करने लगे। मिस बोइ ने बिना कोई आवाज़ किए जल्दी-जल्दी नाश्ता खत्म किया। बच्चे धीरे-धीरे चबा कर बेमन से नाश्ता कर रहे थे। मिस बोइ को दस मिनट उनका नाश्ता खत्म होने की प्रतीक्षा करनी पड़ी।

''ये सब पोषक तत्व हैं, जिनकी स्वस्थ शरीर को आवश्यकता होती है'', टेबल साफ करते-करते मिस बोइ बोलीं फिर लड़की के नाश्ते की प्लेट एक तिहाइ भरी देख कर पूछा, ''तुमने इतना नाश्ता छोड़ क्यों दिया?''

''यह केट के लिए है मिस।''

''केट उस बूढ़े पागल बिलाव का नाम है'', भाई ने मुंह साफ करते हुए बताया।

''बूढ़ा-पागल बिलाव?'' मिस बोइ बुदबुदाई।

''हां, हां वही। बहुत बूढ़ा बिलाव है, जिसके रोयें यहां-वहां झड़ते रहते हैं। पर दूसरी बिल्लियों की तरह वह यहां से जाता ही नहीं।''

मिस बोइ बिना कुछ बोले चुपचाप कुर्सी पर बैठ गईं। बच्चे डाइनिंग टेबल से उठ कर बगल वाले कमरे में चले गये, जहां कॉपियां-किताबें यहां-वहां बिखरी पड़ी थीं और खिड़की के पास बिलाव के कुछ रोयें पड़े थे।

चेहरे पर सख्ती लाते हुए मिस बोइ ने बच्चों को नया पाठ पढ़ाना शुरू किया।

''बिलाव-भूत आम तौर पर आधी रात को आ कर चीखते हैं। वे समूह में चलते हैं और बहुत करुण स्वर में एक-दूसरे को पुकारते हैं...''

लड़की ने कुछ बेचैनी से भाई की ओर देखा, किंतु बिना एक शब्द भी बोले वे चुपचाप सुनते रहे।...

जब पाठ समाप्त हुआ तो मिस बोइ बेहोश सी हो गईं, उनका चेहरा फीका पड़ गया।

भोजन के वक्त बिलाव नहीं आया। उसके रोयें घर में हर जगह बिखरे थे।

बच्चों को देर रात तक जगने की मनाही थी। शाम को पढ़ने के बाद उन्हें अपने कमरे में जा कर, बत्ती बंद कर सोना पड़ा। पर लड़की कुछ बेचैन थी।

''तुम्हें क्या लगता है, वह मर जाएगा?'' उसने भाई से पूछा।

''कौन? वो बदबूदार बिलाव केट? हां, बूढ़ा तो बहुत है।''

''नहीं, मेरे कहने का यह मतलब नहीं था। कई दिनों से उसे किसी ने कुछ खिलाया ही नहीं। वह तो किसी को नुकसान भी नहीं पहुंचाता।''

''यदि तुम ऐसा कहोगी तो मिस बोइ तुम्हें बिलाव-भूतों की कहानियां सुनाती रहेंगी'', भाई ने बहन से कहा, ''मिस बोइ बिलाव-भूतों की बहुत सारी कहानियां जानती हैं।''

''हां, वह मर सकता है।''

पर दरअसल वह मरा नहीं था क्योंकि भाई जब आधी रात को उठा तो स्टोर

हाउस के पिछवाड़े से उसे उसकी कराहट सुनाई दी थी। उसने बहन को जगाने की कोशिश की, पर वह पेट दर्द के कारण पसीने में नहाई थी।

गलियारे में अंधेरा था। बिलाव की आवाज मद्धिम होती जा रही थी। भाई धीरे से बाहर आया। स्टोरहाउस के सामने मिस बोइ का कमरा रोशनी से जगमगा रहा था, मानो कुछ हुआ ही न हो। गहरी सांस लेते हुए उसने पुकारा, ''मिस बोइ! मिस बोइ!''

अब वह मिस बोइ के कमरे के सामने खड़ा था। तेज हवा में मिस बोइ के बिस्तर की चादर फड़फड़ा रही थी। कमरे में कोई भी नहीं था।

घर के पिछवाड़े के बगीचे की मिट्टी और पत्थरों से टकरा कर पुकार की गूंज लौट आई और फिर सन्नाटा हो गया। उसने शीघ्रातिशीघ्र लौटने की कोशिश की परंतु वह बहुत थका हुआ महसूस कर रहा था। रात के सन्नाटे में व्हीलचेयर के पहियों की मार्बल के फर्श पर घिसटने की आवाज से उसे डर लग रहा था। जब वह कमरे में लौटा तो देखा कि बहन के मुंह से लार बह रही थी। उसने बहन को व्हीलचेयर पर बैठाया और चेयर को ध्केलता हुआ बगीचे में ले आया।

बच्चों के लिए जब महिला ने दरवाजा खोला तो वह डरी हुई थी। घर के भीतर लोगों के वार्तालाप की आवाज़ आ रही थी, दरवाजे की ओर दौड़ते कदमों की आवाज़ आ रही थी। लड़की को बिस्तर पर लेटा दिया गया। उसके इर्दगिर्द कई लोग थे। लड़के की व्हीलचेयर एक किनारे पड़ी थी। उसके चेहरे पर मच्छर मंडरा रहे थे, किंतु वह बेखबर सा सो रहा था क्योंकि वह बहुत थका हुआ था।

दोपहर के वक्त तीन पुरुष तथा एक अत्यंत सुंदरी स्त्री मिस बोइ से मिलने आये और एक जीप, जिसका इंजन चक्की की तरह घनघना रहा था, से लौट गये।

कामवाली स्त्री बा... बच्चों का नाश्ता बनाने आती रही। जब वह सब्जी लेने बगीचे में गई तो उसने देखा कि जमीन का कुछ हिस्सा कुचला हुआ था। बच्चे उस वक्त अपने कमरे में पढ़ रहे थे, जब भोजन की घंटी बजी।

इस बीच पिताजी अपनी लम्बी व्यावसायिक यात्रा से लौट आये थे। उनके मरियल से चेहरे की रंगत कुछ काली पड़ गई थी। ''आखिर हुआ क्या था?'' उन्होंने पूछा।

''मुझे कुछ नहीं पता पिताजी। पर हां, मैंने स्टोरहाउस के पिछवाड़े बिलाव

की कराह सुनी थी।''

उन्होंने गहरी सांस ली और बोले, ''पागल बिलावों की कहानियां तो बहुत सुनी हैं कि वे लोगों को काट खाते हैं और लोग मर जाते हैं। मरने वालों में मिस बोइ का बच्चा भी था।''

बच्चे चुपचाप सुन रहे थे। अचानक लड़की बोली, ''पिताजी हमें मिस बोइ चाहिए।''

पिताजी उठ खड़े हुए, वे थके से लग रहे थे। बोले, ''बच्चो! अपने कमरे में जाओ। कल से तुम लोग स्कूल जाओगे।''

दोनों बच्चों ने अपनी व्हीलचेयरें अंधेरे कोने की ओर खिसका दीं।

''भाई, केट किंतु पागल नहीं था।''

''पर हम तो ऐसा ही कहते रहे।''

नये स्कूल के नये सत्र के लिए बच्चों को कुछ जल्दी उठना पड़ता।

लिविंग रूम का दरवाज़ा अभी भी बंद था। पैरपोश मुड़ा-तुड़ा गलियारे के एक कोने में पड़ा था।

स्कूल के नज़दीक हमेशा एक स्त्री खड़ी नज़र आती, जिसके दुबले-पतले शरीर पर मोटी सी पोशाक रहती। वह उन्हें गुजरता हुआ देखने को खड़ी रह कर प्रतीक्षा करती और फिर चली जाती।

(अनुवाद : प्रेम कपूर)

जंग पर जाने के दिन

नुएन की नोक

1949 में जन्मी नुएन थी नोक को उनकी अत्यंत चर्चित कथा 'सेंड यू माई लालाबाई' के लिए वियतनाम लेखक संघ तथा सुरक्षा मंत्रालय के साहित्य पुरस्कार 2015 से पुरस्कृत किया जा चुका है।

मेरे छोटे भाई को डर था कि मां चिंतित हो जाएगी, इसलिए उसने केवल मुझे चुपके से बताया कि उसने स्वेच्छा से जंग में जाने का निर्णय लिया है। उस वक्त तो मुझे अपने भाई की बात पर यकीन ही नहीं हुआ क्योंकि उसकी हाई-स्कूल की परीक्षा को एक महीने से भी कम समय बचा था, फिर उसे युनिवर्सिटी की परीक्षा देनी थी। यदि उसकी बात सच भी हो, तो मुझे विश्वास था कि मेरे भाई को जंग के लिए स्वीकार ही नहीं किया जाएगा।

उस वक्त जंग के मैदान में घमासान युद्ध हो रहा था, और मेरे भाई की उम्र मात्र सत्रह वर्ष थी। उसका चेहरा अपरिपक्व, अंग-प्रत्यंग कमजोर और दाढ़ी'मूंछ तक नहीं आई थी। मैंने कहा ''जब तू हमारे परिवार द्वारा हर महीने खरीदा गया पंद्रह किलो चावल उठा कर सड़क पर दौड़ पाएगा तब मैं तुझे सैनिक मानूंगी।

जंग में दुश्मन का सामना करना बड़ी गम्भीर बात है, कोई मज़ाक नहीं।'' वह हंस दिया। मेरी नज़रों में वह एक अपरिपक्क व्यक्ति की मुस्कान थी।

दोपहर से कुछ पहले यह समाचार मेरी मां को मिला। जब वह काम के बाद घर लौटी तो सीधे न तो रसोई में गई और न ही घर के काम-काज में लगी। आ कर सीढ़ियों पर बैठ गई। उसकी आंखों में उदासी थी, और एक टक जाने कहां देख रही थी। मां को उस अवस्था में काफी देर तक बैठे देख कर मुझसे रहा नहीं गया और मैंने कहा, ''मुझे पता चल चुका है मां।''

''हां, मैं जानती हूँ।'' मां उसी अवस्था में बैठी रही। अपनी बेटी से वह इस प्रकार बात कर रही थी मानो दूर बैठे किसी व्यक्ति से बात कर रही हो।

मां की आवाज़ पिछली रात की आंधी में फड़फड़ाते केले के पत्तों सी थी। मैं आहिस्ता से मां के बगल में जा कर बैठ गई और माथे पर बिखरे उसके सफेद बालों को सहला कर धीरे से पीछे कर दिया। मैं मां को और स्वयं को भी आश्वस्त करते हुए कुछ कहना चाहती थी, पर रुक गई।

एक लम्बी चुप्पी के बाद धीमे स्वर में मां ने कहा, ''मुझे नहीं लगता कि तेरे भाई में उतनी ऊर्जा है। मैं उसका निर्णय बदल तो नहीं सकती इसलिए चिंतित हूँ क्योंकि उसके पैर अभी उतने सख्त नहीं कि घनघोर बमबारी में कठोर पत्थरों पर चल सकें।''

आम तौर पर मां के चेहरे पर मुस्कुराहट रहती। पर आज मेरे भाई की शारीरिक अवस्था देख कर उसके चेहरे पर वेदना की छाप थी। मैं मन ही मन चाह रही थी कि मेरे भाई का निर्वाचन ही न हो, और उसे छांट दिया जाए। किंतु ऐसा होना तो दूर उसका नाम तो स्वयंसेवकों की पहली सूची में ही था।

मेरे स्कूल की युवा-यूनियन ने लोगों को जल-जमाव से बचाने के लिए धान-कटाई का कार्यक्रम बनाया जिसमें घर आने से कुछ दिन पूर्व मैंने हिस्सा लिया था। उस वक्त मैंने जब चारों ओर देखा था तो मुझे भाई दिखाई नहीं दिया था। मुझे केवल मां दिखाई दी पीठ के सहारे चावल रखने वाले लोहे के बक्से में बैठी हुई। उस खाली बक्से से मां के हाथों द्वारा खुरच कर साफ करने की आवाज़ आ रही थी। (बाद में उस क्षण की याद आते ही मन भारी हो उठता)।

मैने मां को हाथों में चावल का एक पात्र लिये हुए उदास चेहरे से घर के

बाहर आते हुए देखा। मेरी ओर देख कर उसने मानो खुद को दोष देते हुए कहा, ''तेरा भाई कल जा रहा है। मैं उसे पूरा खाना देना चाहती थी पर घर में तो बस इतने से ही चावल हैं।''

मैंने एक लम्बी सांस खींची और कहा, ''मां, यह मेरी ग़लती है। चावल मैंने निकाले थे। बाद में उन्हें मुझे पूरा कर रखना चाहिए था ताकि जरूरत के वक्त काम आ सके।''

अचानक मुझे याद आया, मेरे सबसे अच्छे मित्र थाओ के परिवार ने हाल ही में चावल खरीदे थे। मैंने कहा, ''मां, मैं थाओ के घर से चावल उधार ले आती हूँ।''

मां ने हल्के से मुस्कुरा कर अनुमति दे दी।

मेरा सबसे छोटा भाई भी अपने बड़े भाई के साथ विदाई से पहले पड़ोसियों से मिलने चला गया। जब तक वे दोनों लौटे तब तक चावल आ चुका था। उस दिन मेरे परिवार का भोजन किसी औपचारिक भोज से कम न था। सूअर की पसलियों और सूखे प्याज के साथ, एक प्लेट उबले हुए मीठे आलुओं के साथ ही थे एक प्लेट तले हुए अंडे। भूरी मुर्गी ने एक दर्जन अंडे दिये थे। कोई और वक्त होता तो मां उनकी साज-संभाल करती ताकि उनमें से चूजे निकलते। चूजों को बड़ा करने पर खाद्यान्न की बचत हो जाती। पर कल तो मां का बेटा जंग पर जा रहा है इसलिए बचत भूल कर मां ने मुर्गी और अंडे पका लिये थे।

इस खास अवसर पर मेरे दोनों भाई कुछ सयाने हो गए थे। आम तौर पर वे दिन भर आपस में झगड़ते रहते और मुझे निर्णायक बनना पड़ता, पर उस दिन वे दोनों एक-दूसरे से लगभग चिपके हुए थे। छोटा भाई बड़े भाई को उठा-उठा कर भोजन दे रहा था। अचानक मैं घूमी तो देखा कि मां तो कुछ खा ही नहीं रही थी। चुपचाप अपने बेटों को निहार रही थी, उसकी आंखों में आंसू थे।

मां चुपचाप पिताजी की वेदी के सामने प्रार्थना कर रही थी। अस्वाभाविक रूप से शांत थी मां। हालांकि घर से जा रहे बेटे की खुशी के लिए वह मुस्कुरा रही थी। पर तीनों बच्चों को मां के व्यवहार का असंतुलन महसूस हो रहा था।

मेरा भाई मां से गले मिलने को आगे बढ़ा। वह सचमुच एक पुरुष की आवाज में बोलने का प्रयास कर रहा था, ''उदास मत हो मां! जंग के मैदान में अगर

मुझे खबर मिली कि तुम बीमार हो, तो मैं बंदूक कैसे उठा पाऊँगा...'' क्षण भर को रुक कर उसने आगे कहा, ''आशा करता हूँ कि परिवार के सबसे छोटे सदस्य की जंग में जाने की नौबत ही न आए।''

मेरी भी आंखें भर आईं। फौरन, मां की नज़र पड़ने से पहले ही मैंने अपनी आंखें घुमा लीं।

भोर का वक्त था। क्षितिज सूर्य की रोशनी से चमक रहा था। मां दौड़ती हुई मेरे पास आई और मेरे हाथों में मांस रहित नूडल्स रखते हुए बोली, ''आज सुबह उसने कुछ नहीं खाया। जहां वे इकट्ठा होंगे, वहां जा और उसे खिला कर आ।'' ''ठीक है'' कहती हुई मैं मां की रोती आंखों से दूर जाती रही।

फिनिक्स के वृक्षों पर इस बार समय से पहले ही फूल खिल उठे थे। जंग में जा रहे लड़कों की आंखें उन लाल फूलों पर टिकी थीं। मैं भाई के साथ कदम मिला कर चल रही थी, पर मुझे लग रहा था जैसे मैं उससे कदम दर कदम दूर होती जा रही थी। मैंने स्वयं से एक मौन प्रश्न किया - ''जाने कब खत्म होगी यह जंग? जाने कब लौटेगा मेरा प्रिय भाई?

हरे पत्तों से कैमोफ्लाज की गई गाड़ियों में बैठे सभी कच्ची उम्र के लड़के मुझे अपने भाई सरीखे लग रहे थे।

युवा रंगरूटों से भरी गाड़ियां धीरे-धीरे चल पड़ीं। मैं देखती रही हवा में हिलते अपने भाई के हाथ जो मुझसे दूर होते जा रहे थे। केवल मैं खड़ी रही उम्मीद के सपने लिये।

(अनुवाद : प्रेम कपूर)

भारतीय कविताएँ

अभी तक रो रहा है

नवल

हिंदी के वरिष्ठ कवि नवल का अभी हाल ही में निधन हुआ। आपके लगभग आठ काव्य संकलन प्रकाशित हो चुके हैं। आप अपनी प्रेम कविताओं के लिए विख्यात हैं। जीवन पर्यंत आप स्वयं ख्याति से वचते रहे और दूसरों को प्रकाश में लाते रहे। फिर भी अपने पाठकों में बे अत्यंत प्रिय रहे।

अभी तक रो रहा है
एक पांच साल का बच्चा
जिसको नहीं मिल रहा है उसका घर।

नारेबाज़ी करते हुए लोग
लगा रहे हैं आग
घरों से निकल रही हैं चीखें
बदहवासी में भाग रहे हैं लोग
अफरा-तफरी मची है
और वह बच्चा रोते-रोते
अपना घर ढूंढ रहा है।

सत्तर साल पूर्व यही बच्चा
कभी लाहौर की सड़क पर था
कभी अमृतसर की सड़क पर
कभी जेहलम-जगाधरी
कभी दिल्ली की सड़क पर
और छप्पन साल पहले
कभी कलकत्ता की सड़क पर
ढूंढ रहा था अपना घर
इसी तरह की मार-काट और आगज़नी में।

मरने वालों का कोई ईश्वर नहीं था
और जिन्होंने की थी मार-काट
उन सबके ईश्वर सुरक्षित थे

अपने-अपने किलों में
उनके हुक्मरानों की तरह।
लेकिन उस बच्चे का
कोई ईश्वर भी तो नहीं था
ना पहले
ना अब।

वही बच्चा
अब ईश्वर की तलाश में है
जिसने यह पूरी दुनिया बनाई
और लोगों ने जिसके नाम पर
खोल ली हैं अपनी अलग-अलग दूकानें।

और व्यापार में तो
आम बात है
कट-थ्रोट कॉम्पिटीशन।

एक-दूसरे का
गला काटेंगे नहीं
तो दूकान चलेगी कैसे ?
वर्चस्व से बड़ा
कोई रोग नहीं है
इस दुनिया में।

नहीं होगा अध:पतन

अमिताभ चक्रवर्ती

बांग्ला के सुपरिचित कवि अमिताभ चक्रवर्ती एक सेवानिवृत्त बैंकर होने के साथ वरिष्ठ सामाजिक, सांस्कृतिक कार्यकर्त्ता भी हैं तथा विभिन्न सामाजिक-सांस्कृतिक संस्थाओं से जुड़े हैं। आपकी कविताओं के चार संकलन प्रकाशित हो चुके हैं।

मनश्चेतना के गीत
आज जुटाएं भरोसा और विश्वास सभी में
प्राणों में भर कर थोड़ा-सा प्यार-दुलार
सजीव कर दें झुलसती विषाक्त सांसों को
आतंक को कहीं गाड़ कर
मुक्त मन से स्वच्छ मनुष्य
स्वयं को करे जाहिर
झाड़ कर सारी उम्मीदों को
ऊपर से नीचे तक खुला-व्यक्त हो
मन के सारे बांध तोड़ता उल्लास।

पृथ्वी अभी गुज़र रही है गर्भ यातना से
हमारी पालनहार धरती अभी है भयंकर अस्थिर
सृष्टि के प्रथम दिन से
हर शिक्षा ग्रहण कर
उसने दमन किया है अनेक मारक वायरसों का
मानो अतीत की वही धारा
अब कभी नहीं बदलेगी
फिर से हंसेंगे — मनुष्य, फूल, धरती
अब कभी नहीं होगा अध:पतन।

(अनुवाद : प्रेम कपूर)

हैंगर में टंगा वस्त्र

नमिता चौधरी

जन्म: 1949, सुप्रसिद्ध कवयित्री। मूल लेखन बांग्ला में। 25 कविता संग्रह प्रकाशित। 'नंदिमुख' पत्रिका का संपादन। विभिन्न सम्मान एवं पुरस्कारों से सम्मानित।

एक हैंगर पर किसी हुक से
मुझे टांग दिया गया हो जैसे

हिलना डुलना अब मेरी इच्छा के आधीन नहीं
मैं चारों ओर नज़र भी नहीं घुमा पाती हूँ
मेरा समस्त शरीर शिथिल पड़ा है
हैंगर में टंगे वस्त्र की तरह
कुछ नहीं बचा है अब

मेरा गला जैसे हुक से टिका हो
नीचे झुक कर हाथ से कुछ उठा नहीं पाती हूँ

यह कैसा है बचना मेरा
दायें नहीं, बायें नहीं, यहाँ नहीं, वहाँ नहीं
बस टंगी हूँ हैंगर पर वस्त्र की तरह ।

मार्च की सूखी परछाइयाँ

शर्मिला राय

जन्म 1960। अंग्रेज़ी भाषा की कवि, गद्य-निबंध लेखिका। 9 काव्य संग्रह प्रकाशित, विश्व की कई भाषाओं के संग्रहों में कविताएँ संकलित। उर्दू, हिंदी, बांग्ला, स्लोवीनिया, हिब्रू, स्पैनिश और उज़्बेक भाषाओं में अनुदित। अनेक पुरस्कारों एवं सम्मानों से सम्मानित।

मार्च महीने की सूखी परछाइयों के भीतर इतिहास
की छाया है
ईश्वर ग़ायब हो गया है, सड़कें सुनसान ख़ाली और
दुकानों के शटर गिरे हुए हैं।

पूरा शहर ऊँचे-नीचे मकानों के जिग-जैग सा धूसर
और गहरे धूसर रंग में डूबा है,
जिसके बीच कभी कभी पीली धूप की सुनहरी
पतली झालर चमक जाती है।

अब नीम और बड़ के पेड़ बातें करते हैं, पेट्रोल की
गंध में सने बिना।
और पूरा मैदान अब चिड़ियों का है।
दुख होता है देख कर कि असली दुनिया अब
आभासी हो गई है स्पर्श विहीन यांत्रिक।
किसी परी ने अपने जादू से बना दिया है धरती को
चाँद सा ठंडा।

बचपन से हम दुनिया के सात आश्चर्यों के बारे में
सुनते आए हैं
सब मनुष्यों के बनाए हुए। मेरी तरह और दूसरे कई
लोगों ने रॉकेट को
जोड़ा था अपनी सूची में।
हर चीज़ दांव पर लगा हम भूल गए कि दूर नक्षत्रों
में नहीं है हमारी दुनिया।
हृदय को चीरता दुख जलाता है।
और हम तो हैं मात्र मांसल टुकड़े
धरती की त्वचा पर गिरते-फिसलते।

मैं आजन्म प्रेमदासी हूं रावण की

रूमा भट्टाचार्य

रूमा भट्टाचार्य एक प्रमुख असमिया कवयित्री हैं जो धारा के विरूद्ध सोचती और लिखती हैं। आप एक पुलिस अधिकारी होने के साथ समाजकर्मी भी हैं तथा अपनी कविताओं के लिए कई सम्मान भी प्राप्त कर चुकी हैं।

रावण वध के अखाड़े का क्या प्रयोजन?
किस महानाटक या महाकाव्य का
खलनायक है रावण?
रावण एक महानायक है
जीवन के यौवन-काल का।
गुण-दोष यदि मानवीय गुण हैं
तो फिर क्यों तिरस्कृत है रावण?
मैं रावण की प्रेमिका होना चाहती हूं।
मेरी आजन्म एकमात्र साधना का
स्वप्न-पुरुष है रावण
जिसने सीता को
ऐश्वर्य की जंज़ीरों से
बांधना चाहा।
मैं हूं आज की सीता और अब
रावण है मेरा एकमात्र प्रेमी।
मैं अतीत की सीता नहीं
उभयचारी सरीसृप
मैं कृषिलक्ष्मी हूं आज की।
जगत सभा है मेरा एकमात्र लक्ष्य
इसलिए बनना चाहती हूं
सुपुरुष, सुकांतिमय, शौर्यवान, सुनिपुण, पंडित,
प्रेममय, विशाल वक्ष वाले वीर
अश्वमेध यज्ञ के सम्राट रावण की कई जन्मों की प्रेमिका।

मैं प्रस्तुत हूं दस मन्दोदरियों की सौत बनने को
फिर भी मैं प्रेमिका हूं रावण की सहस्राधिक जन्मों की।
मैं दावेदार हूँ मांग के सिंदूर की।
बंद करो
अन्यथा मैं अकेली ही
बंद करूंगी, रावण-वध का अखाड़ा
मैं ही बंद करूंगी, रावण-वध का अखाड़ा।

(अनुवाद : प्रेम कपूर)

कैम्पफायर

डा. इंदु जोशी

गोलाकार नाचते हैं अक्षर
बीच में मैं
गोलाकार थिरकते हैं शब्द
बीच में मैं
गोलाकार गाते हैं वाक्य
बीच में मैं

गोलाकार! गोलाकार!
बीच में मैं
गोलाकार नाचती हूं मैं
बीच में अक्षर
गोलाकार थिरकती हूं मैं
बीच में शब्द
गोलाकार गाती हूं मैं
बीच में वाक्य
गोलाकार! गोलाकार!
आग!   अक्षर
आग!   शब्द
आग!   वाक्य
आग!   अक्षर
आग!   आग
गोलाकार! गोलाकार!

डा. इंदु जोशी एक प्रमुख शिक्षाविद तथा हिंदी की प्रतिष्ठित कवयित्री हैं। आपके दो काव्य संकलन प्रकाशित हैं तथा आप कई पुस्तकों का संपादन भी कर चुकी हैं। आप त्रैमासिक पत्रिका नारी मंच अपूर्वा के अतिरिक्त स्वर समर्थ तथा साहित्य बुलेटिन की संपादिका भी हैं।

गौरैया उदास है

गीता दूबे

1973 में जन्मी गीता दूबे एक शिक्षाविद तथा प्रख्यात हिंदी कवि व समीक्षक हैं। आप कई पुस्तकों का संपादन कर चुकी हैं तथा विभिन्न पत्र-पत्रिकाओं में आपकी कविताएं, समीक्षाएं तथा शोध-पत्र प्रकाशित हो चुके हैं।

आज बेहद उदास है गौरैया
खिड़की पर बैठकर
निहारती है टुकुर दुकुर
खोजती है कोई कोना
मोखा या आला
जहाँ जमा सके वह अपना
छोटा सा खोता,
नन्हा सा झरोखा
कहीं कोई जगह नहीं मिलती उसे।
कामकाजी सफाई पसंद लोगों ने,
बंद कर दी हैं सारी खिड़कियां
धूप और धूल से बचाव के लिए।
कहाँ बनाएगी नन्हीं गौरेया
अपना नन्हा सा घोंसला?
कहाँ जाएगी वह... ?
चारों ओर बिछा है
मोबाइल के टावरों का संजाल,
इलेक्ट्रॉनिक कचरे का बेहिसाब जंजाल,
बंद हो रही हैं उसकी सांसें,
घुटता है दम
अब कोई नहीं रखता
कटोरे में पानी
दाने नहीं बिखेरता
कोई छत पर,

क्योंकि आलीशान महलों
और दड़बेनुमा फ्लैटों में रहने वाले लोग
नहीं जाते छतों पर
और छत भी अब बची कहाँ है।
उसे भी तो लील लिया है
प्रमोटर की अतृप्त लालसा ने।
तो क्या खो जाएगी गौरैया
इस कंकरीट के जंगल में... ?
कौन बचाएगा गौरैया को ?
व्यस्त हैं सभी फेसबुक और व्हाट्स अप पर,
किसी को नहीं चिंता
नन्ही गौरैया की।
नहीं है उसकी कोई यूनियन,
नहीं है कोई प्रतिनिधि।
सिर्फ कुछ सनकी पर्यावरणविद
करते हैं सवाल,
कुछ सिरफिरे कवि
लिखते हैं कविताएं...
तो क्या सिर्फ किताबों के पन्नों में
बची रहेगी गौरैया... ?
कविताओं में चहकेगी गौरैया।
आज सुबह से मथ रहा है
यह नुकीला सवाल
कहाँ जाएगी गौरैया ?
तस्वीर के पीछे बड़े जतन से सजाया था उसने
अपना नन्हा सा संसार
पर उजाड़ दिया है उसे
इंसां के बेदर्दी हाथों ने...

बेहद उदास है गौरैया
चीख-चीख कर फाड़ रही है गला,
जता रही है प्रतिरोध
लेकिन आश्वस्त हूं मैं
देखकर उसका साहस,
उसकी अनथक मेहनत
हताश नहीं है गौरैया
दुगने जोश से जुट गई है
फिर से गौरैया,
बना ही लेगी
अपना घोंसला,
सजा ही लेगी
अपना घरौंदा।
जितनी बार हम उसे उजाड़ेंगे,
फिर फिर बसा लेगी वह
अपनी छोटी सी दुनिया।

पौरुष और स्त्री

विद्या भंडारी

जन्म 1945,
महत्वपूर्ण कवयित्री।
कविता - कहानियों
की आठ पुस्तकें
प्रकाशित, दो
पुस्तकों का संपादन,
संगीत और स्वाध्याय
में अभिरुचि।

तुम्हारे पौरुष के पांव जिंदा हैं
क्योंकि मैंने अपने पांवों को समेट रखा है
रेशम के कीड़ों की तरह।

तुम्हारे पौरुष की आंखें जिंदा हैं
क्योंकि मेरी आंखें झुकी हुई हैं
शर्मीली दुल्हन की तरह।

तुम्हारा पौरुष जीवित है
क्योंकि मैंने अपनी अस्मिता को
छिपा रखा है अपने आंचल में।

तुम्हारा सिर गर्व से ऊंचा है हिमालय की तरह
क्योंकि मैंने समर्पण भाव को
बसा रखा है हृदय में।

तुम्हारे शब्दकोश के पन्ने फड़फड़ाए नहीं
क्योंकि मैं स्वयं एक शब्दकोश हूं।

तुम्हारे पौरुष की ऊंची आवाज बरकरार रही
क्योंकि मैंने मौन की भाषा अपना ली
एक मुनि की तरह।

मैंने प्रतिरोध को अपना मित्र नहीं बनाया
इसलिए ज़िंदा है पौरुष तुम्हारा।

मैं हूं तुम्हारी सांस, पौरुष की सांसें
चलती रहने के लिए।

मुझे महसूस करो।

कवि की पीड़ा

सुशील पांजा

सुशील पांजा बांगला के एक सर्वहारा कवि हैं जो कभी जूट मिल में काम करते थे, पर अब वर्षों से बेरोजगार हैं और अपने जीवनानुमवों को कविता का स्वरूप देते हैं। आपकी कविताओं के कई संकलन प्रकाशित हो चुके हैं।

कवि के जीवनयापन को लेकर
सर्वनाशी खेल खेल रहे हैं
यहां के मिल-मालिक
तीन वर्षों से है मिल में लॉक-आउट!

न वेतन मिला न प्रॉविडेंट फण्ड
बकाया है दो वर्षों का पूजा-बोनस
सारी पार्टियां जानती हैं यह समाचार
जानती है स्वयं सरकार भी
और इनसे कहीं ज्यादा जानते हैं
धंधेबाज, मध्यवर्गी यूनियनों के लीडरान भी

भुखमरी, शोक-संताप में किसी तरह
जी रहा है कवि और उसका परिवार
नहीं वह अकेला नहीं है
और भी हैं कई बंद कारखानों के लाखों मजदूर

अस्वस्थ शरीर लिये एकाकी
घर के अंधियारे कोने में पड़ा है कवि
और बाहर टूटी-फूटी दीवार पर
हवा में आंदोलित हैं नीले अपराजिता फूल...

(अनुवाद : प्रेम कपूर)

सूरज के नाम पर

जितेंद्र धीर

सन 1954 में जन्में जितेंद्र धीर हिंदी के सुपरिचित कवि, गजलकार एवं समीक्षक हैं जिनकी बीस से अधिक संकलनों में रचनाएं प्रकाशित हो चुकी हैं तथा जिनकी कविताओं का एक संकलन इंद्रधनुषी रंगों का सच काफी चर्चित रहा। 1998 में मध्यप्रदेश से गीत गंधर्व पुरस्कार से पुरस्कृत।

कुछ भी तो नहीं
दे सके तुम
सिवा खोखले शब्दों के
        लिखते रहे
        उपलब्धियों का इतिहास
        अपनी मनगढ़ंत
        आँकडों की भाषा में
कलम, कागज, स्याही
लिखने वाले
सब तुम्हारे
        बदलते रहे शासनतंत्र
        व्यवस्था के नाम पर
        प्रयोग करते रहे हमारा
        दंगे-फसाद हिंसा की वारदातों में
        अहिंसा के नाम पर
उजाले की तलाश में
बूढ़ी हो आइ आंखें
पोपला मुंह झुकी कमर
झोंपडी सें रंगी
फूटे शीशेवाली जंगलगी लालटेन
        यही तो दिया है हमें
सूरज के नाम पर।

ग़ज़ल

शाहिद हुसैन शाहिद

10 जनवरी 1948 को जन्मे शाहिद हुसैन -शाहिद' उर्दू भाषा के एक वरिष्ठ कवि हैं जो 1970 से निरंतर ग़ज़लें और नज़्में लिख रहे हैं तथा अपनी साहित्य सेवा के लिए कई सम्मानों से नवाजे जा चुके हैं।

वक्त बडा फितनागर होगा।
खून में डूबा मंज़र होगा।।
कांच के तन पर पत्थर होगा।
आग में लिपटा हर घर होगा।।
हाथ में तेरे खंजर होगा।
दर्द हमारा लश्कर होगा।।
हिचकी लेगा नीला पानी।
खूनी रंग समंदर होगा।।
क्यों है परीशां फिक्र-ए-जहां से।
सामना इसका अक्सर होगा।।
चिकनी चुपड़ी बातें होंगी।
गिर्द-ए-कमर एक खंजर होगा।।
दिल की बातें किससे कहिए।
सबका बदला तेवर होगा।।
'शाहिद' हक पर रहने वाला।
एक दिन घर से बेघर होगा।।

नज़्म

रूचिता कज़ाड़िया

1982 में जन्मी रूचिता कज़ाड़िया राजनीति तथा सामाजिक मुख्य धारा की कविताएं लिखती हैं। आप एक शांतिकर्मी व पत्रकार हैं तथा बीस से अधिक पुस्तकों का संपादन कर चुकी हैं।

1
बॉर्डर नहीं एक ख़ार[1] है ये
बंजरपन का अशजार[2] है ये

2
एक आंधी ऐसी आयेगी
बॉर्डर उड़ा ले जायेगी

3
एक ज़लज़ला[3] ऐसा आएगा
हर ज़ख़्म दफ़्न हो जाएगा

उस दिन ऐ दोस्त ... हम मिलेंगे।
आवारा बॉर्डर का तज़किरा[4] लिखेंगे।

---

1. ख़ार - कांटे; 2. अशजार - वृक्ष; 3. ज़लज़ला - भूकंप; 4. तज़किरा - आत्मकथा

जाने कैसे

अनिता शर्मा

जन्म-1968 एक
काव्य संग्रह
'अंतरंग परिदृश्य'।
प्रमुख पत्र-
पत्रिकाओं में
कविताएँ एवं लेख
प्रकाशित।

जाने कैसे मेरा छोटा सा क़स्बा बन गया
ज़िंदगी से बड़ा
जाने कैसे सँकरी गलियाँ भर गईं स्मृतियों के
समुंदर से एक अप्रत्याशित यात्रा में
जाने कैसे जुड़ी रह सकूँ अपनी कड़ियों से
सारी सीमाओं को तोड़ डालूँ और फिर जुड़
जाऊँ।
खिड़की से बाहर झाँकते हुए गहरी साँस
खींचती हूँ
वही पुरानी परिचित धूल की परत
तैयार हुई थी बरसों में, पल भर में झड़ गई ,
अनुचित है।
जाने कैसे माफियाओं की धरती से
टनों टन कोयला ढोती थी बड़ी बड़ी लॉरियाँ
जहाँ कभी निडर होकर चले जाते थे खदानों
में छिपे हीरों की तलाश में
जिन्हें जड़वा सकें अपनी सोने की अँगूठियों में
जाने कैसे अपनेपन को दर्शाता नीम का पेड़
फैल गया था
ठीक वैसे ही जाने पहचाने चेहरे घुल मिल
एकाकार हो गए थे एक गहरी अंतर्दृष्टि से
झाँकते आर्द्रता से भरे प्रकाश की उम्मीद लिये।

जाने कैसे इस बार स्कूल के अध्यापक नहीं
दबा सके रुंधे गले की वह गाँठ जो समय
की एक लंबी छलांग से उभर आई थी।

और तोड़ दिया था मेरा मिथक।

घड़ी के पास से उठनेवाला कोलाहल
इशारा कर रहा था

मेरी वापसी का समय हो गया है।

मन ही मन आभार व्यक्त किया कि फिर एक
बार नई ताज़ा स्मृतियों का गुच्छा समय ने
मुझे दे दिया है।

जाने कैसे ! हाँ।

मासूम दर्द

दिलनशीन ज़र्रीन

इस संकलन की सबसे छोटी कवयित्री हैं दिलनशीन ज़र्रीन। पहला कविता संग्रह 'लालाज़ार' हाल ही में प्रकाशित।

ये दुनिया बहुत हसीन है
हर तरफ गुल खिलते हैं
हरियाली इतराती है
मासूम मुस्कुराहट की
बहारें भी छा जाती हैं।
पर जब इन नाज़ुक फूलों को
ज़ालिम घायल करते हैं
उन फूलों को जब मसलते हैं
तब हर इंसां का दिल दहलता है
और रूह कांप जाती है।
उनको सज़ा तो होती है
लेकिन, फिर ये सितम कोई और
किसी और गुल पर ढाता है
अक्सर ये गुनाह फिर दोहराया जाता है
इंसानियत शर्मिंदा है।
इंसानियत शर्मिंदा है।

एक बिखरी हंसी

कुसुम जैन

जन्म 1952। मूल लेखन हिन्दी। दो कविता संग्रह। कई भाषाओं में कविताएँ अनुदित। वियतनामी, आइसलैंडिक, स्वीडिश भाषाओं की कविताओं का अंग्रेज़ी से हिन्दी में अनुवाद। विभिन्न पुस्तकों का संपादन।

कुछ है, पड़ा रहता है स्मृतियों में
और हमें जीवित रखता है।
कुछ है, बचा रहता है विस्मृतियों में
और हमें बचाए रखता है।
दोनों के बीच एक रास्ता
आवा-जाही का बना रहता है
कितना कुछ टूट कर भी
बच रह जाता है बहुत कुछ साबुत
अभाव से भरा भावों का प्रतिवेदन
थाह के लिए बेचैन अथाह उर्मिल मन
साँझ की ड्योढ़ी पर आस की टेक लगाए है
एक उम्र अधूरी कुछ थकी कुछ अनमनी
डूबते सूरज के सिंदूरी ढलान पर उभरी
एक हँसी सी बिखर गई है
दो अर्ध विरामों के बीच एक वाक्य की तरह
कितनी दरारों को भर गई.......

भगवान ? ... न... न...

गीतेश शर्मा

89 वर्षीय गीतेश शर्मा की कोरोना के दौरान लिखी कविता, जो काफी चर्चित हुई।

अपनों से दूर
एक गहरा सन्नाटा
और तन्हाई
आवाज़ सुनने को
मन तड़प-तरद्यप जाता है
कौवे की कांव-कांव
जो कभी कड़वी लगती थी
अब सुरीली लगती है
चलो, कोई आवाज़ सुनने को तो मिली
कोयल की कूक तो
कानों में मिश्री घोलती है
देर रात कुत्तों का भौंकना
कभी नींद उड़ा देता था
अब लगता है
जैसे लोरी सुना रहा हो
नींद में खलल नहीं पड़ता
नींद गहरी हो जाती है
चिड़ियों का चहचहाना
लगता है जैसे कोई
मंदिर की घंटियां बजा रहा हो (घंटा नहीं)
यह सब चमत्कार किसने किया ?
भगवान ने ?
अरे न... न...न...
प्रकृति ने
जिसका वाहक है
कोरोना... कोरोना!

भारतीय कहानियाँ

सुबह की चाय

सिद्धेश

सिद्धेश हिंदी के वरिष्ठतम कथाकारों में एक हैं। बांग्ला व हिंदी के बीच महत्वपूर्ण सेतु का काम करते हुए आपने कई बांगला पुस्तको का हिंदी में अनुवाद किया तथा आप कई पुरस्कारों से नवाज़े आ चुके हैं।

सुबह उठकर, पहले प्रभा बाहर बैठक वाले कमरे की खिड़कियां खोल देती है। रातभर बन्द खिड़कियां खुलते ही हवा का झोंका कमरे में भर जाता है। करीने से पर्दे को सरकाने के बाद सुबह-ही-सुबह बरामदे में पड़े अखबार पर एक नजर डालकर अपने दूसरे कामों में लग जाती है। समीर के उठने का इन्तजार रहता है कि कब वह उठे और हाथ-मुँह धोकर खिड़की के पास वाले सोफे पर आ बैठे। तब तक वह चाय और टोस्ट बना लेती है।

खिड़की के बाहर सामने वाले मकान के छोटे-से बगीचे में पेड़ों और पौधों के बीच हवाएं दौड़ती-भागती रहती हैं। कभी-कभी छोटे-छोटे परिन्दे उन डालों पर लुकाछिपी खेलते हैं। परिन्दों की किचमिच कानों से आ लगती है। आम, कटहल और देवदारू की पत्तियों के बीच धीमी-धीमी सरगोशियां होती

रहती हैं। चाय और टोस्ट लेकर जब प्रभा खिड़की के पास आ बैठती है, तब समीर भी तैयार होकर आ बैठता है। इस मकान में आये तीस-बत्तीस साल हो गए, तब से यह क्रम जारी है। दोनों को अवकाश के बाद अब इस समय इन क्षणों का बड़ी शिद्दत से इन्तज़ार रहता है। कब जीवन के बीते समय की घड़ी बन्द हो जाए, किसी को पता नहीं। अकेले हो जाने से पहले अकेलेपन की पीड़ा दोनों मन ही मन में भोगते रहते हैं।

शाम की उदासी प्रभा के चेहरे पर छाई रहती है। खयाल आता है, अपने छोटे-से शहर में रहते उस मकान का, जिसकी छत की नींव काफी दिनों बाद पड़ी थी। पहले खर-फूसों से बने, इसी मिट्टी से बने मकान में कितनी खुशहाली थी, भाई-बहनों के बीच नन्हीं-सी प्रभा ने कितना उत्पात मचाया था। पैरों में जूते न रहने के बावजूद सरपट दौड़ना, शाम होते ही सबकी नजर बचाकर बच्चों के क्लब में शामिल होकर रास रचाना। नाचने, कवायद करने और खेलों में सबसे अव्वल। बड़ी होकर नाच सीखने और सिखाने के पीछे बड़े भैया की डांट कम नहीं सुनी थी। लेकिन वह सब फिर भी नहीं छूटा और फिर कॉलेज में आते ही समीर की नजर से बच नहीं पाई। खूंटे से बंधने के पहले तक जीवन में जो उल्लास, प्रकृति के प्रति सम्मोहन और भविष्य की सुखद कल्पना का सागर लहराता था, वह इस उम्र तक आते-न-आते सूख गया।

अब शाम को प्रभा के चेहरे पर उदासी छाई रहती है। अब वह सत्तर की हुई है। इतने सालों की भागदौड़ के बीच जीवन के मर्म को आत्मसात किया था। पतझड़ और वसन्त के बीच के व्यवधान को बड़ी सहजता से पार करती रही। कहीं कोई क्लेश नहीं, कोई दुर्भावना नहीं, किसी प्रकार की शिकायत नहीं। लेकिन अब? शाम की उदासी चेहरे पर छाई रहती है। अनायास ही हाथ से फिसल जाता है अतीत को पकड़ने का साहस।

बचपन में अपने छोटे-से मकान की नयी बनी छत से जब वह दूर दिगन्त में पसरे पहाड़ों की श्रृंखला को देखती और रात में उन पहाड़-जंगलों के बीच जलती आगों को देखती तो वह मां से पूछती, ''यह रोशनी क्यों, मां?''

''जंगल-पहाड़ पर रहने वाले अदिवासियों के घरों की रोशनी है, बहुत दूर है, इसीलिए ऐसा लगता है।''

लेकिन आग की यह दीपशिखा उसे किसी किस्से-कहानी से कम नहीं लगती।

कोई परी रहती होगी, जो मशाल लेकर दौड़ती-भागती रहती है। उसी सम्मोहन से प्रभा रात को चुपके से खुली छत पर जा चढ़ती। उस क्षण वह परी हो जाती, जो मन-ही-मन पहाड़ के जंगलों में जा छिपती। मशाल उसके हाथ में होती। छत के नीचे मां, भाई-बहन बड़े उतावले हो उसे खोजते, कहां गयी होगी इस वक्त? नीचे उतरने पर डांट पड़ती, ''इस ठण्ड में क्या जरूरत है ऊपर जाने की?''

पिता चुप लगा जाते। पिता जानते थे कि प्रभा अपने भाई-बहनों में सबसे अलग है। जीवन में वह जरूर कूछ गुल खिलाएगी। वे मन-ही-मन मर्माहत होते, लेकिन किसी से कुछ नहीं कहते। सचमुच उसने गुल खिलाया था, बिना किसी को बताए समीर के जीवन में आ गई थी, हमेशा के लिए।

अब प्रभा न सोलह-बीस साल की परी रही और न अपने छोटे-से शहर के मकान की वह छत। सब बिक-बिका गया। अतीत का सम्मोहन यथार्थ के चौखटे से टकराकर क्षीण हो गया। शाम की उदासी उसके चेहरे पर छाई रहती है।

खिड़की खुलने की आवाज से समीर की नींद टूट गई। जरूर प्रभा ने खिड़कियां खोली होंगी उसे जगाने के लिहाज से। लेकिन यह तो उसके सोने के कमरे की खिड़कियां थीं। बाहर की धूप उसके बिस्तर पर आकर लेट गई। वह उठ बैठा। उसने चाहा कि वह थोड़ी देर वैसे ही लेटा रहे। मगर बैठकखाने में चाय पीने और प्रभा के साथ का वह अमूल्य क्षण हाथ से निकल जाएगा।

प्रभा ने अपने जीवन के चालीस साल काम-काज में बिता दिए, लेकिन उल्लास और जिजीविषा में कमी नहीं आई। अपना मकान बनाया, बच्चे बड़े होते गए। पता नहीं चला कि समय कैसे-कैसे खिसकता चला गया। अब किसी के प्रति सम्मोहन नहीं रहा। समय के थपेड़ों में जर्जरित होती रही, भीतर-ही-भीतर। किसी से कुछ कहा नहीं, समीर से भी नहीं। लेकिन समीर जानता है, प्रभा कच्ची मिट्टी से बनी नहीं है, वह आग में तपकर पुख्ता हो गई है। फिर क्या कारण है कि शाम की उदासी उसके चेहरे पर छाई रहती है?

समीर ने उठकर हाथ-मुंह धोए, फिर वह बैठकखाने में आ गया। चाय-टोस्ट रखकर प्रभा अखबार के पन्नों पर झुक गई। कोई बातचीत नहीं। कुछ समय ऐसे ही बीता। केवल चाय-टोस्ट की प्लेटें खनखनाती रहीं। प्रभा की चाय ठण्डी हो

रही है, इस ओर उसका ध्यान नहीं है। एक नजर उठाकर प्रभा की ओर देखा, उसकी आंखें डूबी-डूबी थीं, चेहरे पर फिर वही शाम की उदासी।

''क्यों, क्या हुआ?'' समीर ने टोका।

सोचती हूँ, हम दोनों में से कोई एक नहीं रहेगा, तब?''

समीर चुपचाप चाय पीता रहा। बाहर की तेज हवा बगीचे के पेड़ों से टकराती रही। आम के पत्तों पर देवदारु के पत्ते झुक आये थे। पत्तों के बीच छिपा कोई परिन्दा अपने पर मार रहा था। उसकी छटपटाहट पत्तों के हिलने से जाहिर हो रही थी।

''पता है, पहले कौन जाएगा?'' समीर ने आहिस्ते से कहा।

''ईश्वर न करे, मैं पहले चली जाऊँ।''

''अकेले हो जाने पर कौन तुम्हारी देखभाल करेगा?''

उसके बाद प्रभा चुप हो गई। बच्चे बड़े होकर अपनी दुनिया के मालिक हो गए। लड़की अपनी ससुराल में खुशहाल है। लड़का मकान के ऊपर तल्ले पर रहकर अब भी सामने आता-जाता है। वह दूसरे शहर जाकर थोड़े ही इनकी दुनिया से रू-ब'रू होगा? कहने के लिए दूरी उतनी नहीं है, फिर भी नजदीक रहकर कौन किसकी कितनी खबर रखता है।

अपने मकान के ऊपरी तल्ले पर प्रभा नहीं जा पाती। फूलों के टब सूख गए हैं। छत के सामने जो कुछ दिखाई पड़ता है, न वह बचपन का सम्मोहक पहाड़-जंगल है और न हाथ में मशाल लिये परी घूमती है। अब हाथ की शिराएं सूखकर कांटा हो गई हैं। ललाट पर सिकुड़नें उभर आई हैं। गाल धंस गए हैं। चेहरे पर वही शाम की उदासी छाई रहती है।

एक-एक कप चाय और। समीर ने अखबार अपनी ओर खींच लिया। फिर वही सब। राजनीति में दल-बदल, खून-खराबा। पुलिस जनता में मुठभेड़, पांच की मौत, कई घायल, विज्ञापनों में अधनंगी औरतों से पटे हुए रंगीन पन्ने। प्रभा अपने-आप में डूबी हुई थी। समीर ने अखबार को एक तरफ सरका दिया। फिर कुछ सोच कर बोला, ''चलो, इस बार कहीं घूम आते हैं। अच्छा होगा, उसी पहाड़ पर, जिसे तुम पुराने मकान की छत से देखती रहती थी। दो-चार रोज ही सही।''

''क्या होगा बाहर जाकर, अब तो यहीं...''

लेकिन प्रभा और समीर गये थे, उसी पहाड़ पर जहां प्रभा की परी रहती थी। पुराने शहर जाकर अपने बिक गए मकान की छत की ओर ललचाई नज़रों से ताक-झांक आई थी। पहाड़ पर जाकर आदिवासियों को देखा था। उनके छोटे-छोटे घरों को, रात में जलती ढिबरी की रोशनी में उस परी की छाया को ढूंढ़ने की कोशिश की थी। मगर कुछ हाथ नहीं आया था। सालवन के विशाल दरख्तों की माया चारों ओर दिखाई पड़ी थी। सूखे पत्तों के ढेर, गट्ठर में बंधे डालों को ढोते हुए मर्दों के चेहरों पर जीने की ललक और मजबूत हाथों में कुल्हाड़ी की चमक। प्रभा अपने बचपन में खो गई, परियों की तलाश में खो गई थी।

लौटकर उसने थोड़ी खुली सांस ली थी, मगर कब तक? फिर वही भीतर की दहशत। अकेली हो जाने पर क्या हो, बेटे-बेटी का भरोसा मरुभूमि में जलाशय की तलाश की तरह लगता रहा। प्रभा आज तक दूसरों को देती रही है, लिया कुछ भी नहीं। जो कुछ लिया, उससे दुगुना लौटा दिया है। अब केवल समीर के लिए जिन्दा रहना चाहती है। कभी-कभी उसे भयानक सपने आते हैं। कहीं-का-कहीं भटक गई है, रास्ता नहीं खोज पा रही अथवा ट्रेन पकड़ने की आपाधापी में कुछ भूल आई है। यानी सारे समय अन्दरूनी दबाव को महसूस करती रही है।

बाहर से हवा का झोंका आते ही प्रभा को होश आया, बैठे-बैठे दिन चढ़ आया था। रसोई में जाने का समय। समीर के लिए नाश्ता तैयार करने का समय। ऊपर वाले तल्ले से खट-पट की आवाज आ रही थी। दाई आ गई थी और वही ऊपर-नीचे झाड़-पोंछ में लगी थी।

समीर की भी अपनी दुनिया है। इसे प्रभा बखूबी समझती थी बल्कि अपनी दुनिया से अलग हटकर उसे अपने दोस्तों, मजलिसों में जाने के लिए प्रोत्साहित करती थी। तब वह दिनभर के लिए घर में अकेली रह जाती थी। खाने-पीने और प्रेम के अलावा भी जीने के लिए कोई-न-कोई बहाना तो चाहिए ही।

कई बार समीर बाहर जाने को टाल जाता। कहता, ''अब इस उम्र में जाने-आने की परेशानी उठा नहीं पाता हूँ।''

प्रभा अपने उदासी के क्षणों में भी उसे बाहर भेजकर एक संतोष का अनुभव करती है।

''क्या करोगे, दिनभर घर में बैठे-बैठे बोर होते रहते हो। जाओगे, लोगों से मिलोगे तो मन बहल जाएगा।''

यही बात समीर भी चाहता है कि प्रभा को कहे, मगर प्रभा जब भी किसी कारण से बाहर जाती तो समीर अपने भीतर बड़ा असहाय महसूस करता है। प्रभा को बाहर जाने का एक ही बहाना था। जबसे अवकाश प्राप्त किया है, तब से वह 'टीचर्स फोरम' में हर सप्ताह दो दिन जाने लगी थी। अपने पुराने सहकर्मियों के साथ मेल-मुलाकात के अलावा विभिन्न स्कूलों में कार्यरत अध्यापिकाओं की समस्याओं को मिलकर सुलझाती, स्कूलों में बोनस, ग्रैच्युटी तथा अन्दरूनी समस्याओं को लेकर वे सब आतीं, तब प्रभा फोरम के सदस्यों एवं महिला सेक्रेटरी के कहने पर आन्दोलन में भाग लेती। प्रभा का एकमात्र जुड़ाव इस फोरम से था। वह फोरम चल पड़ा था। स्कूल प्रधान इनकी बातें मान लेती थीं।

लेकिन फोरम के लिए निकलते समय समीर को सब समझा-बुझा जाती, ''देखो, शाम के नाश्ते में यह-वह बना दिया है, याद करके खा लेना। मुझे आने में देर हो सकती है।''

अमूमन वह रात के भोजन के काफी पहले लौट आती। आने के बाद रात का भोजन बनाती। इस बीच फुरसत निकालकर कभी किताबें पढ़ती या पत्रिका उलटती-पलटती। टी.वी. पर कोई अच्छा सीरियल होता, उसे देखती।

इस सब के बीच उसे अगली सुबह का इन्तजार रहता। वहीं से दिनचर्या की शुरुआत होती थी। खिड़की के पास बैठकर समीर के साथ का यह अमूल्य क्षण, चाय-टोस्ट के खत्म होने तक दुख-सुख की बातें। भविष्य की चिन्ता अकेले पड़ जाने का अहसास। कभी अतीत की सुखद यादों में खो जाती, तो उसके चेहरे पर फिर वही शाम की उदासी की छाया पड़ने लगती थी।

कभी-कभी प्रभा को अपना अकेलापन भी अच्छा लगता, समीर को कई बार इसका अहसास करा चुकी थी।

''अच्छा नहीं लगता, रोज का टंटा, एक धुरी पर चक्कर लगाना। मन करता है, कहीं सबसे अलग होकर अकेले जीवनयापन करूँ। क्या हुआ, सन्तानों के रहते कौन-सा सुख मिला?''

समीर कहता, ''तुम्हारे लड़के-बच्चे सब अपनी दुनिया में रच-बस गए हैं, इन्हें तुम्हारे स्वाभिमान की चिन्ता क्यों होने लगी। जमाना बदल गया है। अब वह जमाना नहीं रहा, जब सब मिल-जुलकर सुख-दुख बांट लेते थे।''

''हां, इनके लिए चालीस सालों से खटती-मरती रही। अब जब हमारी देखभाल का समय आया तब किनाराकशी कर ली।''

जबसे लड़के-बहू और नन्हें के दूसरे शहर जाकर रहने की बात तय हो चुकी है, तब से प्रभा जीवन के प्रति और सतर्क हो उठी है। समीर और प्रभा ने जिस तरह जीवन की शुरुआत की थी, उसका परिणाम यह देखने को मिलेगा इसका अहसास प्रभा को ज्यादा कचोटता है। समीर पुरुष है, वह इस तरह के जीवन को झेलने के लिए प्रस्तुत है मगर प्रभा?

उसके चेहरे पर गाहे-बगाहे शाम को उदासी की छाया मंडराती रहती है। शाम के बाद अंधेरे की पकड़, यही सत्य है।

रातभर बारिश होती रही थी, सुबह तक झड़ी लगी रही। सुबह के सात बजे थे। दिन उगने का अंदाजा नहीं लग पाया था, इसलिए समीर सोता रहा था। आकाश बादलों से घिरा था, धूप का नामो-निशान नहीं था। प्रभा अपने निश्चित समय पर उठ गई थी। उठकर सदर दरवाजा खोलकर बाहर टहलने निकल जाती थी। आज नहीं जा पाई।

समीर को पिछले कई दिनों से कहती आ रही थी कि वह सुबह उठकर थोड़ा टहल लिया करे। समीर को शुगर, ब्लडप्रेशर दोनों हैं।

''तुम मेरे साथ उठते क्यों नहीं? डॉक्टर ने भी कहा है कि सुबह उठकर टहलना सेहत के लिए फायदेमन्द होता है।''

समीर कोई-न-कोई बहाना बना देता।

कल ठीक से रात में नींद नहीं आई, इसलिए देर तक सोया रहा, जबकि समीर को नींद न आने की कोई बीमारी नहीं है। डॉक्टर ने उसे आश्वस्त किया है। ''इस उम्र में गहरी नींद आना स्वास्थ्य के अच्छे लक्षण हैं।'' फिर भी उसे दिनभर में तीन गोलियां पानी के साथ निगलनी पड़ती हैं।

समीर ने बैठकखाने से आवाज लगाई, ''क्या हुआ, चाय बन गई?''

''चाय कब की बनी पड़ी है, तुम उठो तब न। फिर से गरम कर रही हूँ।''

प्रभा यह कहते हुए रसोईखाने में ही बहुत देर तक खटर-पटर करती रही। जब आई, तब आठ बज चुके थे। यह समय उनके चाय पीकर उठ जाने का था।

बाहर बारिश थम चुकी थी। सामने वाले बगीचे में भीगी पत्तियों से रह-रहकर बूंदें टपक रही थीं। फूलों के छोटे-छोटे पौधे बारिश की बौछारों से

जमीन पर झुक आए थे। पास के मकान के गेट के पास वाले कामिनी पेड़ से फूलों की सुगन्ध आ रही थी। पेड़ सादे फूलों से लदा था। फूलों के प्रति प्रभा का आकर्षण बहुत ज्यादा है। वह फूलों और पत्तों से गमले सजाती रही है। जन्मदिन, चाहे रवीन्द्रनाथ ठाकुर का हो या नजरूल, उसे उनके जन्मदिन कण्ठस्थ हैं। उसकी याददाश्त जबरदस्त है। समीर को खुद अपना जन्मदिन याद नहीं रहता। वह याद प्रभा दिलाती है। समीर याद कर भी प्रभा के जन्मदिन के दिन ऐन मौके पर भूल जाता है। इस बात की रंजिश प्रभा को नहीं होती, मगर प्रभा ऐसे वक्त उदास रहती है।

शाम की उदासी उसके चेहरे पर छाई रहती है। आखिर क्या करे वह? आगामी आने वाले दिनों की आशंका, अकेलेपन के अहसास से होने वाली पीड़ा का समाधान किस तरह से करेगी? समीर आगे चला गया, तो पहाड़-सा समय कैसे बिताएगी? बेटे का परिवार तो शहर जाने की प्रतीक्षा में था। बेटे का बेटा यानी पोते को अच्छी शिक्षा चाहिए। उसे शहर के अच्छे स्कूल में दाखिला दिलाना था। समीर के भीतर इसकी क्या प्रतिक्रिया है। इसे प्रभा पूरी तरह से समझ नहीं पाती।

समीर ने चाय की चुस्की लेते हुए प्रभा की तरफ देखा अंधेरे के बाद जिस तरह दिन का उजाला फैलता है और उसकी आभा कोने-कोने तक फैल जाती है, उस तरह का आभास प्रभा के चेहरे पर छाई उदासी के बीच से मिला।

''आज ज्यादा देर तक नहीं बैठ सकता।''

''क्यों? देर से उठोगे, तो इस सुख से भी वंचित करोगे?'' प्रभा ने कहा।

समीर ने चौंककर प्रभा के चेहरे पर नजर गड़ा दी। यह कैसा सुख है, किस सुख की बात कर रही है प्रभा? सुबह-सुबह चाय का कप लेकर खिड़की के पास का यह क्षण, जब दोनों दीन-दुनिया की बाधा को ठेलकर बैठते हैं और अपनी पीड़ा, दु:ख, सांत्वना, संवेदना की बातों में समय को भूल जाते हैं - क्या इसी को सुख कहते हैं?

''ठीक है, अभी बजा ही क्या है? साढ़े आठ।''

''नहीं, आज रविवार भी तो है, नन्हे का स्कूल नहीं है। वह भी इतनी जल्दी नीचे थोड़े ही उतरेगा। मां-बाप की भी छुट्टी है।''

''हां, दूसरा दिन होता, तो वह अब तक नीचे का एक चक्कर लगा जाता।''

''एक बार तो जरूर नीचे उतरता। छुट्टी के दिन तो छत पर केवल उसके धप-धप दौड़ने की आवाज मिलती है।''

''ठीक कहा, आज टहलने गई नहीं?''

''कैसे जाती, बारिश हो रही थी? कल से तुम भी मेरे साथ उठोगे?''

''क्यों, कोई जोर-जबरदस्ती है?''

''हां, है। जैसे भी हो, अपने स्वास्थ्य का खयाल रखो, तुम्हें अभी काफी दिनों तक जिन्दा रहना है। जब तक मैं चाहूँ।''

''वाह, मृत्यु क्या किसी के चाहने पर आएगी?''

ऊपर सीढ़ियों पर किसी की पदचाप सुनाई पड़ने लगी थी।

''हां, मृत्यु की इच्छा रखे तो जल्दी आती है। मृत्यु नजदीक आने पर तब लगता है, मैं और कुछ दिन बचता।''

पदचाप धीरे-धीरे नजदीक आती गई। दोनों चौंककर उठने वाले थे कि कान में आवाज आई, ''दादी जी?''

सामने नन्हा फरिश्ता हंसता हुआ खड़ा था।

प्रभा के चेहरे की उदासी क्षण भर के लिए गायब थी।

काली चील

मधु कांकरिया

मधु कांकरिया हिंदी की एक अत्यंत प्रतिष्ठित कथाकार हैं। आपके कई उपन्यास प्रकाशित हो चुके हैं जिनमें 'पत्ताखोर' और 'सेज पर' पाठकों में सर्वाधिक लोकप्रिय रहे।

कोई स्मृति जिन्दगी से बड़ी नहीं होती और न ही कोई सोच। पर कुछ स्मृतियां, कुछ जिन्दा और गर्म अहसास टीस बनकर ताउम्र सालते रहते हैं आपको।

चेखव की एक कहानी पढ़ी थी-एक क्लर्क की मौत। जिसमें एक क्लर्क होता है। एक बार वह थिएटर हॉल में कोई नाटक देख रहा होता है कि अचानक उसे जोर से छींक आती है, छींक इतनी तेज होती है कि छींक के कुछ छींटे सामने बैठी मटकी सी मोटी और गंजी खोपड़ी पर गिर जाते हैं। गंजी खोपड़ी घूम कर और आँखे तरेर कर पीछे देखती है तो क्लर्क के होश उड़ जाते हैं।

वह उसका बॉस था।

बॉस उससे कुछ नहीं कहता, पर अफसरशाही का आतंक, उसके मांस में ही नहीं हड्डियों तक में धंसा था। वह और अधिक चैन से बैठ नहीं पाया, बार-बार

उसे लगता अनजाने ही सही पर उससे भयंकर अपराध हो गया है। उसकी बदतमीज छींक के छींटे बॉस की खोपड़ी पर नहीं पड़ने चाहिए थे, जाने बॉस क्या सोचे, कौन जाने उसे नौकरी से ही...

डर पंख पसारने लगा, बॉस का आतंक कंधे पर बैठे गिद्ध की तरह हर पल उसे अपनी नुकीली नोंक से लहूलुहान करने लगा। अब गई नौकरी! थिएटर ख़त्म किये बिना ही वह घर लौट आता है और सीधे पहुँचता है बॉस के यहाँ। काफी इन्तजार के बाद बॉस घर आता है। जैसे ही बॉस की निगाह उस पर पड़ती है वह गिड़गिड़ाता है-बॉस मैंने जानबूझकर नहीं छींका। मुझे माफ़ कर दें। बॉस उसे कुछ नहीं कहता है बस एक उदासीन नजर उस पर डाल कर रह जाता है। वह और अधिक डर जाता है। बॉस सचमुच उससे बहुत नाराज है इसीलिए उसने मेरी बात का जबाब तक नहीं दिया। उसके वजूद का अंश-अंश इस डर से ग्रस्त हो जाता है कि उससे दुनिया का सबसे बड़ा अपराध हो गया है। बॉस के आतंक के नुकीले कांटे उसे रह रह कर चुभते हैं, पल भर के लिए भी वह पलक तक झपका नहीं पाता है, अपने आप से मजबूर हो वह आधी रात में ही फिर जा पहुँचता है बॉस के घर - सर, मुझे माफ़ कर दें, मैंने जान बूझकर नहीं छींका था, इस बार बॉस सचमुच अपना आपा खो देता है, और चीख कर कहता है-गेट आउट।

सुबह वह क्लर्क अपने कमरे में मृत पाया जाता है।

सवाल यह उठता है कि यह कहानी मुझे क्यों याद आती है रह रह कर!

क्या इसलिए कि इसके सूत्र अवचेतन की किसी गहरी पीड़ा या अपराध बोध से जुड़े हैं?

शायद हाँ, क्योंकि अपराधबोध आसमान में उड़ती वह काली चील होती है जो आपके जरा सा खाली होते ही झपट्टा मार दबोच लेती है आपको। तो किया जाए अपने ही अतीत का पोस्ट मार्टम! क्या हर्ज!

किस्सा कोताह यह कि वे 86-87 के दिन थे, संचार क्रांति का शुरुआती दौर। कंप्यूटर छोटे होते-होते डेस्क पर आने लगे थे, और सस्ते होते-होते छोटे छोटे ऑफिस की भी जरूरत बनने लगे थे। क्योंकि अब जमाना तेज चलने वालों का था इसलिए अब अकाउंट भी लाल रंग के मोटे-मोटे खाते से निकल कर कंप्यूटर के परदे पर दनादन चलने लगे। रातों रात कंप्यूटर हवा पानी की तरह अनिवार्य

बन गया था। जगह-जगह कुकुरमुत्ते की तरह कंप्यूटर सेंटर खुल गए थे। हमारे स्वप्न भी अब कंप्यूटर के साथ जुड़ने लगे थे। अब आसमान उसका था जिसे कंप्यूटर चलाना आता था, स्वप्न उसके दौड़ते थे जिसकी उंगलिया कंप्यूटर पर तेज-तेज दौड़ती थी। पर पुरानी पीढ़ी जिन्हें न कंप्यूटर चलाना आता था, और जिन्दगी की घिस-घिस ने जिन्हें इतना घिस दिया था कि जिनमें नया कछ भी सीखने की उर्जा और उमंग ही नहीं बची थी, कम्प्यूटर के बारे में सोच-सोच उनका रक्त चाप बढ़ने लगा था। उनकी ऊर्जा और स्वप्नों का लीकेज होने लगा था, क्योंकि कंप्यूटर के चलते उनकी जिन्दगी अनाथ हो इधर-उधर भटकने लगी थी।

मैं उन दिनों कोलकाता के प्रसिद्ध टी-एक्सपोर्ट हाउस में ताजा-ताजा कम्प्यूटर प्रोग्रामर बनी थी। मेरा काम था उस एक्सपोर्ट हाउस को computerise करना, कछ इस तरह कि धीरे-धीरे सारी सम्बंधित एवं जरूरी रिपोर्ट कंप्यूटर से ही निकले। अब तक सारी रिपोर्ट एक्सपोर्ट हाउस के typists एवं बाबुओं द्वारा ही तैयार की जाती थी। चूंकि वह एक्सपोर्ट हाउस था। इस कारण इन typist और बाबुओं का भी अलग ही रुतबा था जो मेरे आने के चलते एक दम से धचक गया था। आधे से अधिक typist को पियूनगिरी में लगा दिया गया था, और जो आधे बचे हुए थे वे भी आक्सीजन पर थे, कब गिर जाए उनपर बेकारी या अपमान की गाज। कंप्यूटर उनके लिए एक ऐसा खलनायक था जो न केवल उनकी पतंग काट रहा था वरन उनके स्वप्न और सम्मान को भी देश निकाला दे रहा था। कंप्यूटर से निकली रिपोर्ट की चकमक स्पीड और पर्फेक्टनेस को देख वे ठंडी सांसें लेते, बीते दिनों की जुगाली करते और अपने हाथों से अपनी मेज पर मुक्के मारते। जब कभी कंप्यूटर से निकली रिपोर्ट में मेरी गलत समझ के चलते कोई भूल निकल आती या आंकड़े गलत बोलने लगते, उनके चेहरे पर सौ-सौ गुलाब खिल जाते, हवाएं तेज-तेज चलने लगतीं, उनके होंठ जो इन दिनों नौकरी जाने की चिंता में हँसना भूल गए थे, उनपर हंसी किसी चिड़िया की तरह फुदकने लगती। वे फिर पुराने दिनों का स्वप्न देखने लगते जब वक्त जिन्दगी से भरपूर था, और इतने नीरस काम करते हुए भी वे फ़िल्मी गीत गुनगुनाने, चुटकुला सुनाने और मुख्य मंत्री ज्योति बाबू पर बहस करते हुए ठहाका लगाने की कूबत रखते थे। उन दिनों को सलाम करते हुए वे फिर अपनी

कल्पना में कंप्यूटर को बाहर निकाल अपनी टाइपिंग मशीन और अपने पुराने साथियों को बाइज़्ज़त प्रतिष्ठित करने लगते।

अपने आस पास से असम्पृक्त और तटस्थ मैं उनकी वेबसी का स्वाद लेती, उनके स्वप्नों से खेलती, उन्हें घायल करती तेजी से सिस्टम को computerize करने में लगी थी। उन्हीं प्रयोगों वाले दिनों में एक दिन एकाएक मेरी हार्ड डिस्क क्रैश कर गई। अक्षले दिन एक्सपोर्ट हाउस को अपनी रेट रूस, जर्मनी और जापान आदि देशों के प्रतिनिधियों को भेजनी थी, क्योंकि उसी दिन ऑक्शन होने वाला था। हमारा एक्सपोर्ट हाउस स्थानीय बाज़ार से ऑक्शन से चाय-पत्तियां खरीदता, फिर उनकी ब्लेंडिंग, टेस्टिंग और ग्रेडिंग आदि कर उसे रूस जर्मनी जैसे देशों को मोटे फायदे में एक्सपोर्ट करता था। बहरहाल ऊपर से आदेश आया, सारी रिपोर्ट सुबह तक लग जानी चाहिए। मेरे आने से पहले डेढ़ पसली के फोनी बाबू यह सब देखते थे। वे एक्सपोर्ट विभाग के सबसे अनुभवी typist कम क्लर्क थे। कोई साधारण दिन होता तो वे कप्यूटर की इस दगावाजी पर बहुत खुश होते, शायद मित्रों को दावत तक दे डालते क्योंकि उन दिनों उनका सबसे बड़ा दुश्मन यदि कोई था तो वह कंप्यूटर ही था। पर वह एक महत्त्वपर्ण एवं उड़ता हआ दिन था ,रिपोर्ट उनकी देख-रेख में ही निकलती थी। एक्सपोर्ट डिपार्टमेंट की सारी रिपोर्ट का दायित्व उनके अधीन था। उन्होंने कातर निगाह से मुझे देखा और जाल में कैद पक्षी की तरह फड़ाफड़ाए-सूबह तक 230 पेज की सारी रिपोर्ट कैसे टाइप होंगी? क्या दूसरे कंप्यूटर का इंतजाम नहीं हो सकता? बैक अप (दूसरी floppy में संग्रहीत डेटा) तो है ही आप के पास? मैंने गर्दन उचकाई और अपनी अक्ल से पंगा लेते हए कहा, 'मैनेजमेंट से बात कीजिए', उनका अधबूढ़ा चेहरा हनके से कांपा। आँखों में बॉस का खौफ उभरा। सामने के दो टूटे दांतों से दयनीय हंसी बिखेरते वे लटपटाई आवाज़ में पिनपिनाए -'साहब बहुत गुस्सेवाले हैं, मेरी तो हिम्मत ही नहीं पड़ती, एक बार तो गुस्से में उन्होंने रजिस्टर ही मुझ पर फेंक दिया था।' करीब खिसक कर वे फिर फुसफसाए 'आप पर तो वे बहुत मेहरबान हैं, आपके साथ तो हंसी-मजाक तक चलता है, आपकी बात वे जरूर सुनेंगे, आप ही ज़रा .....' वे खिसकते हुए मेरे इतने करीब आ गए थे कि उनकी साँस, मैले कपडे और बालों में लगे कड़ुए तेल की गंध से मेरा जी मिचलाने लगा था। मेरे लिए यह कोई महामुश्किल कार्य

नहीं था। मैंने एक निगाह घड़ी पर डाली और एक निगाह उनके चेहरे पर डाली जहाँ डर, कुरूपता और मनहूसियत के जाने कितने जाले लटक रहे थे। मुझे उस पूरे माहौल से जितनी अधिक वितृष्णा हो रही थी फोनी बाबू की आँखों में उतनी ही अधिक उम्मीद की किरण कौंध रही थी, वे फिर लटपटाते प्रेम से बोले, आप करेंगी न बात। बोलते-बोलते जाने कैसे तो उनकी बाईं आँख दबी, मुझे लगा शायद इसी मनहूस शक्ल, गंदे कपड़े और अजीबोगरीब व्यवहार के चलते ही बॉस ने उनपर रजिस्टर फेंका होगा। उनकी यातना का दुष्ट आनंद लेती, गर्दन झटकती मैं यह जा वह जा।

दूसरे दिन ऑफिस पहुँची तो बड़ा विचित्र और दयनीय नज़ारा था। जिन्दगी जीता-जागता युद्ध बन चुकी थी। गिरते-डोलते बावन वर्षीय फोनी बाबू को तीन पिऊन पकड़ कर टैक्सी में चढ़ा रहे थे। वे उनके पंजे से निकलने की असफल कोशिश कर रहे थे। बीच-बीच में वे अपनी अकड़ी गर्दन को दांये-बांये हिला रहे थे। उनका दिल अभी भी बुझती लालटेन की तरह भक-भक कर रहा था। वे बुदबुदा रहे थे, 'एखनो चालीस पाता बाकी आछे (अभी भी चालीस पन्ने बाकी हैं।) पास खड़े दूसरे क्लर्क से मैंने पूछा 'माजरा क्या है?' तो पता चला फोनी बाबू रात भर मशीन पर मुंडी झुकाए टाइप करते रहे थे। रात बीत गई फिर भी जब वे घर नहीं पहुंचे तो उनका लड़का पहली ट्रेन पकड़ आफिस पहुंचा उस समय भी वे दीन-दुनिया को भूल अपने अंगों को कछुए की तरह सिकोड़ (वह जनवरी की कुकराती रात थी) अपने आस-पास से निरपेक्ष दनादन टाइप करते जा रहे थे।उन्हें पता ही नहीं चला कि कब रात बीती और कब सुबह फूटी। उनके लिए सब कुछ स्थगित था, मिथ्या था। सत्य था सिर्फ उनकी नौकरी, टाइपिंग मशीन और 230 पेज।

दो औरतें

उमा झुनझुनवाला

उमा झुनझुनवाला एक प्रख्यात नाट्यकार, तथा कवि कथाकार तो हैं ही साव्य ही आपने कई नाटकों का हिंदी में रूपांतरण किया तथा कई मौलिक नाटक लिखे भी। आपको कई सरकारी-गैरसरकारी सम्मानों से नवाजा जा चुका है।

दो औरतें साथ साथ थीं मगर कटी कटी-सी थीं। वजह ऐसी कोई खास बड़ी नहीं थी, फिर भी बहुत बड़ी वजह तो थी। एक औरत के पास हुक्म देने का अधिकार था और दूसरी औरत को उसके मातहत काम करना ही होता था। दोनों एक दूसरे के काम आती थीं; एक दूसरे का काम करती थीं, निर्भर भी थीं; उसके बावजूद एक औरत को दूसरी औरत का होना बर्दाश्त कर पाने में बड़ी मुश्किल होती थी। तमाम पसंदगी और नापसंदगी के दरमियान दोनों औरतें एक दूसरे का मुंह ताकती, पतझड़-सी झरती जातीं।

एक बार हुक्मरान औरत अपने नाखूनों को संवार रही थी। सलीके से किनारे घिस कर खूबसूरत आकार देने के बाद उस पर सुर्ख लाल रंगों की पॉलिश लगाई उसने । दूसरी औरत अचंभित आँखों से देख रही थी सब। उसने एक बार अपने

नाखूनों की तरफ़ देखा। उसके नाखूनों ने उसे शिकायती निगाहों से देखा जैसे, कितनी बेतरतीब हो तुम... देखो मेहंदी की लाली अजीब तरीके से पुती है हम पर... अपने बालों में मेहंदी लगाते वक़्त तुम हमारी मर्जी भी नहीं पूछती, हमारी देखभाल भी नहीं करती... ऊहह : उस औरत ने घबरा कर अपने नाखूनों को अपनी मुट्ठी में बंद कर लिया ताकि वे ज्यादा शिकायत न कर पाएं।

क्या हुक्मरान औरत सही कहती है मुझसे कि मैं किसी काम की नहीं - मातहती औरत ने सोचा।

मातहत काम करने वाली औरत के चेहरे पर दौड़ते भागते भावों की रेस को देखने वाली आँखों ने माजरा समझ लिया। कजरारी आँखें मुस्कुराईं। इन आँखों में ग़ज़ब की कशिश थी कि जो देखे एक बार तो उनकी ओर खिंचता ही चला आए। रस से भरपूर थीं ये हुक्मरान आँखें। जब कभी इन आँखों से नमक बहता, जाने कितनों के ज़ख्म हरहरा उठते; कितने नमकीन टीले ऊँचे पहाड़ बन जाते; तड़पते दिल आह भरने लगते। आँखों का काजल कितने दिलों के लिए मरहम का काम करता, इसका तो कोई हिसाब ही नहीं था। मातहत काम करने वाली आँखें रूखी सूखी थीं; न सपने थे उनमें; ना ही सपनों को देखने का साहस था। उन आँखों के पास अतीत भी नहीं था कि उसके वर्तमान की कोख में भविष्य का अंकुरण हो...। बड़ी सपाट आँखें थीं।

नाखूनों की तरह आँखें भी अपने सौन्दर्यहीन होने का अपराधी इस मातहती औरत की लापरवाही और बेवकूफी को मान रही थीं। हुक्मरानी औरत ने अपनी श्रेष्ठता का दबदबा बढ़ाते हुए उसके गाल को सहलाते हुए ढाढ़स बंधाया कि पाँचों उँगलियाँ बराबर नहीं होतीं; यह फर्क ईश्वरीय है। विशेष फूल और सामान्य फूल ईश्वर की ही देन है। अपने सामान्य होने पर अफ़सोस न करो, बस हुक्मों का पालन किए जाओ। सब एक जैसे नहीं होते।

खिड़की के बाहर वाला दरख्त खिड़की के अन्दर से आने जाने वाली हर साँस की गंध से परिचित था। उसने इस लिजलिजे सौन्दर्य की चिढ़ की गंध को खींच लिया था अन्दर अपने विशालकाय मजबूत तनों के ज़रिए। इसलिए एक बार पत्तों का रंग बैंगनी हुआ था... हुलसा हुआ-सा... हक्मरानी औरत चौंकी भी थी पत्तों के इस अजीबोगरीब रंग को देखकर उसने दूसरी औरत से जब इसका जिक्र

किया तो उसके चेहरे पर उसकी अक्कासी नज़र भी आई -

क्यूं री, सूरज तो उलटी तरफ है: फिर इस रंग की छाया तेरे चेहरे पर कैसे... ये क्या मामला है... ?

- मैं क्या जानूं मालकिन, जो भी दिख रहा है, वह आपको दिख रहा है; मेरी आँखें, मेरी त्वचा, नाक, कान, जिह्वा- सब आपकी ज़बान ही समझते हैं और मानते हैं... तब मैं कैसे कुछ कहूँ..!

जवाब का रंग पिघल रहा था। मातहती औरत रंगहीन होती जा रही थी। मालकिन के कमरे की ज़मीन बैंगनी होती जा रही थी। सब फैल रहा था किसी गंध की तरह। नाक और आँख ने काम करना बंद कर दिया था कुछ पल और फिर उड़ गया सब कुछ।

झिलमिलाते आसमान में कई रंगीन ख्वाबों की सैर होती रहती थी जिसकी डोर चमकीली गालों वाली औरत के सुर्ख लाली से रंगे नाखूनों वाले हाथों में रहती थी। पुरुष के साथ हुक्मरानी की सतरंगी ठहाकों की महफ़िल अभिमानी हो जाया करती थी। अलग अलग रंगों के ज़ायके पुरुष के नथुनों से होते हुए उसकी शिराओं को मजा पहुँचाया करते थे। एक बार बैंगनी रंग की गंध उसके नथुनों में दाखिल हो गई। मालिक और मालकिन की साँसें जब लिपटी हुई थीं, होठों और गर्दन से होते हुए नाभि पर फैल रही थीं कि अचानक वहाँ बैंगनी रंग का घेरा बन गया और अभिमान चटक गया। सकपकाए नथुनों ने अपनी इन्द्रियों की चुगलखोरी पर उलटी तबाही मचाई। हुक्मरानी नाभि सिकुड़ गई।

बरसों पहले पुरुष ने हुक्मरानी औरत के लिए ब्रह्माण्ड में एक जगमगाता कोना ऐसा बनाया था जहाँ हुक्मरानी का अभिमान परवान चढ़ता जाता था हर रोज़। उसकी ठुड्डी की ऊँचाई गर्व से दपदपाती रहती थी। अचानक एक दूसरा कोना जगमगाया... मगर कब और कैसे... ? हुक्मरानी औरत को दूसरे कोने की जगमगाहट घुन की तरह खाने लगी। घृणा गहराने लगी आँखों में, साँसों में; आवाजाही में; यहाँ तक संडास में भी जब वह मल-मूत्र त्याग रही होती थी, तब भी। नहाते वक़्त भी उसकी छाया हुक्मरानी के जिस्म से छूटती नहीं, साहन घिस डालती, घंटों शावर के नीचे खड़ी जाली से जिस्म को इस तरह मसल डालती कि चमड़ी छिल जाती। फिर भी बैंगनी गंध उसे सिर से पाँव के नाखूनों तक पसरती

महसूस होती। अब जब भी औरत और पुरुष की साँसें एक होने को होतीं औरत को उल्टियों का दौरा पड़ने लगता दसरे कोने की जगमगाहट बढ़ जाती तब।

बहुत पहले एक बार खाने की मेज पर कुछ बचा हुआ खाना रखा हुआ था। दोबारा उस पदार्थ को खाने का मन किसी का भी नहीं था। पदार्थ की गंध नासिका छिद्रों को उत्तेजित कर रही थी। मातहत औरत के घर के बर्तनों में रूखा सूखा ही होता था, इसलिए ये गंध उसकी इन्द्रियों को बेकाबू किए जा रही थी। हुक्मरानी की इजाज़त लेकर उसने अपनी इन्द्रियों, नासिका छिद्रों और मचलती जिह्वा को शांत किया। अब यदाकदा जूठन में भी रस मिलने लगा। शुरुआती दिनों में एक के लिए जूठन निपटाना सामान को कचरे में फेंकने से बचाना था और दूसरे के लिए रूखे-सूखे से इतर सुगन्धित रस से जिह्वा और पेट दोनों को शांत करना था। इसलिए जूठन आहिस्ता आहिस्ता माध्यम बन गई अहसान मनवाने और अहसान मानने का। लेकिन इस मनवाने और मानने के दरमियान खिड़की के बाहर वाले दरख्त पर उस गंध के जाले पड़ने लगे थे; लसलसे-से जाले लार से ग्रसित जाले, वासना के जाले। इन जालों से घर के अन्दर की दीवारों पर जाने कितनी ही आकृतियाँ बनतीं, बिगड़तीं, डरातीं, असुरक्षा का भाव उत्पन्न करतीं। सबमें मातहती शक्लें अलग अलग आकारों में उभर कर हुक्मरानी के कलेजे को छलनी करने लगीं।

अब आँखें चार तो होतीं, नजरों का उठना और झुकना भी होता; एक में प्रश्न तो दूसरे में बेहयाई रहती। अक्सर हुक्मरानी को अपने सिंहासन पर मातहती के पिछवाड़े की गरमाहट महसूस होती। सवालों पर झूठे जवाबों की चादर डालने की कोशिश होती। मगर तेज़ आँखों को अन्दर की नंगई नज़र आ ही जाती थी और तब हुक्मरानी औरत की कठोरता ज़्यादा से ज्यादा तीखी होने लगी। संदेह की स्थिति ऐसी हो गई कि धुंधला भी शफ़ाफ़ आईने-सा चमकता नज़र आने लगा। अब श्रृंगार करते वक्त जब चोटी में बेणी लगाती तो जाने क्यों हुक्मरानी हाथों में दुर्गन्ध बस जाती और आँखों का काजल उसे चेहरे पर कालिख जैसा प्रतीत होने लगता, होंठों की लाली में मवाद भरा हआ दिखता आईने में और कमर पर चमकती सोने की तागड़ी किसी तवायफ़ की भद्दी-सी कमर लगने लगती।

एक दिन मातहती लिजलिजी आँखों में अपने बिस्तर की छवि देख हुक्मरानी की आँखों से जो ज्वाला फूटी उसमें बिस्तर खाक हो गया। दरख्त भी झुलस गया उसकी तपिश में - मैं क्यूं सखी, मैंने तो तुम्हें हमेशा आगाह किया है, तब मैं क्यूँ तपिश का शिकार हुआ?

- 'मेरी देह जल रही है सखा; तुमने सब क्यों नहीं सोख लिया? क्यों उसकी आकृतियाँ मेरे जेहन में बनने दीं? अपनी ठंडक तुमने सबके लिए बना रखी थी... और जो सबका, वह मेरा नहीं... जो मेरा, वह किसी का नहीं...

- नहीं, नहीं नाराज़ मत हो... तुम्हें थोड़ी शीतलता की आवश्यकता है। आओ, अपने इस कमरे से बाहर, अपने इस आँगन से बाहर आओ और मेरी शीतलता से अपनी देह की जलन को शांत करो सखी...

और फिर दरख्त एक बहुत ही मीठा गीत गाने लगा हुक्मरानी औरत की पीड़ा की अगन को शांत करने के लिए - भीगती रातें । महकती सौगातें । शीतल...नरम.../ अपने में समाता.../ उपवन.../ वन.../ क्यारियाँ.../ किलकारियां.../ महामाया की लहरियां.../ सौंदर्य सीढियां.... आकार प्रवास.../ हस्ताक्षर अनायास.../ हृदय मणि.../ सृजन ध्वनि...। और मैं तुम...।

इस गीत को सुनते सुनते चंद पल के लिए औरत दरख्त के काँधे पर सर रखकर सो गई। आस-पास हरियाली खिली, दरख्त खुशबूमय हुआ। फिर देह अदेह हुई; पिघल गई; मिट्टी हो गई; खुशबू बन गई और समा गई दरख्त की हर शाखा-प्रशाखा में। देह का अदेह होना चलता रहा... कि स्वप्न-भंग हुआ और हुक्मरानी औरत ने खुद को नमक के टीले में गर्दन तक धंसा पाया। आगे पीछे दो छोर दिखे - एक अँधेरे का और एक उजाले का...। दोनों छोर उसकी पहुँच से बाहर...। उसने देखा, मातहती औरत और पुरुष और भी अनेक अनेक आकृतियाँ - सब अंधेरे की तरफ बढ़ रहे हैं। अँधेरे में बहुत आकर्षण है; सारे गुरुत्वाकर्षणों से परे । अंतरिक्ष के उस काले छिद्र के खिंचाव में सारी अभिलाषाएँ समा जाने को आतुर हैं; समुद्र में घटनाएँ तेजी से घटित होने लगीं : घटनाएँ बादल बनने की प्रक्रिया में व्यस्त हो गईं; बादल नम होने लगे; नमी में उजालों के कण फैलने लगे : हुक्मरानी औरत अपनी बड़ी बड़ी आँखों से

उजालों के उन कणों को अपने अन्दर सुड़कने की कोशिश करने लगी; उन आँखों का गुरुत्वाकर्षण ज्यादा मुलायम था जो मातहती औरत के रोमकूपों को भरता चला गया। मातहती औरत के अंदर हुक्मरानी औरत को लेकर संघर्ष चल रहा था अँधेरे और उजाले के मिलन की एक छोटी सी चाह को लेकर; हुक्मरानी औरत ने उस मिलन को एक नीली रेखा में बदल दिया; एक खूबसूरत घृणित जहरीली नीली रेखा में जहाँ पुरुषार्थी नीला उजाला खरे जिस्म की नर्म चाहतों के साथ अँधेरे की आकर्षक धुन पर लहरों सा नर्तन करते झूमने लगा।

और हुक्मरानी औरत चाँद की मीठी रोशनी में दरख्त के पास बैठी उसके काँधे पर सर रख फटी बिवाइयों और लपलपाती जीभ को आलिंगनबद्ध होते देखती और नमक होती गई।

नमक होती औरत की व्यथा से विचलित दरख्त उम्मीद के हरेपन को धरती के अन्दर से पुरजोर ढंग से खींचता कि इस हरेपन से आसमान का हृदय ज़रूर आकर्षित होगा; उस पर सूरज की किरणें बिखरेंगी; रंगों में विस्फोट होगा; सुनहरे बादल उसकी उम्मीद की प्रतिध्वनियों को समेट किसी करिश्माई बारिश की सृष्टि करेंगे; और उसकी बूंदों की लड़ियों से रक्तिम पुष्पों-सी वेणी बन जाएगी जिससे वह अपनी इस प्रिय औरत की आशा को महकाएगा।

दो औरतों का एक दूसरे का होना, बर्दाश्त न कर पाना जारी था।

तमाम पसंदगी और नापसंदगी के दरमियान एक दूसरे का मुँह ताकना भी मुहाल था।

एक का रोम रोम से घृणा करना और दूसरे का रोम रोम से घृणा सहना रोज़ का नियम बन चुका था।

पुरुष का घोड़े की अढ़ाई चाल चलना आदत बन चुकी थी।

और उधर दरख्त अपने काँधे पर बहते नमक के टीले पर प्रेम का रक्तिम पुष्प उगाने के लिए मनुष्य जीवन पाने की अभिलाषा लिए प्रार्थना में लीन रहने लगा।

पहचान

डॉ. करुणा पांडे

1962 में जन्मी डॉ. करुणा पांडे एक शिक्षाविद तथा हिंदी की जानी-मानी लेखिका हैं। आपके तीन उपन्यास, चार कहानी संग्रह, तीन बाल कहानी संग्रह, बाल-गीत, निबंध, लोक-गीत, आदि अठारह पुस्तकें प्रकाशित हो चुकी हैं तथा अनेक राष्ट्रीय-अंतरराष्ट्रीय सम्मानों से सम्मानित हो चुकी हैं।

शंकर समित, अजय, राजन, राकेश और मैं – हम सभी लोग विचार कर रहे थे कि लोगों के अंदर पैदा हो रहे द्वेष को कैसे दूर किया जाए क्योंकि आज मेरे मोहल्ले में बम ब्लास्ट हुआ था और बहुत से लोग घायल हुए थे। लोगों के क्षत-विक्षत चेहरे देखकर मन बहुत दुखी था। कुछ अस्पताल से प्लास्टर और पट्टी करवाकर लौटे तो कुछ की लाश ही घर पहुंची। समझ नहीं आया कि अचानक बम ब्लास्ट क्यों हआ? किसने किया? क्या यह आतंकवादी घटना थी? पर कहीं कोई हल नहीं सूझ रहा था। मेरे हाथ में भी प्लास्टर चढ़ा था।। हम लोग शाम को एकत्र होकर इस जघन्य वारदात पर विमर्श कर रहे थे और जिनके घर के चिराग बुझ गए थे वहां जाकर शोक व्यक्त करने की भूमिका बना ही रहे थे कि अचानक पुलिस ने दबिश दी और हमारे मोहल्ले के सभी नौजवान लड़कों को

गिरफ्तार कर लिया। हम सब हक्के बक्के थे। यह क्यूँकर हो रहा है ? देखते -देखते हम सब हवालात में थे। हम सबको हवालात में टॉर्चर किया जा रहा था और हम सबके घर परिवार मूल जन्म स्थान और पेशे के बारे में जांच पड़ताल की जा रही थी।

हम अपने बारे में क्या बताते। पंजाब के सिंध प्रान्त में रहते थे। बंटवारा हुआ, पाकिस्तान की सीमा में आ गए। 1972 में बंगला देश बना तो बंगला देश की सीमा में चले गये और बंगला देशी कहलाये। वहां से रोटी पानी को तरसते हुए शरणार्थी बनकर भारत आये। यहीं हमारा जन्म हुआ। हमारे माता-पिता को खुशी थी कि उनका जन्म स्थान भारत था। अब अपने घर आ गए हैं और सुकून की सांस ली।

हमें फख्र था कि हमने भारत में जन्म लिया। बूढ़े माँ-बाप का हाथ बंटाने के लिए हमने मुम्बई जाने का निश्चय किया और मुम्बई की राह ली। ''पूरा हिन्दुस्तान ही हमारा है'' हमारे मन में यह भावना थी, पर हर जगह हमें बाहर का समझा गया, पर भारत हमारी जन्मभूमि है इस अहसास के साथ हम सब सह लेते थे।

आज जब हमने अपने जीवन को स्थिर किया तो बम ब्लास्ट में हमें सशंकित निगाहों से देखा जा रहा है। एक प्रश्न हम खुद से पूछते हैं कि ''आखिर हम हैं कहाँ के ?'' पाकिस्तान के, बंगला देश के, भारत के, और बंटे हुए भारत के किस प्रांत के हैं। आज भी हिन्दुस्तान में सामान्य लोगों को अपने मूल स्थान की तलाश करनी पड़ रही है।

आज जब भौगोलिक रूप से हिन्दुस्तान की एक स्पष्ट राजनीतिक संरचना है फिर भी हमें भारत के भीतर उग रहे प्रति भारत की तलाश करनी पड़ रही है। अलग-अलग प्रान्तों के रूप में कहीं भारत अंदर ही अंदर अपने वजूद को खोखला तो नहीं कर रहा है।

भारत का बँटवारा आम जनता के लिए नहीं वरन नेताओं की महत्वाकांक्षा को पूर्ण करने के लिए हुआ था। जब देश का बँटवारा हआ और राष्ट्र का स्वरूप बन रहा था उन दिनों अलगाववादी गतिविधियों का केन्द्र धर्म था और धर्म के नाम पर भारत और पाक बना। मगर जल्द ही धर्म का स्थान जाति और प्रान्त ने

ले लिया और जातीयता और प्रांतीयता के आधार पर बंगला देश बना। आज जितने भी अलगाववादी आन्दोलन तथा उपद्रव चल रहे हैं, सबका आधार जातीयता और प्रांतीयता है। व्यक्ति जन्म से जिस स्थान में रहता है वही उसका मूल स्थान होता है। अगर बंगाल में एक बिहारी जन्म से रहता है तो वही उसका मूल स्थान होगा, पर वह बाहरी ही कहलाता है। आज हिन्दुस्तान कितने प्रान्तों में बंटा है और प्रत्येक प्रान्त दूसरे प्रान्त से खुद को अलग करना चाहता है। मैं यह सोच रहा था कि तभी हवालात में हवलदार आया और झड़पते हुए बोला - ''क्यों बे, कहाँ का रहने वाला है ? किसके लिए काम करता है ?'' आवाज बहुत कड़क थी।

''साहब मैं यहाँ काम के लिए आया हूँ, एक दुकान में सेल्समैन हूँ, मेहनत-मजदूरी करके घर चला रहा हूँ'' मैंने सीधा सा उत्तर दिया।

''साले झूठ बोलता है, तुम लोग दूसरे प्रदेश से यहाँ आकर गुंडागर्दी करते हो और फिर लूटमार करके चले जाते हो। सच-सच बताना किसके इशारे पर काम करते हो, या तुम्हारा अपना गैंग है'' थानेदार ने गुस्से से पूछा।

''साहब हम निर्दोष हैं, सच कह रहे हैं, हमें नहीं पता हमारे मोहल्ले में बम ब्लास्ट कैसे हुआ। हम सब बेहद दुखी हैं'' मैंने गिड़गिड़ाते हुए कहा। हम चारों गिड़गिड़ाते रहे पर हमारी बात किसी ने भी नहीं सुनी। मुम्बई पुलिस ने हम सबको बम ब्लास्ट में नामजद किया, क्योंकि हम दूसरे प्रान्त के थे। पुलिस को शाबाशी मिली और हमें सजा हुई।

हम जेल में सजा काट रहे हैं–किस बात की–पता नहीं–शायद दूसरे प्रान्त के वाशिन्दे होने की...।

मेरे मित्र शंकर ने कहा–''पहिले तो मुसलमान होना गुनाह था, पर अब तो कुछ भी होना गुनाह है।''

''कुछ भी क्या''

यानी एक अस्मिता से दूसरी अस्मिता की श्रृंखला। व्यक्ति की कई अस्मिताएं होती हैं–धार्मिक, लैंगिक, भाषाई, क्षेत्रीय–इन सभी को लेकर व्यक्ति या कोई जातीय समूह राष्ट्रीय अस्मिता से जुड़ता है।

आज भूमंडलीकरण की आड़ में पूंजीपति और राजनीतिक शक्तियों के दलाल

और माफिया एक समानांतर प्रति राष्ट्रीयता का निर्माण कर रहे हैं। मैंने महसूस किया कि सजा काटते वक्त जेल में रहने पर मेरे मोहल्ले के मराठी मानस हमसे मिलने बराबर आते रहे और हमारे परिवार की देखभाल करते रहे। इन्हीं मराठी लोगों को मुद्दा बनाकर ये नेता लोग द्वेष और अलगाव की भावना समाज में फैलाते हैं।

राजनेताओं और पूंजीपतियों की मिली भगत ही अलगावबाद को जन्म दे रही है, क्योंकि जिन आम मुम्बईवासियों के हक़ छीने जाने की बात उठाकर हिंसा फैलाई गई उन्होंने इन भईया लोगों की मदद की। निश्चित रूप से सिद्ध होता है कि यह सारा खेल पूंजी और वर्चस्व का है और आज के प्रांतीयतावाद का यही यथार्थ है।

मैं और मेरे मित्र बिना गुनाह वाली अपनी सजा काटकर आज एक प्रश्न लिए खड़े हैं कि ''हम कहाँ के हैं? किस प्रान्त के हैं? क्या हम भारतवासी नहीं हैं''...? थोड़ी सी हवा, थोड़ा सा पानी, थोड़ा आकाश, थोड़ी धरती और कम आमदनी में गुजारा करने वाले हम जैसे लोग अपनी अस्मिता और पहचान के लिए दर-दर भटकते हैं।

आज पूंजीपति और राजनेता किसी भी प्रान्त से आकर कहीं पर भी अपना व्यापार और राजनैतिक जीवन शुरू कर लेते हैं, पर उनसे कोई नहीं पूछता कि वो किस प्रान्त के हैं–वरन उनको हाथोंहाथ लिया जाता है। क्या वह दिन आएगा जब हिन्दुस्तान में कोई व्यक्ति जाति, धर्म, गरीबी, अमीरी और प्रांतीयता से ऊपर उठकर सिर्फ हिन्दुस्तानी ही समझा जाएगा? इस प्रश्न का कभी कोई उत्तर पाएगा या एक प्रश्न बन कर ही रह जाएगा।

आज मैं ही नहीं, न जाने कितने लोग अपनी अस्मिता और पहचान को खोज रहे हैं। हमारी क्या पहचान है? कहाँ के वाशिन्दे हैं? हमारा जीवन तो जानवरों से भी बदतर हो गया है। काश! मुझे कोई मेरी पहचान बताये।

आधे उखड़े हुए लोग

नूपुर अशोक

कथाकार-कवि नूपुर अशोक ने हिंदी में कई उपन्यास लिखे। विचारों में नारीवादी। लेखन के साथ व्यापार भी करती रही हैं।

अपने ही शहर में वापस लौटते हुए एक अलग सा रोमांच होता है। शायद परिचित इलाका एक सुकून देता है। वैसे इतने दिन भी बाहर नहीं रहे थे हम, लगभग तीन महीने, फिर भी वापस आते हुए अच्छा लग रहा था। विदेश में भी ये तीन महीने अच्छे ही रहे थे। धूल और धुएं से दूर, बिलकुल शांत वातावरण। ऐसे सुन्दर घर मानो किसी ने बस सजा कर रख दिए हों। लोग तो दिखते ही नहीं थे। और यहाँ देखो, लोग ही लोग। मैने गाड़ी का शीशा नीचे उतारने की कोशिश की तो अमर ने टोक दिया- ए. सी. चल रहा है यार! - हां, पर अपने देश की हवा तो खा लें।

- पहुँच कर खा लेना। कितना पाल्यूशन है बाहर।

मैंने शीशा वापस चढ़ा दिया। पाल्यूशन तो था ही, शीशा चढ़ाते ही महसूस

हुआ कि शोरगुल भी बहुत था।

आजकल ट्रैफिक बहुत खराब हो गया है- पराग ने कहा। पराग, मेरा भतीजा। पर उसे कभी भी भतीजा नहीं समझा, बेटा ही समझा, बिलकुल अपने बेटे समीर की तरह। एक साल का फर्क था दोनों में। समीर जब विदेश चला गया तो पराग के कारण हमें वह सूनापन नहीं झेलना पड़ा जो अधिकतर माँ-बाप झेलते हैं।

वैसे भी संयुक्त परिवार की कुछ खूबियाँ तो हैं ही। आप भीड़ में खो भले ही जाएँ पर अकेलेपन की गुंजाइश कम ही होती है। विदेश में जब बुड्ढों को अकेले बाज़ार में देखती तो तरस आता। ट्रॉली में रोजमर्रा की जरूरतें खुद ही इकट्ठा करते, ट्रॉली ठेलते, बिल चुकाते और कमज़ोर क़दमों से पार्किंग की ओर बढ़ जाते। अमर कहते - देखो कितने इन्डिपेंडेंट हैं। हमारे यहाँ तो पचास पार किया नहीं कि लोग बस सीनियर सिटिजन बन जाते हैं और हर काम के लिए दूसरों पर निर्भर हो जाते हैं। चाय ला कर दो, पानी ला कर दो। उस पर भी शिकायतें। उनका एक ही काम होता है बेटे बहू को गाली देना। ये नहीं किया, वो नहीं किया, नौकरों की दया पर छोड़ दिया...

मैं कहती - मजबूरी का नाम महात्मा गाँधी! कोई और करने वाला न हो तो बेचारे करें क्या। इन्डिपेंडेंट तो होना ही होगा। ब्रेड और टायलेट रोल ख़त्म हो जाए तो खुद ही लाना होगा। वैसे देखो, ब्रेड तो दो ली है और टायलेट पेपर रोल एक दर्जन। ये भी अजीब है, कागज़... छी... इस मामले में हमारा पानी वाला सिस्टम ही ठीक है।

अचानक गाड़ी में ब्रेक लगा। सामने एक ऑटो न जाने कहाँ से आ गया था। पराग शीशा उतार कर ऑटो वाले पर बरस पड़ा। ट्रैफिक वाकई खराब था। सड़क की आधी जगह तो दुकानदारों ने घेर रखी थी। बाकी बची जगह में साइकल, रिक्शे, टेम्पो, टुकटुक, गाड़ियाँ, बसें, पैदल - सब कुछ ठुसा हुआ था। न कोई लेन, न कोई नियम... बाएं-दायें, इधर-उधर... जो जिधर से चाहे उधर से निकल रहा था। सोच कर भी आश्चर्य होता था कि इसी धरती पर ऐसी भी जगहें हैं जहाँ सब कुछ यंत्रवत अनुशासन से चलता है। पैदल चलने वाले भी नियत स्थान से अपने लिए ग्रीन सिग्नल का इंतजार कर के ही रास्ता पार करते हैं।

और गाड़ी चलाने वाले भी पैदल व्यक्ति को सड़क पर देखते ही, गाड़ी रोक कर पहले उसे सड़क पार करने का मौक़ा देते हैं। ट्रैफिक से जूझते हुए हम आखिरकार अपने घर के करीब पहुँच गए। दाहिने मुड़ते ही मैं चौंक गयी। कोने पर हमेशा प्रहरी की तरह खड़ा रहने वाला बरगद धराशायी पड़ा था।

- अरे, यह कैसे गिर गया? मैंने आश्चर्य से पूछा।

- इतनी अधिक बारिश हुई पिछले दिनों कि मिट्टी पूरी ढीली हो गयी। - पराग ने कहा।

- मिट्टी भी भला कभी ढीली होती है? और इसकी तो जड़ें भी काफी गहरी रही होंगी। कोई दो-चार साल पुराना पेड़ नहीं था ये - मैं वाकई अचरज में थी।

घर में घुसते ही चाय की खुशबू से दिल खुश हो गया। कोई आपको अपने हाथों से बनाकर चाय पिलाये तो बात ही कुछ और होती है। खुद बना कर पीने वाली चाय में वह बात नहीं होती। दरअसल अपने हाथ से बनी किसी भी चीज़ में वह बात नहीं होती। उसे बनाने के पहले ही हम अपने मन में उसे बना चुके होते हैं। उसके बाद तो बस सामग्री जुटाना और उस पूरी प्रक्रिया से गुजरना मात्र होता है। पर यहाँ ताज़ा-ताज़ा बनी चाय हमारा स्वागत कर रही थी।

- इंडिया का मज़ा और कहीं नहीं है - मैंने चाय का प्याला उठाते हुए कहा।

-बर्तन धो-धो कर बोर हो गई क्या भाभी?- देवर ने चुटकी ली।

-'अरे भाई, बोर होने से कैसे चलेगा, अब तो वहीं रहना है।

- पी.आर. (परमानेंट रेसीडेंसी) अप्लाई कर दिया?

-हाँ, समीर ने बहुत जोर दिया तो हमने अप्लाई तो कर दिया है। अब देखो कब तक आता है।

-अच्छा है। यहाँ क्या रखा है। अभी तक हमलोग बिजली-पानी जैसी चीजों के लिए जूझ रहे हैं। कल तो रात भर बिजली भी नहीं रही और मच्छरों ने काट-काट कर बुरा हाल कर दिया।

तब तक गर्मागर्म कचौरियां सामने आ गईं। मैंने लपक कर उठा लीं- ये और कहाँ मिलेंगी, वो भी बिना हाथ-पैर हिलाए।

जलेबी खाइएगा- पराग ने पूछा - दस मिनट में ले आऊँगा।

-चलो मैं भी चलती हूँ - मैं देसी हवा खाने का कोई भी मौका नहीं छोड़ना चाहती थी। घर से निकलते ही हम फिर उस बरगद के पास से गुज़रे।

कैसे उखड़ गया यह विशाल बरगद? मिट्टी भी कहीं ढीली होती है? उसके ऐसे गिर जाने से रास्ते में बाधा पड़ रही थी।

-अब गिर ही गया है तो इसे रास्ते से हटाते क्यों नहीं- मैंने पराग से पूछा।

अरे बड़ा झमेला है। पेड़ आधा उखड़ा है। आधी जड़ें अभी भी जमीन में हैं। इसलिए नगर निगम हटा नहीं सकता। वे ज़िंदा पेड़ को नहीं हटाते। इसलिए वन विभाग को बोलना पडेगा।

-तो वन विभाग ही ले जाये।

-हाँ, पर वन विभाग कहता है कि उखड़े हुए पेड़ को हटाना निगम का काम है।

वह सहजता से कह गया पर मेरे अन्दर कुछ अटक गया। क्या नियति है इस पेड़ की - आधा उखड़ा हुआ- कुछ जमीन को छोड़ चुका, कुछ अभी भी जुड़ा हुआ। इतने सालों से इतनी बारिशें झेलने वाला यह वृक्ष इस तरह कैसे....

अगली शाम मैं फिर टहलते हए उसके पास गयी। उसके सामने पहले एक बागान हआ करता था। उसकी लम्बी चारदीवारी अब अलग-अलग मल्टीस्टोरी बिल्डिंगों के गेटों में तब्दील हो गई थी। उस चारदीवारी के पार जाने की हिमाकत करती हुई उन विशाल डालों को काट कर फेंक दिया गया था। चारों ओर उन्मुक्त हवा में प्रसृत ये पृथुल शाखाएं बरगद को एक संतुलित मजबूती देती थीं। पर अब तो दुनिया दो हिस्सों में बंट चुकी थी- निजी सुविधाओं की दुनिया और साझा जीवन की दुनिया। यह बरगद किसी एक का तो था नहीं। निजी सुविधा की दुनिया ने उसकी वे सब डालें काट डालीं जिनकी उपस्थिति उनके लिए एक रुकावट थी। और फिर निरंतर बारिश की मार। कितनी भी गहरी जड़ें हों असंतुलन का भार कब तक झेल पाती।

आते-जाते इस आधे उखड़े बरगद का कातर दृश्य कई बार दिखा। जैसे बार-बार छुए जाने पर दुखती रग भी सुन्न पड़ जाती है, उसी तरह वह बरगद वहीं पड़ा रहा, हम आते-जाते उसे देखते रहे। पर अब वह हमें दिख नहीं रहा था।

निजी सुविधा की दुनिया के लोग अपनी-अपनी जरूरत के हिसाब से उसके

हिस्से काट कर ले जा रहे थे। बरगद की विशालता कट-छंट कर एक ठूठ का रूप लेती जा रही थी। पर कुछ हरी शाखें उसकी जिजीविषा की क्षीण घोषणा में प्रयासरत थीं।

इंडिया लौटने का रोमांच अब उत्साहविहीन दिनचर्या में बदल चुका था। विदेश में जहाँ अमूमन पार्किंग फी दस डॉलर हुआ करती थी, वहां जब कभी पाँच डॉलर की जगह मिल जाये तो हम पुलकित हो उठते थे। अब तीस रुपये की पार्किंग बढ़ कर पचास हो जाती तो हम खीझ उठते थे। मैं अमर को दिलासा देती - जाने दो, एक डॉलर ही तो है, वहां खुशी-खुशी पाँच डॉलर देते थे।

''अरे वहां की बात छोड़ो, यहाँ लूट मचा रखी है।''अमर अभी भी चिढ़े रहते।

सड़क पर चलते हुए टकराती हई भीड़, ऊबड़-खाबड़ रास्तों की ठोकरें, हमें बार बार वहां की चिकनी सड़कों की याद दिलाने लगी। सब्जी वाले से भावतोल करते वहां के सुपर मार्किट का सेल्फ चेक आउट काउंटर याद आने लगता। अमर कहते-उस सेल्फ चेक आउट काउंटर में कितना कम समय लगता था। मुझे लगता कि उसमें कोई कहानी भी तो नहीं होती थी, यहाँ तो सब्जी वाली का - 'ले जाओ दीदी, आजे का तोड़ल है। सबेरे चालीस का बेचे रहे। तीसे में ले जाओ, अंधार हो रहा है। - में मैं सिर्फ सब्जी नहीं, पूरी एक कहानी से भर कर लौटती थी, उस सुन्दर दुनिया की एकरसता से बिलकुल अलग।

पता नहीं अमर को भी वाकई वहाँ की याद आने लगती थी या वे जानबूझ कर उन्हें याद करने लगते थे। उन्हें मालूम था कि चार महीने बीतते न बीतते समीर का बुलावा फिर आने वाला है - आ जाओ, बहुत दिन हो गए।

टिकट बुक करते ही अमर की लिस्ट बननी शुरू हो गई - बेटे के पास जाना है, कितनी सारी शॉपिंग करनी है - सोनपापड़ी, लड्डू, दालमोठ, ब्लैक शू पौलिश, हाँ, वहां चार डॉलर की मिलती है यानी दो सौ रुपये. यहीं से ले चलो....

हम एक बार फिर एयरपोर्ट के लिए निकल पड़े, जाते हुए मैंने देखा बरगद जाने कब पूरा गायब हो चुका था। हाँ अपने पीछे एक बड़ा-सा खाली गड्ढा छोड़ गया था।

देशी घर

नंदिता आचार्य

नन्दिता आचार्य बांगला की लोकप्रिय उपन्यासकार तथा कथाकार हैं। बांगला की विभिन्न प्रतिष्ठित पत्रिकाओं में आपकी रचनाएं प्रकाशित होती रहती हैं।

दीवार से हल्की लाल सी रोशनी चारों ओर छिटकी पड़ रही थी। और टंगी थी कुछ बड़ी-बड़ी ऑयलपेंटिंग। बिरयानी की खुशबू भी फैली थी चारों ओर। इकबाल भाई बोल उठे 'यहां की फिरनी भी काफी मशहूर है।'

मैं तो अवाक् सी चारों ओर देख रही थी। इकबाल भाई के मुझ पर बड़े एहसान हैं, फिर भी दम घुट सा रहा था।

'ब्रेन-करी खा कर देखिए, वह भी मशहूर है।' इकबाल भाई के मित्र आसिफ रज़ा ने मुझसे कहा।... और मैं कहने जा रही थी – पता है, यहां कभी-कभी जीवनानंद भी आते थे।

'गाय की ब्रेन-करी तो खा लेंगी न आप?' मेरी ओर देख कर आसिफ ने प्रश्न किया।

'नहीं, मैं बीफ नहीं खाती', मैंने कहा।

'ओह हो, आपके तो शास्त्रों में मनाही है', कह कर आसिफ मेनू-कार्ड में अन्य डिशें तलाशने लगा।

मैंने कुछ झिझकते हुए कहा, 'नहीं, ऐसा नहीं है। दरअसल मेरे ननिहाल में कई पालतू गायें थीं। बचपन में उनके साथ खेलते-खेलते बड़ी हुई हूं, इसलिए नहीं खाती। साल भर पहले तो मैं कोई भी मांस नहीं खाती थी। चारों ओर थीं बत्तखें, मुर्गियां और बकरियों के बच्चे... सब मुझे बहुत प्रिय थे।

'अच्छा... तो आप बड़ी सेंसिटिव इंसान हैं, समझ गया'(हंस दिए इकबाल भाई)।

मिस्टु मोना, तेरे सिर का स्क्रू क्या फिर से ढीला हो गया?

पैर पटकते हुए मैंने कहा, 'तुम भी ऐसा कहोगे? केवल वहां जाने के लिए ही तो मैं कब से पासपोर्ट बनवा कर बैठी हूं।'

- हूं, तो अब तक गई क्यों नहीं? अब यहां अकेले-अकेले... कुछ दिनों बाद मैं भी निकल जा रहा हूं...

- पिताजी ने जाने नहीं दिया। वे रायॅट के समय भाग कर आये थे, तब छोटे से थे। दंगों का आतंक ही दूर नहीं हुआ था।... फिर पिताजी ऐसे अचानक चले गये...। उसके बाद से वह देश मुझे खींच रहा है, अपनी ओर। वे सब पोखर-नदी-नाले, घर, बाग-बगीचे मुझे अपनी आंखों के सामने नज़र आते हैं। दादू, पिताजी से वहां के बारे में कितना कुछ सुन रखा है।...

- 'जानता हूं मोना। पिताजी के लिए तुम्हें कितना दुःख है...।' वैभव ने रवीन्द्र-सदन स्टेशन में ही सिर झुका कर मेरे माथे को चूम लिया, -- 'मैं सब समझता हूं बेबी।'

- क्या समझते हो?

- तुम्हें। मैं दो दिनों की छुट्टी ले कर तुम्हारे साथ चला चलूंगा। वहां के घर की भी तो कोई निश्चित खोज-खबर नहीं है तुम्हारे पास।

- ओ मां... कुछ दिनों बाद ही तो तुम्हें डेनमार्क जाना है... वर्ना तुम चोरी-छिपे मेरे साथ चलते तो मुझे बहुत अच्छा लगता।

- बाद में चलें तो कैसा रहे? मेरे लौट आने के बाद?

- नहीं... मुझे तो अभी ही जाना होगा।...बरिशाल मुझे खींच रहा है अपनी ओर...। इसमें कोई बाधा मत देना। आज वीज़ा मिल गया है। दो-तीन दिनों में ही निकल जाऊंगी। तुम्हारे डेनमार्क जाने के पहले ही मुझे लौटना होगा।... और देश के घर का पता लगाने के लिए मैंने ऑलरेडी कह दिया है, वहां के एक बहुत बड़े पत्रकार को।... पिताजी तो तब बहुत छोटे थे, बुआएं थोड़ी बड़ी थीं, पर वे भी पता-ठिकाना ठीक से नहीं बता पा रही हैं। पर मैं निश्चय ही खोज निकालूंगी। मैं स्वयं भी तो एक पत्रकार हूं न।

- यह तो अच्छी बात है, पर मुझे तो पता ही नहीं था कि तुमने वीज़ा के लिए एप्लाई कर दिया है।

- अब इस बात पर नाराज मत होना। मैंने नहीं बताया क्योंकि तुम्हें भी बाहर जाना था, तुम्हारी अपनी कितनी व्यस्तता थी।... बताती तो तुम इसी में लग जाते...। मेरी जान-पहचान थी कोई असुविधा नहीं हुई।... चलो दौड़ कर रास्ता पार कर लें। उसी ओर तो है टी-जंक्शन।

- 'तुम लोग भी क्या जमींदार थे वहां ?' वैभव ने जेब से रूमाल निकाल कर मेरा माथा पोंछते हुए पूछा, 'तालाब, काठ का घर... और भी कितना कुछ था न तुम लोगों का ?'

- हां, हां तुम्हें बताया तो था, बड़ा सा तालाब, काठ का घर, सब कुछ तो था। हम जमींदार नहीं थे किंतु बहुत धनी थे। पिताजी के दादा बहुत बड़े व्यापारी थे। उन्होंने काफी धन-दौलत कमाई थी। राजा-जमींदारों को भी वे रुपया उधार देते थे।

- अच्छा ? बाप रे ! किस चीज का व्यापार था ?

- नहीं वह सुनोगे तो खराब समझेगे।

- किसको ? तुम्हारे पिताजी के दादा को ? ऊफ्फ, पागल और किसको कहते हैं। ठीक है, मत बताओ...

- नहीं, नहीं बताती हूं। मुझे शर्म आ रही है। पर मुझे खराब मत समझना। मेरे पिता के दादाजी और उनके भाई लोग काफी शिक्षित थे, किंतु उनका महाजनी का कारोबार था, ब्याज पर रुपये उधार देते। एक राजा ने तो उनके बहुत सारे रुपये लौटाए ही नहीं। उसी सदमे में पिताजी के दादाजी का निधन हो गया। बचपन में एक बार दादाजी को कहते सुना था कि यह सूद के कारोबार के

पाप का ही फल था कि सारी धन-सम्पत्ति जमीन-जायदाद, कॉलेज की नौकरी आदि सब कुछ छोड़ कर एक जोड़ी कपड़ों में उन्हें देश छोड़ना पड़ा...

- तुम कौन सी चाय पीओगी? वही स्पेशल चाय बोलूं मिस्टु रानी! ये सब बातें सुन कर तकलीफ तो मुझे भी होती है, पर आज तुम्हारे देशी-घर के बारे में सब कुछ सुनने को जी कर रहा है। सुनाओगी मुझे?

- धत्! तुम यह मेरा मन रखने के लिए कह रहे हो, तुम्हारी सुनने की बिल्कुल भी इच्छा नहीं है। तुम्हारा तो ओरिजिन यहीं का है। देशी-घर छोड़ने की मेरी तकलीफ तुम क्या समझोगे।... मेरे पिताजी, दादाजी, कोई भी देशी घर में लौट कर नहीं जा सका। एक बार यदि मैं वहां जा पाती तो उनकी उत्कट इच्छा को अपनी दृष्टि से पूरा कर लेती।

- देखो तो सही, मैं कितनी उत्सुकता से तुम्हारी बातें सुनना चाह रहा हूं। बताओ न मिस्टु, अपने देशी-घर, वहां की नदियों-तालाब, लकड़ी के घर और बाग-बगीचों के बारे में।

बड़े-बड़े प्यालों में चाय आई, साथ में गरमा-गरम फ्रेंच-फ्राई।

- पिताजी से, दादाजी से वहां के बारे में कितना कुछ सुन रखा है। हमारे देशी-मकान के चौथे तल्ले पर एक विशाल हॉल-घर था, जिसकी दीवारों पर लकड़ी की खूबसूरत नक्काशी की हुई थी। सिर के ऊपर था टीन का छप्पर, जिस पर बारिश की बूंदें पड़तीं तो अद्भुत संगीतमय सुर सा सुनाई देता। पिताजी की मां बचपन से ही नहीं थीं, इसलिए वे अपनी दादीजी से बहुत प्रेम करते थे। बारिश के दिनों में उनकी दादीजी नाती-पोतों को ले कर अपनी कहानियों का पिटारा खोल कर बैठ जातीं। मेरे कमउम्र दादाजी तब कॉलेज से पढ़ा कर किताबों की दुकान से होते हुए साइकिल पर सवार घर लौटते। उन्हें बरिशाल के विख्यात ब्रजमोहन कॉलेज में नौकरी मिली थी। उनके घर लौटने के रास्ते के दोनों ओर थे नाले और असंख्य वृक्ष। नाले किंतु पहले नदी थे, जिन्होंने बाद में नाले का रूप ले लिया। दरअसल, बरिशाल चारों ओर पानी से घिरा एक द्वीप है, जहां जीवित रहने के लिए मनुष्य को प्रतिदिन संघर्ष करना पड़ता है। सभी कहते हैं कि बरिशाल के मनुष्य संघर्षशील होते हैं। वास्तव में उनकी दैनंदिन जीवन-यात्रा उन्हें संघर्षशील बनाती है।

- वाह! कितनी सुंदर जगह होगी... वहां जाने की इच्छा हो रही है मिस्टु!

- हमारा अपना वहां एक बड़ा सा तालाब था, जिसमें बड़ी-बड़ी मछलियां थीं। बच्चे उस तालाब में तैरते, नाव चलाते। पिताजी के अन्नप्राशन-समारोह के लिए उसी तालाब से तीस और चालीस किलो की दो मछलियां पकड़ी गई थीं। मेरे दादाजी अपनी नई बहू के साथ उसी तालाब के किनारे खड़े हो कर चोरी-छिपे बातें किया करते थे। खुद मेरी इच्छा है कि तुम्हारा हाथ थाम कर मैं भी उस तालाब के किनारे जा कर खड़ी होऊं... हा... हा... हा...

- हां, तो अगली बार मैं चलूंगा ना घूमने... तुम्हारे देश के घर में। ... हां, वो अद्भुत नाम की नदी है न... उसके बारे में कुछ नहीं बताया?

- कीर्तनखोला नाम है उस नदी का... हमारे घर से अधिक दूर नहीं थी वो। बरसात के दिनों में उसमें इतनी हिल्सा मछलियां होतीं कि हम सभी पूरी की पूरी मछली तल कर खा लेते थे। साल में एक बार वहां बाइच-प्रतियोगिता होती थी। उस खेल में बहुत बार मेरे दादाजी जीते। मैं तब बहुत छोटी थी। दादाजी इसीलिए बहुत सारी बातें बताते थे... सारी बातें तो मैं नहीं समझ पाती थी, पर उनकी आंखों की चमक देख कर मुझे बहुत खुशी होती। दादाजी मुझे अक्सर भीष्म के समान लगते, किंतु कभी-कभी वह मुझे अर्जुन सदृश उज्वल भी लगते।

- मिस्टु!... मैं तुम्हें किसके जैसा लगता हूं?

- देखो, बात को कहां से कहां ले जा रहे हो... चलो ठीक है, तुम कृष्ण सदृश लगते हो... शैतान, चंचल।... मुझे छोड़ कर इधर-उधर चले जाते हो।

- हा हा हा... तुम भी तो मुझसे दूर-दूर रहती हो। अभी की बात ही लो, मुझे छोड़कर अपना देश वाला घर देखने जा रही हो...

- हमारे उस घर में प्रवेश करते ही एक कृष्ण-मंदिर था। दोनों ओर थे बड़े-बड़े पोखर और रास्ता सीधे सदर द्वार को जाता था। घर में ही पाठशाला थी, जहां दूर-दूर से लड़के पढ़ने के लिए आते। उन भयंकर प्रतापी व्यक्ति ने शायद... सूद लेने का पाप धोने के लिए ही मंदिर तथा सभी के लिए पाठशाला खोल रखी थी। पता नहीं... अब वहां जा कर क्या देखने को मिले। अब तो वहां भिन्न धर्मावलम्बी रहते हैं। दादाजी हालांकि नास्तिक थे, फिर भी वे कभी-कभी मंदिर के बारे में बताते... आश्चर्य।

- मिस्टु, काफी कुछ हमारे ज्ञान और सोच के बाहर होता है। अब जैसे तुम यहां की नई पीढ़ी की हो, तुम्हारा और तुम्हारे माता-पिता का भी पालन-पोषण कलकत्ता में ही हुआ... फिर भी कितनी ऑब्सेस्ड हो तुम अपने पूर्वजों के देशी-घर को देखने के लिए।

मैंने चाय की चुस्की ली। वैभव की बड़ी-बड़ी उंगलियों को हथेली में भर मैं सोच रही थी कि सचमुच क्या मैं ऑब्सेस्ड हूं ?... क्या पता...

बूढ़ी-गंगा पार कर मेघना के ऊपर से जलयान बढ़ा जा रहा था बरिशाल की ओर। जलयान में सवार होने से पहले ही इकबाल भाई ने ढाका से सुसंवाद दिया था। ब्रजमोहन कॉलेज में खोज-खबर लेने पर उन्हें अंततः हमारे देशी घर का पता चला। किताब की दुकान का भी हल्का सा आभास मिला। जलयान की डेक पर हवा तेज थी। उस तेज हवा में मानो मैं उड़ी जा रही थी। जिस आंगन में पिताजी गेंद फेंका-फेंकी खेलते थे, जिस तालाब में गमछा फैला कर मछलियां पकड़ते थे, कल सुबह ही उस घर के सामने मैं खड़ी हूंगी। आधी रात तक नदी की अपूर्व शोभा देख कर मैं अपने सिंगल केबिन में सोने चली गई। उत्तेजनावश ठीक से नींद नहीं आई। चौमंजिला जलयान नदी का गहरा पानी चीरता बढ़ा जा रहा था गंतव्य की ओर... जहां कीर्तनखोला नदी ने बरिशाल में अपना साम्राज्य बिछा रखा था।

पूरे जलयान में घूम-फिर कर मैंने कई नये मित्र बना लिये थे और वे सभी 'इण्डिया से आई अकेली लड़की' की आवभगत में व्यस्त हो उठे। जलयान के कैप्टेन सारंग तक ने अपने केबिन में बैठा कर मुझे नदी के बारे में विस्तार से बताया। उनका भी देश बरिशाल ही था। उसी देश को देखने आई अकेली लड़की का उन्होंने भी अच्छे से ध्यान रखा। बोले -- रात को दावत में आ कर खाना मेरे साथ खाना। भोर में मैं तुम्हें जगा दूंगा, तब ही चंद्रद्वीप आयेगा।

मेरे गले में दर्द होने लगा...। इतना स्नेह, पिताजी, दादाजी... किसी ने भी नहीं देखा।

थोड़ी सी देर की नींद, फिर भोर-रात के वक्त खुद ही हड़बड़ा कर उठ बैठी।... मैं सपना देख रही थी कि देश के घर के आंगन में बैठी मूढ़ी-नारियल खा रही थी और बगल में बैठे दादाजी मुझे वृक्षों की पहचान बता रहे थे।... रात शेष हो रही थी। हड़बड़ा कर चौथी मंजिल की डेक पर जा खड़ी हुई। बगल में ही

सारंग भाई का केबिन था। जरा सी देर में ही उन्होंने पुकारा -- वो देखो बहन! कीर्तनखोला पर चंद्रद्वीप, तुम पूछ रही थी ना?

धुंधले से अंधेरे में... दूर जाग उठा था द्वीप, जहां के राजा ने हमारे वंश की एक पीढ़ी को प्रताड़ित कर बेसहारा कर दिया था।

भोर हो आई थी। चारों ओर पानी और हरियाली की गंध व्याप्त थी। जाने कहां से आ कर एक बुलबुल पंछी कान के पास अपनी कूक से बेचैन किए दे रहा था। जलयान आ कर घाट पर लगा। इकबाल भाई मुझे लिवा ले जाने के लिए आये थे। जी में आया, उनसे लिपट जाऊँ, क्योंकि वे ही तो दिखाएंगे मुझे मेरा देशी-घर, मेरा देशज वास-स्थान...

- पहले ब्रजमोहन कॉलेज चलते हैं, आपके दादाजी वहां पढ़ाते थे! मैंने प्रिंसिपल साहब से बात कर रखी है।... आपके घर जाने का रास्ता उधर से ही है।

मैंने सिर हिलाया -- ठीक है। किंतु मैं घर को अच्छी तरह से देख पाऊँगी तो? शाम के जहाज से ही तो लौट जाना है।

- हां, हां, अवश्य।... वो देखिए, जीवनानंद का घर... आपके दादाजी के वो मित्र थे न?... यहां की हवा में भी देखिए कितनी मिठास है।

- नहीं, मेरे दादाजी से वे उम्र में बहुत बड़े थे, पर हमारी किताबों की दुकान में अक्सर आते थे। बहुत बड़े-बड़े लोग वहां आते थे।... पर वो नाले कहां हैं? पिताजी और दादाजी से रास्ते के दोनों ओर के नालों के बारे में काफी कुछ सुना था। सुना था कि उनमें ज्वार-भाटा भी आता था।

- हां, हां, देखिए न दोनों ओर... नाले अब पहले जैसे नहीं रहे, संकरे हो गए हैं।

सड़क के दोनों ओर स्पष्ट पानी के नाले थे। गाड़ी बढ़ी जा रही थी कॉलेज और फिर वहां से हमारे घर की ओर।

कॉलेज जाकर वहां की नेम-प्लेट पर दादाजी का नाम देखा। फिर वहां के विशाल मैदान को अवाक् होकर देखती रही, यहीं तो दादाजी अपने छात्रों के साथ फुटबॉल खेला करते थे। इन सारी बातों का मुझे पता है, मैंने सुना है...। प्रिंसिपल सर ने बहुत जोर दिया कि 'मछली-भात खा कर ही जाऊँ'। ऐसा अपूर्व था हमारा देश?

मेरे पास समय नहीं था...। देशी घर भी तो देखना था। मेरी मां, काका-बुआ आदि सब प्रतीक्षा कर रहे होंगे अपने सपनों के इस घर के बारे में सुनने को...

वृक्षों से भरे साफ-सुथरे रास्ते पर गाड़ी चली जा रही थी। लग रहा था जैसे कोई पर्यटन शहर हो। दिन के वक्त भी झींगुरों की तीव्र पुकार सुनाई दे रही थी। उत्तेजनावश दिल धड़क रहा था... तो मैं सचमुच अपने देशी घर में पहुंचने वाली हूं।

गाड़ी रुकी। दोनों ओर स्फटिक स्वच्छ पोखर, नारियल-सुपारी तथा रेन-ट्री की भरमार। अपने स्वप्न के रास्ते पर मैं बढ़ी जा रही थी। यही तो है हमारे घर में घुसने का रास्ता। इन सब के बारे में मैं जानती थी, मैंने सुन रखा था।... किंतु यह क्या? रास्ते के अंत में आंगन के करीब एक नितांत साधारण सा मध्यमवर्गीय दो मंजिला मकान।... मैं चौंक कर पीछे की ओर हटी... नहीं, नहीं, ये हमारा घर नहीं।... कहां गया वह चार मंजिला मकान... लकड़ी की नक्काशीदार दीवारें... सब कहां हैं?

इकबाल भाई हंस दिये, बोले -- आपने जो तथ्य दिये थे, उनके अनुसार तो यही है आपका घर। देखिए, यह रहा मंदिर...

मैंने निगाह घुमा कर देखा रास्ते के उस ओर था एक पुराना जीर्ण सा मंदिर। इसी बीच मकान में रहने वालों में से कुछ ने आड़ से झांकना शुरू किया। महिलाओं ने सिर ढंक रखा था और पुरुषों ने लुंगी पहन रखी थी। पुरुषों के चेहरे कुछ रुष्ट से नजर आये। वे एक सपाट चांटे की तरह धड़ाम-धड़ाम, मुंह पर दरवाजे बंद कर रहे थे।

इकबाल भाई दौड़ कर मेरी ओर आये और बोले -- आप प्लीज़ अपसेट न हों। मैं देखता हूं...

अगल-बगल से लोग बढ़े आ रहे थे और मैं बुत बनी मौन खड़ी थी, आंगन में अकेली। उनकी बातें मेरे सिर व देह पर बरस रही थीं।

- हां, यही तो था चक्रवर्तियों का घर, यहीं थी पाठशाला। बहुत दिन हुए, वे सब के सब इण्डिया चले गये...।

मेरी धुंधली नज़र के सामने से दरवाज़ा खोल कर जाने कौन थे, जो बढ़े आ रहे थे। इकबाल भाई मेरे कान में फुसफुसा कर बोले -- दरअसल, ये लोग डरते

हैं।... अब यह एनिमी प्रॉपर्टी है न, इसलिए।

कुछ ही देर में लुंगी पहने पुरुष और सिर ढंके स्त्रियां मेरे पास आईं और बोलीं -- आइए, आइए, यहां बैठिए, नाश्ता-पानी कीजिए।

मैंने अपने शुष्क होठों पर जीभ फिराई और कहा -- मैं घर देखूंगी...

वे बोले -- आइए, दिखाते हैं।

ओढ़ने से ढकी स्त्रियों के पीछे-पीछे मैं घर में घुसी। सब कुछ अनजान सा था। किचेन में कई हांड़ियां एक साथ रखी थीं। मेहमान, यानी मेरे लिए कच्चे नारियल का पानी लाया गया, जो अत्यंत मीठा था। जो महिला नारियल पानी लाई थी वह तनिक मुस्कुरा कर बोली -- यह बहुत पुराने नारियल गाछ का नारियल है, शायद आपके दादाजी के समय का।

मैं तालाब के पास जाकर खड़ी हुई, बगल में ही था वृक्षों से भरा बगीचा। मैं फुसफुसाई -- बगीचे देख कर आती हूं।

लुंगी पहने पुरुष समवेत स्वर में बोल उठे -- पर यहां तो कोई बगीचा नहीं है।

मैंने घूम कर इकबाल भाई को देखा और कहा -- नहीं, थे। हमारे कई बगीचे थे और लकड़ी का एक चौमंजिला मकान भी था जिसमें चौथे तल्ले पर एक हॉल-घर भी था, विश्वास कीजिए...।

हाथ में धारदार कटारी लिये लुंगी पहने हुए जो पुरुष मेहमान के लिए कच्चा नारियल काट रहा था, उसकी जुबान भी उतनी ही धारदार थी। वह बोला -- हम लोग भी कोई झूठ नहीं बोल रहे हैं। इतने वर्ष बीत गए हैं। सब कुछ क्या पहले जैसा रहता है?

... अब चलना होगा।... तालाब के पानी में हाथ डुबाया तो पानी मानो बोल उठा, इतने अर्से बाद आने का समय मिला?... सीने में एक हलचल सी मचाते हुए सहसा एक जलपंछी चहक उठा। पचपन वर्षों से मेरे परिवारजनों का जमा गुस्सा-वंचना-गर्व मानो मेरा पीछा कर रहे थे।

अपने स्वप्नों के रास्ते से मैं धीरे-धीरे निकल आई।... जर्जर मंदिर में झांक कर देखा। देवमूर्ति खड़ी थी, एकाकी... अस्पष्ट सी...

थोड़ी देर बाद ही जलयान छूटेगा।... सबसे आखिर में दादाजी की किताबों की दुकान देखने पहुंची, जो वे अपने प्रिय छात्र कादिर को सौंप गए थे। प्रोफेसर

कादिर अभी बहुत मशहूर व्यक्ति हैं, विदेश में रहते हैं। और वह दुकान भी अब काफी मशहूर बरिशाल का सबसे अभिजात रेस्तरां है, जहां बैठकर आसिफ गाय की 'ब्रेन-करी' खाने का आग्रह कर रहा था और मैं उसे रुंधे गले से बताना चाह रही थी -- पता है, इसी दुकान में जीवनानंद आते थे तथा सभी विख्यात लोगों का अड्डा जमता था यहां।

आसिफ का किंतु मेरी बातों की ओर ध्यान नहीं था। उसका सारा ध्यान तो अतिथि सत्कार की ओर था। बोला -- तो फिर आप मटन बिरयानी खाएं। याद रखेंगी बरिशाल की मटन बिरयानी। हम भी खाएंगे पर पहले ब्रेन-करी।... आप भी चख कर तो देखें...

वही जलयान था, जिसमें मैं आई थी। कैप्टेन सारंग ने दूर से ही देख कर हाथ हिलाया -- बहन! कैसा लगा देश का घर?

इकबाल भाई ने सामान उठा कर केबिन में रख दिया। नाभिमूल तक कंपाता हुआ भोंपू बज उठा। यह पहली वार्निंग थी... इकबाल भाई मेरी ओर देख कर हल्के से मुस्कुराए -- फिर आइएगा... बरिशाल की नदी तो ठीक से देख ही नहीं पाईं...

'हां, हां, जरूर।' मैंने सिर हिलाया।

नियत समय पर जलयान चल पड़ा। डेक पर खड़ी हो कर मैंने देखा इकबाल भाई किनारे पर मुस्कुराते हुए हाथ हिला रहे थे। क्रमशः वे दूर होते जा रहे थे। इतनी देर तक रोक कर रखे आंसू आंखों से गालों पर लुढ़क पड़े।

अपनों की पहचान

आरती सिंह

1969 में जन्मी आरती सिंह हिंदी की एक लोकप्रिय कवयित्री व कथाकार हैं तथा महिला काव्य मंच की बंगाल शाखा की महामंत्री हैं।

महेश की जब आंखें खुलीं तो उसने यशोदा की भुनभुनाने की आवाज सुनी। वह बिस्तर पर लेटे-लेटे ही बोला 'क्या बात है? आज सुबह से ही शुरू हो गई हो। कम से कम सुबह के समय तो शांत रहा करो।' वह चिढ़ाने वाले अन्दाज में बोला।

यशोदा बोली - 'तुम्हें क्या है? आफत तो मेरी जान की है। सारे बर्तन जूठे पड़े हैं। आज सुधा फिर काम करने नहीं आएगी। लेने को तो सात सौ लेती है और काम के नाम पर कभी आती है, तो कभी नहीं आती। मैं अकेली जान क्या करूँ? बच्चों का नाश्ता तैयार करूँ, तुम्हारा खाना तैयार करूँ या तुम्हारा टिफिन। मांजी भी सुबह-सुबह पूजा-पाठ करने बैठ जाती हैं। यह नहीं होता कि थोड़ा हाथ बंटा दें।'

'यशोदा, तुम मां से यह आशा मत किया करो। उनके बुढ़ापे के दिन हैं। अब उन्हें आराम करने दो। प्रीति और रमेश को उन्होंने ही तो पाल-पोस कर बड़ा

किया है। याद है, जापा के बाद वह तुम्हें हवा भी नहीं लगने देती थीं।' महेश समझाते हुए बोला और स्वयं बिस्तर से उठकर बाथरूम में जाने को हुआ तभी यशोदा ने कहा - 'देखो जी, मुझे कोई शिकायत नहीं है, आपकी माताश्री से। मैं तो बस इतना ही कहना चाहती हूँ कि एक आदमी खटते-खटते मरता है और दूसरा आराम करते-करते।'

'तो आपके कहने का मतलब है कि मेरी मां आपका चौका-बर्तन कर दिया करे।' महेश झुझंलाकर बोला।

'आपको तो बात का बतंगड़ बनाने की आदत है।' यशोदा ने कहा।

महेश बिना उत्तर दिये बाथरूम में चला गया। यशाोदा भी भुनभुनाते हुए फटाफट काम निबटाने लगी।

पार्वती ने पूजा घर में बैठे दोनों का वार्तालाप सुन लिया था। यह कोई नई बात तो थी नहीं। उन्हें प्राय: इस तरह जली-कटी सुनने को मिलती थी। वह आज तक पुत्र-पौत्र के मोह-जाल में फंसकर हंसते-हंसते सब कुछ सह जाती थीं। किन्तु न जाने क्यों आज उनसे यह सब न सहा गया। उन्होंने महेश से बात करने का फैसला कर लिया। क्योंकि वह नहीं चाहती थीं कि उनके कारण घर में किसी प्रकार का क्लेश हो। वह अपने पुत्र महेश को प्राणों से भी ज्यादा चाहती थीं। उन्हें आज भी वह दिन याद है, जब महेश के पिता की मृत्यु एक दुर्घटना में हो गई थी। उस समय महेश मात्र बारह वर्ष का था, छठी कक्षा में पढ़ता था। इस घटना के बाद उनके रिश्तेदार उनसे ऐसे कटे मानो लटाई से पतंग।

पार्वती अपने पति के बचाए पैसों से कुछ दिन तो आर्थिक समस्याओं का सामना करती रही। किन्तु जब पैसे समाप्त हो गए, तो जीवन निर्वाह कठिन हो गया। वह अपने होनहार पुत्र की पढ़ाई को बीच में रोकना नहीं चाहती थी। इसलिए स्वयं कुछ करने की ठानी और सफल भी हो गई।

पार्वती की जान-पहचान बहुतों से होने के कारण उसे सिलाई-बुनाई का काम खूब मिलने लगा। वह कमर तोड़ मेहनत इसी आशा में किए जा रही थी कि महेश किसी तरह पढ़-लिखकर, सम्मानित ओहदा प्राप्त कर ले ताकि उसका जीवन सफल हो जाए।

विश्वास लगन के साथ की गई मेहनत अवश्य सफल होती है। ठीक उसी प्रकार मां-बेटे की मेहनत रंग लाई। महेश को सेल-टैक्स विभाग में उच्च

आफिसर का ओहदा प्राप्त हो गया।

पार्वती अपने पुत्र से बहुत खुश थी क्योंकि अब वह उसे कुछ करने नहीं देता। उनके आराम का पूरा-पूरा ख्याल रखता। इसलिए उसने अपनी पत्नी को पहली रात में ही बता दिया था कि उसकी मां को उसे हर हाल में खुश रखना होगा।

यशोदा सास का पहले बहुत ध्यान रखती थी। परन्तु ज्यों-ज्यों उसके ऊपर जिम्मेवारियों का बोझ बढ़ता जा रहा था, त्यों-त्यों वह सास की ओर से विमुख होती जा रही थी। अब उसे वह बोझ लगने लगी थी।

पार्वती सब कुछ समझते हुए भी शांत बनी रहती। क्योंकि अब वह समझ गई थी कि उस घर से उनका अवकाश प्राप्त करने का समय आ गया है।

आज छुट्टी का दिन था। बच्चे खेल में व्यस्त थे। यशोदा किसी काम से पड़ोस में गई हुई थी। महेश बिस्तर पर लेटे-लेटे अखबार पढ़ रहा था। पार्वती उसके बगल में बैठकर कोई धार्मिक पुस्तक पढ़ रही थी। वह मौका देखकर बोली - 'बेटा, एक बात कहूँ?'

'कहो।'

'बुरा तो नहीं मानोगे?'

महेश अखबार रखकर उठ बैठा और बोला - 'क्या बात है, मां। ऐसे क्यों पूछ रही हो? क्या मेरे ऊपर से तुम्हारा विश्वास उठ गया है या मुझमें कोई खोट नजर आने लगी है?'

पार्वती ने कहा - 'ऐसी कोई बात नहीं है, बेटा।'

'तो फिर क्या बात है मां कि तुम्हें मुझसे इजाजत लेनी पड़ रही है।' महेश द्रवित होकर बोला।

'बेटा मैंने एक वृद्ध आश्रम में बात कर ली है। मैं वहीं रहना चाहती हूँ।'

'क्यों मां यहां कोई परेशानी है क्या?'

'परेशानी तो कुछ भी नहीं, किन्तु यहां पहाड़-सा दिन कटता नहीं। वहां अपने जैसों के साथ बातचीत करके, आराम से दिन काट लिया करूँगी।

'तो क्या, इसी दिन के लिए मुझे पाल-पोस कर बड़ा किया था? मैं यह सब सुनने से पहले मर क्यों न गया?'

'ऐसी अशुभ बात मत बोल मेरे बच्चे।' पार्वती रोते हुए बोली।

'क्या तुम्हें यशोदा ने कुछ कहा है?'

'नहीं, मुझे किसी ने कुछ नहीं कहा।'

महेश मां का हाथ अपने सिर पर रखते हुए बोला - 'मां, मेरी कसम खाकर बोल कि तुमने यह फैसला क्यों किया ? क्या तुम्हारा महेश बदल गया है या तुम महेश का मुँह देखना नहीं चाहती या......।' अपनी बात समाप्त किए बिना महेश बच्चों की भांति फूँट-फूँट कर रोने लगा।

पार्वती भी उसके गले लगकर रोते हुए बोली - 'नहीं, मेरे बच्चे, ऐसी कोई बात नहीं। मैं तो तुम सबको खुश देखना चाहती हूँ।'

'मां, यशोदा उतनी बुरी भी नहीं कि तुम उसे सदा के लिए त्याग दो।' महेश आंसुओं पर काबू पाते हुए समझाने वाले अंदाज में बोला।

'नहीं बेटा, बुरी तो मैं हूँ कि आज तक अपनों को पहचान न सकी।' तभी दोनों बच्चे दादी-दादी कहते हुए वहां आ गए। पार्वती ने आंसू पोंछ, दोनों को गोद में बैठा लिया।

पार्वती मन ही मन समझ गई कि उनका बेटा उन्हें इतनी आसानी से जाने देने वाला नहीं। धीरे-धीरे दोनों इस बात को भूल गए।

एक दिन अचानक महेश को कार्यालय के काम से हफ्ते भर के लिए बाहर जाना पड़ा। इस दौरान यशोदा के ऊपर काम का बोझ और अधिक बढ़ जाने से वह पहले से अधिक वाचाल हो गई।

पार्वती यशोदा के वाचालपन और उग्रता को बर्दाश्त नहीं कर पाई। इसलिए महेश के नाम एक पत्र छोड़ कर स्वयं वृद्धाश्रम चली गई।

दरवाजे पर दस्तक होने पर यशोदा ने पूछा - 'कौन है ?'

'मैं।' महेश की आवाज पहचान कर यशोदा ने झट से दरवाजा खोल दिया।

महेश ने जूता खोलते हुए पूछा - 'बच्चे कहां हैं ? शाम हो आई। क्या वे अभी तक स्कूल से नहीं लौटे ?'

यशोदा बोली - 'नहीं, स्कूलवाले सभी बच्चों को घुमाने ले गए हैं। इसलिए आज दोनों को लौटने में थोड़ी देर होगी।'

महेश ने मां को न देख पूछा - 'मां कहां है ? दिखाई नहीं दे रही।'

यशोदा ने आलमारी से एक पत्र निकाल कर महेश को दिया। महेश फटाफट पत्र खोलकर पढ़ने लगा।

प्रिय महेश बेटा,

सदा खुश रहो। ईश्वर तुम सबको लम्बी उम्र दे। बेटा, तुम मेरे लिए चिन्ता न करना। मैं वृद्धाश्रम जा रही हूँ। तुम्हारी अनुपस्थिति में मुझे जाना नहीं चाहिए था। किन्तु तुम्हारे रहते मेरा घर छोड़ना शायद सम्भव न होता। तुम यशोदा को भला-बुरा मत कहना। क्योंकि इसमें उसका कोई कसूर नहीं है। हां, अन्तिम क्षणों में मैं तुमसे अवश्य मिलने की कोशिश करूँगी। बेटा कभी दुःखी न होना। यही मेरी अन्तिम इच्छा है। ईश्वर तुम्हें हर पथ पर सफलता दे। इसी कामना के साथ पत्र समाप्त करती हूँ।

—तुम्हारी मां

महेश सिर पकड़कर बिस्तर पर बैठ गया। तभी बच्चे आ गए। बच्चे चिन्तित दिखाई दे रहे थे। यशोदा ने दोनों बच्चों से अनेक प्रश्न किए। किन्तु दोनों चुप रहे। किसी प्रश्न का उत्तर नहीं दिया। अचानक रमेश मां की तरफ देखते हुए बोला - 'मां एक बात पूछूँ?'

यशोदा प्रफुल्लित हो मुस्कुराकर बोली - 'जरूर पूछो।'

रमेश बोला - 'मां दादी कहां है?'

यशोदा इस प्रश्न से घबरा गई। किन्तु स्वयं को संतुलित कर उग्र होती हुई बोली - 'कितनी बार बताऊँ?

रमेश ढिठाई से पेश आते हुए बोला - 'नहीं मां, दादी काशी नहीं गई है। आप झूठ बोलती हो। आज हम वृद्धाश्रम घूमने गये थे। वहां दादी की तरह बहुत सी औरतें थीं। टीचर ने हमें बताया कि इन सभी का घर परिवार है। किन्तु इनके अपनों ने इन्हें घर से निकाल दिया है। दादी काशी नहीं, वृद्धाश्रम गई हैं। मैं भी जब बड़ा हो जाऊँगा, तब आपको भी वृद्धाश्रम भेज दूँगा।'

नन्हीं प्रीति भाई का साथ देती हुई बोली - 'मैं भी बड़ी होकर आपको घर से निकाल दूँगी।'

यशोदा अवाक् हो दोनों बच्चों को निहारती रह गई। वह सोचने लगी, 'बच्चे इतने सयाने कब हो गए?'

महेश बच्चों को गले से लगाते हुए बोला - चिंता न करो बेटे। मैं आज ही दादी को ले आऊँगा।'

यह सुनकर बच्चे खुश हो गए। महेश क्रोध भरी निगाहों से यशोदा को देखने लगा। यशोदा को लगा, मानो उसके शरीर में बिजली कौंध गई हो।

मेरा घर

डॉ. फ़ातमा खातून

डॉ. फातमा खातून उर्दू की एक जानी-मानी कथाकार हैं तथा उर्दू कहानियां और उनके सामाजिक संदर्भ पर गवेषणा के लिए आपको पीएचडी की डिग्री भी प्राप्त हुई है।

शीला और रमेश की प्यारी बेटी रूपा घर में अपनी मासूम बातों से जैसे फूल बिखेर रही है। .... बाबा हमारे गाँव का घर कितना सुंदर है ना। आप इस बार खुशी से गाँव चलेंगे ?

रूपा सिर्फ दस साल की होने के बावजूद बला की हसाद (भावुक) थी। उसे अपने आवाई(पुरखों) गाँव व बस्ती के छोटे से घर से हद दर्जा लगाव था। वहाँ के खुले माहौल में खेलना, खेतों की हरियाली, पोखर के पनघट में दोस्तों के साथ डुबकी लगाना उसे काफी पसंद था। मगर रमेश को मज़बूरन मज़दूरी के लिए गाँव-घर छोड़कर बम्बई शहर में रहना पड़ा। शीला और रूपा को भी बाद में ले आया। अपने घर को छोड़कर शहर की तंग गली में उस पोशीदा खोली में रहने को मजबूर होना पड़ा। शीला और रमेश तो हालात से समझौता कर चुके

थे क्योंकि बड़ों को हालात के मुताबिक़ बदलने में वक्त नहीं लगता।

मगर मासूम दिल रूपा को आज़ाद परिंदे की तरह मुकैय्यद (कैद) होकर रहना गंवारा नहीं था। रूपा को रह-रह कर अपने गाँव के घर, वहाँ के आँगन की याद आती रहती। लेकिन वक़्त हमेशा बदलाव लाता है। धीरे-धीरे रूपा ने शहर में जीना सीख लिया। अचानक मुल्क में कोरोना नामी ऐसी बबा (रोग) फैली जिसने महामारी की शक्ल अख्तियार कर ली। सरकार ने पूरे मुल्क में लॉक डाउन कर दिया जिसका सबसे गहरा असर मज़दूरों पर पड़ा।

किसी की नौकरी चली गई, किसी का कारोबार बंद हो गया, हर तरफ नफी-नफी (हाहाकार)।

रमेश को भी अब काम मिलना बंद हो गया। घर में फांके पड़ने लगे। सबलोग घरों में मुकैय्यद (कैद) होकर रह गए। सरकार मदद का एलान करती मगर वह मज़दूरों तक नहीं पहुँच पाती। रमेश को उसके दोस्त कैलाश ने बता दिया था, हमलोगों का शहर में गुजारा नहीं हो सकता इसीलिए हमलोग गाँव जाने का इरादा कर रहे हैं।

रमेश ...... मगर लॉक डाउन की वजह से तो गाड़ियां बंद हैं।

कैलाश...... तो क्या हुआ, हमारे साथ दस और लोग हैं। सब मिलकर पैदल का सोच रहे हैं। पहले के जमाने में भी तो लोग काफिला बनाकर चलते ही थे। हम भी चलेंगे। क्योंकि यहाँ रहे तो वैसे भी भूखों मर जाएंगे।

कैलाश की बातें रमेश के दिल में घर कर गईं। उसने भी शीला के साथ मश्विरा करके गाँव जाने का इरादा कर लिया।

रूपा घर जाने की खबर से ही खिल उठी। उसकी भूख का एहसास भी जाता रहा। वह अब जल्द से जल्द अपने घर जाना चाहती थी।

आगामी सुबह रमेश सबको लेकर बाकी मज़दूरों का हमराह बनकर अपने घर के सफ़र को निकल पड़ा। कुछ जरा सा ही सामान रमेश और शीला ने सर पर उठा लिया और रूपा की मखमली उंगली पकड़ कर चलने लगे।

दो दिन हो गए। खाने की चीजें अगर रास्ते में कोई दे देता तो ले लेते। किसी तरह सफ़र कट रहा था। चलते-चलते रूपा की चप्पल टूट गई और उसके पाँव जमीन की तपिश से झुलसने लगे। शीला से बेटी की हालत देखी नहीं जा रही थी। वो कभी उसे गोद में उठाकर चलती, कभी उसकी उंगली पकड़कर। मां की

ममता ज्वार मार रही थी कि बेटी को पलकों पर बिठाकर ले जाए। मगर वो मज़बूर थी।

रमेश भी रूपा की हालत देखकर दिल मसोस कर रह जाता।

चलते-चलते दो सप्ताह गुजर गए। अब रूपा में चलने की ताकत ही नहीं थी। वह कई बार गिर चुकी थी। मां बार-बार उसको हौसला देने की कोशिश करती।

मां बोलती ...... देख रूपा, हमारा घर आ गया।

इतने लम्बे सफ़र के बाद उनकी हालत भी खराब होने लगी। चलते-चलते गर्मी और प्यास की शिद्दत जिस्म को निढाल कर रही थी लेकिन रूपा की आँखों की चमक मंद नहीं पड़ी। रूपा...... जल्दी चलो ना, मां। हमारा घर आने ही वाला है। गुडडू और सबके साथ खेलने में कितना मजा आएगा।

धीरे-धीरे उनका खाना ख़त्म होने लगा। रास्ते में कुछ लोग मदद के लिए सामने आते दिख रहे हैं।

शीला..... राधा चाची ने तेरे लिए हलवा-पूड़ी बनाकर रखी है। हमारे आँगन के पेड़ में आम फल गया है। तुम जी भरके खाना।

रूपा में फिर कहीं से कूबत आ जाती और वह चलने लगती।

तकरीबन पचास मीटर की दूरी से उसका घर दिखने लगा। वह ख़ुशी से झूम उठी। आज वह खला में उड़ रही थी। उसने मां को आवाज़ दी.... मेरा घर और फिर वह अपने दुखों से आज़ाद हो गई।

उसकी रूह भगवान से पूछ रही थी .... मेरा घर।

लाशें बोलती हैं

डा. प्रभामयी सामन्तराय

डा. प्रभामयी सामन्तराय ओडिया व हिंदी की सुपरिचित कवि कथाकार हैं जिनके चार कविता संग्रह प्रकाशित हो चुके हैं तथा जो ओडिशा के एक सरकारी कॉलेज में अंग्रेजी की प्राध्यापिका भी हैं।

धीरे-धीरे आंखों के परदे हट रहे थे। बहुत तकलीफ हो रही थीं। आंखें खोलने में मानो शरीर की सारी मांस पेशियों को जोर लगाना पड़ रहा हो। लेकिन कुछ दिखाई क्यों नहीं देता? अंधेरा, सिर्फ अंधेरा...। क्या मेरी आंखों की रोशनी चली गई है या फिर दुनिया की, पता नहीं। अंधेरा कहीं गाढ़ा है तो कहीं फीका। बहुत ठंड भी लग रही है, एक कंपकंपी सी भरी है शरीर में, हाथ-पैर भी हैं या नहीं पता नहीं चल रहा। हाथ-पैर हिल नहीं रहे हैं। बदन टूट रहा है अजीब सी बदबू आ रही है, मुझसे, आस-पास से और दूर से भी। एक सन्नाटा छाया हुआ है। सिर्फ लहरों के थपेड़े खाने और जल-प्रवाह की आवाज सुनाई दे रही है। सन्नाटा इतना गहरा कि सैलाब की आवाज चीख बनकर कानों में गूंज रही है।

अब तक मैं महसूस कर रही थी खुद को और आस-पास की दुनिया को। घर

की चारदीवारी में भी अंधेरे से डरने वाली लड़की खुले मैदान में नए-नए बने श्मशान में अकेली पड़ी हुई थी। अब मुझे याद आये मेरे परिवार वाले। कहां गये सब? दिखाई नहीं देते। कहां गये मुझे छोड़ कर? वे छूट गए या फिर मैं? ठंडक इतनी मानो चुभ रही हो। पूरा बदन पीला है। कपड़े हैं कि नहीं, सुध नहीं। सदा ओढ़नी से ढकी रहने वाली मैं भूल गई थी, कपड़ों के बारे में। ढूंढ़ना चाहती हूँ अपनों को, लेकिन हिल क्यों नहीं पा रही मैं? न सिर हिल रहा है, न हाथ-पांव, न शरीर। बहुत मुश्किल से हिल पा रही हैं तो सिर्फ पलकें।

अकेलेपन का डर सता रहा है। किसी के न होने का ग़म सता रहा है। शायद मेरे मन का अंधेरा बाहर के अंधेरे से कुछ ज्यादा ही था फिर भी मन में शंका पैदा हो रही थी। पास में पड़े पेड़ और चट्टान से चिपका पत्थर। अनजाने नगर में श्मशान भी शहर लगता है लेकिन जब आंखों के सामने बस्ती श्मशान बन गई हो तो हर चीज खौफ पैदा करती है।

मन की वेदना गला घोंट रही थी। अपनों की याद हर पल सता रही थी। कहां होंगे सब? जिन्दा भी हैं, या...। आगे की सोच कर सिहर उठी थी। नहीं... नहीं... सब लोग होंगे। अच्छे होंगे। कहीं मुझे ढूंढ़ तो नहीं रहे होंगे? कैसे मिलूंगी उन सबसे? कोई तो मदद करो...।

यह रात इतनी गहरी, इतनी लम्बी क्यों है? मानो पूरी जिंदगी इसी रात में समा गई हो। बस- पानी... पानी... पानी... पर शरीर का चमड़ा जगह-जगह से फट गया था जैसे अकाल पड़ने पर जगह-जगह से धरती फट जाती है। घूमने आई थी यहां। भगवान के दर्शन के लिए हम सब आये थे यहां। सोच रही थी झूठ है यह कहावत कि इनके दर्शन से सारे दु:खों का हरण हो जाता है। सोच रही थी, काश हम सब यहां न आये होते...। यह सैलाब न आया होता तो जिंदगी कितनी सुन्दर रहती। दूर से नज़र पड़ता मंदिर पर मंदिर के चारों तरफ बर्फ का हिस्सा सैलाब में बह गया था। मेरे जैसे कई लोग निश्चल पड़े हुए थे इधर। मन में बात उठी, तुम क्या उद्धार करोगे? तुम तो अपने पास बुला कर विनाश कर रहे हो। अगर तुम्हारे पास सबको बचाने की ताकत नहीं तो तुम भगवान काहे के? और अगर शक्ति होते हुए भी तुमने सबको नहीं बचाया तो भी तुम भगवान नहीं हो। अगर सब कुछ तुम्हारे इशारे पर होता है तो यह सब भी तुम्हारे इशारे पर हुआ है। घिन भर आई मन में इनके लिए जिन्हें लोग भगवान कहते हैं। मेरी सोच

पर काले परदे पड़ते जा रहे थे...। कोई बहता हुआ आया जिसने मुझे उसकी तरफ देखने को मजबूर कर दिया।

मां... मां... मां... छोटी बच्ची थी। मैं बोल उठी - बेटा रो मत, इधर आ मेरे पास। तुम्हारा नाम क्या है? कोई जवाब नहीं बस रोना और सिर्फ रोना। रो-रोकर बेचारी थक गई तो आवाज अपने-आप बंद हो गई। रह गई केवल सिसकियां...। सिसकियों के बीच रह-रह कर मां, मां, पुकारती रही। कहां होगी उसकी मां? छोटी-सी बच्ची बिना मां के बिलख रही थी। उसको सुस्त देखकर मेरे अंदर की करुण काया सिहर उठी। यह इंसान है या भूत? शरीर का रंग और बालों का रंग आपस में मिल गये थे। बेचारी बयान नहीं कर पा रही थी अपने दर्द की दास्तान लेकिन उसकी आंखें खुद बयान कर रही थी, अपनी आपबीती, उसकी सिसकियां मेरी रूह तक को झकझोर रही थीं। एक पल को मैं अपना दर्द भूल गई। ऐसा लगा इस बच्ची के दर्द के आगे मेरा अपना दर्द कुछ नहीं है। जाने कहां से ताकत आ गई। मुर्दा हाथों में हलकी-सी जान लौट आई और धीरे से उसके सिर पर हाथ फेर दिया मैंने। थोड़ा-सा स्पर्श पाकर वह मुझमें और भी सिमट गई। कौन है, कहां से आई है? एक पल को वही मुझे सबसे अपनी लगी।

अंदर का डर दूर हो रहा था इस बच्ची से मिलकर ठीक वैसे ही जैसे रात का अंधेरा सिमट रहा था भोर की किरणों के साथ। सुबह की प्रतीक्षा इतनी शिद्दत के साथ मैंने कभी नहीं की थी। सुबह की रोशनी भी बुझी-बुझी सी थी क्योंकि मीलों दूर तक काले बादलों का साया पसरा हुआ था। अजीब बात है, जिस सुबह का इंतजार इतनी बेचैनी से कर रही थी उसे देखकर रूह कांप गई। फैलते उजाले के साथ खौफ भी बढ़ता जा रहा था। रात के अंधेरे से दिन का उजाला ज्यादा भयानक था। मैं देख रही थी और महसूस कर रही थी हर एक का दर्द। पलकें खुद ही सिमट गईं। यह कौन-सी उजड़ी जगह है? काश! यह सुबह कभी न आती। कुछ पलों के बाद फिर से आंखें खोलीं यह सोच कर कि शायद यह मंजर एक सपना था, लेकिन नहीं..., हकीकत मेरे सामने थी। कुछ भी अपनी जगह पर नहीं था, न घर, न पेड़, न पत्थर, न पहाड़, न इंसान। सब कुछ बिखरा पड़ा था। कल तक जहां जिंदगी की खिलखिलाहट थी वहीं आज मौत का सन्नाटा पसरा था। किसी उजड़ी नगरी की निशानी के तौर पर खड़े इन खंडहरों के पत्थर

चीख-चीख कर बीती - रात के कहर की दास्तान बयान कर रहे थे। वीराने को देख-देख कर जब थक गई तो अपने-आप मुंद गई आंख। सिनेमा की तरह बीते दिनों का मंजर सामने आने लगा। मैं अपने मम्मी, पापा और भइया के साथ चारधाम गंगोत्री, यमुनोत्री, केदारनाथ और बद्रीनाथ छुट्टियों में घूमने आई थी। बहुत खुश थे हम। यकीन नहीं हो रहा था कि जिस हिमालय को हमने किताबों में पढ़ा था, वह हमारे सामने था। सिर्फ सामने ही नहीं, हमारे चारों ओर फैला हुआ था। जिस गंगा के पानी को हमने एक छोटी सी बोतल में घर के पूजा-घर में देखा था, वह बह रही थी पहाड़ों का सीना चीरते हुए। कल-कल की आवाज पहाड़ों से टकरा कर गूंज रही थी। बादल और आकाश द्वारा बनाई गई इमारतों, मकानों और रास्तों को देख मैं शाबासी दे रही थी इंसानी दिमाग को, सराह रही थी उसकी बुद्धि को। सोच रही थी, इंसान चाहे तो क्या नहीं कर सकता, किस-किस को नहीं झुका सकता, अपने सामने। हालांकि प्रकृति को मात देते-देते वह खुद उससे मात खा गया था। जरूरत से ज्यादा प्रकृति से छेड़छाड़ उसकी सेहत के लिए नुकसानदेह साबित हो चुकी थी। पहाड़ी रास्ते में जब हम भाड़े की गाड़ी में ऊपर की तरफ जा रहे थे, खुशी के साथ-साथ मन में भय भी बढ़ता जा रहा था। जितनी तेजी से हम जमीन को छोड़ते हुए ऊपर उठ रहे थे उतनी ही तेजी से दिल भी धड़क रहा था। घुमावदार मोड़ थे। सांसें अटक जाती थीं। सामने से आने वाली गाड़ी को जब हम पार करते थे तो आंखें मुंद जाती थीं। इतनी ऊँचाई में भगवान के दर्शन से ज्यादा मैं गंगा, पहाड़, बादल, मकान, बस्ती आदि देखने को व्याकुल थी। पहाड़ी रास्ते के मोड़ पर मम्मी के मुंह से निकला 'हे भगवान!' और आपस में बातचीत के साथ हम आगे बढ़ रहे थे। रास्ते में, ऊपर के पहाड़ से टकराता हुआ बादल देखने, तस्वीर खिंचाने और भुट्टा खाने की मेरी जिद, सब एक-एक कर अतीत से उभर कर मेरे सामने आ रहे थे। बीमार मौसम भी हमें बीमार नहीं बना पाया था। बादल, बारिश, ओले सब अच्छे लग रहे थे पहाड़ों के बीच। डर तो लग रहा था लेकिन डर से ज्यादा उत्सुकता थी जो डर को हावी नहीं होने दे रही थी।

मन के घोड़े पर सवार मैं पहुँच गई केदारनाथ। यकीन नहीं हो रहा था कि हम केदारनाथ पहुँच गये हैं। मैंने कल्पना की थी कि जगन्नाथ मंदिर से भी बड़ा मंदिर होगा केदारनाथ जी का। लेकिन केदारनाथ जी का छोटा-सा मंदिर था

पहाड़ों के बीच। काफी सुंदर लग रहा था। अतीत की खूबियों को समेटे खड़ा था हिमालय के बीचों बीच कुछ मकानों और होटलों को अपने साथ लिए। याद आया अपना कमरा जहां हम रुके हुए थे जिसकी खिड़की से मैं देर तक खड़ी होकर बाहर ताका करती थी, शाम का मंजर, प्रकृति का खूबसूरत नजारा। अचानक फिर लोगों का चीखना-चिल्लाना, दौड़-भाग और सैलाब। हम आये तो साथ ही थे पर कब साथ छूटा याद नहीं। बह गई मैं पानी की तेज धार में, मम्मी, पापा चिल्लाते-चिल्लाते, बचाओ, बचाओ चीखते-चिल्लाते। दम घुट रहा था। पानी नाक में, सर में चले जाने से बेचैनी सी हो रही थी। दर्द में बेबस बहती चली जा रही थी। मेरा बदन जो पानी में डूब गया था अब धीरे-धीरे हल्का होकर पानी में तैरने लगा था। मुझे बहाते-बहाते जब पानी थक गया तो यहां लाकर पटक गया शायद।

दर्द का मंज़र ताजा हो गया। बच्ची को और कस कर अपने सीने से जकड़ लिया। शायद अपने-आप को दिलासा देना चाहती थी कि मैं अकेली नहीं हूँ। दर्द भरी पुकार के साथ कोई शायद यहीं आ रहा था। मैंने पलकें उठा कर देखा, एक हट्टा-कट्टा आदमी था जिसकी ताकत प्रकृति के आगे हार गई थी। मैंने उसका हाथ पकड़ लिया। उसका एक पैर घुटने से गायब था। लेकिन झूल रहे थे मांस के लोथड़े। कुछ देर बाद उसकी आंख खुली, तब तक मैं उसे निहार रही थी। वह मुझे ऐसे देख रहा था, मानो कोई भाषा नहीं थी उसकी आंखों में, बस अधखुली आंखों से टुकुर-टुकुर मुझे देखे जा रहा था। अचानक उसने रोना शुरू कर दिया। एक आदमी को दिन के उजाले में एक लड़की के सामने रोते देखकर किसी और परिस्थिति में मैं शायद अचंभित हो जाती, लेकिन इस घड़ी में मैं खुद उसके साथ हो ली क्योंकि अपने से बड़ा कोई अगर आपके साथ हो तो धैर्य पाने और हलका होने में देर नहीं लगती। वह बिलख रहा था अपनी पत्नी और बेटे के लिए। शायद जी भर के गला फाड़ के रोना चाहता था। क्या पता उसकी आवाज उसकी पत्नी और बेटे के पास पहुँच जाये। मैंने उसे जी भर के रोने दिया। शायद बहते आंसुओं के साथ उसका गम भी थोड़ा कम हो जाये। कुछ देर बाद मैंने पूछा, 'आपका नाम क्या है ?'

'मैं निहार अपने परिवार के साथ बिहार से उत्तराखंड घूमने आया था। हम बहुत खुश थे। मेरा बच्चा...।' बोलते ही रो पड़ा। वह बहते आंसुओं के साथ

बोले जा रहा था... 'मेरा बेटा रास्ते भर पूछता रहा,' केदारनाथ कब आयेगा, पापा? हम उसे दिलासा देते हुए करीब पांच बजे केदारनाथ पहुँच गये। दर्शन भी हो गया लेकिन तब तक तेज बारिश शुरू हो गई थी। हम लोग कुछ देर रुक कर जल्दी से गौरी कुण्ड लौट आये। वहां से सीतापुर होते हुए रामपुर पहुँचे। वहां सारी रात गुजारी। 16 तारीख को भी भारी बारिश हो रही थी। घोड़े, खच्चर, गाड़ियों और आदमियों की अच्छी खासी तादाद थी। दोपहर बाद खबर मिली गौरीकुण्ड और सोनप्रयाग पूरी तरह बह गया है। अपने जिंदा बचे रहने के लिए भगवान का शुक्रिया अदा किया। उसी दिन एक छोटी गाड़ी से हरिद्वार के लिए निकल पड़े। रास्ते टूटे हुए थे। बहुत तकलीफ के साथ चार दिन उसी गाड़ी में गुजारे। फिर सरकार की मदद से काम चला। रास्ता खुला तो आगे बढ़े। हमें क्या पता था कि आगे तबाही हमारा इंतजार कर रही थी। मुश्किल से 5 किलोमीटर आगे बढ़े होंगे कि भूस्खलन हुआ। ऐसा लगा जैसे पूरा पहाड़ ही हमारी गाड़ी पर आ गिरा हो। मैं गाड़ी में किनारे बैठा हुआ था। टूट कर गिरने वाली चट्टान के भारी दबाव से दरवाजा टूट गया और मैं छिटक कर बाहर आ गिरी। और लुढकते पत्थरों के साथ न जाने कितने नीचे आ गिरी। मैं दर्द को ठीक से महसूस कर पाता इससे पहले ही दर्द ने मेरा साथ छोड़ दिया और नीचे सैलाब के तेज बहाव के साथ यहां आ पहुँचा। न जाने क्या हुआ होगा मेरे बेटे और पत्नी का, इसके आगे वह कुछ और न बोल सका। कुछ आगे कहने से उसके होंठ शायद कांप रहे थे। कुछ देर बाद बोला, 'घर से निकलते वक्त मैं बोला था कि रोहन को साथ नहीं ले चलें, अगर हमें कहीं कुछ हो गया तो मेरा बेटा रोहन तो बचा रहेगा। लेकिन वह कहां मानने वाला था। जिद्दी अपनी मां पर गया है न! साथ में आया। काश! मैं उसे साथ न लाता। काश! हम लोग यहां न आये होते...।

मैंने उसे दिलासा देना चाहा लेकिन मेरे हाथ-पैरों में भी कहां जान थी। बेबसी में आंखों से दो बूंद आंसू निकल पड़े। फिर सन्नाटा छा गया। न जाने कितने पल बीत गए। शायद हम सब यही सोच रहे थे कि हम सब यहां न आये होते या फिर यह जानलेवा बाढ़ न आई होती तो क्या हो रहता अभी...।

तभी अचानक बहते पत्थरों की तेज धार के साथ दो जन और आ गये जिनको सैलाब यहां ला कर छोड़ गया। हम सब थोड़ा-सा सरक गये ताकि वे

अपने बिखरे शरीर को संभाल सकें। उनमें से एक की उम्र शायद मेरे पापा जितनी होगी, यानी कोई पचास या पचपन साल। रास्ते भर पानी, पत्थर, कादा की चोट सहते उनका सारा शरीर झुलस गया था। शायद जोड़ों में ज्यादा तकलीफ हो रही थी उनको, दर्द से सिहर रहे थे। और दूसरी एक औरत थी, बूढ़ी औरत। सिर्फ साया और ब्लाउज था उसके बदन पर। इससे पता चल रहा था कि आर्थिक स्थिति अच्छी रही होगी उसके घर की, क्योंकि मेरे गांव में इस उम्र की औरतें यह सब नहीं पहनती। वे पहनती हैं सिर्फ मोटी सूती साड़ी। कुछ देर रोने-धोने के बाद दोनों ने अपनी दास्तान बयां की।

शायद कुछ ज्यादा ही तकलीफ हो रही थी उस औरत को। एक तो यह गहरी चोट, ऊपर से बुढ़ापा। बहुत मुश्किल से आधे-अधूरे लफ्जों में बोली, मैं अपने बेटे, पतोहू, बेटी, जमाई, पोते, पोतियों के साथ केदारनाथ दर्शन के लिए झारखंड से आई थी। यमुनोत्री से कुछ किलोमीटर पहले चमोली के पास जब हम पहुँचे, भारी बारिश के चलते जहां हम रह रहे थे वह जगह बर्बाद हो चुकी थी। दोनों तरफ से रास्ते बह गये थे। हम वहीं फंस गये। मेरे बच्चे उस समय को देख बिलख-बिलख कर रो रहे थे। मेरे अंदर का कोना-कोना कांप रहा था। मैं भी बयान करना चाहती थी अपने मन का खौफ, लेकिन मैं टूट गई तो इनको कौन संभालेगा, यही सोच कर अंदर ही अंदर मरी जा रही थी। करीब 10 घंटे तक हम लोगों ने यह खौफ का जीवन जिया। फिर एक बड़े सैलाब में वह जगह बह गई। मैं अपने पोते का हाथ पकड़े हुई थी लेकिन पानी उसे मुझसे छीन ले गया। सैलाब मेरे जीवन की पूंजी, मेरे परिवार को मुझसे छीन ले गया। पता नहीं, कौन कहां होगा। लेकिन उम्मीद है कि सब लोग कहीं न कहीं अच्छे से होंगे, जहां भी होंगे। भगवान है, वह इतना निष्ठुर नहीं हो सकता। सब हैं... सब होंगे... यही फुसफुसाती रही।

नज़र उस आदमी पर पड़ी तो वह बोला, 'मैं अपनी पत्नी, दो बेटियों और रिश्तेदारों के साथ 8 तारीख को उड़ीसा से केदारनाथ के लिए रवाना हुआ था। 15 तारीख को गौरीकुंड पहुँचने के बाद मैं अपने परिवार के साथ केदारनाथ पैदल चल कर गया। मेरे रिश्तेदार अपने परिवार के साथ खच्चर से गये। वहीं से हम लोग अलग हो गए, फिर नहीं मिल सके। 15 तारीख से ही मौसम खराब होने की वजह से बारिश शुरू हो गई थी। इस मौसम में भी हम लोग केदारनाथ का

दर्शन करके रामबाड़ा होते हुए गौरीकुंड लौट आये थे। फिसलन भरे रास्ते में गिरने से मेरी बच्चियों को काफी चोट लगी थी। गौरीकुंड में कोई गाड़ी नहीं मिली। एक अनजाना डर हमारे अंदर घर कर रहा था। सूखा खाना और पानी कीमती चीजों की तरह बाजार में काफी ऊँचे दामों पर मिल रहा था। कुछ न सूझा तो हम फिर पैदल चलते-चलते सोनप्रयाग पहुँचे। बहुत मुश्किल से जंगल विभाग के पान्थ निवास में दो कमरे मिले जो थोड़ी ऊँचाई पर थे। रात के आठ बजे के करीब गांव के 30-35 लोग प्रलय की आशंका से आतंकित होकर वहां रहने आ गए। एक कमरे में हम लोग रहे, दूसरा कमरा उनके लिए छोड़ दिया जिसमें उन सब लोगों ने रात गुजारी। 16 तारीख को भयानक बारिश और बाढ़ को लेकर लोग इतना डरे हुए थे कि रात आंखों-आंखों में गुजार दी। किसी की आंख में नींद नहीं थी। पलकें नींद से बोझिल थी लेकिन किसी को सोना मंजूर नहीं था। १७ तारीख की सुबह दरवाजा खोला तो कहीं कुछ नहीं था। सब कुछ सैलाब में बह गया था। चारों ओर सिर्फ पानी ही पानी था। आंखों के सामने बहती जा रही थीं गाड़ियां। बहते चले जा रहे थे मनुष्य, पशु और भी न जाने क्या-क्या? इस दिन वहां से निकल कर कहीं और जाने की हिम्मत नहीं थी। खाना, पानी सब खत्म हो चुका था। दूसरे दिन पान्थ निवास की रखवाली करने वाला आदमी अपने गांव की हालत देखने के लिए 'पान्थ निवास' को बंद करके जाना चाहता था। ऐसी स्थिति में आगे बढ़ने का निश्चय किया। लेकिन कहीं कोई रास्ता नहीं था। मजबूरन हमें पहाड़ों पर चढ़ कर जाना पड़ा। बीच-बीच में भूस्खलन, कांटा, पानी, पत्थर, सबका सामना करते हुए आगे बढ़ते जा रहे थे। मैं आगे-आगे चल रहा था ताकि स्थितियों की परख कर सकूं। पत्थरों को जांच सकूं। इसी परखने में जिस पत्थर पर मैंने पैर रखा वह अचानक ही खिसक गया और अपने परिवार के सामने ही उस पत्थर के साथ मैं भी बह गया। इस बहने में बदन में काफी चोट लगी। एक जगह किसी पत्थर से सर टकराया और आंखों के सामने धुआं सा छा गया।'

हमारी बातें अभी खत्म भी नहीं हुई थीं कि आसपास की जो थोड़ी सी जगह बची हुई थी उसे भरने और तीन जन बहते हुए आ पहुँचे। इनमें से एक तो पंद्रह-सोलह साल का लड़का था, एक युवक का आधा जला शव और तीसरा एक साधू। हमने उनको भी जगह दे दी, प्रकृति के बनाये आशियाने में।

लड़का अपनी आयु के मुताबिक चंचल था। जो उसके रोने में भी झलक रहा था। हम सब उसकी ओर सवाल भरी नज़रों से देखे जा रहे थे। उसने बताना शुरू किया, 'मैं अपने मम्मी-पापा के साथ घूमने आया था। हम लोग मंदिर के पास एक होटल में रुके थे। मुझे अपनी बहुत सारी तस्वीरें खिंचवा कर दोस्तों को दिखाने का शौक था। इसलिए बाहर घूमने निकल गया। मैं घूम ही रहा था कि अचानक पानी का सैलाब आया। मैं डौड़ा और जो घर सामने आया उसी पर चढ़ गया। कहीं और जाने का न समय था न मौका। मैं दो और लोगों के साथ कमरे में चला गया। देखते ही देखते बंद दरवाजे और खिड़की से पानी घर के अंदर घुसने लगा। हम कुर्सी पर खड़े हो गए, फिर कुर्सी को बिस्तर के ऊपर रख उस पर खड़े हो गए। लेकिन पानी को रहम नहीं आया और उसी कमरे में हम तीनों की जलसमाधि हो गई। कुछ देर बाद मकान भी बह गया और कौन कहां चला गया पता ही नहीं चला।'

हम उस अधजले शरीर को देखे जा रहे थे, पता ही नहीं चल रहा था कि पैर किधर है और सिर किधर? वह एक जला हुआ मांस का लोथड़ा ही तो था लेकिन बेखौफ हो वह बोल पड़ा, 'मैं प्रवीण एमआई-17 वो 5 विमान का पायलट। हम गुप्तकाशी और केदारनाथ में फंसे लोगों का उद्धार करके लौट रहे थे कि एक दुर्घटना में विमान के साथ हम सब जल गए। हम लोग उसकी बातों को सुनने से ज्यादा उसके अंदाज को देख रहे थे। कोई अफसोस नहीं, उसे कोई दर्द नहीं, पूरी तरह बेखौफ पड़ा था।'

तीसरा जो अपनी शक्ल से साधू लग रहा था, बोल पड़ा, 'जब सैलाब आया तब मैं मंदिर में ही था। अचानक आई विपत्ति से बचने के लिए कुछ न सूझा तो मंदिर के घंटे को ही पकड़ कर झूल गया। पूरा एक दिन एक रात इसी तरह मंदिर के घंटे से झूलते हुए गुजारा। पानी थोड़ा कम हुआ तो नीचे उतरा। नीचे लाशों का ढेर लगा था। बच्चों, बूढ़ों, आदमी, औरतों की अनगिनत लाशें थीं। मेरी नज़र इन लाशों के गहनों पर पड़ी। इनके हाथ, पैर, गला काट कर मैंने गहने इकट्ठे किये क्योंकि मैं एक आश्रम बनाना चाहता था। जान बचाने के लिए एक पहाड़ के ऊपर आश्रय लिया। तीन दिन वहां बिना खाना-पानी के रुका रहा। हिम्मत धीरे-धीरे दम तोड़ रही थी। चौथे दिन जिंदगी ने साथ छोड़ दिया और पानी के बहाव में कितनी दूर बह गया पता नहीं...।' यह बोल कर वह खामोश

हो गया। लेकिन मेरा रोम-रोम क्रोध से ऊब उठा और पहली बार किसी अनजान के लिए इतनी नफरत महसूस की थी। अचानक ही मुझे उससे अधिक तकलीफ लगने लगी और उसकी ओर से नज़र खुद-ब-खुद हट गई। मैं अपने मन की सोच को नई दिशा देना चाहती थी। ज्यादा देर तक इस साधु के बारे में सोचना नहीं चाहती थी जो किसी भी तरह से इन्सान कहे जाने लायक नहीं था।

मैं सोच रही थी, बारिश तो पहले भी होती थी, लेकिन इस बार क्यों इस कदर कहर बरपा रही थी प्रकृति अपनों पर। यह विपदा प्राकृतिक नहीं बल्कि मानवकृत है। यह ढेर सारे हाइड्रो-प्रोजेक्ट बनाना, वर्षों से जंगल काटते चले जाना, नदी किनारे कानून की धज्जियां उड़ाते हुए बड़ी-बड़ी इमारतें, मकान बनाना, नदी किनारे से भारी मात्रा में बालू की चोरीृ, डाइनामाइट लगा कर पहाड़ों को उड़ा देना, कमजोर पहाड़ों पर मिट्टी लगा कर पेड़ लगाना, सुरक्षा न करना, प्रदूषण फैलाना-आदि वजहें हैं इस विपदा की। चंद लोगों की पैसाखोरी प्रकृत्ति ही जिम्मेदार है असंख्य निरीह और मासूम लोगों की जान लेने की। हम तो घूमने आये थे। क्या पता था, दूसरों के गुनाह की सज़ा हम भुगतेंगे। वे हजारों लोग जिन्होंने इस हादसे में अपनी जान गंवाई है, हम उनमें से कुछ हैं। हम छोड़ गये हैं अपने पीछे रोते बिलखता परिवार। सारा शरीर गल गया है। बदबू फैली हुई है। नाउम्मीदी में भी उम्मीद है अपनों की। अपनों को क्या पता। कभी ढूँढ़ता हुआ हमारा कोई अपना आ पहुँचे और भटकती रूह को सुकून मिल जाये।

गीतेश शर्मा

जन्म से हिन्दू, आस्था से मानवतावादी और मिशन के रूप में पत्रकारिता तथा सांस्कृतिक-सामाजिक कार्यों को स्वीकार करनेवाले गीतेश शर्मा का जन्म 4 अगस्त,1932 को लखीसराय, बिहार में हुआ था।

आपने कुल 24 पुस्तकें लिखीं—16 हिन्दी में और 8 अंग्रेज़ी में। *धर्म के नाम पर, जननायक हो चि मिन्ह और भारत, बाबा नागार्जुन और कोलकाता, विद्रोही कवि नजरुल इस्लाम, भारत : नेहरू का अवदान, भारतीय संस्कृति और हिन्दुत्व* आदि उनकी महत्त्वपूर्ण हिन्दी पुस्तकें हैं। अंग्रेजी पुस्तकों में प्रमुख हैं—*इंडो-वियतनाम रिलेशन्स : फर्स्ट टू ट्वेंटी फर्स्ट सेंचुरी; ट्रेसेज ऑफ इंडियन कल्चर इन वियतनाम*, स्वीडिश लेखक थॉमस एंडरसन एवं कुसुम जैन के साथ लिखित *डबल फैंटेसी, वियतनाम लिबरेशन वार : रोल ऑफ कलकत्ता, परवर्टेड सोसायटी, दा नांग द सिटी ऑफ वंडर्स, वियतनाम 1982-2017 : रुइन्स टु इनक्रेडिबल प्रोग्रेस।*

बांग्ला, स्वीडिश एवं वियतनामी भाषाओं में रचनाएँ अनूदित। अनेक देशों की यात्राएँ जिनमें बांग्लादेश, नेपाल, पाकिस्तान, भूटान, बैंकाक, सिंगापुर, वियतनाम, ब्रिटेन, फ्रांस, जर्मनी, स्विट्ज़रलैंड, डेनमार्क, स्वीडन, नार्वे, अमेरिका, कनाडा और सोवियत संघ शामिल हैं।

सम्मान एवं पुरस्कार : हिन्दी साहित्य सम्मेलन, प्रयाग का 'सारस्वत सम्मान', आर्गेनाइजेशन ऑफ अंडरस्टैंडिंग एवं फ्रेटर्निटी का 'हार्मनी अवार्ड', बिहार सरकार का 'राष्ट्रीय एकता पुरस्कार', बल्गारिया सरकार का 'दिमित्रोव मेडल', उत्तरपथ (स्वीडेन) द्वारा 'सेलेमा लेगर–लॉफ गोल्ड मेडल', वियतनाम यूनियन ऑफ फ्रेंडशिप ऑर्गेनाइजेशन का 'नागरिक सम्मान', वियतनाम राइटर्स एसोसिएशन का 'नागरिक सम्मान' तथा वियतनाम का सर्वोच्च नागरिक सम्मान 'ऑर्डर ऑफ फ्रेंडशिप'।

प्रेम कपूर : महानगर कोलकाता के वरिष्ठ नाट्य-समीक्षक, पत्रकार व जाने-माने अनुवादक हैं, जिन्होंने वियतनाम के हो चि मिन्ह, हू थिन्ह, हाम आन्ह, के अतिरिक्त अलेक्ज़ेंडर पीटर क्रोपोत्किन, नज़रुल इस्लाम, सुकांत भट्टाचार्य, विमल मित्र, सुभाष मुखोपाद्याय, बिमल दे जैसे अंतरराष्ट्रीय ख्यातिप्राप्त लेखकों की कृतियों का अनुवाद किया है। इतिहास, प्रकृति-विज्ञान, चिकित्सा-विज्ञान, यात्रा-वृत्तांत, कविता, कहानी, बाल-साहित्य आदि विषयों से संबंधित 25 से अधिक पुस्तकों का अनुवाद करने के अलावा विभिन्न पुस्तकों का संपादन भी किया है।

कुसुम जैन : जन्म 1952, हिंदी कवयित्री। दो काव्य-संग्रह प्रकाशित-सच के साये में, कविता : *दुख की नदी*। एक संग्रह बांग्ला में प्रकाशित–*रोटी और कविता*। उड़िया, अंग्रेज़ी, स्वीडिश आदि भाषाओं में अनुवाद। बांग्ला, वियतनामी, स्वीडिश, बुल्गारियाई, आइसलैंडिक कविताओं का अंग्रेज़ी से हिन्दी में अनुवाद। विभिन्न पुस्तकों का संपादन। स्त्री-पुरुष समानता, विवेक और विज्ञानसम्मत मानवीय मूल्यों की पक्षधर।

डॉ. प्रभामयी सामंतराय : केंद्रापाड़ा कॉलेज ओड़िसा में व्याख्याता। इससे पूर्व वे डिप्लोमैटिक अकादमी ऑफ़ वियतनाम में अंग्रेज़ी पढ़ा चुकी हैं। दो कविता संग्रह प्रकाशित हैं और हिंदी से ओड़िया में दो कविता पुस्तकों का अनुवाद किया है। वियतनाम-भारत मैत्री संबंधों को प्रगाढ़ विस्तार देने के लिए वियतनामी भाषा का शिक्षण प्राप्त कर रही हैं।

Geetesh Sharma

1932-2021, by birth Hindu, by faith Humanist, by mission Journalist, cultural and social activist.

Authored 24 books – Sixteen in Hindi and Eight in English. In Hindi most acclaimed books *Dharma Ke Naam Par, Jananayak Ho Chi Minh Aur Bharat, Baba Nagarjun Aur Kolkata* (presents legendary People's poet Nagarjun), *Vidrohi Kavi Nazarul Islam, Bharat : Nehru ka Awadan, Bharatiya Sanskriti aur Hindutva*, English titles include–*Indo-Vietnam Relations : First to Twenty first Century, Traces of Indian Culture in Vietnam, Double Fantasy*, jointly with a Swedish writer Tomas Andersson and Kusum Jain, *Vietnam Liberation War : Role of Calcutta, Perverted Society, Da Nang the city of Wonders, Vietnam 1982-2017, Ruins to Incredible Progress*.

His works have been translated in Bengali, Swedish, Vietnamese languages.

Widely travelled in India and abroad countries such as Bangladesh, Nepal, Pakistan, Bhutan, Bangkok, Hongkong, Singapore, Vietnam, Britain, France, German, Switzerland, Denmark, Sweden, Norway, USA, Canada, Former USSR etc.

Recipient of Various Awards that include Saraswat Samman by Hindi Sahitya Sammelan, Prayag, Harmony Award by Organization of Understanding and Fraternity, National Integration Award by Govt. of Bihar. Georgi Dimitrov Medal by Govt. of Bulgaria, Selama Lagarlof Gold Medal by Uttarapath (Gothenburg, Sweden), Civil Award by Vietnam Union of Friendship Organisations, Civil Award awarded by Vietnam Writers' Association, Order of Friendship, Highest Civil Award by the Govt. of Vietnam.

Prem Kapoor : Besides being a senior Drama Critic, journalist and writer Prem Kapoor is an eminent translator who has translated some of the works of Ho Chi Minh, Huu Thinh and Ham Anh (Vietnam). Apart from Vietnam, he has translated renowned writers Mubarak Ali, Alexander Peter Cropotkin, Kazi Nazrul Islam, Sukanto Bhattacharya, Bimal Mitra, Subhash Mukhopadhyay of International fame. He has translated from English and Bengali to Hindi and from Hindi to English works related to History, Nature Science, Medical Science, Travelogue, Novels, Short stories, poems, Children literature and edited a number of books.

Kusum Jain born in 1952, two poetry collections in Hindi, one in Bengali. Her poems have been translated in Bengali, Odia, English, Swedish. She has translated poems of Bengali, English, swedish, Icelandic, Bulgarian from English. Edited many books. By conviction an atheist and humanist with scientific thinking.

Dr. Pravamayee Samantaray : Dr. Pravamayee Samantaray is a lecturer in English, Kendrapara Autonomous College, Odisha. Formerly, she was teaching at Diplomatic Academy of Vietnam, Hanoi. Except being a poet, translator, social - cultural activist, she is the Secretary of Indo-Vietnam Solidarity Committee. Two of her poetry collections have been published and has translated two poetry collections from Hindi to Odia. Currently, she is learning Vietnamese language to boost the bilateral relationship between India and Vietnam.